SCHOOL-AGE CHILD CARE

An Action Manual

RUTH KRAMER BADEN

ANDREA GENSER

JAMES A. LEVINE

MICHELLE SELIGSON

**Wellesley College Center for
Research on Women**

 Auburn House Publishing Company
Boston, Massachusetts

This book was prepared with the support of the Carnegie Corporation of New York; the Ford Foundation; the General Mills Foundation; the William T. Grant Foundation; the Levi Strauss Foundation; and the National Institute of Education, grant number NIE-G-80-0009. The statements, findings, conclusions, and recommendations included herein do not necessarily reflect the views of any of the sponsoring institutions.

The photographs at the beginning of each part of the book were taken by Andrea Genser. The locations at which they were taken are as follows:

Parts One, Two, and Three: The Hephzibah Children's Association, Oak Park, Illinois.

Part Four: The Santa Monica Children's Center, Santa Monica, California.

Part Five: The Madison After School Day Care Association, Madison, Wisconsin.

Library of Congress Cataloging in Publication Data
Main entry under title:

School-age child care.

  Bibliography: p.
  Includes index.
  1. Day care centers—United States—Administration. I. Seligson, Michelle, 1941–   . II. Baden, Ruth Kramer, 1933–   .
III. School-Age Child Care Project (Wellesley College)
HV854.S27 1982   362.7′12′068   82-11503
ISBN 0-86569-112-6

Printed in the United States of America.

SCHOOL-AGE CHILD CARE

An Action Manual

SCHOOL-AGE CHILD CARE PROJECT

Michelle Seligson, Director

PREFACE

This book derives from the work of the School-Age Child Care Project, an action-research project based at the Wellesley College Center for Research on Women. It deals with one of the fastest-growing family dilemmas in the United States: caring for the young school-age child when school is not in session.

Thanks to the support of the Ford Foundation, Carnegie Corporation, Levi Strauss Foundation, William T. Grant Foundation, General Mills Foundation, and National Institute of Education, we have spent the last several years immersed in the problems—and solutions—of school-age child care (SACC). Our work since 1979 has included many facets—research, technical assistance, training, and demonstration—and it continues to expand in response to national needs.

Actually, the origins of our work can be traced to the serendipitous meeting of Michelle (Mickey) Seligson and Jim Levine in 1976. As assistant director for the Human Relations–Youth Resources Commission in Brookline, Massachusetts, Mickey had been responsible for helping several parent groups set up after-school day care programs in the town's elementary schools. These programs were modeled after two pioneer programs organized and run by Brookline parents. She was being deluged by requests for help from parents, school principals, even mayors' and governors' offices from as far away as Hawaii. Indeed, mention of the Brookline program in two national magazines, *McCall's* and *Ladies' Home Journal,* had brought over fifteen hundred letters requesting information and help.

The Brookline program was a natural for Jim to visit as he began research for *Day Care and the Public Schools,* a report to the Ford Foundation describing different types of public school involvement in the controversial day care arena—infant care, family day care, preschool care, and school-age care. In 1978, when the report was published, Jim too began receiving letters from people all over the country who wanted help with school-age care. They wanted to know *how to do it;* they knew they had a desperate need, but had only vague notions about how to go about putting a quality program together.

That's when Mickey and Jim got together to create the School-Age Child Care Project. They brought together a team of researchers, writers, and day care experts to devote full time in helping to ease the national dilemma with school-age child care. Andrea Genser, former public school teacher and day care director, came to the project after her experience coordinating the Title XX day care training program at Boston's Wheelock College. Wendy Gray, a student of day care policy with direct experience in school-age care, came from the Heller School at Brandeis University. And Ruth Kramer Baden brought her expertise as a writer and consultant to educational institutions, in order to help us translate our research, experience, and ideas into this book. In 1981 Ellen Gannett, a seven-year-veteran director of a school-age program, joined us as a staff member.

From its inception, the School-Age Child Care Project was designed to be pragmatic, to use research as a tool for action. We wanted to find out what communities other than Brookline were doing to meet their need for school-age child care. What creative models could be found in America's cities, suburbs, and rural areas? Were there any patterns that seemed to repeat themselves again and again in "successful" programs?

As we began to plan our research and the book that would result from it, we had to make some hard decisions. How many different kinds of programs would we explore, and for which age group?

We knew that the term *school-age child care* could encompass many possibilities: these included self-care (the "latchkey" practice used by many families—so called because children wear house keys around their necks and let themselves into empty homes); informal care (children spending afternoons at one another's homes where a relative or older sibling is at home); the "patchwork" approach (families arranging a schedule for children which might include music or drama classes one day, swimming or gymnastics at the local Y another day, and going home or to a friend's house on other days); family day care (a paid arrangement used by many families, in which school-aged children spend their after-school hours at the home of a "provider" who cares for small groups of children in her home); and finally, the formal day care program, operated either by a preschool day care center, a community agency such as the Y, or by a group renting or receiving free use of public school space for the program.

We also quickly became aware as we began our research that school-age children come in different ages, stages, and needs. While population statistics lump school-age children together as a group of six- to thirteen-year-olds, in reality many children enter school at age five when they begin kindergarten. Parents were most concerned about finding suitable and accountable child care for the youngest children, those between the ages of five and eight—kindergartners through third grade. Although parents were concerned about their children in all age groups, most of the formal programs were being requested or organized for the five- to eight-year-olds, and to some extent the nine-to-elevens (the eleven- to thirteen- or fourteen-year-olds did not appear to be served by or interested in day care programs). Also, the programs themselves tended to focus primarily on the needs of the younger children.

Although we would have liked to cover the waterfront of the issue—how all these children from five to thirteen were faring during the hours when school is not in session and what resources were being used by these children and their families—we chose to focus on care for the younger children and to expand the knowledge that many parents, personnel from schools and social services, and community groups were asking for: How do we organize and set up programs for these young children? How can we best meet parents' needs for accountable and safe child care? How can we make a difference in the lives of children and families?

We were happy to learn that during the course of our work, two national resource groups took up the task of learning about the older children—from ten or eleven to fourteen—and applying that knowledge by developing a range of opportunities to meet the needs of the older child for independence and the development of skills, as well as for nurturance and care.[1]

To find out what solutions were being developed at the community level throughout the United States, we did extensive field research. By telephone, we contacted leaders in day care, early education, and the community schools movement in almost all the states. These knowledgeable colleagues steered us to programs that, in their opinion, were "outstanding" for one reason or another: they had created a stable administrative structure, used resources effectively, had figured out how to make a program work for five-year-olds and

---

[1] These two groups are the National Commission on Resources for Youth in Massachusetts and the Center for Early Adolescence in Chapel Hill, North Carolina.

ten-year-olds at the same time, and trained staff effectively. There was no single ingredient we were looking for, no special formula we had predetermined. We simply wanted to get a fix on the "state of the art," to identify interesting and innovative ways of doing school-age child care that might be replicated, in whole or in part, in other sections of the country.

Had we our "druthers," we would have visited each and every one of the almost two hundred programs that our community experts directed us to. However, time and budget constraints precluded that approach. Instead, we did telephone interviews with the directors of most of these programs, trying to get a feel for what each had to offer: the population it served, the types of activities it made available for children and families, its administrative and fiscal structure. From this round of data gathering, we selected twenty-five programs to visit, making sure to include programs that represented each major geographical region of the country—urban, suburban, and rural areas—and different approaches to school-age child care.

Our site visits brought us to cities as far flung as New York, Seattle, Chicago, Baltimore, Santa Monica, Minneapolis, and Nashville. Our staff spent a week or so at each program interviewing the key people who were involved in its development and operation, learning how it worked, and—most importantly—learning what stumbling blocks had to be overcome to make it work. Everywhere we went, day care directors, teachers, board members, and school administrators—all people with unbelievably demanding schedules—made the time to help us see and understand their programs. Because of their immersion in their programs, they didn't have time to do research or write books. But there was much they wanted to share with others, and they saw us as "information brokers" who could help translate what they had done in a way that would be useful to people who were just beginning to grapple with the complexities of putting together a good school-age child care program.

We started to do that brokering long before writing this book. As we proceeded with our research, we continued providing the technical assistance that Mickey Seligson had started years before in Brookline. All of us had some experience with school-age child care—as directors, teachers, and parents—and we combined it with what we were learning in the field. And so, a school principal who called us from Colorado might benefit immediately from what we had just learned from a principal in Virginia. A parents' group in Texas might pick up what we had just gleaned from a swing through Minnesota.

Whenever it made sense, we put one party directly in touch with the other.

During the last two years, we have received calls or letters from all fifty states. We have received requests from parents, service organizations such as the YMCA and Camp Fire Girls, school principals and superintendents, school boards, employers, and government agencies—each of whom wanted to know how to meet its community need. The demand for information is so great that currently we average 2,000–3,000 requests for technical assistance each year—500 by phone and 1,500–2,500 by mail.

Indeed, the demand for help increased so quickly that in 1981 we expanded our technical assistance activities. Thanks to continued support from the Ford Foundation, Carnegie Corporation, and Levi Strauss Foundation, we launched a demonstration component of our project in each of eight communities: Santa Monica, California; Oak Park, Illinois; Rochester, Minnesota; Albuquerque, New Mexico; Buffalo, New York; Eugene, Oregon; Nashville, Tennessee; and Fairfax, Virginia. In each location, groups that already have some expertise in school-age child care are now serving as technical assistance "affiliates" of the School-Age Child Care Project. The demonstration component vividly illustrates the guiding premise behind all of our work: that solutions are really to be found at the community level, and that they can best be developed by mobilizing people with similar interests to help one another.

This book is one more illustration of that premise. Any expertise it provides comes directly from the many people who took the time to share with us what they had learned by doing: the countless parents, directors, teachers, community leaders, and school administrators who were so busy creating their community solutions that they didn't have time to write them up. Our deepest appreciation goes to all of them.

A few individuals made their time, skills, and other resources available in particularly special ways, thereby enabling us to play our active roles as researchers and information brokers: Judy Paquette, Administrative Assistant, and Joan Johnson, Project Secretary, spent countless hours typing and retyping the manuscript, keeping track of its many drafts, laboring over proofreading and the many details that accompany the production of a book this size. All of this was done with concern for quality and with unfailing good humor. Wendy Gray, Project Associate during the early research phase, visited programs in several states, and contributed her research skills to the data that forms the substance of the book. Louise Sullivan worked with us as editor to shape the manuscript and make it ready for publication, and we appreciate her intelligent and thoughtful suggestions throughout that process. Ellen Gannett, Project Associate, read the final draft and, from her many years of program experience, ably pinpointed several areas in need of clarification. Cliff Baden of Wheelock College helped us with the chapters on financial management at the conceptual stage and, later, in reading final copy. We were fortunate to be able to work at the Wellesley College Center for Research on Women, which provided a stimulating and supportive environment.

We thank all of the experts who are out there providing care for school-age children for making this book possible. We hope that our book, in turn, will make it possible for more communities to meet the challenge of school-age child care in the years ahead.

THE AUTHORS

Wellesley, Massachusetts
June 1982

ACKNOWLEDGMENTS

We are especially indebted to the many program directors and staff, parents, school principals and superintendents, school board members, classroom teachers, school secretaries, school custodians, social service agency staff, and community leaders who spent so much time with us during interviews sharing their knowledge, their problems, and their advice. We are particularly grateful to those children who patiently explained their thoughts and feelings to us as we, armed with tape recorders and notebooks, tried to capture some of their daily experiences in school-age child care programs. Space does not permit mention of all these individuals, so we have listed the states, communities, programs, and agencies we visited. In many cases, more than one program was affiliated with or administered by a single agency.

In *California:* Santa Monica Unified School District; Santa Monica Children's Centers; Child Care Information Service, Santa Monica; Riverside County Schools, Children's Services Unit; YWCA, Riverside.

In *Colorado:* City of Boulder; YMCA Child Care Program, Boulder; Mile High Child Care Association, Denver.

In *Connecticut:* Office of Child Day Care, State of Connecticut, Hartford; Windsor Child Care Program, Windsor; Y Fun Family Program, Wethersfield.

In *Illinois:* Hephzibah Children's Association; Oak Park Public Schools; Family Service and Mental Health Center, Oak Park.

In *Maryland:* Anne Arundel County Health Department; Department of Social Services, Day Care Division, City of Baltimore; Institute for Child Study, University of Maryland; Maryland Committee for Children.

In *Massachusetts:* The Children's Center of Brookline and Greater Boston; Community Day Care Center, Inc., Lawrence; Lawrence (School) Extended Day Program, Brookline; Tina Seamore Learning Center, Newton.

In *Minnesota:* City-Wide Latch-Key Programs of the Minneapolis Public Schools; Greater Minneapolis Day Care Association; Hennepin County Family Day Care Association; Adventure Club, Robbinsdale; Community Education and Services, Robbinsdale Area Schools; Brooklyn Park Parks and Recreation Department.

In *New Mexico:* Albuquerque Parks and Recreation Department; Community Education Program, Albuquerque Public Schools; Cariño Child Care Information and Referral Service; YMCA Central Branch, Albuquerque.

In *New York:* Bank Street Extended Day Program; Chinatown Planning Council, New York City.

In *North Carolina:* After School Day Care Program, Durham County Schools; Department of Social Services, Durham; Phillips Extended Day Magnet School, Fred Olds Extended Day Magnet School, Raleigh; Wake County Public Schools, Raleigh.

In *Oregon:* Eugene Latchkey; 4-J School District; 4-C Council, Eugene; Portland Public Schools; YMCA Latchkey Program, Portland.

In *Tennessee:* Davidson County School-Age Day Care Task Force; Eakin Care Program; City Road After School Program; McGavock Community School, Nashville; Tennessee Department of Human Services, Licensing Division in Nashville and in Johnson City.

In *Texas:* El Paso Public Schools; Central Area YWCA, El Paso; Extend-A-Care, Austin.

In *Virginia:* Arlington Public Schools; Extended Day Program, Arlington; Fairfax County School-Age Child Care Program; Fairfax County Office for Children; Reston Children's Center, Reston.

In *Washington:* YMCA, Seattle.

In *Wisconsin:* Madison After School Day Care Association, Madison; Family After School Program, Milwaukee.

Special thanks go to the following individuals and organizations whose written materials we relied on heavily in certain chapters of the *Action Manual:* Kay Hendon, John Grace, Diane Adams, and Aurelia Strupp (*The After School Day Care Handbook,* Dane County 4-C, Wisconsin); Lawrence Kotin, Robert M. Crabtree, and William F. Aikman (*Legal Handbook for Day Care Centers*); Kathleen Murray (Bay Area Child Care Law Project Publications); Roger Neugebauer (articles in *Child Care Information Exchange* on administrative models, budget and finance, personnel, and curriculum); Robert Posilkin, Department of School Facilities, Montgomery County (Maryland) Public Schools (articles and program materials); Elizabeth Prescott and Cynthia Milich

(*School's Out! Group Day Care for the School Age Child*); Elizabeth Prescott (several unpublished papers, speeches, and interviews); Joe Perrault and Nancy Travis, The Child Care Support Center, Save the Children, Atlanta, Georgia ("Recruiting and Enrolling Children" and other materials on administrative issues); Peggy Pizzo (*Parent to Parent: A Look at Self-Help and Child Advocacy by Parents,* a report to the Carnegie Corporation).

A number of people gave graciously of their time in conversations with us during the research and writing stages, and we thank them: Roz Anderson, Joan Bergstrom, Rosalie Blau, Irwin Blumer, Mary Anne Broeman-Brown, Gerri Bugg, Cambridge Child Care Resource Center staff, Cathleen Cavell, Jacqueline Clement, Elaine Collins, Nate Finklestein, Jan Fish, Pat Gardner, Betsy Hiteshew, Ann Kahn, Gwen Morgan, Multi-Cultural Project staff, Cambridge, Massachusetts, Jim Olivero, Nancy Pullum, Fran Roberts, Jim Robertson, Pat Rowland, William Ryan, Richard Scofield, Robert Sperber, Linda Stoller, Rudi Vanderburg, Diane Warner, Jenni Watson, Docia Zavitkovsky, and Natalie Zuckerman.

Finally, we wish to thank John Harney and Eugene Bailey of Auburn House Publishing Company for their patience and understanding in working with a diverse group of authors, each having a rather definitive idea of a final product.

THE AUTHORS

CONTENTS

LIST OF IMPORTANT SAMPLE FORMS

SCHOOL-AGE CHILD CARE
An Action Manual

Part One

OVERVIEW

INTRODUCTION

Day care for the young school-age child—before school, after school, and during school holidays and vacations when parents must work—is a national problem that affects more and more families every year. For the increasing number of two-paycheck, dual-career, and single-parent households in America, three hours of kindergarten or six hours of elementary school cover only part of the working day and leave much room for anxiety. It is difficult to get an accurate picture of the actual numbers of children who are left alone or whose parents report that they leave them with brothers or sisters only a year or two older. Senator Alan Cranston of California testified in 1979 before the Senate Committee on Labor and Human Resources that "Census data tells us that at least two million school-age children between the ages of seven and thirteen are simply left alone without any supervision." And this figure does not include the number of five- and six-year-olds who may be in similar situations.

Signals of need are not coming just from parents. Classroom teachers and school principals express concern about children who arrive at unsupervised playgrounds an hour before school officially opens and who hang around, on those same playgrounds, into the late afternoon. And community service agencies—the Y's, boys' and girls' clubs, and recreation centers that are scattered throughout the land—realize that although not officially in the child care business, their facilities and programs are, in fact, being used more frequently for that purpose.

The enormous need has begun to receive national attention only within the past several years. Before that, most discussion of day care focused on the preschool child. In the late 1960s and early 1970s, psychologists and policy makers were particularly concerned about young children with working parents (though usually they only mentioned working mothers); they examined the effects—both positive and negative—of enrolling young children in Head Start or day care centers for up to nine hours per day. The fact was, however, that the parents most likely to be working full time were those with children already in school. By the mid-1970s, American society had crossed an important demographic watershed: for the first time in history, more than 50 percent of mothers of school-age children were employed outside the home. As this book is being written, that figure has leaped to just over 65 percent. In 1981, sixteen million children between the ages of five and thirteen had working mothers, according to a report of the U.S. Department of Labor. There is no going back.

While the need is on the rise, so are the solutions to meet it. From Virginia to Colorado, from Nebraska to Louisiana, communities are developing a rich and varied assortment of child care programs to complement the school day. Where these are being developed, children don't have to hang out on the block, or stay alone in an urban apartment or a suburban home watching television. Instead, in the best of programs, they have a familiar and comforting place to unwind at the end of the school day. They can have a snack, talk about the day's events with their friends and with trained staff, and then choose from a variety of activities. They can take outings to the local park for a game of touch football or "capture the flag," go on trips to the local recreation center or Y for swimming, or visit the local library or museum. Or they can stay at their program base to work on arts and crafts projects, cook, read, or catch up on homework. Similarly, before school they have a place to read, do homework, talk with friends, and even have breakfast.

The variety of models being used to meet the need is remarkable. School-age care is being provided in or by a wide variety of groups, including park and recreation departments, churches, Y's, day care centers, family day care homes. In a trend that is increasing faster than any other, new programs are being offered as a result of collaborations between public schools and other organizations. The programs are housed in the schools, but they are administered—and have been spearheaded—by a variety of local parent groups, civic organizations, and nonprofit agencies, such as: the YWCA in El Paso, Texas; the State Office of Child Day Care in Hartford, Connecticut; the Camp Fire Girls in Sparks, Nevada; the Chinatown Planning Council in New York City; and a parent group in Nashville, Tennessee.

In the Boston suburb of Brookline, after-school care is available in each of the town's nine elementary schools. Although each program is administered by a separate parent-group organized as a not-for-profit corporation, all programs operate as part of the Brookline Public Schools in accordance with a highly formalized set of guidelines adopted by the Brookline School Committee. Brookline's Extended Day Program has been so successful that the school committee has voted to include "specific space designated for Extended Day" in all future building plans.

In Lawton, Oklahoma; Raleigh, North Carolina; Santa Monica, California; and other communities, the addition of day care services to the regular elementary school program is being used as a "magnet" to effect voluntary racial desegregation. In Lawton, for example, families from any section of town do not pay any fees to send their children to a specially designated "school for working parents," open from 7:00 A.M. until 6:00 P.M. The Family Service Association of Lincoln, Nebraska, and the Children's Center of Reston, Virginia, have developed family day care programs specifically for school-age children. Before or after school, children go to a home near their elementary school and can then play in the neighborhood. In Chinatown, New York City, the Chinatown Planning Council has set up an after-school program that features instruction in the English language, a skill most parents want their children to have.

These creative community solutions to the dilemma of school-age child care are just a beginning, for the need is enormous now and will only increase in the years ahead. In the future more parents will share the care of their children with the school and with a program or programs that supplement the school day.

Such sharing does not represent an abdication of responsibility by parents. Rather, the use of day care reflects the reality of working life in America and the creation of "the new extended family," so aptly described by Ellen Galinsky and William Hooks in their book of that title. In the absence of more traditional kinship networks, parents—along with friends and colleagues who are deeply concerned about their children's care—are in effect creating a new institution that can preserve the values of the past. After all, parents are already sharing their children with another institution—the schools. Moreover, empty classroom space in many schools throughout the nation provides a relatively inexpensive resource. Developing care for the school-age child is, in the best sense of that business-world phrase, a "target of opportunity"; a need that many communities can start responding to *now.*

This book will help you design, develop, implement, and operate a program for the school-age child. If you are a parent desperate for care, we will show you how to identify others like yourself, form an action group, do a community needs assessment, and find the support you need to get a program in place. If you are a school principal faced with working parents who need day care—or with declining enrollment and the need to develop a service that will attract more families to your school—this book will show you how to develop guidelines that allow the day care program to flourish without impinging on your regular school staff or facilities, and how to create a supportive atmosphere in which classroom teachers and day care staff can work cooperatively. If you are the program director of a child care organization, Y, or recreational organization, we will show you how you can expand your program or develop a new program in cooperation with the public schools. And if you are the superintendent of schools or school board member, we will outline the considerations you will have to balance in deciding if you want day care to be operated in your district. We will also show you how to draw up a contract that recognizes the interests and responsibilities of both the school district and the day care provider—one that covers all the nitty-gritty details such as insurance, janitorial services, and access to parking areas.

While we hope this *Action Manual* will meet your needs and the needs of your community and constituency in very practical ways, we emphasize that it is not a cookbook that offers the one magical recipe for school-age child care. Indeed, we do not think there is one particular model that will fit each and every community— different communities have very different needs. A program that works beautifully in one community cannot always be transferred lock, stock, and barrel to another, although parts of it may be transferred and adapted. There is no one right program for every child: some children do better in family day care homes, others in group settings.

What this book offers is a set of models to examine, enabling you to combine and/or adapt those features that best fit your own community needs. It offers a way of thinking about school-age child care, its planning and implementation, which can be applied in many communities, though they won't always produce the same results in each community. And it points toward a variety of ingredients or resources that can be used, to a greater or lesser extent, to develop a program.

One of the resources we emphasize is the use of the school as a base for the operation of school-age child care. We do so for a variety of practical reasons: classroom space is becoming more and more available; many parents prefer to have their children at the same location throughout the day; and the use of school facilities at low or no rent permits parent fees to be reduced and/or staff salaries increased. School space also has its disadvantages; we point these out, too.

We also emphasize a model of service delivery that we call "the partnership," because it involves two community agencies combining their resources to provide care. Often we refer to partnerships between schools and other community groups. The partnership model is one we find most promising for school-age child care, whether or not the schools are involved, because it often involves the most effective use of community resources.

One model that we describe, but do not emphasize, is family day care. Family day care offers some unique advantages to children and parents, especially when provided as part of a "system" of day care homes. But caring for children in a home rather than in a school, community center, Y, or other institution has many ramifications that would require a separate book—and we point you to several good ones.

All of the guidance we offer here is designed to produce a high-quality child care program. "Quality" is a complex and often elusive concept, for it includes virtually every component of a program—its staff, curriculum, administration, finances—and the ways they complement or trade off against one another. Throughout, we will be pushing you toward an ideal of day care, though we are well aware that you will continually have to play your sense of the ideal against the reality of specific situations. We do not compromise on the quality of programs in this book, but want to challenge you to develop the best programs you can with the resources you possess.

The passion behind this very pragmatic book—behind all the nitty-gritty details and technical information about how to make a program work—is a concern for children and their families. It's a concern that was communicated again and again by the many people who shared their programs with us. We hope that by clearing the way for you through everything from needs assessment to incorporation, budgeting to enrollment procedures, and staffing to evaluation, this book will make it easier for you to express your concern for all our children.

Chapter 1

PROFILES OF DIFFERENT PROGRAMS

Programs come in as many varieties as the groups and circumstances that shape them, and each of them is unique. Later you will read about the separate steps that must be taken to establish a program—forming a group, getting approval, finding money and space. You will have to consider what may appear to be discrete program issues, such as providing a range of activities or affordable transportation. But each program is greater than the sum of its parts. Keep in mind that we are talking about real programs, such as the ones presented in this chapter. They exist in specific communities where parents, educators, community organizations and institutions, as well as program staff, are dealing with a range of issues and finding successful solutions.[1]

The Adventure Club—Robbinsdale Area Schools
Suburban Minneapolis, Minnesota

A community education department responds to school-age child care needs in a seven-city school district.

The beginnings of the Adventure Club were not auspicious—this suburban community was convinced it didn't need school-age child care (SACC). The program was initiated because one principal was concerned with the numbers of unsupervised children he was seeing

---

[1] Some of the information in the program profiles will have changed since the original data were collected.

around his building after school. Some of those children who got into trouble in the late afternoon were returning to the school to get help.

When the program did open, it started very slowly—no one knew how to get it off the ground. In its first year it served only six children, and went through several staff members. But the Adventure Club learned how to attract the people who needed its services by reaching out to them with more attractive programing and energetic public relations efforts.

Now in its fifth year, the club serves two hundred children. Three programs held at three schools runs from 6:45 A.M. until 6:00 P.M. Since these schools have both regular morning and afternoon kindergarten sessions, the program serves kindergartners. Special programs are also offered.

The program's success is due in large measure to its ability to build links with other community organizations. It is administered by the school district's community education department. The parks and recreation department cooperates by allowing children in the program to attend recreation activities, such as floor hockey and soccer, at no cost. Parks and recreation department members also come in for two or three weeks and give a special course in gymnastics or drama, and the department publicizes the program.

The summer program is a collaborative effort between the Y and the summer school. The Y offers about five different options to children. For example, they can attend summer school enrichment courses in the morning, and then take a bus to the Y for its recreational program from noon until 6:00 P.M. (The Y offers its programs in the schools and in its own contemporary building.)

Adventure Club staff members and school personnel work closely together for the benefit of the children. For example, on a Monday the school nurse might conduct an in-service training course for Adventure Club staff who are working with a special needs child who is coming off medication. On Tuesday, the supervisory staff will meet with a school social worker who will explain the different resources available to program personnel.

The Adventure Club has also been able to cooperate with the schools to institute a breakfast program at two of their sites. A wide variety of hot and cold breakfasts is provided through the school lunch program at no additional cost. The cost comes out of the program budget and is subsidized by the federal school lunch program (USDA). The schools pay for the necessary staff.

The cost of the program is very appealing. Fees are reasonable

—$25.00 a week for before- and after-school care; $12.50 if only one of these periods is used; and $45.00 for a kindergartner who attends, for example, before school, during the morning when regular school is in session, and then again in the late afternoon, after his or her afternoon kindergarten session is over.

Ninety percent of the program is paid for by parent fees, with the other 10 percent coming from various funding sources, especially the cities. Three cities set aside between two and four thousand dollars each year to subsidize low-income families in the community. This funding enables the program to offer parents a sliding fee scale, so that it is available to all who need it.

At the Adventure Club, there is a strong focus on providing children with a wide variety of options. At their school sites they use a base room for woodworking, crafts, dramatics, and building. They also use the school's gymnasium and outdoor play area, as well as an additional resource room. A variety of outdoor winter sports is provided, and every program has access to a skating rink.

Parents play an active role in the program, although, as is often the case, their involvement has declined a bit since the early, difficult days. Parents are members of the Adventure Club Advisory Committee. They are active lobbyists, writing letters and talking to school board members to help them understand the need for programs, and to encourage them to save school space for SACC.

Like any SACC program, the Adventure Club has problems. Tight money is a concern. The district is experiencing the declining enrollments and school closings many other communities face, while the need for SACC grows. Administrators are trying to determine what their criteria for expansion should be. They feel they haven't developed a good plan yet for deciding when to open new programs, or even how much of their time should be spent devising one. While it attempts to ask these questions about the future, the program deals effectively with its present challenges.

Hephzibah Children's Association
Oak Park, Illinois

A nonprofit agency collaborates with public schools and community agencies to provide school-age child care in both school-based and out-of-school settings.

The Hephzibah Children's Association in Oak Park, Illinois, began more than eighty years ago as an orphanage called the "Hephzibah Home." As the times changed, so did Hephzibah. In the

1950s the agency became a weekday children's residence. In 1973 Hephzibah went through its last major transition when it was faced with new state policies about residential care, as well as dwindling numbers of children at the home. At this same time, concerned members of the community were trying to find a solution to a pressing problem—care for children before and after school. After many meetings and much discussion, the community group, which included representatives from Hephzibah, came up with a solution: Hephzibah and one public school should work together to provide school-age child care. Hephzibah would run the program and the school would provide space and other resources.

This decision was reached at a time when the Oak Park Public Schools were concerned about low enrollments in some schools and were also thinking carefully about how they could maintain the community's racial balance. It was hoped that offering child care at this school would be an incentive to parents from other parts of the school district to send their children there, and that this would help to integrate the schools and increase enrollments. It worked. In the first year, this one school's enrollment increased by seventy children, and more than half of these were minority children. What made it all possible was the adoption of a policy that permitted children to transfer to other schools within the Oak Park school district in order to take advantage of the SACC program. The district provided transportation to the program.

The agency has put much energy and effort into achieving financial stability. It receives a wide range of funding from both public and private sectors.

Because Hephzibah has built strong links with a variety of community agencies, it is able to offer children a wide range of activities at little or no cost—ice skating provided by the recreation department, swimming at the Y, ballet and movement at the Academy of Music. Other services, such as those of a part-time social worker, are also available because of the program's success in networking and collaborating with others.

The good working relationship between the school district and Hephzibah continues. The transfer process within the school district has been streamlined, but the written form that is now used to facilitate that process represents years of hard work.

In fact, setting up the program "was long and hard and there were many setbacks," according to one initiator. But, she adds, "Today, Hephzibah administers school-age child care programs at its original home location and at two school-based sites. Approximately two hundred children in grades K–5 are receiving care before and after school and during school vacations. If you do a good job, it will mushroom."

The Eakin Care Program
Nashville, Tennessee

A parent-run program in a public school.

A 1976 needs assessment at the Eakin School in Nashville, Tennessee, proved what many parents had known for a while: they needed good, safe child care for their school-age children. One parent, the president of the school's parent-teacher organization,[2] would get telephone calls from other parents, and was impressed by the sense of urgency: "I'm a nurse—I can't call for a child at 2:30 in the afternoon!" By 1977, parents had organized a program at the Eakin School, assisted by the principal, who worked with them to have the program officially approved by the school board. This original group of parent organizers had been involved in other projects at the school and had established a good reputation as efficient workers, so the school principal had little trouble with the concept of a program that was not run by the school system operating in "his" school.

Getting approval wasn't easy—the school system had been dealing with many special interest groups that year and was sensitive to still one more demand. But the Eakin parents were patient, and their proposal to the school superintendent was given a sympathetic hearing.

The program started with twelve children but quickly grew. Over sixty children are now registered. The program's bylaws provide for the inclusion of the principal as a member of the governing board and the personnel committee, but the program is run by the parents who use it. They hire staff, develop program policies and philosophy, and are accountable to the school principal and the school system for the successful operation of the program. The school contributes rent-free space and utilities, but parent tuitions support all other costs. Fees were $11 per week for the before- and after-school child care at the time of our visit in 1980.

Children range in age from five to eleven, and all participate in activities and projects together. The philosophy of the parents is a significant factor in the design of the daily activities, which stresses

---

[2] Hereafter, all parent-teacher groups—PTAs, PTOs, and others—will be referred to as PTOs.

opportunities for children to make choices and to have freedom of movement within the limits of safety.

The Eakin Care program was unique in Nashville as the first parent-run, public-school-based program. It has served as a model for other parent groups and schools elsewhere in the state. A school-age child care task force was developed at the same time as the Eakin Care program. A group of agency representatives, parents, and school personnel formed this task force to iron out some of the problems of getting started and to create a climate of acceptance of school-age day care in the community.

There are problems—parents must be managers of this small corporation while working at their own jobs. But most parents seem to feel that it is worth the effort to have a program available which really reflects their goals for children and helps them by providing dependable child care.

The State of Connecticut's Innovative Grant Program for Day Care

A collaboration between a state agency and community groups to provide school-age day care services.

A governor's interest in day care resulted in legislative action in 1978 so that funds would be granted, through a state agency, to support some of the start-up and operating costs of some school-age child care programs in Connecticut. The overall goal of the innovative grants program was to demonstrate that innovative programs could be developed to address unmet needs in cost-effective ways and could become financially self-sustaining. It is now possible for an agency to expand its services to include a school-age program, or for new groups to initiate a nonprofit program, using the money earmarked specifically for this purpose.

In 1980 eight programs were operating under this grant program. They served approximately 356 children in different locations, with each program administered by different community groups. The Office of Child Day Care was the thread that tied these programs together and provided technical assistance on start-up and program operation, along with the special funding. Using a set of guidelines developed for school-age programs under the grant program, the Office of Child Day Care required that the programs maintain a 1:10 staff:child ratio, recommended that a sliding fee scale be used with a maximum fee of $25 per week, and developed a sample fee scale for programs to use.

Many of the programs are run by local YMCAs, but other community groups also participate. A unique before- and after-school program run by a Youth Service Bureau serves Head Start children and kindergartners enrolled in nearby elementary schools. This program was designed to help parents of Head Start children find and keep good jobs by providing all-day child care, as well as day care for kindergarten children whose school schedules create problems for working families needing child care.

The original allocation was $100,000—money that has gone a long way to help meet school-age child care needs in Connecticut. However, the grant program will not continue to fund indefinitely the programs selected for support. Programs are expected to become totally self-supporting at the end of three years, so money is allocated at a decreasing rate during each of the three years. Local governing bodies in the towns served by these programs are urged to take an active role in sponsoring their programs so that local support will become available.

The state of Connecticut has helped to expand the use of community resources for families and children. School codes make unused public school space available for both full-day programs as well as SACC, and the state encourages and helps towns to pay for the renovation of unused classrooms so that community groups can use them. Agencies and local groups which would have had a hard time getting a program off the ground have been given a helping hand, and school-age child care for the "working poor" and for middle-income families not eligible for federal assistance has received an unusual boost.

One of the goals (and by-products) of this project was to stimulate and encourage other communities in the state to support school-age child care by demonstrating that a variety of administrative models are available options.

Eugene Latch Key, Inc.
Eugene, Oregon

A community schools department collaborates with a nonprofit agency.

At an early meeting of a group of people interested in solving the school-age child care problem in Eugene, an invited guest from a

YMCA in a neighboring city told the group that it would cost $50,000 to run one program and "everyone fell off their chairs"!

The planning group, composed of representatives from the local Y, the state social services department, the City of Eugene planning department, 4-C, girls' club, and the community schools department, decided to put together a program that would make use of the resources available in the community—and to stretch those resources to organize a program that would be affordable to parents and would "fit in" with the structures already established to meet community needs for services.

Their efforts resulted in the creation of Eugene Latch Key, a nonprofit organization that would operate school-age day care programs in several schools in the community, supported and nurtured by the community school program which was to provide space and shared resources. The program now operates in seven schools and serves close to 300 children before and after school, on vacations, and during school holidays. Its small administrative staff works hard with parents and community supporters to build a strong financial base, emphasizing diversity in the funding sources supporting the program. The original staff were CETA employees; many of these workers were hired by the program as it developed support from parent fees, state day care subsidies, USDA and state vocational rehabilitation monies.

Two of the most significant resources the Latch Key Program has are the free use of public school space and the support of the community schools program. But Latch Key is financially and administratively independent of the community schools, although the two programs are seen as one by many in the community. This independence is the program's greatest asset: the school budget does not reflect costs for the Latch Key program. Operating in schools designated as community schools means that Latch Key has the use of facilities already available for community school activities and that the program can pay its own way for any extra costs not already covered by community schools funding. Were school budget funds to be cut from the community schools program, Latch Key would continue to exist.

School officials value the program as a much-needed service to families in Eugene, and also appreciate the support parents give to the school system in return for the schools' contribution.

Satellite Family Care Program
Reston Children's Center
Reston, Virginia

A parent cooperative administering home-based care for school-age children with parents involved in policy setting, fund raising, and advising the program.

The Satellite Family Care Program was begun when the center's after-school program—serving toddlers through sixth graders—reached the overflow level. The program was developed as a way of meeting the needs for care, while at the same time providing flexibility to children and their families. For the children involved, it's like having a home away from home.

A number of "homes" are available, each with a caregiver who is a parent with children of her own. A total of sixty children are served, from kindergartners through twelve-year-olds. There are never more than five other children assigned to each caregiver. The advantage of this program is that each home is located in the child's own neighborhood. Caregivers generally live no more than three or four blocks away from the child's home. Children can go out and play with their friends, go to Scouts or lessons, return to the home, go out again—and take part in all of the activities they would if their own parent were at home. They are always under the supervision of a caring person.

Some providers have a more planned approach to activities than others, offering crafts, cooking, field trips, or library visits. Children are also able to visit the main center, but most don't choose to because their friends aren't there.

A program of this type would only work in a neighborhood where children can easily and safely go out into the streets to play. The Reston community provides a very planned, protected environment. Apartment units in townhouses are surrounded by swimming pools, basketball courts, and other facilities that invite children to come out to play. In addition, providers of care are generally women with their own children who don't wish to work outside the home and don't depend upon income from providing child care in order to survive.

Most of the program's income is generated by parent fees, but there is some financial support for families—the Reston Children's Center participates in the USDA's reimbursement program. There is a scholarship program financed by a combination of county subsidies and the center's overall operating budget.

Although this program is not school-based, the schools have, in a sense, become a partner to the center. The Reston Children's Center arranged for the family day care providers to visit children's classrooms so that they would have a better sense of who "their" children were. Also, caregivers meet with principals and send them the center newsletter. The arrangement has worked very well. Both parents and children are very enthusiastic about the informal partnership, because it shows them how committed the providers are to the children's well-being. One visitor has called the satellite program "the best of the new extended family."

Part Two

GETTING STARTED

INTRODUCTION

For many people, starting a school-age child care program is a new experience, and may seem overwhelming. "Where do we begin," they ask, "and how can we be sure it will be successful?" Others may already have established programs and developed much know-how, but would like to improve or expand existing services.

The task is not overwhelming. Many diverse groups have established programs successfully. Each of the components of the start-up process presented here is one that our project, and the many people who shared their experiences and hindsight with us, considers crucial in establishing a program or in improving existing services. Comments, tips, and caveats from those who have successfully initiated programs are included, as well as discussions of common problems, potential obstacles, and strategies that have been used to avoid or overcome them.

This part will take you through the step-by-step process of getting started, from the initial perceptions of one or two people that there is a community need for school-age child care to the formation of a planning group and the work it must accomplish. This work includes assessing needs, and then designing a program of good quality that will reasonably fill them.

There is no one right way to make it happen, and we are not presenting a recipe. Program initiators come from many different locales and constituencies: from small suburbs and large cities, from social welfare agencies, local public school systems, parent-teacher organizations, and churches. What works for one group may be inapplicable or inappropriate for another. You will need to tailor each task to the pattern of your own community.

Although the steps are described separately, the process is not a linear one. Everything hinges on the work that has come before and that will follow. At times your group will perform a juggling act as it simultaneously assesses needs, explores the resources available to it, and designs a program that will realistically meet the needs of the community.

The most important work you will need to accomplish as you get started is to build alliances within your community and to learn how to gain access to the community's resources—both personal and material. Solid building takes time. Many months—perhaps more than a year—may pass between the first shared awareness of need and the establishment of a program. As one veteran citizen advocate from Virginia admonishes, "Know that community organization is a long haul of continuing work."

Good luck.

Chapter 2

FIRST STEPS

No matter what form and scope school-age child care programs eventually achieve, they always originate in the perceptions of one or a few people that children's needs for after-school care are not being met. You may not be aware that there are others who share your concerns, but the signals that a problem exists are probably being received by a number of people coming from diverse bases in your community: parents, staff members of agencies, principals, and other school personnel.

Going it alone is very hard; the broader your base of power and support, the easier your task will be. How do you connect with people that recognize the problem? How do you convince others that a problem exists? And how do you then mobilize your community's resources?

This chapter will take you through the process of perceiving need, connecting with others, and forming an effective action group. It will then describe one of the earliest and most important tasks you will have to perform as you get started—conducting a needs assessment.

Perceiving Needs

Signals of need may come from many different places. As a parent, it may be painfully obvious to you that it is almost impossible to find reliable after-school care for your children; the arrangements you have been able to make with such difficulty are not working satisfactorily; the community you live in has, to your knowledge, no adequate provision of services.

The community itself may be sending out signals that a need exists. The old neighborhood support systems that used to work seem to have collapsed. The women who used to be home to "keep an eye on the kids" have entered the paid labor market; fewer neighbors are around to provide a home base for children when the school day is over, or to keep them until it's time to go to school. Anyone whose eyes are open can see children hanging around with no place to go; accidents occur and parents cannot be reached to provide help and/or medical consent; acts of vandalism are increasing. Here are the signals that led some communities to start programs.

In a southern state, teachers at an elementary school became aware of an increasing number of single parents in the neighborhood and also of a growing number of "latchkey" children who let themselves into empty homes after school. A principal in the Midwest became concerned after a number of incidents: "A child swallowed a lollypop, stick and all, after school on his way home. There was nobody at home and he came running back to school . . . . Kids were getting home and getting into other kids' apartments and raising all kinds of Cain . . . . There were no adults at home; there were all kinds of accidents. When I saw this kid sitting in the back of the car eating his cereal for breakfast, I knew it was time for us to get involved."

A YWCA in Oregon and another in Texas realized that an increasing number of working parents needed school-age child care in their communities when they started getting more phone calls and requests for help. And in Colorado, the director of a YWCA summer camp noted that parents were dropping their children off at 7:00 A.M., long before the program officially opened. A member of a community education department in Florida became concerned when he found kids running around unsupervised at 7:20 A.M., a full hour and forty minutes before the school doors opened.

While individuals, social agencies, and school personnel may perceive the need and feel it is their responsibility to help their constituents, they may also recognize that the establishment of a SACC program will help fill some other needs of the institution or community, such as revitalizing neighborhood schools or achieving racial integration.

■ *Keeping Neighborhood Schools Open.* Declining enrollments and the threat that neighborhood schools will close have
prompted many parents and principals to unite their efforts to establish SACC programs. A group of parents in the South who wanted to
keep their school "alive and viable" and thus "stabilize" their
neighborhood saw the establishment of a SACC program as a way to
achieve their goal; the principal of their school realized that a SACC
program might reverse the trend of declining enrollment. Parents
and principal worked together to set up a program and obtained a
commitment from their city to provide funds.

At a school in North Carolina, three teaching positions were lost
after a 1977 drop in enrollment. The handwriting was on the wall.
However, many families with two working parents or single-parent
heads lived in the school district, and the principal saw "a natural
population in need of school-age child care." A program was begun in
1978; enrollment did increase and is expected to continue growing.

■ *Racial Integration.* In several communities SACC is being
used as an incentive to achieve racial integration. In 1977, for example, as a response to court-ordered desegregation, an Oklahoma town
designated one of its elementary schools as a "School for Working
Parents." Open from 7:00 A.M. until 6:00 P.M., the school is available
to *all* families from any section of town with no charge for the extra
hours of child care.

To achieve voluntary racial integration without forced busing,
public schools in one southern county took a similar approach. An
extended day program was begun in a "magnet school," a predominantly black school where the ratio of blacks to whites did not comply
with court-ordered ratios. The drawing power of the SACC program
attracted a large number of white families, so that compliance with
legal ratios and desegregation was achieved and forced busing was
avoided.

The use of an extended day program as a magnet device to
achieve integration does not work at all schools. When the southern
program described above was established, there were problems of
underenrollment. It took several years before the program gained
acceptance by the community and attained its goal of true racial integration. The long battle was finally won through hard work (including
much publicity), determination, and commitment.

■ *Preventive Services.* Some agencies may decide to set up
SACC programs because they perceive a need to stop problems before they start. They view SACC as a social service strategy to deal

with family situations where there is actual or threatened child abuse and neglect, and as a preventive service in cases of truancy, runaways, drug and alcohol abuse, other forms of delinquency, and teenage pregnancy.

Connecting with Others

School-age child care is not the problem of only a few people, it is a *community* problem, and the solutions have to be created by a coalition of citizens responding to an expressed community need. "It's a mistake to sit there alone and try to do the whole thing by yourself. You need to work with others," said a veteran director in California.

Find others who share your concerns, who confirm your perceptions that the need for SACC is a pressing reality, and who may also want to start a program.

- Parents need to get together with other parents and with schools and agencies.
- Agencies should connect with their constituents, with other agencies and organizations, including community education departments, and with schools.
- Schools should connect with the families whose children attend and with other community resource people.

How Do You Connect with Others?

Talk informally with neighbors, friends, other school parents, the principal, teachers, and other school personnel. "Check with school social workers," advises one organizer. "They have some insight, some inside scoop on who will help you. They know of parents who have a need and aren't getting it met." Talk with the staff of community agencies, such as Y's, boys' and girls' clubs, and with other child care groups, such as preschool programs. Contact your local information and referral system (I&R). Often, an hour or two of telephoning by one or a few people will tell you who else recognizes the need for SACC and whether they are willing to join you in efforts to seek a solution.

In the state of Washington, individual parents approached their elementary school principal asking, "What do I do with my kids after school?" The principal was also concerned because he had noted that children were hanging around the school after it closed, without any proper supervision. The principal spoke to the youth director of the YMCA about the possibility of the Y starting a SACC program in his school.

In Tennessee, the superintendent of one county's schools decided to explore SACC. He found that parents, school principals, community education coordinators, and a Day Care Council were also very concerned, and they joined in efforts to set up programs.

In one Massachusetts town, the League of Women Voters—many of whose members were parents of school-age children—decided to mount a group effort to see whether there was widespread community need for SACC.

Forming an Effective Action Group

The key to getting a program established is to build a constituency that wants the program and will push for it. Whether the impetus first comes from a group of parents or from a principal, there must be prime movers who will then work on others, such as the superintendent and the school boards. (Superintendent of schools in Massachusetts)

After you've connected with others and confirmed that there is a general need for SACC, your next step is to form an action group or task force of "prime movers." There are many ways to start the ball rolling. Sometimes one person within a school administrative structure—a principal, a superintendent, or a member of a parent-teacher organization—sees that there is a need, presents the problem, and asks for the go-ahead to pursue a solution. Often this means conducting a formal study, or "needs assessment," to determine who needs SACC. After the study confirms that there is a need, a group will be formed.

Other individuals may decide to create a specific group that will conduct a full-blown study to pinpoint specifically what needs exist—what age groups need care, in what locations, and during which hours—and then move forward to design and implement a program. In Wisconsin, a group of residents met to discuss the needs of children and families in their community. They decided to conduct an assessment, and after they had the results, they contacted PTO presidents and the superintendent of schools to communicate their findings. They then formed a community advisory committee to "implement a response" based on the indications of need from the survey. That response included establishing program goals and objectives, exploring possible sites, and serving as the community's SACC liaison with other organizations.

Form a Broad-based Community Coalition

All the SACC programs we have talked with have told us that the key to their programs' eventual success was the formation of a broad-based community coalition. Although a group of parents, an agency, or a school principal may have initiated discussion about a possible program, you must soon include people who represent a wide variety of community affiliations, interests, and backgrounds because you must have a broad-based constituency that will support, advocate, and press for the program.

Gaining community approval—and continued support—for a SACC program is usually not an easy task. A Y director stated the problem frankly: "There is a stigma attached to day care. To break down that barrier you must involve the community in what you're doing." Therefore, your best strategy is to ask as many community representatives as you can to join you in your campaign, or in its early stages. All directors who shared their tactics with us came up with the same game plan:

> The best strategy for gaining support and approval is to build a consortium of different interest groups. In our case, there was a parent group, a principal, and an agency. Without all these three groups working in unison and trusting each other the program might not have become a reality.
>
> You have to capture the community—the whole community, not just the schools—build a broad base of support. For our initial meeting we called together thirty or forty organizations. It was the only time we had all those organizations together, but it was important to get their support. That took a lot of phone calls beforehand.

Involve different social classes. When you are hammering out a philosophy and designing the program, the greater your group's diversity, the more cross-fertilization of ideas there will be, and the more likelihood that your program will truly serve different needs.

Involve the "power brokers" in your community. "It doesn't do just to have an interested group of parents. You have to have people who have decision-making powers—gate openers," counsels a director from California. One parent from a small town observed, "Every community has its 'movers and shakers'—find them." Another explains, "We had the Day Care Council working with us, but we also had the school principal on our task force. Without that key person, the program would never have gotten off the ground."

School administrators cannot be expected to organize programs alone, nor, generally, can parents. Parents who need child care are usually working. However, sometimes parents may be the only people who will be able to get the job accomplished, because they have proven their credibility with the school principal, superintendent, or school board. In Massachusetts, Tennessee, New Mexico, and Wisconsin, to mention a few states, busy parents, many of them working, initiated programs. They could not have done so, however, without the school's cooperation. "Parents have more clout with the school administration than anyone else," remarked an organizer from the Midwest. But parents may not be aware that they possess leverage and power. Principals with whom parents have established relationships of trust and accountability may be totally responsive when these parents communicate their needs and their desire to work together to find a solution. It is important for parents to realize that they are their school's constituency, and that they are the taxpayers whom a school committee or town council represents.

Figure 2–1 is a resource list of individuals and groups you should approach as you prepare to call your first meeting to form your action group. Use it now as you plan whom you'll invite, but refer to it at any time when you are looking for help—when you are exploring resources that might be available to your program, or when you must enlist further support. Not all of these people or groups will want to join you now, but they comprise a storehouse to which you can continue to return six months or three years from now. It's a good idea to keep a file on anyone you contact, noting whether they've indicated support, could suggest other contacts, or have offered to help you in some future tasks.

Which of these people can and will help you depends on the kind of program you want to establish: where you'd like to have it located, what kind of money is needed, the politics of your community, and whether SACC is a totally new concept or has been implemented nearby.

Community schools (sometimes called "community ed," "CE" or "lighted schools") can be a major resource. These are publicly supported buildings which are used, either wholly or in part, for activities that are open to all members of the community, after and sometimes during the regular school day. The community schools concept is

SCHOOL-AGE CHILD CARE RESOURCE LIST

- Parents and parent groups, including parent-teacher organizations
- Religious organizations: councils, boards, clergy, members
- Local advocacy groups, especially those involved with children's issues
- School personnel:
  1. Principals, teachers, social workers
  2. Central administration: superintendents, school boards; other administrative bodies
- Departments of community education (sometimes called community schools)
- Recreation departments
- Federal, state, county agencies, especially those that are advocates of children and/or that may provide resources for children with special needs
- Local agencies, especially those connected with child care and children's services. Some of these may be responsible for issuing licenses to child care programs.
- Local licensing bureaus: health, fire, etc.
- Other child care centers: proprietary and nonproprietary
- Citizens' councils
- Members of state, county, local governments
- Special groups in your community: for example, League of Women Voters, Lions, Kiwanis
- Other professional people: for example, staff of universities, lawyers and accountants to help with specific tasks
- Representatives from local industry and business

Figure 2–1

built on the idea that "The schools belong to the community and (that) social service and governmental agencies were created specifically to meet the needs of the people and to serve the community."[1] CE maximizes the use of public school facilities, thus making the best use of tax dollars.

Community schools are often administered by a community or adult education department that is part of the school system. Almost any school can be designated a community school: elementary school, middle or junior high, high school, or unused or outmoded school buildings. Other municipally-owned facilities in the community—recreation centers, old factories that can be renovated, etc.—can also become part of the CE system.

---

[1]Dennis Palm, "Community Education: A Municipal Function," Parks and Recreation Department, Brooklyn Park, Minnesota.

Many kinds of activities and courses can be offered to people of all ages to meet their recreational and educational needs. School-age child care programs are an example of the kind of services that community schools can and do provide for families in the community.

Local social welfare agencies can be very helpful in initiating programs within schools. They often have long-standing relationships with school power structures, and sometimes members sit on the same boards. They have proven their accountability and earned their trust through years of working together. In one Oregon city, the school system now views the Y as a reliable initiator of SACC programs on school turf. In North Carolina, many different groups were seriously considering establishing programs, but when the city's Day Care Council became involved, "it really eased the way."

Agencies which have already had dealings with the school board, churches, and other elements of the local power structure can often direct you to the right person (or persons) to approach. (Be aware, however, that there are sometimes local issues and factions which are not apparent.) Their support should be used with discretion and knowledge of your community's power structure.

Keep in mind, too, that agencies sometimes feel that they can serve community interests best by remaining impartial. Some state agencies will make suggestions on strategies for gaining support or will offer to provide technical assistance, but feel that their future power as child care advocates would be weakened if they allied themselves with one particular group. The director of one state office of child care in the Northeast took such a position, explaining, "*Getting together locally has to be done locally.* We have to be aware of any opposition and will try to bring disparate forces together. If our office intervened, it would skew our impartiality; we have to be careful about not antagonizing one local group or another."

Hold the First General Meeting

Your group may decide to put up announcements—in supermarkets, laundromats, on community church and synagogue bulletin boards, and other public locations. When one program announced that a public meeting would be held, one hundred parents showed up, including a legislator and a selectman. One PTO sent fliers home with the school children, after obtaining permission from the principal. (See Chapter 12 for further suggestions on publicity.) You may wish to send letters to those whose support you particularly want, asking them either to attend the meeting or to join your task force. Explain briefly what your concerns are, what evidence of need there is so far, and why you feel a task force is necessary.

In Rochester, Minnesota, after a general survey found that there were many young children in need of care, a public forum was called to "review the need" and "discuss possible solutions." The Child Care Resource and Referral, Inc., sent letters to key community leaders, citing the survey. Fliers were also posted so that parents were alerted to the meeting. (See Figures 2–2 and 2–3.)

Requisites for an Effective Group

Whether you are a fledgling group that is just beginning to explore the possibility of starting a program, a coalition that has already conducted surveys of need, or an established agency exploring with others the possibility of expanding its services, there are certain requisites that ensure that your group operates most effectively. They are:

- Development of good group process
- Commitment to the common goal
- Establishment of formal, capable leadership within the community
- Division of tasks

The development of good group process means communication: taking the time to share ideas and discuss differing needs and expectations, in order to form a preliminary consensus of what is needed and a very general idea of the ideal kind of program you would like to establish. This communication of needs and ideas will be the most important function of the first meeting or first few meetings, because through it a general, shared, group understanding will develop. During the hours of input and exchange among its diverse members, the group will begin to form cohesiveness, its own identity, and commitment to the goal of establishing a SACC program.

> You have got to commit yourself so that the program will be a success. You have to gain access to and mobilize all the resources and personnel that are necessary to make this a success or, at least, acceptable. Make folks aware that you are going to be taking an adventure and that you are committed to the adventure. (*Community Education Director*)

■ *Developing Commitment.* Without developing a group commitment, the tasks that will shortly be assigned will not be accom-

CHILD CARE RESOURCE AND REFERRAL, INC.

"a community agency dedicated to serving young children and their families."

November 10, 1980

Dear Friend,

We are extending a special invitation to concerned citizens
and community leaders to participate in a public forum on the
need for after school care and supervised activities for
elementary-age children in Rochester. The forum will be held
at the University of Minnesota Rochester Center, 1200 South
Broadway in Rochester, Room 120, on Monday, December 1st from
7:30 to 9:00 P.M.

Your opinions and suggestions are needed regarding a problem
of children caring for children in Rochester. A recent survey
of elementary school-age children indicates that many of them
are unsupervised, or supervised by young siblings, before and
after school while their parents work. Acknowledging the
undesirability of this situation, parents are frustrated by
the lack of good alternatives.

Parents and representatives from the schools, health, law enforcement and social services will review the need and discuss
possible solutions. You are invited to participate in this
creative problem-solving discussion and share your ideas and
concerns with us.

Thank you for caring.

                            Sincerely,

                            Dr. Roy House, Jr.
                            President

                            Tutti Sherlock
                            Executive Director

P.S. To help with our planning, please call our office at
288-9388 to let us know if you will attend. RSVP by
November 26th.

1312 N.W. 7th Street - Suite H • Rochester, Minnesota 55901 • 507/288-9388

Figure 2–2

- please post -

"Hey Joe, can you play ball after school?"

P A R E N T S . . .

ARE YOU FRUSTRATED BY THE LACK
OF CHILD CARE FOR YOUR SCHOOL-
AGE CHILDREN?

DO YOU HAVE TO SCRAMBLE ON SCHOOL
HOLIDAYS TO FIND GOOD ALTERNATIVES?

COME TO OUR PUBLIC FORUM ON THE
NEED FOR AFTER-SCHOOL CARE AND
SUPERVISED ACTIVITIES.

WE WANT YOUR IDEAS TO DEVELOP
SOLUTIONS.

DATE: MONDAY, DECEMBER 1
PLACE: FRIEDELL BUILDING
        1200 SOUTH BROADWAY
        ROOM 120
TIME: 7:30 - 9:30 P.M.
SPONSORED BY: CHILD CARE RESOURCE
                AND REFERRAL
               1312 NW 7 STREET
               288-9388

"Naw...I gotta watch my kid brother until mom and dad get home from work."

Figure 2-3

plished, or the "long haul of community organization" referred to earlier will be abandoned.

■ *Establish Formal Leadership from within the Community.* Programs had been successfully initiated in a Wisconsin city, but when the group that started programs in the city wanted to start SACC programs in rural areas where there was need, they were viewed as "outsiders." The communities, suspicious of city people and the concept of day care, would have no part of them. "They needed some kind of leadership, but no one down there either wanted to take it on or had the knowledge about it."

A program established by parents in the Southwest floundered because of the lack of a formal leadership structure. One parent recalls, "There was funding possible from Community Development but no one was really solid enough to get it. There were great ideas about getting money, but without a formal leadership structure, there was no way to make connections."

■ *Determine and Divide the First Tasks.*   Once an initial consensus and commitment have been formed, the work of the group begins. Many tasks need to be accomplished. Although they will be described separately in the following pages, some of them must be performed simultaneously. (Not all groups will need to tackle each of them.) Since there is so much to do, organize your members into working groups, and divide the responsibilities.

Your immediate tasks will be to conduct a needs assessment and design a program. To accomplish these, you will have to move out into the larger community, exploring and tapping its resources. Then, as you move toward implementation, you will need to gain approval; investigate and obtain incorporation and tax exemption; clarify legal issues of licensing, liability, and accountability; create written agreements; and develop outreach and public relations activities as you open for enrollment.

Strategies for Accomplishing Your Tasks

None of the work ahead of you can be accomplished without approaching other people in the community and asking for and mobilizing their help. While you are accomplishing each of your separate tasks, you will be performing one overriding function: bridge building, proselytizing, gaining further allies. You must continually build alliances and a local constituency that will advocate and press for the program—not only to implement it, but to ensure that it continues successfully. The objective, as one organizer phrased it, is to "capture the city." How is this achieved?

First, you must get the attention of those whose help you need. This may mean enlisting the aid of others to help get a foot in the door—literally, "door openers."

- Find mentors.
- Learn what the power structure is, and who the individuals in it are. Who are the key people, advocacy groups, and agencies that might provide support, power, information, expertise, contacts, knowledge of the politics of the community?
- Send people who are consumers as emissaries. For example, parents whose children attend a particular school should visit the principal to sound him or her out about using the school's space; someone who is an active member of the local YWCA would be the choice to explore with the Y the possibility of expanding its summer program to include care during the school year. Parents have more clout with the school administration than anyone else—use them to speak for themselves.
- Send people or agency representatives who have already established positive relationships with the organization the group wishes to "sound out" and/or who have a reputation for providing good services for children.
- There's strength in numbers. If you have support from the community ed group, for example, ask a member to go with you when you ask for space in a school. Two groups are better than one.
- Observe protocol. One of the first people you should talk with is the one in whose building you'd like space for your program. Be careful to go to the principal and/or the superintendent in the beginning. They don't want to be the last to know.
- Put the relationship on a personal basis first. Don't just walk in and ask for something. Instead say, "Tell me what you do."
- Be pleasant, communicative, and firm—described by one as the "Mr. Nice Guy approach." He added, "Don't get discouraged too easily. Keep pushing, but don't be pushy." The principal of a school that now offers a SACC program recalls,

> I told them that I was not the slightest bit interested, that I was busy enough as it was. But they were persistent! They made me feel guilty about how all of this beautiful space and facilities were being underused. So we agreed to do a needs survey. And I told them that we did

*not have any parents here who wanted their kids staying after school.
And I was surprised at the results! About fifty to seventy-five parents
were interested, which really surprised me.*

- Be confident. Sell your product well. Know you have a good
  thing.
- Provide information. Explain what SACC is. (See Chapter 3,
  "Designing the Program," and Chapter 4, "Getting Approval,"
  for additional suggestions.) Through your public relations,
  make sure that the community understands day care services in
  the public schools. It is important to emphasize the developmental aspects of day care services—many people think that
  day care is a welfare program. There are a lot of myths concerning day care services which need to be dispelled. People
  who misunderstand can infect others with their misunderstanding.
- Explain and establish the need. Approach the problem on the
  basis of *need,* not the *values* of day care. "Values are controversial," according to one director in the Southwest, "but what the
  community needs can be documented." In discussing need,
  buttress your argument with your original perceptions and
  those others have shared with you. Mention that you are about
  to conduct a formal needs assessment—you may enlist the
  cooperation of those with whom you're talking.
- Listen to the viewpoints, problems, and apprehensions of those
  you approach. They are very real. Be particularly sensitive to
  the "turf" issue—the fear that the program will encroach upon
  regular school programs or others' authority. This is a potent
  issue, and must be dealt with by clarifying lines of authority and
  responsibility. Be sure you're not usurping or undermining the
  other person's position.
- Show that you can help each other—point out SACC's benefits
  to the school or agency and to the community. With mutual
  contributions, districts are more inclined to work together and
  with programs.
- Community ed and parks and recreation departments may be
  especially receptive to the benefits of running or cosponsoring
  a SACC program.
- Try to gain cooperation first. This is not yet the time to exert
  direct pressure by going over peoples' heads to their bosses or
  enlisting the intervention of politicians. (See Chapter 4.)

Assessing Needs

One of the first tasks a planning group should undertake is to conduct a needs assessment. This is a survey of your city or neighborhood that asks the specific questions a group must have answered so that it can, first, substantiate to others the pressing need for SACC, and then design and plan a realistic program that will fill those needs.

Why Conduct the Survey?

The immediate purpose of the survey is to find out how many people need a school-age child care program and to obtain a general picture of what their needs are. You may choose to survey the small "target" area you are concerned with—such as one school—or an entire city or county. Just knowing the number of families with school-age children in a neighborhood isn't enough; there has to be a means of finding out who *wants* and *would use* a SACC program, the kinds of care they require and prefer, and an idea of what they can afford to pay. As one director in California stated, "You must know and study the community first, before you begin planning. Understand the expectations of parents. Understand what kind of community you are dealing with —whether it's affluent, impoverished, or somewhere in between."

The needs assessment is both a political and a practical tool:

- To justify and establish the credibility of your goals by documenting the need for a SACC program;
- To gather community support and/or as a basis for calling a general meeting to address the problem;
- To help you design a program that will realistically meet community needs by obtaining information on the extent and type of need, and a financial profile of prospective parent users (see Chapter 3);
- To use as a powerful political tool for persuasion of the "powers that be";
- To overcome opposition based on objections that a new program is not needed and/or competes with programs that already fill the need for SACC;
- To comprise part of the proposal you may have to present if you must request formal approval from the group that is empowered to provide it;
- To buttress your request for funding, especially from federal sources.

An organizer in Maryland advises: "The strongest tool for convincing officials is a needs survey, together with a great deal of newspaper and other media coverage on the need for school-age child care."

It is one matter to inform a principal that a majority of the parents whose children attend his or her school work full time, and that many children are left to their own devices after school. It is another, stronger tactic to present the principal with a documentation of the extent of need, including the specific information that in forty of the school's families, the children between the ages of six and nine are unattended and unsupervised after school; that thirty of those families have indicated they are willing to pay X amount of dollars a week in order for their children to attend a quality after-school program; that they would prefer that this program be located in their neighborhood school. The statistics cited in the letter shown (Figure 2–4) make it difficult to refuse the invitation that was extended.

When representatives of your planning group are, for example, standing before a local governing body asking for permission to use space supported by taxes for a child care program, but lacking clear documentation of need—including numbers—your case will be very difficult to plead, and your request may be tabled until you can conduct a survey. "Responsibility to the taxpayer is very important. You have to establish the need for the program," a director from Virginia points out.

The needs assessment will *not* tell you, by itself:

- Whether you can satisfactorily fill the needs,
- Whether you should have a program,
- If you can offer one that is of good quality and is financially viable,
- What kind of program should be designed,
- Whether those who need it will use it.

The results obtained from the survey will provide only an approximate picture of need; most program organizers don't count on assessments to give them an accurate measure. Nevertheless, we advise that you conduct one. Even when informal perception of need is enough to give the go-ahead for establishing a program, and getting approval is no problem, you will still need specific information to design your program.

FAMILY AND CHILDREN'S SERVICE

201 Twenty Third Avenue, North
NASHVILLE, TENNESSEE 37203

October 25, 1977   615 327-0833

Dr. Bob Innes, Director
Child Development Specialist Program
Peabody College
Nashville, Tennessee

Dear Bob:

The Tennessee Office of Child Development and Family and Children's
Service has for over a year been concerned with the lack of after
school care for children in Davidson County. The need for programs
which serve children (K-6) of working parents has been highlighted
through two specific surveys. In the Donelson Community some 177
parents expressed a need for an after school care program for some
275 children.

The Tennessee Office of Child Development and Family and Children's
Service were instrumental in initiating an after school program at
Eakin School and are currently involved in developing a similar
program in the Donelson Community. Our concern at this point is
to consider after school care with the total community in mind. Our
indications show an overwhelming need for programs of this type in
several sections of Davidson County. We are therefore creating a
task force to act as a coalition in support of after school care
in our Community. Enclosed you will find a narrative which will
give you a brief history of our efforts in this and will further
explain why we feel a task force is necessary at this point.

We invite you to attend a meeting at Family and Children's Service,
201 23rd Avenue, North, on Thursday, November 17th at 10:00 A.M.
to further explore what this task force could do in support of
after school care in Davidson County.

If you are interested in serving on this Committee, please contact
Family and Children's Service (327-0833) before Thursday, November
10th. We thank you for your cooperation in this endeavor and look
forward to working with you.

Sincerely,

Amy Potter   Louise Burgess
Mid-Cumberland Child   Family Advocate
  Development Coordinator   Family and Children's Service
Tennessee Office of Child
  Development

A United Way Member Agency *Member Family Service Association of America—Member Child Welfare League of America, Inc.*

Figure 2–4

When Should We Do the Assessment?

Long before you offer a program! Assessments to determine and validate the extent of need for SACC are often conducted before any official group is established to move ahead in designing and proposing a program. Do the assessment *before* you make your decision to offer a new program, or begin to design one. This may seem obvious, but many groups have jumped into the water without knowing the depth. The assessment may show you that there is, in fact, not enough need or interest to warrant a program, or that you cannot provide a quality program that will adequately fill the actual needs.

If you already know that need is pervasive, but want precise information on such consideration as who would use a program, where they would like it, and what they can afford to pay, the timing of your survey should be planned according to when you would like the program to begin. If you want to open your doors in September, do the assessment in plenty of time to design the program, get it approved, and set it up right. This may take more than a year to accomplish.

Who Conducts the Survey?

This depends on which is the most logical group in your community to do the job, and also on which resources are available to you. Whatever route you use, be sure you observe protocol and obtain prior permission to conduct your survey from the appropriate people: the principal or superintendent if it is a survey within his or her school or district, your clergyman if you are calling a meeting of your congregation to ask them questions.

Here are some suggestions for possible routes to use:

■ *Schools.* This is easiest and most logical. The schools are generally where your population-in-need is; there will probably be an existing structure that can be used, and it is often the cheapest course, since mailing costs are eliminated.

Within individual schools or entire school systems, SACC surveys have been done by PTOs, individual classroom teachers, room parents, and administrative staff that exist to handle external "business." Many school systems have special departments of research and statistics that may either help you with your survey or conduct it for you. In Utah, the State Board of Education conducted a needs assessment in two large school districts. Community schools or community education departments should be considered as prime vehicles for conducting your survey. They are mandated and already set up to do comprehensive needs assessments of different age groups within a community, and then to determine whether providing space in school buildings would help meet those needs.

It is often difficult to gauge the number of children who will be in kindergarten within a year or two, and who might need and use the program. Some people have used kindergarten screening or preregistration periods, or have asked preschool day care centers in the neighborhood to survey this age group. Schools sometimes gather information on approximate numbers of kindergartners they expect; you might survey incoming kindergarten children with younger siblings to determine future need and numbers.

Sometimes it is difficult to obtain access to the schools. One reason is that principals don't want to be seen as responsible for the survey or its results. Assuring him or her that the group conducting the assessment will be careful to assume all responsibility for the survey may allay fears. Some principals fear it will jeopardize the home-school relationship, or are initially opposed to the idea of day care in their schools. (See Chapter 4, "Getting Approval," for sources of opposition and strategies for handling them.) When the director of a YMCA child care program in Colorado asked principals to inform parents and teachers that the Y would be making programs available within their schools, she quickly learned not to use that approach:

> The principals didn't see themselves in the role of bringing information to their clients. It was an insult to them to think of the schools caring for kids from 8 to 3 and of us taking care of kids before and after school. They didn't like to think of themselves as doing day care. A lot of them were not interested and saw no relationship between our program and the children in their schools.

■ *Agencies.* If gathering the information you want is difficult to do through the schools, don't go over heads or tread on toes. There are other routes you can use. Try community agencies—sometimes they are permitted to work through public school systems. Also, they might either conduct their own independent surveys or include the questions you want answered on one they're about to do. We suggest checking out child welfare agencies, the local health and welfare council, Y's, or information and referral systems. For example, in one city in the Southwest, an initial community needs assessment was done by the city's department of social services; this resulted in a program based at the YMCA. Six years later regular community-wide needs assessment for all types of child care are the responsibility of the Volunteer and Information Center, a United Way–funded service that does information and referral and volunteer placement for a variety of social services. CETA workers conducted a door-to-door survey for a Children's Association in the Midwest.

■ *Cities or Counties: Planning and Recreation Departments.* A city department of planning in Maryland did a study that indicated that there was a minimum of 6,200 children in need of SACC.

■ *Civic Groups.*   The Women's Club in one city, and the League of Women Voters in another, circulated questionnaires in the public schools.

■ *Devise Your Own Creative Solutions.*   A local high school or college class that is learning techniques of demographics, statistics, or research methods might be happy to take on a survey task. Many SACC groups conduct the assessment themselves.

What Form Should the Survey Take? How Big Should It Be?

Both the form and size of the survey will depend on many factors:

- Who your "target population" is (who you've decided to limit the survey to)
- How much acknowledgment and perception of need there already is
- Your financial and human resources
- Who is conducting the assessment
- What kind of information you want

There is no one way in which the questions must or should be asked. Suit your survey to your needs: what are you trying to find out, and from whom? Use whichever method is most feasible and efficient to obtain and retrieve the information you need.

The use of sophisticated instruments does not always ensure that you will come up with information that is really useful for your purposes. Some surveys are so large, and the return rate on printed questionnaires is universally so small, that it may be difficult or misleading to make generalizations or predictions from the answers you do retrieve.

You will have to decide on the scope. In one Massachusetts town, when parents wanted to begin a pilot program in one school, only that school population was canvassed. The PTO conducted the survey, and thirty children were found to need after-school care. On the basis of this information, a program was proposed to the town's school board, and it was approved.

It's not carved in stone that a needs assessment must be done in writing. Surveys may be done:

- By printed questionnaires, fliers;
- By telephone;
- By door-to-door surveys;
- Verbally, by calling a general meeting.

Retrieval

Veterans of the printed survey method will attest that retrieval is the greatest problem in getting reliable information: "We only received nineteen out of six hundred fliers back, even though we knew more people needed and wanted the program." People don't like to fill out forms. In the deluge of printed matter that assails us all, forms get misplaced on the kitchen counter; sometimes they get lost on the by-ways between school and home. Before a method of distribution is chosen, try to anticipate these problems and devise ways of dealing with them. If you do take the paper route, a good plan is to follow up the distribution of printed forms, about a week after the first round is made, by conducting phone calls. If your survey is a large one, however, printed forms are the most expeditious means of gathering your information.

In some communities a bilingual form, printed in Spanish on one side and in English on the other, for example, may obtain the largest response and the best profile of what is needed and who would use the program. In one Florida county the survey was written in Spanish, Vietnamese, and English.

If you mail questionnaires, enclosing a stamped, self-addressed envelope will increase your rate of return, but you must, of course, weigh the benefits against the financial costs.

You may decide not to use forms. If you choose to conduct the survey by telephone or door-to-door, keep a list of questions by your side and enter each response, so that later you can compile and analyze your information.

If you want to canvass one specific group, such as a religious congregation, you might call a general meeting for all interested parents, obtaining on-the-spot information about interest in and need for a program.

What Makes a Good Needs Assessment Instrument?

The survey should be simple to answer and designed so that the information you receive from it can be easily analyzed, compiled, and summarized. Clarity is the most important feature of your survey: the questions and definitions must be clear and precise. For example, by inquiring, "Do both parents work in your family?" you may be implying that only paid *work* qualifies one for using the program, and unwittingly exclude those cases in which a parent is attending school and is in need of child care. Respondents shouldn't feel that they don't qualify for a program because of the definitions on the questionnaire.

If the survey is not clear, the information you do obtain may vastly underrepresent actual need. In one Connecticut town, the parents of seventy children indicated on a questionnaire sent out during the planning stages of the program that they needed child care. The program was set up to accommodate these children, but once it opened, fewer than twenty-five signed up. It became evident that the cost was too high and the actual need was for more part-time care—a few days a week, not five. But the questionnaire hadn't asked about costs or part-time care. Specific questions about what parents could afford, how many days a week, and for which hours they required care might have smoothed the program's early days.

Brevity is the soul of insuring a higher return rate. Ask the questions you need to have answered, but try to keep the survey as brief as possible.

How Do You "Do" the Survey?

- Decide on the information you need, and prepare questions that will obtain it.
- Ask the questions and record the answers.
- Compile the information. Use a tally sheet for the number of "no," "yes," "maybe," and other kinds of responses.
- Summarize the results so that you can use them.

■ *What Information Do You Need?*   Each group will probably word its own needs assessment based on the information it wants to gather about its specific community. However, questions generally should be included that find out not only who *needs* care for school-age children, but also who *wants* it, who would *use* it, and what they feel they are able to *pay. The answers to these questions are not always the same.* In addition, try to obtain some idea of what kinds of care is needed (hours, special days) and where the preferred locations for your proposed program would be.

It is strongly advised that you ask for the names, addresses, and phone numbers of the respondents. Some groups, concerned about the issue of confidentiality, decided not to request this information. Later, when the program was ready to open, and enrollment was low, they were unable to get in touch with those parents who had indicated they would definitely use a child care program.

Specifically, some of your questions should ask the following:

- Name, address, telephone numbers (home and work)
- All children in family: ages, grade levels
- School(s) attended and neighborhood(s)
- Extent of need (wording should be very clear here):
  — Ages of children in need of care now
  — Ages of children you anticipate will have need
  — Special needs children
  — Hours care is needed: before school, after school, both
  — Days: every weekday, a few days a week, summers
  — Hours and days when the need is most serious
- What are present arrangements? Are they adequate?
- Would you use a child care program if one were available in an accessible location and in a price range you could afford?
- What could you afford to pay? (Give several choices, and ask parents to set a maximum limit on what they could afford.)
- Would your child need a scholarship, if it were available, to attend?
- What location would you prefer? (neighborhood school, central city location, etc.)
- Would you need to have transportation provided? For which hours? (morning, split session, afternoon)
- What kinds of activities would you like the program to include?
- Would you be able/willing to help with the program? Planning? Working?

You may want to include a space for comments, but be prepared for some that oppose the concept of school-age child care, especially when programs are based in schools.

Figure 2–5 is an example of a survey used throughout the schools in Winchester, Massachusetts.

■ *Special Tips for Conducting the Survey.*   State who is responsible for the survey, and its purpose. It's important to let people

TO: WINCHESTER PARENTS

FROM: The Winchester League of Women Voters and the Community
         Schools Association

DOES WINCHESTER NEED AN AFTER SCHOOL CHILD CARE PROGRAM?

This year the Winchester League of Women Voters (LWV) is conducting a study of after school child care programs. Such programs
have evolved primarily, though not exclusively, to meet the needs
of working parents. They are geared toward the elementary school
age child, providing a stimulating but comfortable environment
during non-school hours, vacations and holidays. The Winchester
LWV has designed this questionnaire to determine if a need exists
here in Winchester for the type of programs now being offered in
several neighboring communities. Please answer the questions
below and return one questionnaire per household to your child's
teacher or school office by FEBRUARY 11, 1981. All responses
will be treated confidentially.

1a. Are you currently making arrangements for after school care
    for your elementary school aged child/children on a
    regular basis?

            ____ YES, 5 days/week   ____ NO

            ____ YES, less than 5 days/week

1b. If yes, would you consider or prefer an after school full-
    or part-time child care program of recreational/educational
    activities as opposed to your present child care arrangements?

            ____ YES, consider   ____ NO

            ____ YES, prefer

    If you answered NO to question 1a, please answer c and d
    below.

1c. Would you take advantage of such a program even though you do
    not have the need for after school child care?

            ____ YES   ____ NO

1d. Do you anticipate having this need within the next five years?

            ____ YES   ____ NO

2. If a well conceived, quality after school child care program
    were initiated in Winchester, would you be willing to pay
    for it via a reasonable fee or tuition?

            ____ YES   ____ NO

    If YES, at what point would you find the cost per child of
    an after school care program prohibitive?

    ____$15/wk   ____$25/wk   ____$35/wk   ____$45/wk   ____higher
                                                            than $45/wk

3. Please indicate how important each of the following features
    would be in deciding whether to use an after school child
    care program.

	Very Important	Somewhat Important	Not Important
a) Cost			
b) Transportation			
c) Types of activities offered			
d) Coverage on school holidays/release days			
e) Other			

4. The following is a list of activities frequently offered in
after school programs. Please put a check next to the five
activities you would most like to see offered in a Winchester
program.

Dance	Exercise classes	Tutoring
Movies	Woodworking	Foreign language
Gymnastics	Arts and crafts	Free play
Cooking	Music	Other (list your
Homework/reading room	Drama	suggestions)
Field trips	Sports	_____

Please use the back of this form for any other suggestions or to
comment on further needs/problems not addressed by this questionnaire (e.g., extended-day kindergarten, after school program
geared toward junior high age group). If you would like to be
contacted with more information if and when a program is developed,
fill in your name and address below.

Name _____   Telephone _____

Address _____   School District _____

Figure 2–5

know—on the form, if you use one, in an accompanying cover letter,
or verbally, and in any public announcements—what organization is
conducting the survey, including the name and phone number of at
least one contact person. Be careful not to raise parents' expectations.
You should make clear that the survey is an exploration, and in no
way a promise that a program will definitely be established. In one
town, on the same day that a League of Women Voters' survey was
distributed through the local public schools to see whether there was
enough parent interest to begin serious work on a program, the
president of the League received a call from a mother who asked, with
desperation in her voice, "When can I enroll my child?"

See Figure 2–6 for an example of a well-worded cover letter.

Providing the organization's name and a contact person will also
spare those not responsible from unwanted phone calls. A program
coordinator in Virginia explained, "We don't want to put undue pressure on the principals in the schools . . . having people knocking on

FAMILY AND CHILDREN'S SERVICE

201 Twenty Third Avenue, North
NASHVILLE, TENNESSEE 37203

January 16, 1978   615 327-0833

Dear Parents:

    We are looking into the need for some type of after-school
care program for children (grades K-6) in the Madison community.
This program would provide supervised recreation and creative
activities for children whose parents work later than the school
closing time.

    We need to know how many parents could use this service.
We would appreciate it if you would answer the attached questionnaire as completely as possible. Please send the completed
questionnaire back to the school by your child tomorrow. We
will then gather these forms from the school, evaluate the need,
and send you our findings.

    Thank you for helping us with this project.

Sincerely,

Louise C. Burgess, M.S.W.   Amy Potter
Family Advocate   Regional Coordinator
Family and Children's Service   Tennessee Office of Child
                                       Development

AP:db

A United Way Member Agency   *Member Family Service Association of America—Member Child Welfare League of America, Inc.*

Figure 2-6

the doors saying, 'We demand this service!' We don't want to create false hopes."

Share the results of the survey with all those who had a part in it: parents, children, congregation, principals, press, etc. It might be possible to do a follow-up press release, which will help you to generate more publicity and interest.

One director of a county office for children recalled the difficulties she encountered in having assessment promises fulfilled:

> Last year was an election year. There had been no needs assessment that year because of an administrative transfer. Each supervisor was promising their constituents that they would get them mailed out but they hadn't. We didn't like that because there was too much politicking involved there.

If you can, use newspaper and other media coverage. (See Chapter 12, "Publicity and Enrollment," for further discussion of publicity techniques.) This will help generate interest in your survey, making it more likely that people will cooperate in answering the questions or in returning printed forms to you. Many radio and some television stations will make free public service announcements; generally local newspapers will print a press release, especially if it is hand delivered and you get a chance to speak personally to the editor responsible for community news. Include a name and phone number on the press release, so that either the editor or interested readers can call a spokesperson for additional information. (But be prepared for the possibility that your publicity may generate the first manifestations of opposition, possibly from irate taxpayers—"Is this a good use of our tax dollars?"—or from private day care operators—"Unfair competition!" However, never fear the power of publicity.)

■ *How Do We Compile the Information?* Total the responses, and then break them down for each question. Some groups use a tally sheet, marking down each response of "yes," "no," or "need is for before-school," etc., to each question, and then totalling the number of same responses to each question. Others use one of the questionnaire forms, entering the totals for each response on it. If you are sending questionnaires to a number of schools, and you later want to break down the responses by schools, use a different colored paper for each school—it makes it a lot easier to sort and break down the responses when they are trickling in.

Figure 2–7 is a sample of a questionnaire distributed to the seven schools (parochial and public) in Milton, Massachusetts, and a breakdown of some of the results.

LEAGUE OF WOMEN VOTERS
of Milton, Massachusetts

The Milton League of Women Voters is conducting a study of our community's needs for after school day care. Would you please help us by completing this questionnaire and returning it to us in the accompanying envelope by March 31st? Thank you.

Name of Contact Person: _____
Telephone Number: _____
Address: _____
_____

***** Please submit one questionnaire per family *****

1. How many children in your home are in grades K-6? _____

2. List the grade each child is in (K-6). _____

3. How many parents in your household work outside the home?

_____ 1 parent   _____ Both parents

4. Does your child go to a day care center or other organized program?

_____ Yes   _____ No

5. If an organized and supervised after school care program was started in the area of your child's school, would you take advantage of it?

# Responses	# Children
142 Yes	224
193 No	326
41 Maybe*	74
376 Total	624

If yes, would you take advantage of such a service at a maximum cost of $25 per week?

__107__ Yes   __30__ No   __5__ Maybe

6. If an after school program is started in the area of your child's school, could you provide transportation home?

__104__ Yes   __32__ No   __6__ Maybe/Blank

Name (optional) _____

Address _____

*There was no "Maybe" category on the survey, but parents wrote it in or put question marks. The person who worked on the analysis of the responses reported, "We didn't know how to interpret the 'maybe's--they might have meant, 'First we'll wait to see how good the program is.'"

Figure 2-7

(Adapted from *Starting School-Age Day Care: What Are the Considerations?* Prepared by the Davidson County School-Age Day Care Task Force in Nashville, Tennessee.)

■ *How Do We Summarize the Results?* Present them so that they have meaning, are easily understandable, and place your cause in the best possible light. Don't be discouraged if the return rate is lower than you expected or hoped. Use your other perceptions of need in deciding whether to move ahead with your plans. You will have to decide the best way to present your figures.

The Milton League of Women Voters changed the raw numbers into percentages when they later presented a report of their study. However, they were advised that it might not be to their advantage to do so. Statistics such as the ones in their survey may be deceptive, or are more easily manipulated than plain numbers. For example, 38 percent of those who returned the survey answered question 5 by saying they would use a SACC program. Someone who wished to oppose a program might use this percentage as proof that there was not sufficient need or interest to warrant starting one. Presenting the fact that parents of 224 children indicated they would use a program makes a more powerful statement. There was a 28 percent return rate for all the surveys sent out. What is the significance of the 72 percent who did not return the questionnaire? Does that mean that 72 percent are opposed? Not interested? Too busy to fill it out? Or are many of them waiting to see what happens before they make their decisions? The 28 percent return rate is, in fact, surprisingly high; if anything, it points to unusual interest.

It's a good idea to develop a "profile" of the parents and children who would use the program. The detailed form shown here (Figure 2–8) might be for your own use when you later design the program; the "short form" (Figure 2–9) contains only essential information that you would present to a board for approval to move ahead in designing and implementing your program.

What Do We Do with the Results of the Assessment?

- If you have not already contacted officials, you can use the results to get their attention.
- If you have waited for the results of the survey before forming an action group, you now have the basis for calling people together to create a task force.
- You will use the survey to decide whether a program is indicated, and you will use it as a general guide in designing the program (Chapter 3).

A DETAILED PROFILE

I. *CHILDREN*—Who needs the program?
   # of Children   _____
   Age Ranges (Grades)   _____
      Kindergartners?   _____
      Special Needs?   _____
II. *LOCATION*—Where is program (are programs) needed?
   Neighborhoods   _____
   Schools Attended   _____
   Where do parents prefer to have program(s) located?

   _____
   What are the transportation needs of children and parents?
      from home to program   _____
      from school to program _____
      from program to home   _____
   Can parents pay for transportation? _____
III. *TIME*—When is care needed?

                                             No. of Children   Ages
      HOURS:
         Before school   _____   _____
         After school   _____   _____

      Are there split sessions?
         Beginning when:
            A.M.   _____
            P.M.   _____
         What are differences in school hours?   _____
         What are kindergartners' hours?   _____
      DAYS: On which days is care needed?
         Monday—Friday?   _____
         Part-time (e.g., three days a week)?   _____
         Snow days?   _____
         School vacations?   _____
         Summer?   _____
IV. *MONEY*
   What is the range of price parents can
      afford to pay?   _____
   What is the maximum amount they can pay?   _____
   How many will need significant financial
      support?   _____
   How many may be eligible for special funding?   _____
   How many cannot afford to pay any amount?   _____
V. *GENERAL INDICATIONS*
   How many have indicated they would use the
      program?   _____
   What kind of program have they indicated
      they would like?   _____

Figure 2-8

A "SHORT" PROFILE

(#) _____ children, ages _____, special needs (#) _____,
    need a program in the _____ neighborhood.
They (*will/will not*) need transportation.
The program is needed for (days) _____
    and (hours) _____.
(#) _____ can pay a range of $_____ a week (or day), with a
    maximum amount of $_____.
(#) _____ will need financial support.
(#) _____ families have indicated they would use such a program.
They would like the program to (offer, emphasize, achieve the goals of)
_____.

Figure 2–9

- Finally, you will use the results when you go for formal approval; if you need to submit a proposal, the survey will be a part of it.

Now that you have some concrete information, you can move to the next task: designing a program to help meet the needs expressed in the results of your survey.

Chapter 3

DESIGNING THE PROGRAM

You have conducted a survey of the need for school-age child care and analyzed the results. You are now ready to consider the following questions:

- What kind of program is needed?
- What kind of program do we want?
- Can an existing program(s) be used, expanded, or improved to meet the need and provide what we want?
- If not, should a new program be established?
- Can we design and deliver a *viable, successful* program that will meet the needs of children, parents, staff, and community?

To answer each of these questions, you will need to study the results of your needs assessment; consider the options you have as far as available resources are concerned; weigh the advantages and disadvantages of each option; and make choices that come as close as you can to filling needs, without sacrificing basic standards.

Using Existing Programs

Before you make the decision that a new program should be designed, find out if there is an existing program (or programs) that could be changed or expanded to fill the need for SACC. A children's center in Massachusetts enlarged a preschool program to include school-age children, because the program had the extra space available to do so; in a small southern city, the community education coordinators expanded a summer program held at an elementary school into a program that operated during the regular school year as well.

Sometimes departments or agencies that have not considered the provision of school-age child care as part of their "mission" may be encouraged to enlarge the scope of their services. Examples might be a community schools department that offers evening classes for adults, a youth-serving agency such as a Y or boys' club, or a preschool day care center. In New Mexico, a community parks and recreation program began providing SACC in addition to its open-rec program.

If you are an agency or other group that is already offering SACC, but would like to improve your services, compare the different elements of your program with those options, standards, and recommendations presented in the following pages. (You can also refer to later chapters, for example, "Personnel" or "Resource Development," for more detailed suggestions.) If you haven't conducted a needs assessment recently, you may wish to do so to make sure your program is meeting the real needs of the families you wish to serve.

Designing a New Program

If you have concluded that there are no existing programs that can be used to meet the needs you have perceived and that are expressed in the needs assessment, you are ready to begin the exciting but difficult process of designing a new program. There are no set formulas or "right" decisions for program design. Since every community and situation is unique, the only correct decision is the one that best meets the needs of your community. A good program, wherever it is placed, is a good program. There are, however, common areas where decisions must be made, as planners consider location, finances, administrative structures, and basic standards that must be maintained. We will make recommendations to help guide you in making the decisions that are "right" for your individual program.

It is important for program designers to understand the ways in which decisions made about one program area affect all other areas. Although staff or transportation may seem to be discrete considerations, they are not. As you plan your program, you will be forced to consider a number of factors simultaneously. Throughout the design process, the greatest balancing act will be the pull between your desires for a quality program and the realities of your budget constraints. Finances—cost of program and available income—will weight all of your decisions. For this reason, it is essential that program design and budget preparation be done side by side. You will have to make trade-offs—perhaps a less ideal space in exchange for free rent, or a slightly higher rate of tuition in order to provide safe and reliable transportation.

Take one step at a time. Be realistic about what you can and cannot do. Remember that you neither can, nor must, fill all the needs in the proposing or planning stages of a program—and sometimes never. Some planners have found that pressure is exerted on them to start programs for certain groups, or in certain locations. Try to resist the pressure from these groups to fill their individual needs. A community organizer told us, "Set up a pilot program, fund it modestly, evaluate it as it goes along. If it works, it gets bigger. You have to be willing to not meet all the needs at once if you want it to work in the long run. We've told that to several communities around here. They didn't listen to us and they weren't successful."

You will not solve all the problems at once. You may feel it is wise to delay some decisions until a later date. In one Massachusetts community, a planning group decided to put off the purchase of any major equipment until they could later determine the best allocation of the funds they had.

Although ideally the program should be designed before it is proposed and initiated, in reality, its shape is constantly evolving: often some major decisions will be made while the program is in its beginning stages of operation, and as it grows and external circumstances change, so will its characteristics.

Using the Needs Assessment

A common question is, "How do we know if there is enough need to justify a program?" Sometimes this is difficult to determine. Obviously the more precise and detailed the information from the survey is, the better able you will be to make your decisions about whether to offer a program, where to locate it, and how much to charge. Remember that evidence of need is not sufficient to make the decision to push for the creation of a program. You will need to weigh the results of your survey against other factors—particularly what parents say they can afford to pay—and available resources against program needs.

How do you know that those who have indicated on the survey that they need the program will use it? You don't. Remember that respondents may tell you that they need SACC, and even what they can or are willing to pay. This does not necessarily mean they will use the program once it is offered. One program organizer repeats the experience of many:

> We surveyed parents in the community. Twenty-seven parents said they would use the program. Out of those twenty-seven, only twelve responded later when we started the program. Some had moved out of the community, and some maybe felt that they didn't want to give the program a try.

Some parents don't want to jeopardize their already-existing— although perhaps not too satisfactory—child care arrangements for a program that hasn't gotten off the ground. Others may not be able to afford the program once it opens. Or perhaps, in the time lag between assessment and actual start-up, parents have moved out of town or made other arrangements. Needs assessments are not foolproof; they give no guarantee that parents who expressed strong interest will actually enroll their children.

In designing your program, use the needs assessment results as a general guide, not a blueprint. Take a long look at the survey information, and the information you may have gathered in other ways. What kind of picture of need is taking shape?

- How many children are potential customers? What is their age range? Are they predominantly in kindergarten through third grade, or do you have a smattering of fourth- to sixth-graders? In some communities, seventh- and eighth-graders' parents may seek an organized program.
- Are there children with physical or emotional handicaps who need day care?
- Do most of the children go to and leave school at the same time, or do you have split shifts?
- Are there geographic pockets of concentration—certain school neighborhoods, for example—where demand is largest? Or is the need spread across the community? What does this mean in terms of transportation?
- Where would parents prefer to have the program located? What are their transportation needs?
- What is the range of prices parents have indicated they can afford to pay? How many are eligible for federal or state social service funds? What percentage of families responding to the questionnaire would need significant financial support from Title XX or other funding programs?
- How many have indicated they would use the program? What

kind of program—academic emphasis, recreational—would they like?

Consider Your Community's Resources

Now that you have a rough outline of need, consider primary sources of assistance and cooperation. There are three kinds of resources that exist in every community: human resources, information resources, financial resources. No matter how they are categorized, we agree with the community ed director who says that "communities are rich in resources." Your task is to find them and to learn how to tap into them. (Refer to Chapter 2, p. 27 for list of potential resources.)

Some existing programs and services may be of special help by providing specific information and/or technical assistance. (See Appendix for list of programs to contact for technical assistance and licensing agencies.)

Information and referral services will refer you to community groups relevant to your area of interest. Some referral systems provide information solely on available child care services. Others, such as those I&R's funded by the United Way, will refer you to a variety of services. If you do not know whether such a system exists in your community, the local city hall probably does. Communities may have a directory on resources and youth, or a publication that lists all local commissions.

Some child care information and referral systems will also provide technical assistance to you and can tell you what program to visit in a nearby neighborhood, or who else is interested in starting a program. They may be able to help you with program design, proposal writing, possible funding sources, or how to apply for licensing. Consider seeking help from your local licensing agency, child welfare organizations in your vicinity, or other day care programs.

Visit model programs. A North Carolina superintendent and assistant superintendent of schools visited different magnet schools around the country and were very impressed with the extended day programs they saw. As a result, they were instrumental in developing similar models in their own community. The extended day programs of the Brookline Public Schools in Massachusetts have served as a model for a number of groups who wished to initiate their own SACC programs.[1]

---

[1] See James A. Levine, *Day Care and the Public Schools* (Education Development Center, Newton, Mass., 1978), for a full profile of the Brookline, Massachusetts, extended day programs.

Be sure to think about community facilities that may be used in addition to those at your program site. In the Southwest, a YMCA-sponsored SACC program is held in schools where the only spaces available to them are the gymnasium, cafeteria, playgrounds, and some stage sections in the gyms. Because these constraints would prevent the Y from running the kind of program it would like to offer, it has built additional activities into the SACC program schedule: all children swim at the Y once a week, and there is at least one additional weekly field trip.

In a small Massachusetts city, a program that is based in a church and at the center's own building has surveyed its surroundings and been able to maximize local resources for the benefit of the children it serves. They use the gymnasium and pool at the YMCA, the public library for reading and homework, a bowling alley, and a movie theatre. Van trips are made into the surrounding countryside.

Consider schools. Many planners—who often include school personnel—look to the schools as a potential resource during the early stages of program development. In considering how you might collaborate with the schools, remember that there exists a wealth of possibilities that range along a continuum, from schools that are willing to transport children to a center or family day care home after school to others that want to administer their own program. In these times of funding cutbacks in all areas, planners—whether they are parents, agency directors, school personnel, or others—should consider the general ways that community/school collaborations can maximize the use of already-existing resources. (See the chart on p. 72 for advantages and disadvantages of different facilities. Refer to Parts Three and Four for discussions of policy issues and administrative models involving the schools.)

Using schools as resources doesn't always work, or work well, however. You should be aware of potential problems, such as threatened school closings and consolidations. When communities reach the point of closing schools down, it usually means these schools are no longer economically efficient to operate. One director of a program that uses school space worries, "Declining enrollment could squeeze us out—we could get shoved out at any time. We really have to look at the positives and negatives of being in school space." Schools may also increase the financial charges to programs, affecting the parents' ability to pay or making SACC's cost to them prohibitive. School boards may oppose your proposal to locate your program in the schools. If regular services are being cut, it may be hard to justify adding another. While the program's actual cost to the schools may not be significant, the school board may be worried about resistance from taxpayers. (See Chapter 4, "Getting Approval," for suggestions on overcoming opposition.)

When communities don't want day care programs to be in schools, and mount opposition to the idea, it may not be the right option for that community and other solutions may have to be developed. No program will work well in a school system or in an individual school that has strong resistance to the idea.

Using buildings that are already heated and lighted means less expense for a tightly budgeted program. As an associate superintendent in the South told us: "Even if you turn the heat off at 3:00 P.M., the building would still be warm at 5:00. We have people in there cleaning the buildings. School children don't go home at 3:00 P.M. anyhow; there are always children in the building doing homework."

Schools can provide essential resources to programs housed within them. These resources may be received either as in-kind (no-cost) donations, or the program may pay for some of them:

- *Space:* This may be the program's "own" room, not used by anyone else—an unused classroom, a community room, a cafeteria corner, or, possibly, a music room that is shared by the music teacher during the school day and the program afterwards.
- *Utilities and energy:* The costs of heating, cooling, and lighting the building are often charged to the program in proportion to its use.
- *Custodial services:* Many school systems have agreements with custodians' unions that a school-employed custodian be on the premises of a school after the school day; in other cases, custodians will be paid overtime after school, or on certain school holidays and vacations.
- *Other kinds of school resources:* These might include use of other facilities (library, home ec rooms, gymnasium); maintenance supplies (cleaning materials, paper towels, etc.); telephone (installation and monthly bills); materials, consumable supplies, etc. (purchased in bulk together with the school); administrative time of school personnel; building security; trash removal.

Programs may use space, utilities, and custodial services and only one or two of the other school resources. Telephone services, for example, may be purchased by the program and paid for out of income generated. Some schools are more heavily involved in collaborating with outside groups, and have school staff whose time is assigned to working with tenants and negotiating the use of space and other resources. In Montgomery County, Maryland, the school system has a "Policy on Joint Occupancy." This policy promotes the rental of school space to outside groups as a way of getting a financial return on the large number of empty classrooms in the area's schools. (See Chapter 10 for a description of how this policy works.)

It is not necessary to have your program located in a school to collaborate financially with one. Programs may work in tandem with the schools by sharing transportation costs, purchasing low-cost meals from school-run kitchens, participating in their bulk purchasing of supplies, sharing staff, etc. Be certain to explore all of the possibilities.

Community schools or adult education departments may be another school resource. Community or adult education programs that are tied in administratively with a school system usually receive some financial and in-kind support from the schools. This support varies, depending on the nature of the relationship. Use of space, bookkeeping, accounting, billing, and personnel salaries and benefits may be part of the arrangement. Other resources may also be available: special staff, materials, equipment, and transportation. When community education programs provide SACC, it is either as the administering agency or as a partner with a community group. When community education runs programs in community schools, financial support is usually derived from parent fees, or from contracts and grants with social service agencies. When community schools act as *partners,* they can provide space, some portion of administrative time, technical assistance, and some sharing of school resources.

Setting Up the Program's Building Blocks

In designing any program, there are specific areas where decisions must be made. You will need to answer the following questions. We suggest you use them as a checklist as you tackle the design of your program.

1. What is the basic philosophy of this program? What are our goals?
2. Who will the program be for? How many children? What are their ages? Will we include kindergartners? Special-needs children?
3. When will this program operate? Which days? During vacations? Summers? Snow days? Which hours? Before school? After school?
4. Where will the program be held? (location and space)

5. Will meals be served?
6. What activities and experiences will be planned?
7. Will there be a need for transportation? How will it be provided?
8. Will other community facilities be used? Which ones?
9. What will the program cost?
10. Where will the money come from?
11. Who will administer the program: overall direction and policy making? Day-to-day decisions?
12. What kinds of staff will we need to hire?
13. Who will be accountable—and for what?

"Think big, but start small." The content and shape of your program will undergo many changes during its formative years, and well it should. Have ambitious plans, but begin cautiously, adding and expanding as experience leads the way. It is difficult for planners to disappoint their constituents, but many of the SACC programs that have attempted to "do it all" are no longer around to provide care to anyone. We recommend that you begin with a segment that you feel you can do and do *well*, work out the kinks and the details, and let the program grow organically. Being able to carry out your program in well-planned stages will help to guarantee its longevity.

■ *Develop a Philosophy and Goals.* The development of a philosophy is crucial in designing a program. It is the foundation upon which the program rests, and will provide the basis for all decisions you make now in your design process and after the program is in operation. One program director stated its importance this way: "The reason that we have survived is that we have a philosophy and a point of view."

A philosophy is nothing more—and nothing less—than your common-sense answers to the questions, "What do the children in this program need?" and "What do we want to give them?" You should be able to state your philosophy verbally and in writing, after agreeing on your basic goals and objectives. This means that your planning group, the people who are hired later to staff the program, and policy makers should be in agreement on the central philosophy. There is no one "best philosophy"—there is only the philosophy that best expresses and fills the needs and values of the people involved in your program, and of your community. To verbalize your philosophy:

• Ask questions: "What do we want for our children? What kinds of experiences are important for them to have?" Trust yourselves. You know the answers.

- Be open and flexible, so that your philosophy and goals incorporate the values of people of different backgrounds, incomes, and cultures.
- Think about the ways a SACC program is unique. It is neither the home nor the school; it doesn't attempt to replace either of these, but it does complement each. Children in SACC programs are away from home for many hours, and they move through several different environments in the course of their day. There are children of different ages and stages of development in the program; these differing needs must be met.

Your philosophy must be translated into reality through the program you plan and later institute. Philosophies are meaningless if they remain well-turned phrases in brochures and are not given life through the program in operation. (See Part Five, "Day-to-Day Operation," for suggestions on shaping and implementing a curriculum to achieve this goal.) The following are our recommendations of general standards a program should maintain. Keeping these standards in mind as you design your program will help to ensure that the program really does implement your philosophy.

The program should meet children's needs. It should be based on an understanding of the needs of children who are at different stages of development. These needs are social, emotional, intellectual, and physical. It meets these needs by creating an environment that:

- Offers children a base of warmth and security provided by caring adults, in which they can all grow and respect and enjoy each other;
- Fosters autonomy: initiative and independence, cooperation and self-control, choice and the assumption of responsibility;
- Permits freedom within set limits;
- Encourages creativity;
- Provides activities reflecting and filling these different needs while respecting cultural diversity.

The program should meet parents' needs. A parent from the state of Washington told us, "The parent is buying peace of mind when his or her child is enrolled in this program." It meets parents' needs by:

- Offering a safe, accessible, affordable program;
- Providing warm, trusting, competent, responsible staff who understand and meet the needs of the children;
- Respecting and incorporating their needs, values, and cultural diversity in the policies and activities of the program;
- Including parents in decision making.

The program should meet staff's needs. It should value and respect them, and demonstrate this value and respect by:

- Hiring appropriately trained staff who also have relevant work experience;
- Paying them the highest possible salaries and benefits;
- Providing them with a quality work environment;
- Having staff:child ratios within the 1:8–1:12 range.

The program should meet the community's needs. It should incorporate the values and respond to the concerns of the community. It will achieve this by:

- Encouraging the participation of people of different racial, ethnic, cultural, and economic backgrounds;
- Providing good quality care to children, who will benefit from its provision;
- Sharing and building upon existing community resources;
- Respecting other agencies and groups who share the concern for children's and families' well-being;
- Giving the community a feeling of pride.

■ **Who Will the Program Be For?**   What does your needs assessment tell you about the numbers and ages of children in need of care (older children? kindergartners?) and children with special needs? You will have to decide now whether you will establish eligibility criteria for the program. Making decisions about eligibility and admissions usually involves a number of different considerations and may be done in a variety of ways. Some programs set no priorities and enroll children in the order that they come through the door. While this may seem equitable, it means that the program staff has no control over ingredients such as boy/girl mix, ages of children, numbers of children with special needs, etc. Other programs set priorities based upon their fiscal limitations, needs of parents, etc.

Some programs limit the numbers of children at different age levels, for example, 50 percent kindergarten through first grade, 40 percent second to third grade, and 10 percent fourth grade and up. Others give a limited age range for enrollment (for example, six to ten years) and leave it at that. If your program serves a wide age span, planning is more difficult because of the diversity of interests and abilities; however, it does mean that older children can assist with younger ones and/or walk a younger brother or sister home.

Whether or not to include kindergarten children is controversial. On the one hand, public school half-day kindergarten sessions present the greatest care problems for parents, since surround care is desperately needed. Also, in many communities, the half-day session changes in midyear, causing carefully constructed arrangements or schedules to fall apart. Parents with kindergartners may well be your community's most desperate group in need of care—and the one with fewest available options. Serving kindergartners may mean a full-day program which allows you to have full-time staff. However, five-year-olds may seem "years" younger than their six- to twelve-year-old cohorts, and programing must address this problem.

You will want to balance the needs and the financial picture with other factors. For example, although you might want to serve kindergartners during your first year of operation, the transportation arrangements, additional hours, and needs of the younger child might convince you to begin by caring for six- to ten-year-old children and to expand downwards during your second year and upwards during your third year. On the other hand, if the bulk of your potential users have kindergarten-age children, this would suggest beginning with a program focused on younger children (five to eight years) and adding older children in subsequent years.

Another question you'll want to consider is whether or not to admit children with special needs, and, if you do, what age limits to set for them. Programs that admit children with handicaps are aware that they can only handle certain numbers of special needs children, depending upon the children's disabilities and the amount of staff attention required. Programs that do accept children with special needs offer a wonderful opportunity to *all* of the children in the program. As one SACC staffer said, "Having handicapped kids in our program is one of the best socialization experiences for all kids." It teaches all children to accept differences, and can give the special child a chance to gain confidence and acceptance by other children. It also can provide support to parents who often have incredible difficulties in finding programs that will accept their children. It is, however, not without its hardships. Staff must be top-notch, not only able to accommodate the special needs of the child, but also able to help the rest of the children deal with the issues that arise. Planning must be done carefully, with consideration given to activities and, possibly, with special provisions made for special-needs children.

We recommend that SACC programs base their decisions about whether or not to serve children with special needs upon several key criteria: the nature and severity of the handicaps; the implications for the program—and the child—of mainstreaming; whether there is a special school available that has, or could have, a SACC program; actual practices of your agency and/or school; and extent of need and agencies willing to collaborate.

We also recommend that SACC programs serve children with special needs in one of two ways: (1) mainstream children and have special resources (funds or collaborations to receive staff help from specially-trained individuals; transportation; materials; staff support and training), or (2) have a self-contained program that serves only children with special needs (provide SACC for multiple-handicapped children in special schools or programs).

In either case, a program director from the Midwest advises, "Hire staff who have the experience or willingness to work with special needs children. Staff who have the background tend to be great."

■ *Program Size; Group Size and Staff:Child Ratios.* When considering the size of your total program, you will want to ensure that you have enough staff to effectively plan, manage, and carry out the program. As your program grows, so does the paperwork, the financial management details, and other administrative duties. A teacher-director may be able to collect tuitions, pay staff, order supplies, and work directly with children in a small program (under twenty-five children). However, bookkeepers, administrative assistants, cooks, nonteaching directors, etc., may be needed as your enrollment increases.

Program size will depend on standards of agencies you copartner with, as well as your own. In one western city, when the YMCA proposed setting up programs in schools, the school board insisted that each school's program be limited to twenty children; they felt that a larger number would lead to a program that was too rigid and structured, and this was antithetical to their philosophy and goals. The Y, in agreement with this philosophy, accepted the stipulation.

The space available to you will also set limits on program size:

> Space is our biggest limitation. We have a waiting list at some schools. At one school, we could have a bigger program if we had the space. (*Director in the Midwest*)

> It never pays to put children in too small a space that's unfamiliar to them. It doesn't work for the staff and it doesn't work for the kids. (*YWCA Director, Pacific Coast*)

In general, a minimum of thirty-five square feet of indoor space per child is used as a rule of thumb. Some programs care for as few as ten children; others have as many as eighty children at one location.

Program size will also be determined by the number of children you need in order to offer variety and diversity of experiences. In terms of cost effectiveness, a decisive factor will be the number of children you need to collect fees from in order to break even financially and to achieve your standards of quality.

You may need to set policies on the number of children the program will admit because both overload (too many children) and underload (too few) can create problems. Overload places too great a burden on your finances, staff, and facilities, and as a result you are unable to provide intimacy and individualized attention. Underload makes for insufficient income, staff layoffs, and inadequate grouping and diversity of experience.

In making decisions about totals, you must consider *group size* and *staff: child ratios.*

> *Group size* is the total number of children assigned to a caregiver or team of caregivers. In most cases, groups occupy individual classrooms or well-defined physical spaces within larger rooms.
>
> *Staff: child ratio* is the number of caregivers divided by group size. Higher or more stringent staff: child ratios are those with a smaller number of children per adult. For instance, a ratio of 1:5 is higher, or more stringent, than a ratio of 1:10.[2]

In some states, group size is a mandated licensing requirement; in others it is left up to the individual program. No matter how it is dealt with by your state, consider the impact of group size upon the children, upon the staff, and, consequently, upon the total program. It's important to consider this issue from the child's point of view. Children who have been in school all day need to be in small groups and to have some time for solitary activity. A group size of thirty may feel like a repeat of the school day to them.

You will have to balance what you can afford with what is best for the children. Licensing standards are usually minimum standards and we suggest that you use them as a rule of thumb, adding a generous dollop of your own common sense. As one program director so aptly stated, "The group should be small enough for each child to receive some individual attention and big enough to get a softball game going!"

---

[2] Richard Ruopp et al., *Children at the Center*, vol. 1 (Cambridge, Mass.: Abt Associates, 1979), p. xix.

We recommend a group size of sixteen to twenty-four children. As for staff:child ratios, we agree with the program director who said:

> There is no one who could give more than ten children what they need in terms of individualized attention. Children may need help with their homework, want to learn how to swing a baseball bat, etc.

Staff:child ratios should be coordinated with group size. For example, if you want a group size of eighteen children, with a staff:child ratio of 1:9, you will need two staff; and if you want groups of twenty-four or sixteen, and a staff:child ratio of 1:8, you will need two or three staff.

As you balance the numbers you should consider how certain ratios will or will not allow you to offer certain activities or experiences for children. Your goals and the planning of your program content should determine your decisions regarding ratios and group size. Of course, if you are forced to have ratios and size that you feel are not workable for the types of activities or orientation you are planning, you must either restructure the program content or juggle your numbers.

The tradeoffs with both staff:child ratio and group size revolve around costs and quality. Larger groups with lower ratios may certainly be less expensive, but they minimize the individualized attention and the activity choices open to children. Smaller groups with more stringent ratios cost more, but allow for more staff attention to each child and a broader range of activities.

■ *Days and Hours of Operation.* Days of program operation can vary widely. School-based programs that wish to define themselves as "an extension of the school day" often do so by providing care only on days when school is in session. Other programs may be open daily, on the basis that no-school days are when parents and children are most in need of care. There are also the programs that take a middle ground, perhaps staying open daily during the school year, but closing during the summer months.

While year-round programs are probably what most parents need if they are working, at school, or in training programs, such programing may not be feasible for you. For a school-based program, you may have to pay exorbitant costs (custodial, utilities) when the school buildings are closed—costs that you may not be able to pass along to parents. On the other hand, daily programing allows for a continuity and depth that can be especially rewarding and exciting for staff and children.

Setting minimums on the number of days a child may attend the program implies that you don't want to enroll children on a part-time basis, and that you don't want drop-ins. You may want to set minimums because you believe that sporadic, drop-in, or part-time attendance will not promote the kind of atmosphere you are trying to create. Large daily variations in attendance could mean that on any one day you could be under- or overstaffed. However, you may need drop-ins because you need the additional money.

In thinking about whether you will allow unenrolled children to occasionally come into the program at will, or to be guests, you must consider accountability. Who is responsible if something happens to the child? If no enrollment forms have been filled out, whom do you contact? If an unregistered child has an accident, will your insurance cover it? It may; some insurance policies cover any child in the space that is insured. But it may not. Accountability and careful record keeping are vital in a program that allows drop-ins.

If part-time care is an option, whether it is flexible or fixed has different implications. Variable hours (six hours a week, taken anytime) may be advantageous to parents, especially those who have changing work/school schedules, and this flexibility may result in additional children coming to the program. However, it can also become confusing to children and to the program. Is today Dennis's day for day care? If transportation is involved, this can add another layer of confusion—with arrangements and details that change daily! Having fixed schedules permits the program to plan staffing and activity arrangements, and to know exactly who will be in attendance when. It also allows you to balance children's attendance, so that you can be certain that on any one day you will be within your licensing limitations, and that you will be staffed appropriately.

Will the program be open or closed when regular school is, or is not, in session (holidays, vacations, nonschool storm days)? This decision will depend on whether the facilities you use are available; if not, whether you can make special agreements to keep them open; or whether you can make alternative arrangements. It also depends on the values and practices of the community you serve, the costs involved, and your ability to meet the needs expressed.

■ *Should You Serve Meals and/or Snacks?* If so, which ones? Who will pay for the food? Supplying meals or providing time and space for them will be determined partly by your hours, partly by your facilities (do you have refrigerators, stoves, and preparation areas?), and partly by the wishes and needs of parents and children. Whether federal assistance is available, whether what the government provides is adequate, and whether the impending cuts in funding do take place are other determining factors. One program staffer felt that "the nutrition program doesn't meet the needs of school-age kids," while another worried that because they fed the children so much, they'd go home and not want to eat dinner. Early morning programs often provide breakfast. In some school-based SACC programs, SACC and the schools can collaborate.

Serving meals, especially breakfast, can make mornings at home easier and less hectic for families, while allowing children to eat later than they would at home. However, some parents would rather feed their own children and may object to a SACC program doing so. Serving meals takes planning, facilities (or special arrangements with a food service), staff time, and money. The trouble may be worth it, though, as it may "sell" some families on the program.

Most programs serve a snack of some type, or encourage children to bring their own. Serving a snack to school-agers can involve them in cooking, nutrition, and even menu planning and shopping. It will mean time and money, but in this way the program has some control over the quality of food served and what quantities are being consumed. Individual financial circumstances and/or eating habits won't be a factor, although special diets should always be respected. School-age children, often reluctant to experiment with new foods, will be provided with such an opportunity if cooking and snack preparation is the program's responsibility.

■ *What Activities and Experiences Will Be Planned for the Children?*   Detailed planning is not a task to be accomplished now, when you are creating an overall blueprint for your program. (Refer to Chapter 15 for a discussion of shaping your SACC program.) However, certain questions must be addressed at this point because they are related to such areas of program design as space, cost, staff, etc. To answer them, refer to your philosophy, and the indications parents gave about the kind of program they wanted when they answered the needs assessment.

Will children spend most of their time at the program site, or will they become involved in community activities? Will most activities be in small groups or large ones? What types of activities, materials, and experiences will there be? Will provisions be made for both the older and the younger children?

■ *Space and Location: Where Should the Program Be Housed?*   If there is any one area of program design that is inextricably linked to all the others, it is the space you choose for the program. High-priced space will either force you to cut expenditures in

> With many schools closing and space becoming available, we felt it was appropriate for schools to provide physical space. We tell the county government where space is available, and the county can decide what it wants to use. Whatever school space is available, we are pleased to offer it—the space is there, the heating is there anyway, the janitors are there anyway. (*Virginia Board of Education Member*)
>
> I suggest that inner-city parents who are church members get their churches to donate space for SACC. The program could then charge fees on a sliding scale, with additional money to establish neighborhood programs obtained through fundraising and through working with the local business, industry, and unions. (*Maryland Social Services Director*)

other areas (for staff or supplies), or to raise tuition rates until they are out of reach for many families, or both. In addition, the space you choose will affect the types of activities and experiences that are available to children in the program, either because of the constraints of the actual physical space or because of the program's accessibility to other local community resources that might be used by the program.

For these reasons, many programs opt for space that is available for the lowest price—in some cases, space that is free. Given the costs of salaries, materials, and other necessities, many SACC programs find that they can offer a reasonably-priced, high-quality program to parents when no-cost or low-cost space is part of the package. Although such in-kind donations of space may not cost money, they may extract another price from SACC programs in terms of the program's status, feelings of tenuousness, or accusations that the program is "getting a free ride." Those SACC programs that have the most success with free or low-cost space are very careful to show how the program contributes to the host institution and how free or low-cost space translates into a direct benefit to parents. Whatever your options, we advise you to consider all of the "costs" involved.

Finally, the location you choose may require program staff to organize extensive transportation to and/or from schools in the community—thus adding to the program costs—or present problems for parents who transport their own children.

Your needs assessment has told you where your prime users live; what types of transportation they need or can provide; what tuition range is affordable; approximate numbers and ages of children in need of care; special needs of children that might affect space (wheelchair access, etc.); and days and hours of care needed.

As you set out to see what the community has to offer, be very clear about what your rock-bottom space requirements are, since compromise and negotiation are likely to be your constant companions. Also, think as creatively as possible. Although a given space may not *appear* to be a likely home for your program, ingenuity and a little money may transform it completely.

Space options for SACC programs include the following general types of facilities: schools (public, private, community, and those no longer in operation as schools); churches and synagogues; community and municipal agency/buildings (Y's, boys' and girls' clubs, park and recreation centers, libraries, and community centers); nursery schools and day care centers (those serving younger children); and commercial property (storefronts, offices, and rental space in industrial parks).

You are looking for a low-cost or free option and for this reason the purchase of a building, except in unusual or unique circumstances, is generally out of the question. In addition to our list of possibilities, don't overlook local business and industry and the ways that they might be a resource. Knowledge of local licensing requirements (in places where SACC must be licensed) and zoning requirements is essential, and often regulatory agencies can serve as a great resource—with ideas on where to look, on whom to talk to, and—maybe—on assessing the "licensibility" and associated costs of various possibilities. (For a full discussion of licensing, see Chapter 5.) Also, don't forget that real estate agents, local politicians, and other well-connected individuals and groups can be tremendous sources of information and assistance.

Figure 3–1 outlines the most common options, with the tradeoffs they present from the perspective of the different constituents. From the point of view of cost, accessibility, and program environment, it appears that school-based programs are often the most viable. However, as you examine the chart, you must superimpose the facts and figures that relate to your own community and to your own needs and priorities. For example, your community's schools may not have an iota of unused space, or they may not welcome outside use of school facilities. This may mean that a church located down the block from the school may be a better bet. Or, perhaps, all space available in Y's, community centers, or churches must be shared, which is not in keeping with your basic standards.

As one group found out, there may be advantages to what, at first, might appear to be unacceptable space conditions. The director of a program that is housed in school cafeterias and administered by the YMCA in Colorado explains:

> The advantage of school space is that it reduces the transportation problem, which is particularly acute in our community, and it allows flexibility in responding to needs. Because the program is not dependent for its activities on school classroom space being available, it will continue to operate even if school enrollment increases, as it is expected to do in the next few years. It will not be "bumped," and, since the programs can't use classroom space, they are quickly disassembled and reassembled at other schools when the program has to lose one site and/or open another one. We compensate for this in our program planning by making great use of the YMCA facilities, planning trips, and using other community resources.

Sweet (sometimes) are the uses of adversity.

On the other hand, some space defeats the purposes of a program, such as that in use at one elementary school. The group is limited to the use of the auditorium and the cafeteria, and outside facilities are not available. The director said,

> It is loud, it echoes, it is not comfy and cozy, it is not nice to come home to. The kids get there and they feel that they are still in school and it makes for discipline problems and emotional problems. My personal assessment is that I put the best staff I could possibly think of in that program because of these problems. But after a year of working there with really excellent staff, my assessment is that this space is not conducive to what we want.

In making our specific recommendations on space, we agree with the Wisconsin group that lists the following requirements for an ideal setting. It would:

- Meet licensing and building code requirements without added expense (at least thirty-five square feet per child indoors and seventy-five square feet per child outdoors).
- Be convenient to the families who will use the program.
- Be in close proximity to the schools children attend.
- Permit children to add features that will give them the feeling that the space is "theirs."
- Have indoor space that provides for private group times, group quiet activities, and active games and sports.
- Have adjacent outdoor space suited to the many types of outdoor games and activities.
- Have ample and appropriate storage for equipment and materials.

ADVANTAGES AND DISADVANTAGES OF MAJOR OPTIONS

	Facilities	Needs of Children	Needs of Parents
Schools			
Advantages:	Extends function of schools; enhances image; builds parent support. May increase enrollment or help with desegregation efforts.	Familiar and suitable space; oriented for school-agers; availability of additional spaces—gym, lunchroom, playground, etc. Convenient—no long bus rides—and allows maximum time to be spent in program; in child's own neighborhood; may give continuity to child's day.	No transportation costs or worries; consider school a "safe" place; deal with one environment/institution; program easily accessible for pick-up; affordable.
Disadvantages:	Another program to worry about; fears regarding liability, accountability, and costs.	Same environment all day; institutional restrictions and limitations; possible negative associations with school accrue to program.	May have negative feelings about school.
Churches/ Synagogues			
Advantages:	Generates income for institution; gesture of good will and community involvement.	New space they haven't been at all day; may be equipped for use by children; may feel "less institutional."	May be in the neighborhood for many families.
Disadvantages:	Daily use by children may be hard on facility; may limit other activities.	May not have adjacent outdoor space; have to walk or be transported to site; may be unknown territory.	Cost of space may be high; transportation may be complicated and/or costly; some parents may be uncomfortable with "religious" location; may not be convenient for some families.

Figure 3–1

Needs of Staff	Needs of Community	Needs of Programs
Allows communication between school teachers and SACC staff.	Draws people to public schools and to the community. Good use of taxpayers' dollars.	No transportation costs; may have flexible locations to meet changing needs; custodian, facilities, equipment, utilities are already on premises; building set up for SACC; has potential for lowest cost to program; well located with access to other city resources.
School personnel may not welcome staff; may lack access to cooking and food preparation facilities; staff may need to "take down" the program daily.	Use may be questioned by private sector or taxpayers.	Space is often shared or has common usage; SACC program may be moved if school activities are seen as taking precedence; storage space may be limited; program may be unable to alter or change space; may be unavailable during summers, vacations (or costs may increase dramatically).
More autonomy; don't have to be part of school environment if don't want to; cooking facilities are usually available.	Use of already-existing community facility.	Generally open and available year round; rent may be subsidized.
May have to set up and take down weekly; may have constraints due to other uses of space; no contact with school personnel.	Might limit other uses of space.	Need for transport; costs for space may be high and may need to pay for maintenance, utilities, etc.; use of building by others during program time may limit program; licensing may be costly or problematic.

ADVANTAGES AND DISADVANTAGES OF MAJOR OPTIONS

	Facilities	Needs of Children	Needs of Parents
Community and Municipal Agencies/ Buildings			
Advantages:	May tie in with other programs at agency; may enhance reputation; may add to usage figures and membership; may be a multiple use of facility; additional revenue.	New space they haven't been in all day; may have excellent facilities (pool, gym) for children.	May be well located for many families.
Disadvantages:	May limit other activities from using space.	Need to be transported or to walk; may have lots of other programs going on; may not be close to home or school.	Children will need to walk or be transported; may not be convenient for some families.
Nursery Schools and Day Care Centers			
Advantages:	Additional revenue for institution; may provide option for "graduates."	Space oriented to children; may be familiar to some of the children.	May be a known environment; may be convenient for some families.
Disadvantages:	May be unable to give exclusive use.	May be inappropriate space for older children; may be "bored" with space if attended preschool program; need to walk or be transported.	May not be convenient for many families; transportation may be complicated and/or costly.

Figure 3–1 (continued)

Needs of Staff	Needs of Community	Needs of Programs
May have excellent facilities at their disposal; more autonomy; don't have to be part of school environment if don't want to.	Use of already-existing community facility.	Generally open and available year round.
May not have exclusive use of space; may not be welcome by other staff; no contact with school personnel; may have other constraints due to other uses of space.	Might limit other uses of space.	Costs for space may be high—may need to pay for maintenance, utilities; licensing may be costly or problematic; need for transport.
More autonomy; don't have to be part of school environment if don't want to; cooking facilities may be available.	Use of already-existing facility.	Generally open and available year round; may make better use of facility/space; may help subsidize program rent; may already be licensed.
May not have exclusive use of space; no contact with school personnel; may have constraints due to other uses of space.		Space may not be appropriate for older children; transportation will be needed; may be costly; may not have exclusive use of space.

- Be appealing and attractive to the eye—inviting children to come in, relax, and enjoy.
- Always be available for the time it is needed.[3]

In addition, we would add that the space should be safe, low in cost, located near other community facilities so that they may be used by the program, and located in a place where others want and value the program. (See Part Six, "Day-to-Day Operation," for a fuller discussion of issues related to space.)

Space is generally the resource whose boundaries are left woefully unclear. We urge you to clarify, in writing, what you will be giving and getting in terms of space, other resources, and funds. (See pp. 288–90 for a full discussion of figuring rental and utility costs for programs.) Exactly *which* space—rooms, exterior grounds—may your program use? For exactly which days and hours? With whom, if anyone, will you be expected to share it? Will anyone "bump" you out of the space? Will you be permitted to make alterations in the space—for example, erect a partition to divide a large hall into more intimate areas? What are the program's responsibilities in using this space? If it is a classroom, must chairs be returned to the tops of desks at closing time? Which supplies and equipment can you use and which are you expected to pay for and replenish?

As our final recommendation, we urge SACC programs to push for exclusive use of *some* portion of their space. Having exclusive use gives the children a sense that the program is really theirs and circumvents the struggles that often occur when space is shared. Although it can be done, and done well, space-sharing takes ingenuity, patience, and time. If this is your only available option, be aware that you are making a compromise, do everything possible to clarify the use of the space with your "partners," and plan your program accordingly.

■ *Transportation.*   Some programs provide no transportation and are serving their parents and children well; others have extensive before- and after-school routes that cost thousands of dollars per year but are essential to their operation. And still others fall somewhere in between.

Explore all avenues and balance their cost with your feelings about what is good for children. Analyze the direct relationship be-

---

[3]Kay Hendon et al., *The After School Day Care Handbook: How to Start an After School Program for School-Age Children* (Madison, WI: Community Coordinated Child Care/4-C in Dane County, Inc., 1977), p. 60.

tween enrollment (upon which you are basing all of your budget cal-
culations) and the provision of transportation. If you expect that, at
first, enrollment will be dependent upon your ability to transport a
certain number of children from a nearby school, this must be built
into your budget. Regional differences in the frequency and the limits
of public school busing, population density, geographic factors, and
the quality and quantity of public transportation will all have an impact. Transportation during program hours must also be considered.
Will children have access to community facilities? Will there be field
trips? Will transportation needs change throughout the year?

Information from your assessment of need that is relevant to the
transportation issues includes where children live; which schools they
attend; school opening and dismissal times; whether parents can pick
up and/or drop off their children; ages and special needs of children;
hours and days of care needed.

Your options will be greatly affected by the money you have to
spend (and the lack of it), your program size, where you are located,
when you need the transportation and for how many children, and
the distances you will travel. If you are school-based, you may find
that your only transportation needs come during program time, when
children are travelling into and out of the community. Or perhaps
you are well located within walking distance of most of your community's resources, but need to transport children to the program after
school. Weather conditions can also greatly affect your transportation
needs—what may be a perfectly acceptable walk in California may be
out of the question in Minnesota.

Where can you look for transportation resources?

- Parents (individuals or carpools)
- Public transportation (buses, subways)
- School buses
- Private transportation companies, taxis, hiring individuals
- "Pooling" with other agencies and/or sharing systems
- Purchase or lease of van, bus
- Human service agencies (may have volunteers who will help
  provide transportation)

Schools may serve as a transportation resource in a range of different ways. Some communities have extensive school busing networks and are willing (especially if a *parent* requests it) to pick up children and drop them off anywhere within their bus routes. Others
may let you rent their buses and drivers at a low rate for field trips, or

may negotiate with you to provide the needed transportation for a price. One program, which has school-based sites as well as its own building, receives a good deal of "free" transportation from the schools. This is especially critical for the program's before- and after-kindergarten component; otherwise transportation for these children would become financially out of reach.

In weighing the different options, the major factors to consider are costs, accessibility, impact on children and families, and effects on the program. It may seem that children could easily walk by themselves. However, what about the "wanderers" who would arrive there an hour late? Can the five- and six-year-olds handle the responsibility? This arrangement may not provide enough peace of mind to parents who are paying you so their worry may be minimized. Another solution might be having staff walk children to and from the site. In this case, the only cost is for the staff time required. However, weather conditions, distance, and numbers of schools served by the program might make this an undesirable alternative.

Using public transportation is likely to be affordable and feasible in communities where excellent, reliable systems exist, and where children are used to the method and parents are comfortable with the option. It is not really an adequate solution for the youngest children or in places where weather conditions or long waits pose problems.

Arranging your own transportation to and/or from schools to the program is likely to mean dealing with logistics: different starting and dismissal times, different rules for different schools, and knowing which children come and go when. If you do all of the transporting yourself, the arrangements and details will be within your control; if you hire it out, you may relinquish control without minimizing your involvement with the details. Involvement with school busing may mean dealing with many bureaucratic layers: school board approval; okaying changes through the school's transportation personnel; having each family fill out forms and send written notes when there are changes. On the other hand, the price may be right, it may be familiar to the children, and it may minimize parental worry. These factors may far outweigh all other considerations. Transportation and taxi companies often juggle many different contracts, and, for this reason, they may not be wholly reliable. However, because of the volume they handle, they are often able to offer special rates that may be within your price range.

Purchasing a vehicle is a possibility only for a large agency that has many uses for the vehicle and has enough going on to hire a driver and keep him or her busy all day. However, a few agencies with differing needs may purchase a van together and find that over time it is most cost-effective. Before you make this decision, you must figure costs and project overtime.

Expecting parents to do anything but early morning or late afternoon transportation is contrary to the very purpose of SACC programs. However, before- and after-school carpools can be helpful and may go a long way toward establishing networks among parents.

Some programs build transportation expenses into their budgets, charging the costs to all parents. Others separate out the fees and only pass them along to parent users. Dividing the costs equally keeps the price down for individual families, but some people may resist paying for a service that they don't use. Charging the parents directly for daily transportation may well be the most equitable policy, but when translated into actual fees, may force them to look elsewhere for SACC. Many programs solve this problem by subsidizing the costs, figuring that they stand to gain by doing so. (See Chapter 9 for suggestions on budgeting.)

What are our recommendations? Consider transportation options and possible locations for the program simultaneously since the two are directly related. You may prefer to begin providing transportation to or from a few areas and see how it goes. Later you can extend your services to more sites, when experience has taught you what you can and can't handle. You will find that once you have provided transportation, parents will object if you take it away.

Programs should do some figuring early on so that transportation costs may be considered alongside other factors. Your method(s) of transportation should be:

- Safe, reliable, and consistent.
- Planned so that children spend the shortest possible time on a vehicle.
- Low in cost.
- Practical, manageable, and convenient for SACC staff and parents.
- Adequate for the needs of the program in terms of enrollment and activities.
- Projected over several years so that changes won't put the program in jeopardy.

■ *Administrative Structures: Who Will Run the Program?* Your program will need some official group that will be responsible and accountable for running it—for making decisions on both day-to-day and long-range issues and policies. You will need to establish structures that you feel will administer the program well and that will be committed to providing school-age child care that will meet the needs of children, parents, and staff. In addition, any group granting you approval will want to make certain that your administrative structure is sound and well thought out.

> Designing the administrative structure and the management —how it will work, where it is going to be and who is going to be in charge of what—is a very crucial area. You want people planning it who understand how things work—how the local government works, where the levers of power are —in order to design something that you can predict is going to have success. (*SACC Program Organizer in the South*)

As you consider your needs and the possibilities available, you will find that there are really two types of administrative structures needed—one for the overall program (external) and one to oversee the daily operation (internal). (See Chapter 7, "Administration," for a full discussion of the two types, including their advantages and disadvantages.) In fact, the group that holds the titular power of responsibility and/or approval of policies and budget, such as a school or YMCA board, may serve as a superadministrative structure, but may have almost nothing to do with the actual running of the program. For example, a county school department in the South is the umbrella organization for programs that are run in nine schools. Each program has its own director. The community education department, as one of the interested organizations that contributes to the success of the program, does some of the administration, but serves mainly in an advisory capacity; it does not share in the decision-making process that is part of the day-to-day operation.

Contrasted with these "official" governing bodies is the "operative" group—the people, generally including the director of the program, who are responsible for the day-to-day decisions. These might include who will actually be hired, where the children will go on a particular field trip, and how to handle specific problems, such as late arrival of parents. One Minnesota community education director explains the chain of command in this way: "The day-to-day things we don't take to the community education advisory board; but if we change the SACC director's position to full time, we have to go to the advisory, the superintendent, and then to the school board."

The administrative structures you choose will have an important impact on the program. One choice might result in an intricate web of hierarchies with individuals and groups that must be consulted on each and every decision. Another might saddle your program with disinterested or uninformed decision makers who have little understanding of a SACC program's needs. While these are extremes, they help to explain why many groups use ingenuity in forming their own combinations of administrative bodies.

Although for the most part your decisions about an administrative structure will be based upon the type of program you want and the options available, there is also information in your needs assessment that will help you to choose a structure. This includes parents who are interested in working on the program, hours and days of care needed, and type of program parents want (recreational, arts, etc.).

Who are your possible managers? School-age child care programs are run either by parents or by institutions or agencies. Most programs are in some way a collaboration between groups, with the schools being a popular partner. People who wish to initiate SACC programs can either adapt the following models according to their own community profiles or devise their own collaborations:

- *Administered by one agency:*
- Public-school operated
- Community-school operated
- Private- or parochial-school operated
- PTO-run (not much data on these, but certainly an option if theré is sufficient time and dedication)
- Community agencies (Y's, day care, rec departments)

- *Administered collaboratively:*
- Parents and public schools (based in schools, operated by parents or by PTOs)
- Community agencies and public schools (based in agency and/or school)
- Community agencies and community school departments
- Parent groups and churches (based in church)
- Recreation department and schools (based in school and/or rec department facilities)

This list is intended solely as a guide. You may think of other groups in your community, county, or state that might be approachable, such as Rotary and Lions' Clubs, League of Women Voters, Junior League, etc. Or there may be other institutions that could house, spearhead, or collaborate on a program.

In considering potential administrators, ask: Will the partner we're selecting do a good job? Will it take school-age child care seriously? Can it set up effective administrative structures, so that there are open lines of communication between the two groups? Does it have an objective that is different from ours? (Another group might see the program chiefly as a money-making venture.)

If the agency will pay only lip service to providing SACC, then it will not pay attention to the program once it is in operation. The agency staff will not put money into the program, won't hire qualified staff, will not trouble-shoot, and will not serve as its advocate when it is time for budget approvals or when continuation is in jeopardy because of financial cutbacks.

You will need to work out expectations with any institution you are interviewing as a possible administrator. What does it expect to do for the program, and what does it hope to get out of it? *School-age child care programs do not make money,* and an agency with that as a major reason for running one should be disabused of this expectation.

What are the tradeoffs of major options? Program planners should continually ask, "What are the costs?"—both in terms of the philosophy of the program they hope to establish, and in terms of money. If you choose a certain route, what are the rules you will have to adhere to? What are the advantages it offers, in terms of know-how, good track record, dedication, and savings in dollars? You may decide that the price of a particular group running a program is too high in terms of philosophy and ideals, or that the administrative cost will cut into the budget too deeply to allow for adequate staff salaries.

Programs run by schools or community schools departments have administrative structures already in place, and have all of the resources of the schools available to them. However, the school administration may not fully understand SACC or may have a motive for wanting to administer the program that is quite unlike yours. Major issues your group should consider are quality, flexibility, autonomy, and parent participation. If school funds support the program, budget cuts could have a fatal effect on its longevity.

An independent, nonprofit agency (a Y, day care) already has mechanisms for adding SACC to its program offerings, although it may become just *one* of the agency's many endeavors. However, depending upon the size of the agency and its orientation, many parents and/or planners may feel more comfortable with a smaller nonprofit agency running the program than with a large school system, in which the bureaucracy may be overwhelming.

Collaborations can bring the resources of *two* partners together to best administer a SACC program. When programs are jointly administered, it must be clear who is responsible for what, so that responsibilities don't fall through the cracks. Although a parent group that runs a program in a school space may have a strong sense of commitment and caring (since the program is for *their* children), they are likely to find that the very reason they need the program prohibits them from sustained involvement over time. If the program is largely supported by parent fees, with negligible funding from the school, it will be on firmer ground when school programs feel a financial squeeze.

As you weigh the different factors, you will find that it may be difficult to clarify the issues of program autonomy and the decision-making process. However, if an agency is to run the program, or run it in conjunction with you (or another group), you should do whatever research and questioning possible to find out what policies and rules will have to be followed.

> You have to know the school, what it is about—its philosophy. Is there an active parent body? You can't say, "This is our program, and we're going to do such and such—use the halls, playgrounds, etc." You need to follow the policies of the school—and if you really think about them, they make sense. Maybe you shouldn't be in the school if you don't agree on the policies, procedures, philosophy, etc. (*School principal*)

> If a responsible group like the Y can run programs, it's better than the school. A lot of things go into making Latchkey work properly. If the school had to take on that job, they'd have to tack it on to already burdened job responsibility. (*Y Director*)

No matter who is chosen to administer your program—a Y or a community schools department—and whether it is managed by a collaboration of two institutions or solely by one organization, we recommend that:

- Lines of responsibility, accountability, and costs be agreed upon, be clear to all, and be in writing.
- There be a place for the involvement and input of parents in real, meaningful ways.
- The SACC program be welcomed by all institutions.
- The administrative group(s) be committed to the idea of providing SACC, and have the time to run a program well.
- You know exactly which existing policies and procedures will apply to your program; which codes, rules, and regulations

(closure on snow days, no use of gymnasium) you will have to
adhere to, and how policies are set.

- You know what "administrative services" (secretarial, bookkeeping) will be provided.

A program planner whose program has been in existence for over
ten years illustrates one creative solution to the question of "Who will
run the program?":

> The way we decided to design the program, and the way we were success-
> ful in having this accepted, was to have the county government and the
> schools as co-administrators. We didn't want it all in the school system for
> several reasons: there was an obvious lack of enthusiasm for wanting to
> do it—the school administrators really didn't want to. They were being
> pulled kicking and screaming into doing it. So, knowing the ways of
> bureaucrats, we didn't want to dump it completely in their hands because
> they would easily see that the program didn't work—quickly. And yet
> we felt that the program must have some sort of blessing of the school
> system—be an official part of the system in some way—in order to make
> those official contacts with the principals. And that would force a little
> bit of cooperation from principals. We were successful in getting the de-
> sign of the thing set up that way, with co-administration.

■ *Personnel: What Kinds of Staff Will We Need to Hire?*
Day-to-day running of the program is the responsibility of the
director and, to some extent, other staff people. The *quality* (and to
some extent the *quantity*) of SACC staff has a direct impact on the
overall program to be offered to the community. (See Chapter 8,
"Personnel" for a thorough discussion of all staff issues.) Staff who
have prior experience, child-related training, and a commitment to
SACC are most likely to be able to plan and implement an exciting
program that meets the diverse needs of the children in care. Also,
staff who receive "a living wage" in a work environment where they
are valued and where their needs (for sick days, health insurance,
vacation, etc.) are considered, are likely to remain in the job over time,
and this provides stability to the program.

Before you set out in search of the "ideal" staff members, some
important decisions must be made that will directly affect hiring. The
program hours you decide upon, the numbers of children you will
serve, and the ages of children in care will have an effect on how you
set up staff work hours or staffing patterns. You will want to consider
the options available to you in your particular community and how
this will affect your staffing decisions. For example, program planners
in college and university towns will want to consider how to tap this
labor source; communities with many teenagers looking for employ-

ment may want to hire teenage assistants. An in-depth exploration of your community may turn up interesting possibilities for collaborations.

What are the tradeoffs of different options? When it's a question of staffing, weighing the advantages and disadvantages of different staffing options is difficult because of the human factors involved. The major variables have to do with salaries, work hours, staff: child ratios and group size, backgrounds and qualifications of staff, use of volunteers, and "division of labor" among staff.

If you pay high salaries you will probably attract and keep quality staff, especially if raises and benefits are built in. However, it will place a financial burden on the program, since salaries represent approximately 70–85 percent of program costs. If you pay staff a yearly salary that is well above minimum wage, you might be forced to cut expenses in other areas or look to sources of income in addition to parent fees.

Although work hours for staff will be greatly affected by the program's hours of operation, there will still be a range of approaches possible: staff may work part time (even if the SACC program operates all day) or full time (either via split shifts, combining jobs, or because the program is open all day or close to it).

Clearly, and sometimes unfortunately, lower cost to the program is the greatest advantage to hiring staff who have less variety or experience in their background and training. Although most programs don't go out hunting for inexperienced, young staff who remain in the job for only a year or so, many find that, with the salaries and working conditions they offer, their choices are limited.

What are our recommendations? Our most important recommendation is to pay great attention to all of your staffing decisions and to carefully consider how each one affects the program. We urge SACC program planners to:

- Pay staff as much as possible, and include benefits such as "sickdays" and vacation time.
- Attempt to hire some staff members on a full-time basis.
- Be guided by the following staff: child ratios and group size ranges:
    Ratios: 1:8–1:12.
    Group size: 16–24.
- Consider the special needs of the children (younger/older, handicapped), how they will be served by the type of staff you wish to hire, and what the financial implications will be for the program.

■ *Getting the Money, Spending the Money, Keeping the Money.*   Finances relate to every area of program design. Decisions about whether you can begin a viable program and about the design must be made side by side with an honest appraisal of financial questions. Your program's quality will be a reflection of the decisions you make about how you will spend your income. (Refer to Chapter 9 for a more complete discussion, including the advantages and disadvantages of different options.)

One of the most difficult struggles you will have as you design your SACC program is the continual pull between the funds you have to spend (parent fees, grants, in-kind contributions, etc.) and the expenses facing you. Do the expenses determine the income or does the available income dictate the expenditures? The answer: *They both do to some extent.*

Probably every question on your needs assessment instrument is related to finances in some way. However, the most critical information you will glean is what parents *can* and *would* pay for SACC if it were provided.

In exploring your resources and options, there are three major questions to consider. First, *where will the money come from?* For most SACC programs, parent fees provide the bulk of the funding. Programs may set up flat fee systems (everyone pays the same amount), sliding fee scales (the fees people pay are set up on a graduated scale and vary according to ability to pay), scholarship programs, or some combination of all three.

Existing funds may be reallocated. If the initiating group is a multiservice agency, it may already have funds available, or money that can be reallocated. In the Southwest, a YWCA used surplus federal funds from their preschool day care program to start up after-school programs located in schools.

Government money, especially on the local level, may be available. This is especially true if groups or individuals are well connected into local networks and keep abreast of funding possibilities. Says one successful fundraiser: "I feel other groups in the country could convince their local officials, too, if they had a persuasive needs survey and could elicit media coverage of the need for school-age child care in their community or city."

The schools are an excellent resource, not so much of actual money but rather of in-kind donations of space, utilities, transportation, etc. When you're looking for financial resources, such in-kind donations are as good as gold!

Private sources of funds—individuals, foundations, corporations, or other donors—are another possibility. Although exploring the foundation and corporate route takes research, contacts, and time, it may provide you with the start-up funds you need.

Remember that most groups sew together a patchwork quilt of finances, using funds from many of the above sources. (Refer to Chapter 10 for a complete discussion of resource development.)

The second question is, *how will the money be spent?* It is likely that funds will be spent differently by different programs, depending upon how each is designed. For example, a school-based program is likely to have few or no transportation costs and may spend the bulk of its money on staff, rent (utility fees, custodial services, etc.), and program supplies. A YMCA-based program may need to allocate funds for transportation from a number of schools, but not for rent and utilities. By and large, however, the major expense of SACC programs (70 to 85 percent) is for personnel.

In addition to the regular operating expenses, your program will need start-up money to get off the ground. Some of the one-time-only costs include licenses; renovations and/or purchase of space, materials, and equipment; and staff salaries prior to opening.

Third, *how will funds be managed?* Fiscal accountability—which includes developing systems and establishing procedures for managing the money—is crucial. (Refer to Chapter 11 for a complete discussion of financial management.) This area is closely linked to administrative design, since you must clarify issues such as *who* is responsible for providing funds for start-up and operation, and whose salaries will be paid for by which "partner" in the collaboration.

There are tradeoffs in each of the three financial areas: income, expenses, and management. If you depend too heavily on any single source of income you may well put your SACC program in jeopardy. One school superintendent pointed out, "If you just use school funds, you're going to have a fatal flaw. In a budget squeeze, the cost of that program would be cut." However, many programs find that because of the time and energy it takes to solicit funds from other sources, it is far easier to rely solely on one form of income—usually parent fees.

Each parent fee system brings its advantages and disadvantages. Flat-fee systems are the simplest to set up, allow programs to accurately estimate income, and may seem most equitable to parent users. Unfortunately, they rule out financial assistance for those parents who can't afford the fee, and so they work against program diversity. Scholarship programs and sliding fee scales enable SACC programs to offer subsidies, which may boost enrollment and encourage diversity; however, these systems can be complicated to work out and programs may not be assured of receiving sufficient income from parent fees to cover program expenses.

Other income—government funds, private sources, and school support—comes each with its own set of pluses and minuses. Government funding may involve much paperwork, and its provision in the near future is tenuous. However, it might still bring a large chunk of money into a SACC program—money that often helps the program to serve a broader slice of the population. Private funds from business, foundations, individuals, and service clubs usually come without bureaucratic red tape, but there may be stipulations that it be used for specific areas of the program—facility renovations, purchase of equipment, etc. Unless you have good connections or a known track record, such money may be hard to acquire.

Receiving funds and in-kind resources from the schools has its advantages and disadvantages, too. When you work in collaboration with the schools, you are best able to keep parent fees down and staff salaries up—an advantage that goes a long way toward ensuring program stability, quality, and longevity. The costs of personnel, transportation, and rent are usually substantial enough so that tradeoffs or compromises may be necessary. If you decide on a location where transportation is not necessary, and where you pay a minimal rent—a school—funds may be freed to increase staff salaries and, perhaps, to add benefits. On the other hand, when costs are high for transportation and rent (as well as personnel), you will be faced with tough questions: Should we lower staff salaries? Should we raise parent fees to offset the expense? Should we seriously look elsewhere for a facility or additional funding?

What are our recommendations? Build a broad base of financial support. In this time of spiraling costs and the threat of cutbacks in funding, develop a conglomeration of financial help from as many different sources as you can. This is necessary not only to initiate the program, but to ensure its survival.

Begin in your local community first. Funding sources are often literally right in your own backyard. Each community has its own financial mechanisms, its own political structures that hold the purse-strings. You will need to learn what these sources are, so that they can be tapped.

Obtain start-up funds. No program can be set up without them. Before your new SACC program ever opens its doors, it will need to pay for staff, equipment, supplies. It may also need to pay rent, heat and electricity costs, custodial fees. Some of these expenses may have to be paid to providers before the program begins. Established agencies that add SACC as a new component may have fewer problems finding start-up money than individual programs will.

At the onset, there will be a cash flow problem, with more going out than is coming in. This is because most programs are not fully enrolled at the beginning. They cannot count on sufficient income from clients to underwrite initial costs, no matter how beautifully balanced the budget is on paper. The program will need cash to carry it from opening day to the point where it is breaking even—in reality, not on paper.

Get the most from already-existing resources. Try to build bridges with agencies, institutions, and groups. Collaborations may not bring funds into the program, but may allow your program to receive services or other benefits that are more valuable than actual dollars.

Work to make the cost of the program low enough so parents can afford it and high enough so that good quality is ensured. The cost of the program to parent users will ultimately determine whether your program survives. It may be an excellent and exciting program, but if it is financially out of reach of most potential consumers, you will soon be out of business.

In allocating expenditures, give staff salaries the highest priority. If you must pay high prices for utilities and rent, you may find yourself with great physical space, but with a staff that is underpaid and constantly in transition. Low staff salaries and meager benefits affect staff quality and morale.

Build in mechanisms that ensure fiscal accountability. It is essential that programs carefully work out their plans for carrying out all of the financial management tasks. Who is legally liable if bills are not paid? Who will take the responsibility for bookkeeping: for paying the bills, collecting fees, managing the payroll? Who will audit the books? These and other financial questions should be carefully worked out well in advance of start-up.

■ *Who Will Be Accountable, and for What?*   In each area of program design discussed above, we have recommended that you consider and clarify exactly who will assume responsibility for the different components—finances, administration, etc. Who will assume which costs? Which group will run the over-all program?

Look back now over each category you've made decisions about, and make sure you have assigned specific responsibilities for each one, including a definition of what those responsibilities are. (See

Chapter 5 for a discussion of legal accountability, and Chapter 7 for a chart of the tasks of administration.) Accountability is one of the most crucial elements in your design, and in the eventual success of your program. Attending to it now will prevent or ameliorate many future problems or conflicts about who is responsible. Everyone involved in the program will know exactly what is and is not expected of them. This is a particularly sensitive point when partnerships are being established.

You will soon be seeking informal or formal approval. Whether it comes from a church, school board, or agency, be assured that you will be asked very specific questions about accountability. (Chapter 4 discusses approving boards' concerns with this issue.)

Weighing the Ideals and Realities: Should We Have a Program?

You have established a philosophy, goals, and standards—you have formed an ideal of the kind of program you would like to provide; you have studied the results of your needs assessment, and know what is needed; you have assessed available resources, your options, their advantages and disadvantages; and you have considered our recommendations. Now, you will have to weigh ideal, need, and reality—the three are never congruent—to see what you can come up with, where you will have to compromise, and where you cannot. You will be adding and subtracting angel cake and bread—high staff salaries against what people can afford to pay.

If, after assessing all the choices and conditions, you conclude that you cannot offer a program that will achieve your goals and maintain your minimum standards of quality, *do not start a program now.* First, see if you can make further, more acceptable negotiations—including the application of stronger political pressure. Try harder to find more acceptable resources, such as cheaper or more accessible space. Consider seeking technical assistance. *Wait.*

If none of these efforts is successful, do not push ahead to establish a program. It will not be successful. However, if you conclude that you *can* provide a program that will meet the needs of some parents and children for a SACC program, will meet the needs of staff, will hew to your basic philosophy and goals, will not sacrifice rock-bottom, essential standards, and will be financially viable, you are justified in presenting the program you have designed for approval and implementation.

Part Three

MOVING AHEAD TOWARD IMPLEMENTATION

INTRODUCTION

Your group has gathered the information it needs and designed the program. You must now obtain cooperation and approval from "the system" before you can put your program into operation.

There are steps you must take before your program can open. Some will be your first administrative tasks. Although you will not be able to actually complete some until after you receive approval, you should begin to investigate them now:

1. Continue to build alliances and gain support of key school people, including personnel, board, PTOs, parents.
2. If necessary, prepare a proposal and make a formal presentation for approval.
3. Investigate and begin the process of incorporation as a nonprofit organization; develop bylaws; investigate tax exemption.
4. Clarify issues of licensing and liability; set up clear lines of accountability.
5. After obtaining approval, complete the processes of incorporation, tax exemption, licensing and liability coverage; draw up written agreements.

Although we discuss the necessary steps in a specific order, legal issues should be investigated before you go for formal approval, and accomplished immediately afterward. Chapters 4 and 5 will discuss all of the mechanisms and strategies for successfully accomplishing these tasks.

Once you make it clear that you are very serious about initiating a program and ask for the firm commitment of others, you turn a crucial psychological corner. Although some groups encounter no difficulties (or any opposition is hidden or mild), others may now meet opposition that is up front, organized, and as serious as you are. You will have to disarm this opposition.

"Develop a full feasibility plan before you approach the administration—lines of responsibility, liability, etc. Otherwise, it will be easy to knock you out when you make your presentation," advises one organizer. If you don't think through and resolve these issues before you appear before a board, the targeted opening date may be delayed by several months or longer—or even prevented completely. Rather than being "knocked out," you will be successful in implementing your program.

Chapter 4

GETTING APPROVAL

What Kinds of Approval Are Needed?

This will vary in each community. Generally, all groups will need "informal approval." This is the tacit consent, acceptance, or blessing of the community in which you live, and/or of the group within whose jurisdiction you wish to establish your program. If all you need is informal approval, you will not have to appear before an official body—a church or school board, for example. No program can open, however, even one that is to be totally self-supporting, without at least the acquiescence and acceptance of its neighbors: the personnel within the school building, or the clergy and other members of a religious organization.

Even if you have the full blessing of the school community, you must visit the principal, discuss the details of your program, and obtain his or her consent. Probably, you will also have to make a formal appearance before the school board in order to use the building, answering many questions, perhaps presenting a proposal, and then being "voted on."

Most groups will have to obtain formal approval from the groups or individuals (usually a board) who are invested with the power to say yea or nay to your program. You will also need approval from the bureaus who grant licenses, permits, insurance, and corporate and tax-exempt status. Groups who have a choice as to whether or not to obtain formal approval usually choose to do so because it helps them to gain legitimacy. This prevents any opposing forces from challenging the legality of their program.

Strategies for Gaining Approval and Overcoming Opposition

Formal approval doesn't happen out of the blue. It is achieved by careful behind-the-scenes preparation: developing and using the support and power of others, and confronting and overcoming your opposition.

Some groups have been welcomed into and approved by their community immediately. Others meet moderate opposition that quickly fades once the program opens; others have had to wage open battles, not only in order to get approval, but also to keep the program alive and well. "Try to exhaust all the positive avenues first," as one organizer observed, "and then apply political pressure." Now may be the time to "pull out the big guns."

How do you begin? Learn who the power structure is—key people, advocacy groups, and agencies. Get the support of the power structure. The allies you identify and establish now will facilitate gaining approval. As one organizer said,

> Every small town has people you can pull together. I would think at least 75 percent of the towns in this country have a self-generating power structure: there's always a lawyer, a doctor, etc.

Send these people as your mentors, door-openers, and advocates, as well as others—consumers, representatives of groups with good track records.

Observe protocol. Learn the informal and formal rules for making decisions in your community, including who the real decision makers and "power brokers" are. Find out from whom you must obtain formal approval, and what the process is.

Know you have a good product and sell it well: explain what SACC is; dispel myths; talk about need for child care in the community; listen to the viewpoints of others, being especially sensitive to the issues that concern them; show that you can help each other.

Learn who oppose SACC and try to understand why they do. Confront them and rebut their objections with facts. Use your contacts, pressure, and clout. Go over heads now, if you have to, and mobilize your support before the date of formal approval. Get the laws behind you: by getting your program approved by all the proper official empowering bodies, including licensing bureaus; by attending to issues of liability and accountability; and by instituting new policies, if need be. Make SACC an election issue.

Key People: Allies and Opposition

A successful activist told us, "Get their attention first and then change their minds—that's how it works. To all the people we found who were interested, we said, 'Call your supervisors, call your board of education, school board members, superintendent. Write letters.' We had months of doing that to put it on the public agenda."

You will need the support of key people and groups to help you "get a foot in the door," to lobby for you, and to use their contacts and power on your behalf. Sometimes you will have to survey people informally to find out who's sympathetic. These individuals may be able to advise you on the best ways to approach the power structure and present the potential program to them, and from whom to expect opposition. Acquiring this information is preferable to "walking in blind" to a superintendent or school department. In one school, a teacher assisted a group by telling them the best way to present their program to other school personnel. She would present an issue, get feedback, tell them if their timing was right, and who was going to oppose them. Ask these people to speak to organizations they belong to. Get legitimate groups to back you, such as day care councils or PTOs.

Ask them to help you gain entrée where you need it. Sometimes one person can mean the difference between success and failure:

> The only reason we have day care in the public schools is because the principal at one school was a working mother. She remembered a time in her life when she needed day care herself, and there was none. We visited her and she agreed to try it in her school on an experimental pilot basis for nine months. The school board hadn't wanted to take responsibility and force the program on principals. But when Jane volunteered, it really opened the way. She was the principal of two schools, so we started in two sites. And now that the pressure was off the other principals, they became more willing to gather information about the program, with an eye toward beginning one in their schools. (*Program organizer*)

Sometimes one right contact can change defeat into victory:

> The greatest obstacle was actually the associate superintendent who just didn't want the program. So what we did was that we identified significant others to reach the superintendent—we found a person who went square dancing with him and we told her to get to talk to him about how important it was. We flattered him, we did everything, but it

was really this woman who went square dancing with him once a week and talked about it with him weekly who really turned the tide. I knew I couldn't go over his head. If we did this, the whole thing would have come to a halt. (*Organizer*)

Put "key people" who are supportive of SACC, and who would approve your program if they had a say in it, on your task force and boards. This might mean putting on your board a school principal or the director of the official group that will be responsible for your program. Or, place parents who are strong advocates for SACC on the community education board, if community ed is the group whose support and approval you need to start a program.

Identify key organizations and individuals and "sell the program." Most often, you will have to meet informally with the key people whose approval you need in order to do this.

Now that you have the results of your needs assessment and have carefully designed a program, you are well equipped for this public relations task of educating and informing your public. Come well prepared, and explain the need. (Remember our earlier advice to argue the need, not the values of day care.) You must know how much the program will cost, where the money will come from to finance it, and what kind of program it will be, including its scope and size. You may wish to send sample packets of information on your survey and program design. Be sure to point out the benefits to the community and to the institution you're approaching.

Be particularly careful to explain the lines of responsibility: who will assume which costs, liability, and the responsibility for the overall administration and day-to-day running of the program. Be clear on what you are asking of the person you're meeting with, and what you are not asking—for example, you would like to use school space, but the program will be responsible for its own administration.

Respect the viewpoints of others and be flexible. Suggest or accept compromises if you feel they will not jeopardize the integrity of the program. Principals should participate in hiring a program director.

Don't overwhelm an individual or group by presenting elaborate plans. Approach the school board with one or two issues at a time. You may want to begin by suggesting a pilot program in one or a few locations.

■ *The Psychology of Institutions.* You, as a seeker of approval, are on the outside: "They"—the board or government, the school, or the agency—are inside. Respect the differences in your positions— but don't be cowed.

> Once you break down the barriers, it's easier. But first you have to recognize what the barriers are. (*Director from the South*)

Institutions, by their nature, have certain common characteristics. All institutions, and many individuals, are defensive of what they consider to be their "turf." They may also fear that their power will be usurped, or that they will be burdened with responsibilities they don't see as theirs. You must present your request so that it doesn't diminish the responsibility and decision-making power of the people whose approval you want. Be sure you're not usurping or undermining their position.

Institutions resist change and are suspicious of new concepts. "Anything new is difficult," is the way one director expressed the problem. They may resist assuming any role they regard as outside their jurisdiction or responsibility. In a southern state, the school board initially was opposed to SACC "because it was very new and very different." Now, however, their attitude has changed, largely due to extensive public relations work (the most recent was television advertising) that was done to increase community understanding of and support for the program. One organizer, whose group is now beseeched by principals to open more programs, told us:

> There were some ill feelings on the part of the principals toward our planning council because we were moving into their domain. They felt we would be an alternate power source and thereby threaten their existence.

Institutions do not like to take risks: it exposes them to the possibility of criticism and/or censure. Two very effective ways to encourage bureaucracies to "take a risk" are to organize groups (of parents, especially) who are vocal and will demonstrate that they support the risk-taking, and to prove that the risk is minimal, because the program is well thought-out and will be financially viable.

■ *Confronting and Overcoming Opposition.* Figure out what the real objection is. Then figure out what you can do about it. You may have to listen very hard before the real issues emerge—turf, power, fear of censure or financial loss, guilt—from behind the institution's smokescreen. The smokescreen may take the form of such emotionally laden charges against school-age child care as:

- It's a communist plot.
- It's a welfare program.

- When I was raising children, I stayed home with them and I don't see why mothers can't do that now.
- It adds to the further disintegration of the family.
- The family should take care of its own, not pay for day care or have governments pay for it.
- Children can take care of themselves—they always have, and they always will.

You must also be aware and become convinced, warns Bettye M. Caldwell, a leading national advocate for child care, of the extent to which people who oppose you may organize to defeat your program.[1] Ms. Caldwell, who argues that day care strengthens, rather than weakens, families, speaks of (1) the number of people who hold differing views from those probably espoused by a majority of persons in the child development field; (2) the intensity with which those views are held; and (3) the extent to which such people are organized to see to it that their views become the official ones.

Above all, remember this general advice from the director of a successful large urban program that faced, and overcame, enormous city-wide opposition from the mayor, labor leaders, and school personnel:

> The reason that we have survived is that we have a philosophy and a point of view. You must believe in this stuff. You need to persevere. You have to be able to come out of that corner every time you're knocked down. A lot of people hate it. Some think it is God's worst sin to have day care. The obstacles are enormous. But you have to believe in kids, and you have to persevere.

Following are typical concerns of some of the major groups that may suddenly become vocal—especially at public hearings where you go for approval—now that you clearly mean business. We also list some suggestions for dealing with these concerns.

■ *Members of the Community—"Taxpayers."* When taxpayers express opposition, it is usually based on fears that a school-based program—especially one where in-kind resources are contributed by the school system—will cause taxes to rise. This may be a special concern of older residents. Such opponents fail to recognize the costs to the community of vandalism and of increasing social problems that are partially the result of unsupervised, bored children.

---

[1] Bettye M. Caldwell, "Reflections on the 1980 White House Conference on Families," in the *Newsletter of the Society for Research in Child Development* (Winter 1981).

The argument that the use of unused school space is cost effective, and an efficient as well as worthwhile use of taxpayers' dollars, is cogent here. Housing SACC programs in publicly financed buildings that once closed at 3:00 P.M. makes very good financial sense. One program director told us, "Taxpayers said, 'I am finally able to use something that my tax money pays for!'" Remember that parents are taxpayers.

In many communities today, cutbacks in federal, state, and local funds for after-school activities—not only at schools, but throughout the community and for many day care centers as well—means that there will be fewer recreational opportunities for children. SACC can provide some extra experiences for children.

If your programs will pay rental, custodial, or energy fees to schools, you may not have much opposition. The director of a multi-center program that pays large fees points out:

> How can the school turn down the fees? Most schools are strapped for funds. You're not coming to ask for support in the position of a beggar.

From Virginia come suggestions of additional benefits that can be pointed out: SACC draws people to the community—"We have people moving here and telling school board members that they moved here because of extended day. We hear it especially from younger working parents." It fills the needs of a wide spectrum of economic levels—"Originally SACC started in the schools where parents had modest incomes. Now we have extended day in the most affluent areas of the county. The demand is there."

■ *PTOs Sometimes Voice Opposition to Proposed Programs.* Often it comes from members who are not in the paid labor force, and is based on general opposition to working mothers. It is sometimes stated in this form: "I don't work. Mothers should be home with their children," or "I stayed home with my children and I don't see why mothers can't do that now." Ironically, this same source of opposition may come from working parents. They may feel guilty about working outside of the home, even though they must. Or they may be reacting to the general stigma that is still attached to day care in some communities. In one community where the PTO voiced opposition, a director said, "You kind of assume, because some are working mothers, that they would obviously know what we are all about. But it is not always true." She advises, "You must meet your PTO president, and don't try to change people's attitudes. We know there are a lot of people who don't like working parents, and you just can't get personally offended because they don't agree with your philosophy."

In one town, PTO opposition was resolved and overcome because the school board and administration supported the program. Those parents who use day care will have to take the lead in saying that it is not only all right, but beneficial to their children.

Opposition comes from men more often than from women (and from male principals more often than female administrators). One director explains, "Men don't relate to the issue at all. They don't understand it, and they look down on child care. So it's important to talk with them about it and give presentations."

■ *Members of Boards (Agencies, Schools, and Others).* Their major concern is their vulnerability to criticism from constituents or from their superiors in their organizations. If boards are being asked for their sponsorship, the money issue is paramount: in one city where the central downtown YMCA enthusiastically proposed latch-key programs, one director reported, "Very often, branch directors were not terribly enthusiastic about the program. Some thought it was 'a communist plot,' or that mothers should be at home, or that it would lose money." Note that what seems to be a genuine fear—loss of money—is masked by irrational or emotional issues.

■ *Proprietary (For-Profit) Day Care Providers.* These, as well as others, may perceive the program, especially if it is held in schools, as in competition with private providers in the community. Providers who operate centers without any relationship to schools worry that the school-based program has an edge on the day care "market" in the community. This concern may be shared by for-profit and nonprofit centers.

A school board chairman was actively lobbied by a day care center operator to oppose the use of school resources for a SACC program run by the community education department; in another community, day care center owners sued the school board for "competing unfairly with private enterprise." (The suit lost in court because the judge ruled that the school board had broad powers which included offering day care services to the community.)

However, some program organizers have had the following experience:

> We have a couple of day care centers where the school buses drop kids off, and we wondered about being in competition with them, and that

they would raise some flap about it. That was naive on our part: as it turns out, the day care centers did not enjoy having our kids dumped on them at 3:00 P.M., and they were delighted when we started a program here which would take away that burden from them. (*Principal in the South*)

In Durham, North Carolina, an Interagency Council on Community Education and Recreation (DICCER) has helped to minimize such problems. Different community groups are represented on the council and there is an opportunity to air feelings and to resolve problems.

One school-based program chose to limit operation only to those days when school was in session, because:

> If schools don't extend the program to vacations and holidays which might compete with the private sector, then we can avoid the charge that we're providing day care that competes with them.

While we don't necessarily recommend this approach, we do suggest that program planners take the time to assess how the private providers may feel about day care in schools or other public facilities and try to establish good feelings and open communication on the subject.

■ *School Systems: Boards, Members of Central Administration, Principals, and Other School Personnel.* When programs seek approval from school systems, they often hear: "The school is not a social agency—our business is reading, writing, and arithmetic." Some school superintendents, however, see their roles as more comprehensive. Some counter-arguments expressed by school superintendents:

> Extended Day eases the anxiety of parents. If schools move in that direction it's better for families and for kids and is therefore better for the schools.
>
> SACC enhances the role of educational providers, especially those who see their role as providing for the community needs of the people who use their schools.
>
> SACC is an exciting, innovative idea, and thoughtful educators are innovators.
>
> Politically, you have a group of parents who are supportive of the schools. It's certainly very important these days to have a vocal and supportive group of parents. Every superintendent could use that.
>
> We're very sympathetic to the needs of the mothers who are trying to raise their kids on their own, and by having decent child care, we're providing a necessary service, and we like that idea.

There are additional ways SACC can benefit school systems:

1. It can help maintain—or increase—enrollments. A school district that offers SACC will attract families to it. In addition, as one superintendent told us, "I have no question that our town kept its public school population from entering private schools (which had longer activity hours than regular schools) because we had an extended day program."
2. It may facilitate desegregation.
3. It is self-supporting: there need be no cost to the schools.
4. When the program pays rent, the system benefits financially.

You must point out these ways SACC can benefit the schools.

If you want to house your program in a school, and to have a partnership with a school system, you will have to obtain the agreement and approval of everyone in that system at each administrative level—the school board, the superintendent, and the principals—before you go for official approval. Remember that even if a principal is sympathetic, he or she will not go out on a limb for the program without the backing of the superintendent, and if the superintendent is not behind the program, the school board will probably not approve it. Nor can you ignore the misgivings of teachers, custodians, and other school personnel, although generally you will deal with these people directly when the program is in operation.

Approach the proper person at each level, find out whether he or she supports the program, and hammer out any concerns and problems—no matter how minor they may seem to you. You must get things cleared up in advance. Enemies on the school board can get in your way. Whether you move up—or down—the ladder, however, all organizers agree on one basic fact: *obtaining the principal's support is the key to getting approval.* No program will succeed without the backing of this individual.

> The schools are one of the most difficult places to negotiate with. You can approach a church, and they'll say yes or no, and you can kind of negotiate with them because they *have a sense of mission,* and they are able to make *their own decision.* But you approach the principal of a school that is part of a large school district, like New York or Los Angeles, and, first of all, he has the power to make very few decisions. The decision *has to go up through many levels,* and it only goes up if he says he agrees with it and would really like it to happen. And then there's always the counterpoint to that—"Well, you wanted it! Therefore anything that goes wrong will be your fault!" *(Program organizer from the Northeast)*

Approach any and all levels of the school system by holding informal meetings. Invite school personnel to talk with parent groups, and demonstrate that you have a great deal of parent support by using it. In one midwestern state we were told, "SACC evolved because a lot of parents in the school supported the program, and would go to the teachers and to the principals and say, 'We want the program, we need your support.' So parents played a big role in whether or not the program succeeded. They pushed hard for it. And they got it." School boards and individual personnel do not want to fight parents in their own school districts.

School boards often cite the absence of any school board or other policy on the use of school space by any outside groups—or for purposes of day care—as a reason to oppose and veto SACC.

There may be opposition to the philosophy of using schools for day care. As one YMCA director commented, "It was quite okay for us to provide special after-school activities at the schools, but taking care of somebody else's kids after school by establishing a formal child care program was something else—that's day-to-day care, and they didn't like it." Or it may be that the board is not opposed to day care *per se,* but to the use of the schools by *any* outside group. Boards may worry that opening schools to your program will bring demands from many different interest groups. In areas where community education departments offer programs that are held in school space, boards and administrators will probably be more open to the idea of allowing entry to SACC, especially if the program comes under the CE umbrella.

School boards and administrators can no longer justifiably defend a policy of prohibiting the use of school space to its community members. They are as interested as anyone else in demonstrating to the taxpayers their ability to manage space and finances efficiently and effectively.

Sometimes, in order to overcome school board or other opposition, you may have to legitimize and/or change what you call "the program." To legitimize SACC, you must obtain a mandate from the school system in the form of policies promulgated by the school board or district, and the school administration, that will permit the use of school space for purposes of a SACC program. When such policies are established, SACC will be institutionalized within the system. After this, it becomes easier to get approval for other new programs. In a Massachusetts town that had no policy on the use of school space by SACC programs, parents and school board members together created the guidelines for the school system's policy that allowed SACC to be held in the schools. Once SACC was a legitimate part of the system, other new programs burgeoned.

You may have to emerge from the local arena and enlist the aid of key state officials to gain legitimacy. Some states have legislation encouraging schools to share resources. Both Oregon and Connecticut have enacted legislation supporting the use of schools for day care.

Oregon's legislation:

> Any district school board may contract for or operate programs providing activities before and after usual classroom hours for school-age children residing in the district. Such programs may be supervised by persons other than persons holding teaching certificates. The district school board shall establish rules of eligibility for participation in such programs and may collect fees for participation thereon. The fees shall be used for the support of the programs. (*House Bill 2069 as amended*)

Connecticut's laws on use of school facilities for other purposes:

> (a) Any local or regional board of education may provide for the use of any room, hall, schoolhouse, school grounds or other school facility within its jurisdiction for nonprofit educational or community purposes whether or not school is in session. (*Title 10, Sec. 10-239*)

Your state may have similar legislation, or legislators may be interested in sponsoring an amendment to existing laws; try to encourage their support of the idea.

State legislation can, however, only suggest that schools share resources. It is up to the district or local school board to develop policies for their communities. Boards of Education can set some broad policy directions, as in this excerpt from the Boulder Valley Public Schools in Boulder, Colorado:

USE OF SCHOOL BUILDINGS AS CHILD CARE CENTERS

> The Board of Education authorizes use of public school buildings before and/or after school for child care programs for school-age children when the building is not in use for the regular school program.
>
> All authorized programs will be self-supporting. Any costs incurred by the school district directly related to a child care program will be charged to the program, including but not limited to custodial services and utility costs.
>
> The local school is expressly prohibited from assuming responsibility as the sponsoring agency unless specific authorization is first obtained from the Board of Education.

Responding to the "increased interest in the concept of joint occupancy of available space in schools and in the community use of schools," the Montgomery County (Md.) Public Schools Board of Education developed very specific policies that would allow the superintendent to select tenants who would "complement, support, and benefit the educational program." Surplus space for school-age programs and other community services is leased by the schools in accordance with a set of priorities developed by the board of education, which includes a range of groups and organizational types such as private nonprofit agencies, public-supported county agencies, and private enterprise (religious day schools; private medical, legal, or business practices). (See Chapter 10 for financial arrangements of this policy.) Local school systems can also develop policies and guidelines for approval procedures for groups wishing to use school facilities. (See the Appendix for examples of policies school systems can adopt.)

Sometimes, in areas where day care has negative connotations or conjures emotionally based opposition, referring to or calling a program "after school" or "extended day" rather than "day care" will help avoid problems. One program decided to change its name from "Latchkey" to "Adventure Club" with good results. Some programs have been creative in naming themselves—for example, the Brookline After-School Special (BASS) in Massachusetts.

You must demonstrate that the general design of your program is very sound, especially in areas that relate to accountability. School boards will require absolute assurance that they will not be sued, that the program is fiscally solid and therefore will not cause them to incur financial liabilities or be a drain on them, and that it will be well run on a day-to-day basis. If you think the school board is particularly concerned with the management of the program, you may want to give it representation in the group that will run the program.

■ *Principals.* We reiterate: *no* program will be approved if it does not have the support of the principal. Some principals see their roles as totally divorced from any connection with day care, and resent the idea that their schools are being used as "social welfare agencies" or "baby sitting," rather than for purely educational purposes. Another reason that principals initially (or over the long run) oppose SACC is that *they* are the ones especially vulnerable to criticism—from parents whose children are in the program, from teachers and custodians, superintendents, and school boards—if anything goes wrong with the program. Principals are vitally concerned with issues of accountability: Who is liable in case of accident and lawsuit? Will the program be well-run? They are afraid that inept or inadequate people will be running the program and that the end result may be a call to the principal. So, advises one director, "Do PR (and *assure the principal* you will do it) and be sure that people know whom to call when there is a problem—*not* the principal."

Finally, the "turf" issue is potent—principals fear that the program will encroach on their space, their authority, and will interfere with the regular educational program going on in their school.

The way to overcome principals' opposition is through communication. The following advice is from successful program initiators:

> See to it that principals are made aware of a need in the community for the program.
>
> Arrange for principals to meet with parents who are already in a program and to find out from them how it has helped.

Opposition based on any of the fears discussed above may emerge as a simple and adamant declaration that there is just no space available. Sometimes, the absence of space is an absolute fact. But often, with a little help, space can be found. Dr. Robert S. Posilkin, coordinator of the Joint Occupancy Program of the Montgomery County (Maryland) Public Schools, gave us the following suggestions, based on his own experiences, for dialogue between a principal and a SACC advocate.

ADVOCATE: We would like to use some rooms in your school for a SACC program.

PRINCIPAL: I just don't have the space.

ADVOCATE: What if there were fifteen new homes built in the area? Would you say, "I have no space for these children at my school?" You have two free rooms that aren't used all the time.

PRINCIPAL: I have to use those two rooms for art.

ADVOCATE: Are you, as a manager, using space effectively? Can you justify using two rooms? The standard in our district is one art room per elementary school.

PRINCIPAL: *(Perhaps unable to justify use of two rooms, now presents the real issue.)* The school is for the educational program. SACC will disrupt it.

ADVOCATE: We agree that the school is for the educational program. SACC will not interfere with it. Give it a year, and we'll prove it. Our lease agreement with the school system will stipulate that adverse impact on the educational program is prohibited. Also, you can't justify keeping other groups out, when the school is already filling other community needs. And, as a school employee, with programs paying rent, you'll be making money for the schools.

A strategy that has worked in many communities is to organize the parents very early. They can be a tremendous counterforce against the principal. The principal is not about to fight the group, because that would mean he would be fighting his own students' parents.

Listen to the problems of the principal. Above all, discuss and consult with him or her about the program. When principals are informed about how the program will actually work, their fears abate and their support grows.

Sometimes when concern over one mechanical detail is allayed, opposition evaporates. Before going for board approval, one organizer met with the two school principals, the secretary, custodians, and the rec department director. He explained the program, how it would be worked out, and asked them how they felt about it. One principal said they didn't really have an opinion either way, but that their main concern at that time was that the school would have to take responsibility for what the day care office should be handling. When he was assured that each day care center would have a phone of its own in addition to the office phone, that all business would go through the day care office, and they wouldn't be bothered, that seemed to help. (See Chapter 7, "Administration," for suggestions on making such partnerships work.)

■ *Community Education Departments.* Sometimes called "community schools," these groups should be regarded as a potentially very strong ally: their mandate is to offer services to people of all ages within the community. With connections both in the schools and in the community, community ed departments can provide the perfect bridge for groups trying to cross over. This was the case in one city in the Southwest, where a YMCA operated six programs in the public schools with the informal agreement of the superintendent of schools and the individual school principals. The community education department was instrumental in bringing the need for SACC to the attention of the Y, and in promoting the use of shared school space as part of its own mandate.

■ *Agencies.* People in agencies may also voice the opinion that the proposed school-age program is in unfair competition with services they already provide. If your needs assessment is well done, you can demonstrate that this is not so. Or you may have to show that the quality and kind of program you wish to initiate differs from that of the agency. You might invite them to join you in your efforts, since you are both concerned with providing needed services to families and children.

■ *Religious Institutions.*   You will need to convince members, clergy, boards, or councils that it is a good idea to support a SACC program in their space.

Using Political Savvy, Power, and Pressure

Political sophistication is essential to confront and overcome opposition. You must understand the politics of your community and work within the power structure. Some groups have succeeded only by the unabashed use of naked power and pressure.

Your group may have to undertake a long campaign to gain acceptance and approval. Campaigns are won at the grass roots level by an organized, concerted effort to bring out every voter and power broker on election day. Before your formal approval day, you may have to do a great deal of political work. Be aware that your campaign may take a year or longer. If you have to fight hard, the following strategies will help you gain approval now and avoid threats to the program after it is established.

1. Get the laws behind you to gain legitimacy. The law is a powerful ally. Make sure you use it by observing correct protocol and fulfilling all legal requirements for your program.

Find out who is legally empowered to grant official approval (it may be several different groups) and what the process is. If you must be approved by your local school board or city board of selectmen, how do you get on the docket for their hearing? You may have to make a written application in order to be heard. If the board meets only once a month to conduct business, it may take some time for you to get an audience.

If you will not be permitted to operate until a policy on use of school space by SACC programs is established, learn who sets the policy and how you get it implemented.

Which state and local bureaus grant licenses? Begin troubleshooting early by looking into the means of obtaining licensing and liability coverage. Also investigate the processes of incorporation and obtaining tax-exempt status.

In one city, when the owner and director of a program sought approval, she did so by placing the program in the category of an "educational facility," not a "day care" program. She had learned that, according to her city's laws, an "educational facility" needed approval only of its site plans by the local governing body, the board of aldermen. She realized that "by doing this, the program was insuring its survival, since all that could legally happen was that the board could put reasonable restrictions on the program. It could not reject us—we had the law on our side, by calling ourselves an educational institution."

In another town, where both parents and principal wanted to start a school program, they knew that the issue of liability—who would assume the responsibility for insurance—would be of major concern to the school committee whose approval they needed. So before they appeared for formal approval, they visited the town counsel and sought an opinion: the counsel advised that the program could not be covered by school insurance, but would have to take out its own. At the formal hearing for approval, liability did turn out to be a major concern of committee members, and the planners were prepared to respond with the "official word"—the town counsel's interpretation and recommendations. They were favorably received, and the program was approved.

2. Make SACC a general government concern—put it under the aegis of a government (county, town) structure rather than a welfare department. Individual mentors can come and go, and even bureaus or departments can be terminated, along with the programs under their umbrellas—but the political structure continues. Get local government attention: inform elected representatives and other officials, school board members, and county supervisors, enlist their aid—and remind them that you vote.

3. Approach the political power structure: enlist its aid, win it over, or fight it. You may find that power and opposition are coming from only one person, or from a number of people.

4. Be careful about enlisting the support of pressure groups who are not directly involved with your SACC issue. In one southern city, pressure for a SACC program to be held in a school came from individuals who were complaining, in general, about the school system, and it had a negative impact. Instead, success was achieved by a supportive principal and a local Citizen's Council who met together with the district superintendent. He listened and promised he would present their plan, with his own approval, to his superintendent. One organizer commented, "A citizen's group, with a proposal, with the principal's support, is better than others trying to expedite the decision by making a lot of noise." Sometimes even local community agencies can be regarded as "outsiders" by other groups, and their intervention can be a disadvantage.

5. If you wish to establish a number of programs (county- or city-wide), you may have to attack each district in a different fashion.

Start with the president of the school board and the superintendent, then find out where the power is centered in each district and approach each person who holds that power.

6. "Use intervention now, rather than remediation later," is the excellent advice of a strategist from the West Coast. If key people are now strongly opposing your program, you must either circumvent them or appeal to their superiors. Don't be afraid to go over heads. One very savvy director had located funds for her program and enlisted the enthusiastic support of a principal who offered her school space. As she moved toward implementation, a regional supervisor from the department of recreation told her, "This is not space that the principal can give you. This is recreation space." "It was definitely a turf issue," the director now sees with acute hindsight. "I should have gone back to the city council to nip this in the bud, but I didn't at the time." It took many more months of frantic pressure and maneuvering before the program was allowed to open.

One activist advises:

> Make your interest known at the decision-making level. We went straight to the top because we knew that is where the decisions were being made, and that is where you have to change peoples' minds.

7. Get a political network going. You may have to make SACC an election issue by educating candidates, helping elect SACC proponents to the school board, and defeating opponents. Learn from experienced veterans of SACC organization:

> You have to educate the powers that be on the school board, and that means getting involved in elections and making sure your candidate's running. And that's how we got crunched last year. We didn't have any effective network.

> There were ways that people who were active in the community learned who was politically vulnerable, and who could exert pressure on them—for instance, there was one administrator who kept putting up different reasons for opposition to SACC. Some of us knew he had political ambitions, and we knew some of the political powers behind the scenes. We contacted those powers, and said "Hey, you tell him that unless he cooperates with us, he hasn't much political future." That's one telephone call from a couple of the right people. That's the way. Later, when we had a series of meetings with the administrators, we got most of what we wanted.

> The parents should pressure the principal. They can dominate the PTO advisory committee. In fact, not too long ago, there were two slates of candidates who were running for PTO offices. One represented the day care constituency, and the other represented the principal's constituency. The parents came out in force for the pro-day-care candidate.

As you know, there are declining enrollments in schools and day care is an added leverage to keeping them open . . . . For the last two years in our county, extended day care has been a plus force in local politics.

As a community citizen taxpayer, when it comes time to vote, to interview, and to determine someone's suitability for the school board, the idea of community schools being used for SACC should be explored with them.

The Formal Presentation

Everything you've done up to now has been leading to those few hours when representatives from your group will appear before an empowering body to formally request approval. If you've done your homework well, you'll receive the green light to implement your program.

Call in the Troops

Publicize your imminent hearing by sending letters home with children (see Figure 4–1) and/or placing announcements in local papers and strategic community sites. Encourage supporters, advocates, and especially parents, who need and would use the program, to be in the audience when your hearing takes place (but be aware that this publicity may bring out some organized opposition).

Although in a few cases the "go ahead" is achieved by a few phone calls, most groups will have to make a formal presentation.

Who Makes the Presentation?

This depends somewhat on your sense of who will best be received by the agency or board. Remember that people who use that agency, church, or school have the most clout. If possible, these people should be well known to the approving body, with proven track records of reliability. Send people who can make a skilled presentation. Be sure to name one or two people as contacts, so that later, if board members want added information, they have someone to call.

What kind of approach is best? Be positive. Use moderation. Assume that the people you are appealing to are your allies. Stick to the facts—the need for a program.

In What Form Should the Presentation Be Made?

Which form you choose depends on the degree of formality required by the body you're dealing with. The presentation can be written,

EXTENDED DAY PROGRAM

GREENWOOD—YEUELL DISTRICT
WAKEFIELD, MASSACHUSETTS

Dear Parents,   September 3, 1980

An Extended Day Program is being proposed to the Wakefield School
Committee on Tuesday, September 9, 8:00 P.M. by the Greenwood-
Yeuell parents group formed after a Needs Survey was taken by the
PTO last spring.

The program will be staffed by qualified people and will serve
the Greenwood-Yeuell district, grades kindergarten through 5.
Hours of operation will be from 2:45 - 5:30 P.M. daily, Monday
through Friday. Fees will range from $9.00 to $20.00 per week
depending on the number of days the child is in the program.
Scholarship money will be available on a limited basis. Payment
must be made in advance every two-week or four-week period.

Fees: 2-day program: $9.00 per week
        3-day program: 13.50 per week
        4-day program: 18.00 per week
        5-day program: 20.00 per week

	2 days	3 days	4 days	5 days
2-week period:	$18	$27	$36	$40
4-week period:	$35	$52	$69	$75
	(save $1)	(save $2)	(save $3)	(save $5)

There will be a meeting of interested parents at the Greenwood
School on Monday, September 8, 7:30 P.M. to answer any questions
or problems you may have concerning our proposed Extended Day
Program. It is hoped to have the program in operation by October 1980.

This proposal needs your support! Your attendance at both meetings
will be appreciated, but particularly, your attendance at the
School Committee meeting on September 9th!

A questionnaire is attached — if you are interested in this program for your child, please complete and return to the school
immediately.

Sincerely,

Anthony Hober
Chairman of the Parents Group

Figure 4–1

oral, or a combination of the two. Even if you do not need to prepare
a written proposal, bring *something* in writing. Refer to the components of the proposal listed in the following paragraphs for suggestions, whether or not you have a more formal, written proposal.

Preparing the Presentation

Anticipate questions before they are asked—and know the answers.
Be able to present a carefully designed program. Remember that legal

protection and financial responsibility will be uppermost concerns to those you are approaching, whether for formal or informal approval. Be prepared to demonstrate that your group is responsible, because it has thought about and established clear lines of accountability by investigating licensing, liability coverage, incorporation as a nonprofit organization, and tax-exempt status. The approving body will want to know, "What is the program going to cost us?"—whether "us" is the county government, the city recreation department, or the school system (if you are collaborating with the schools). They will also want a clear explication of where the money will come from to pay for the program.

The Formal Proposal

Most groups will be required to present a formal proposal. This could be a brief (a few pages) written document—or a very detailed one, depending on the requirements of the group you are soliciting. If you are requesting money from a funding agency, your proposal may be very long and detailed. (See the Appendix for an example of a proposal.)

Evidence of need in your community or neighborhood should be included in your proposal. Present the clearly and succinctly summarized results of your needs assessment. Your statement about the survey's findings does not have to be full of statistics or go on for three pages. (Officials appreciate brevity—if they want to see more data, you can give them your complete study.) It need only be powerful and persuasive. You might want to use the short profile form presented in Chapter 2. The Wakefield, Massachusetts, parent committee, in their proposal before the school committee, made only this simple statement about needs: "We are recommending an extended day program in the Greenwood-Yeuell district based on a needs survey taken last spring by the PTO. Over thirty parents showed an interest in and need for this service." They were approved.

Evidence of need might include concrete examples, such as the number of children who appear at a school at 7:15 A.M. and/or evidence of increasing after-school vandalism. One group shot film of children "hanging around" after school, and showed it at a hearing.

If it is possible, arrange for advocates and possible users to speak at the hearing. You might wish to include letters—*on official letterheads*—from people with appropriate credentials. (A sample from Orange County, Florida, is shown in Figure 4–2.) A district attorney, for example, might attest to the increasing amount of juvenile

State of Florida
Ninth Judicial Circuit of Florida
COUNTIES OF ORANGE AND OSCEOLA

2000 EAST MICHIGAN STREET

ORLANDO, FLORIDA 32806

ROM W. POWELL
CIRCUIT JUDGE

TELEPHONE
420-3281

MEMORANDUM

TO: All Commissioners, Board of County Commissioners;
         All Commissioners and Councilmen, All Municipalities

FROM: Circuit Judge

DATE: June 25, 1980

RE: County Public Schools "Home Base Child Care Program"

I wholeheartedly endorse this Home Base Child Care Program.

The 16 months I recently spent on the Juvenile Court Bench convinced me that one of the primary factors in juvenile delinquency
is that many children are without supervision after school from
2:15 P.M. (1:30 P.M. on Wednesdays) until 5:30 P.M. or 6:00 P.M.
when the working mothers return home. One of the primary factors in truancy is that many working mothers must leave for work
before the child leaves for school.

This program fills a need that has existed for some time, and
should assist in materially curbing delinquency and truancy in
this county.

I trust you will give this program favorable consideration
(when applications are made for licensing of the homes and
granting zoning exemptions).

Figure 4–2

delinquency in the area and support the benefits SACC would provide. You may also wish to present a general outline of the problem
from a national perspective. (See Bibliography for helpful materials
and pertinent data.)

A *"statement of purpose"*—the philosophy and goals of the proposed
program—should also be included.

Specific information about the program you are proposing is necessary. Spell out the general elements in your design, especially:

- Where the program will be held, the hours of operation, and the age groups to be included;
- Costs of the program and the sources of your funds (attach a budget, and be prepared to explain each item);
- Accountability: who will assume responsibility for overall decision making, day-to-day operation, fiscal accountability, and liability coverage.

Example of a Hearing

Following is a report of a school committee hearing. Members' approval was sought by a group of parents and the school principal who wanted to establish a program in a public school. The group had first presented their idea for a program four months earlier, to give the committee a sense of their intentions and to receive initial approval. Now the planners had returned with a full proposal. Some of the questions the school committee asked indicate their concern with accountability.

"What room will be used? Is it a vacant one or will it be shared?"

"What about liability insurance, etc.?" (To which a parent responded, "We wouldn't open our doors unless we had insurance.")

"Custodial help—is this an extra expense that doesn't show up on the budget?"

"Who will be responsible for the general building supervision—the principal? What about after-school hours?"

"I'm concerned about the custodians' union. You may have it worked out with the custodians in the building, but. . . ."

"What will the program do in the case of illness of a child? Will there be a nurse on call or on duty?"

A few school committee members expressed their concern about having the program in one school instead of opening it to town-wide enrollment. The response from the principal and some of the parents was that their plan was to "start small, let it grow of its own accord."

The proposal indicated that the principal would supervise the SACC staff. One school committee member asked just how that would be done. It was explained that the principal would be a member of the parents' committee that would perform that particular function.

"What will happen when the A.M. kindergarten kids get switched to a P.M. session in the middle of the year and vice versa?" (This was an important question, since children in morning kindergarten got out at noon and couldn't really use the program—which wouldn't begin until 2:30.)

Another committee member asked, "How will transportation costs be paid? By individual parents using the service? By the program?" (This member noted that there was no dollar amount listed for transportation on the estimated costs page of the budget.) The principal responded, "There will be no cost to the town. We have arranged to hire a driver with a special license and van to transport any children coming from outside the district who need transportation. Individual parents will foot the bill."

A school committee member asked the representative from the superintendent's office what that office's response to the program was. The representative answered, "We think the concept is very timely. It answers a crucial community need and it enables community ed to provide a service to the district. The closer we get to the community, the better education we provide. And we are sensitive to the cost factor. There is no cost to the town."

"We should be getting legal advice . . . . What did the town's counsel say about all of this?"

"How can we be assured that there will be continued support to have this program?" (Probably the school committee didn't want to have to run the program.)

One school committee member began his remarks with, "It's unfortunate that we have to implement this type of program." The same school committee member said after approval was voted, "The program has to fly or die by the work of the parents involved."

Not every board will ask so many detailed questions; probably this committee did so more from a need for reassurance that the planners knew what they were doing than from their desire for such specific knowledge of details.

The final motion the committee made was that the program be accepted as a pilot program (not to exceed one year) pending the approval of the town's legal adviser and that it be reevaluated after the year. There was a unanimous vote of approval, even though one member was obviously opposed to it. Because the group had done their homework, they got their "A."

When Boards Must Choose

At times school administrators must choose one group to administer a school-based partnership program from among several proposals submitted by different groups, each of whom wants to run the program. It is difficult but important to steer clear of politics in this situation. For example, what if one of the proposals is submitted by a recently unemployed teacher who was laid off for budgetary reasons but left the system with a good reputation? As a school administrator, you might be tempted to choose that proposal because of loyalty to a former school employee. But suppose that the proposed program is going to charge parents more than you know they can afford. Or perhaps the curriculum outlined is just too much like the regular school curriculum, and you realize that the teacher will not be able to make the transition from being a great classroom teacher to being a good day care teacher. The point is that the decision should be made on the basis of the quality of the proposal, the qualifications of the group submitting the proposal, and the way the group intends to meet its own goals and yours for a program in your school system.

One way to make this choice in a fair manner is to convene a child care committee in the community. This committee could be a subcommittee of the school board or of a municipal agency concerned with children's services—for example, the health department. Some communities already have child advocacy groups which could send a representative to be on this committee. Parents who will use the program could also be members. It is important that the committee itself be seen as impartial, and not liable to make the decisions for political reasons.

Outcomes of the Presentation

There are a number of possible outcomes of your presentation. First, *the decision may be postponed.* This usually occurs because the board wants more information or requests a revision of some of the plans you've presented. Listen carefully to their reasons for not granting immediate approval, and try to figure out what is behind them. Are they right—does your plan need some tightening up or further clarification? If so, you may need to add something to your design that will satisfy these misgivings. Is there some issue that was not expressed, such as behind-the-scenes opposition and lobbying from a special-interest group? You may have to do further public relations or political work. Or, possibly, you will have to establish a new policy for the use of schools by SACC programs before your program can be approved.

Your proposal may be rejected. Ask yourself the questions raised above in the discussion of postponement and begin planning new strategy, based on the suggestions in the earlier part of this chapter.

The board may want you to negotiate. You will have to decide whether you can afford to give in on certain issues, or whether you cannot sacrifice program philosophy and goals.

Your proposal is or will shortly be accepted. If approval is certain, immediately—even while you are waiting for notification of formal approval—take the following steps:

1. Begin the process of incorporating and obtaining tax-exempt status. Then you will be able to purchase necessary equipment and supplies tax-free.
2. Make formal applications for licensing and insurance, and for funding, if applicable.
3. If you are an agency, begin the procedures for any changes that must be made, such as in agency regulations, policies, or additional insurance.
4. Firm up all agreements in writing. This may now include legal agreements such as contracts and leases.
5. Begin the search for and hire a director, *if* you have a firm commitment about use of a facility. (These steps are discussed further in Chapter 5, "Legal Issues," and Chapter 8, "Personnel.")

This is an exciting, exhilarating time. Much work lies ahead, but for a moment, stop and congratulate yourselves. You've gotten started and the program is poised at the point of implementation.

Chapter 5

LEGAL ISSUES

Programs need to safeguard the well-being of the children they care for, and protect the program and the people who run it. In addition, everyone—the community, empowering boards, any partnering agency staff, parents, and children—wants assurance that the program can be relied upon to "take care." Clarifying legal issues and establishing legal responsibility is one way of ensuring accountability.

As a caretaker of children, your program will have to comply with a number of legal requirements. For example, you will have to obtain official approval from the city, state, or federal bureaus that are empowered to grant licenses and/or to impose specific regulations.

It takes a lot of time to get things done. As we will explain later, there is often such confusion over legal issues with regard to SACC that you may need months to cut through reels of red tape. It is a good idea to assign responsibility for checking out all the procedures, "regs," and insurance to one person, or to a small task force. A lawyer would be the ideal person to handle this job. In some cases, one phone call to the state board that licenses day care programs and another to an insurance agent will give you the information you need; in others, especially those regarding tax exemption, we regret to say, the talents of a Sherlock Holmes will be required.

Incorporating as a Nonprofit Corporation;
Seeking Tax Exemption

Becoming a nonprofit corporation is a means of providing protection and financial benefits to the program during its operation, and of establishing legal and financial accountability.

Unless your program is sponsored by another incorporated institution, in most cases you will not be granted approval—nor will you be permitted to operate the program officially—until you are incorporated. Boards of sponsoring or partner institutions, and/or others from whom you must gain approval, will be concerned with reducing the risk of personal liability as much as legally possible. They are also likely to insist that program operators or officers be clearly identified as responsible and accountable before they permit your program to operate. Therefore, you must demonstrate to those whose approval you seek that you have investigated incorporation and tax exemption, and are prepared to accomplish both tasks.

One parent group in Wakefield, Massachusetts, said in its proposal to a school board:

> The program will be incorporated as a nonprofit institution for several reasons: personal liability is reduced, programs are exempt from some taxes, and proposals can be written for grants from state and private agencies and foundations. A lawyer has volunteered to serve this program.

Once the organization has incorporated as a not-for-profit institution, it can then apply for tax-exempt status. This will mean that you will not have to pay federal or state corporate income taxes or some state sales taxes.

Many states will require centers to incorporate in order for them to be eligible for government funding. You are more likely to receive financial support, including grants, if you are a nonprofit corporation with tax-exempt status.

For these reasons, as soon as your organization (or the organization sponsoring the program) is granted approval, you should move ahead quickly to become a legal nonprofit corporation, and then to seek tax exemption. The process of incorporation alone can take anywhere from a few weeks to six months.

Becoming a nonprofit corporation doesn't mean that you are automatically granted tax exemption. They are two separate processes. The steps are: (1) File incorporation papers as a nonprofit corporation with your state government and (2) once the state has approved this status, file with both the federal and state governments to obtain tax exemption. The two processes are closely related, however—you must apply for tax exemption under a specific category, and this category must be justified by information you provided earlier on your incorporation papers and accompanying bylaws.

Let's define the terms as they relate to SACC programs. A *corporation* is a legal entity that exists separately and independently from the individuals who make it up. As a legal entity, the corporation—*not* any individuals who are managing it—is legally responsible for anything the organization does, or doesn't do. If you decide to become a corporation, you can do so as either a profit-making or not-for-profit organization. You don't even have to become a corporation. (For information on different legal options—sole proprietorships, limited partnerships, and for-profit corporations—see the Bibliography.)

A *not-for-profit corporation* is an organization that defines itself in legal documents as the provider of an educational or charitable service, such as school-age child care. This definition of purpose must satisfy Internal Revenue Service (IRS) criteria and categories for meriting tax-exempt status. This means that the corporation *cannot define itself* as an organization that seeks to be a profit-making business, with the profits to be distributed among the members of the corporation for their personal financial benefit. However, not-for-profit programs *can* make a "profit"—that is, a surplus—as long as the money goes back into the program for staff salaries, scholarships, equipment, etc. (In some states, no legal distinction is made between "nonprofit" and "not-for-profit." In others, there is a difference in their legal status. You will need to check this out in your individual state, to learn what the differences mean in terms of the operation of the program.)

▪ *Tax-Exempt Status.*   Nonprofit corporations whose stated purposes fit certain IRS categories can file with both federal and state government tax bureaus so that they will not have to pay certain taxes and will become eligible for benefits that are not accorded to other organizations. You do not have to file for this status, but it is clearly to the advantage of SACC programs to do so.

Incorporating as a Nonprofit Corporation

Studying and investigating incorporation will be one of your first managerial tasks.

▪ *What Are the Choices?*   You can choose to be an unincorporated organization—if you can get approval. We do not recommend this choice, although there are some exceptions: some programs choose *not* to incorporate, but, rather, to use a sponsor institution as a channel or conduit for funds which are available only to nonprofit organizations.

If a sponsor agency is already a legal corporation, probably tax exempt, it can serve as an "umbrella" for its own program. This means that schools, churches, Y's, municipal and state agencies may not need to initiate the process of filing for incorporation or tax exemption if these institutions are administering the program themselves. Any group that is seeking to collaborate with a larger body but *wishes to maintain control of the administration* of the program may want to incorporate as a legal entity.

This section addresses those groups and organizations starting SACC programs that are independent of any larger, already incorporated agency.

■ *Why Should a Program Incorporate?*   Incorporation protects you and any others responsible for the program—the board members, the agency, or the school—from personal or institutional liability. This is because the corporation has a legal identity and existence that is separate from those individuals who began the organization or who are running its program. As *the* legal entity, it is the corporation that is responsible for anything the organization does. Therefore, it is the corporation, and not individuals, that will incur any legal or financial liability in most situations.

The board can formally vote approval of an "indemnification resolution"—a statement that no officer of the board or directors of the corporation may be held personally liable. For example:

> No officer or director will ever have to pay any money as a consequence of any action . . . unless it was a direct result of gross negligence on the part of the officer or director, and if any payment is to be made for any reason not involving gross negligence, such payment will be made from the funds of the organization, either directly or as reimbursement to the officer or director.[1]

This statement can be part of your bylaws.

Nonprofit incorporation gives you a built-in administrative structure. The most important administrative feature of the not-for-profit corporation is the requirement that there be a board of directors legally responsible for the organization. Even though some states

---

[1]Lawrence Kotin, Robert K. Crabtree, and William F. Aikman, *Legal Handbook for Day Care Centers* (Boston, Mass., 1981), p. 40.

don't require the corporation to have members, all require the existence of a board to oversee business.

The process of incorporation means that you will have to take on
the responsibility of creating several internal structures in order to set
policy and to establish procedures for decision making, governance,
program operation, and continuity in program governance. These
structures and other procedural policies are usually part of the
bylaws, which you may or may not be required to include in the articles of incorporation. If and when you apply for tax-exempt status
you are also bound to adhere to government regulations on nondiscriminatory policies and goals for the actual program.

So, although applying for incorporation may be an inconvenient
and time-consuming task, the resulting framework you create will
actually guide you in establishing an organizational structure for almost every task you and others in the program must accomplish!

The stipulation, in your articles of incorporation, that parents
must be board members means that parents may have a greater investment in the program. A board of directors may be composed
either wholly or partially of parents whose children are enrolled in the
SACC program; larger programs run by social service agency boards
may have parent advisory boards—which may or may not be active
forums for parents to express their needs or desires for the program.
*Regardless of structure, when parents serve on boards as active participating
decision makers, programs benefit.* Parents may have a greater stake in
working with the program, and children see their parents as part of
the day care experience, rather than separate and removed from it.
The bylaws in Figure 5–1 from Eugene Latch Key, Eugene, Oregon,
spell out the inclusion of parents on the board.

BYLAWS

ARTICLE III.   BOARD OF DIRECTORS

Section 1.   The corporate powers of the Agency are vested in the
Board of Directors, who shall control all matters of policy and expenditure of funds of the agency.

Section 2.   The Board of Directors shall include as a minimum:
    a.   1 selected parent of an enrolled child from each school at-
        tendance area program
    b.   1 representative from community schools
    c.   1 representative from Lane County 4-C's
    d.   such other positions as authorized by Directors

Figure 5–1

■ *Is a Lawyer Necessary to Incorporate?* Yes—and no! The process of incorporating does involve some paperwork, a knowledge of state law, and the steps required to file. However, once a layperson learns what the requirements are, he or she can file the right papers at the right time—many have done so and have been successful. The office of the secretary of state or other state agency charged with incorporation duties may give you enough good advice to incorporate without a lawyer. Nevertheless, since your success in obtaining tax-exempt status is directly related to the way you respond to certain categories in the application for nonprofit incorporation, a lawyer would be helpful—either to point out the tricky areas or to do the actual work. Since each state does have its own regulations, and some are more complex than others, a lawyer would facilitate the process.

See if you can find a lawyer who will volunteer some time. This is called *pro bono* work—work that is donated to community service. You might be able to convince a lawyer who's running for office to help out. Other groups that can refer you to free legal assistance are the local bar association and affiliate groups, such as an association of women lawyers.

■ *How to Incorporate.* Here are the steps to follow:

1. Locate the state agency responsible for incorporation of organizations and request a form. This agency may be the secretary of state's office, the office of the attorney general, or the department of corporations. A form for filing as a nonprofit corporation will be sent to you, along with instructions for all procedures. Each state has its own procedures and forms, and sets its own requirements and fees. The procedures are generally simple. The fees may range from $1 to $50.

2. Choose your "incorporators." These are the people who will be empowered to sign the legal documents necessary to officially create the corporation, and who hold the first meeting at which this creation takes place. Incorporators no longer have any duties, responsibilities, or power once the initial meeting is called and the program has been legally incorporated, unless these people serve in another capacity within the organization (such as members of the board of directors).

3. Prepare the articles of incorporation: This may also be called the "articles of organization" or "certificate of incorporation." The articles will include:

- The name of the initial incorporators (board of directors)
- The date of your annual meeting and the date of the end of your fiscal year

- A statement on the purposes of the organization and its legal powers
- The organization's membership and their rights and duties

4. State the purposes of the organization. Choose your words carefully! The way you state the organization's purposes in the articles will have an impact on your success in obtaining tax-exempt status later. You must make a choice now as to how you describe the organization's purpose: you can define your purpose either as (1) educational or (2) providing day care.

If you say that your purpose is to provide day care, you will probably not experience any difficulty now in becoming a not-for-profit corporation. However, you may not be approved later on by the IRS as a tax-exempt organization if, as a day care center, the majority of those you serve are not from low-income families. IRS definitions and qualifications for tax exemption will be discussed more fully in the following pages. What is pertinent now, as you prepare your articles, is that the IRS's exemptions relevant to SACC programs are for (1) an educational institution or (2) a charitable organization.

Therefore, your future chances of receiving tax exemption are greater if, in the articles of incorporation you now state as your purpose that you provide educational and child development opportunities for the children you serve. Note that in the articles of organization (Figure 5–2), the purposes stated are "to provide a varied educational and enrichment experience. . . ."

The authors of the *Legal Handbook for Day Care Centers* suggest that:

> To be safe, it is usually a good idea to include a sentence restricting the organization's purpose "to those permitted under section 501(c)(3) of the Internal Revenue Code of 1954 or its successor sections in subsequent revenue codes.[2]

5. State the organization's powers. This is a straightforward statement that the organization seeking to incorporate claims all powers permissible to not-for-profit corporations in your state, such as the powers to buy, sell, and lease property; make and receive loans; etc.

6. List members of the corporation. Find out which names and designated officers your state requires on the document. Some states have waived the requirement of listing members, permitting those who serve on the board to be "the members."

---

[2]*Ibid.*, p. 24.

The Commonwealth of Massachusetts

PAUL GUZZI

Secretary of the Commonwealth
ONE ASHBURTON PLACE, BOSTON, MASS. 02108

ARTICLES OF ORGANIZATION
(Under G.L. Ch. 180)

Incorporators

NAME   POST OFFICE ADDRESS

Include given name in full in case of natural persons; in case of a corporation, give state of incorporation.

NANCY COLEMAN	18 Mayflower Street	Newton Highlands, Mass.
JEAN NELSON	11 Cedar Road	Newton Centre, Mass. 02159
ROBERT LEVY	30 Pine Brook Street	Newtonville, Mass.
CHARLOTTE ROSS	52 Pierce Street	Newton Highlands, Mass. 02168

The above-named incorporator(s) do hereby associate (themselves) with the intention of forming a corporation under the provisions of General Laws, Chapter 180 and hereby state(s):

1. The name by which the corporation shall be known is:

BYRD SCHOOL EXTENDED DAY PROGRAM

2. The purposes for which the corporation is formed are as follows:

To provide a varied educational and enrichment experience to a regularly enrolled student body, consisting of children from grades kindergarten through sixth, primarily from the Byrd school district of the City of Newton school system, as an adjunct to their regular public or private grade school education.

Said corporation is organized exclusively for charitable, educational and scientific purposes, including for such purposes the making of distributions to organizations that qualify as exempt organizations under section 501 (c)(3) of the Internal Revenue Code of 1954 (or the corresponding provision of any future United States Internal Revenue Code).

Figure 5–2

You can have as many members of the corporation as you want. Members of the corporation elect the officers of the board of directors. People who are on the board may also be members of the corporation—or, the board may be one group and the membership another. (Some programs set up a parents advisory committee as a unit separate from the board. If the board and the membership are separate, then each group is required to hold separate meetings, and to maintain its own reports and records.)

7. Prepare the bylaws. The rights and duties of the members of the corporation, the board of directors, and program personnel are spelled out in the bylaws. Although not all states require bylaws in order to incorporate, the IRS does require them before it will grant tax-exempt status. Bylaws are of great help to you, however, because they provide a codified framework for the way your program will conduct business: its rules, the way in which decisions are made, the delegation of power and authority. Since bylaws can always be amended or changed by the membership, they should be used as guidelines that are flexible so that they can reflect the changing needs of the program. You can write anything in your bylaws except statements that an IRS reviewer might see as contradictory when he or she is considering approval of your application for tax exemption. (See Appendix for a copy of the complete bylaws of the Eugene Latch Key Program in Oregon.) Every program will tailor its own bylaws according to its unique purposes and wishes.

At the minimum, your bylaws should include the following:

Name of the program or organization.

The purpose(s) of the organization, both general and specific. For example, "The program aims to promote child development in Rosehip County through the operation of before- and after-school child care programs during the school year and vacation time."

The board of directors—who's on it; how many members it has; the role of officers of the board; election procedures; term of office of directors and officers, etc. You should define the board's powers and the scope of its authority. For example: "The corporate powers of the agency are vested in the board of directors, who shall control all matters of policy and expenditure of funds of the agency." Specify how decisions are made and by whom. (Do all staff members on the board vote or are they represented by one or two staff members?)

The staff. This provision specifies that there will be staff filling certain roles within the organization. For example: "There shall be a director (or administrator, coordinator) and such other members of the staff as the board of directors shall deem necessary to carry on the work of the agency."

The bylaws may state that the director is empowered by the board to perform such duties as hiring of other staff, informing the board of all aspects of the operation, keeping a record of all communication and information "of value to the agency," and that the director is the "medium of communications between all departments of the agency and between the agency and the community."

Bylaws can also address the need for links of communication with partner agencies. In Oregon, bylaws of the Eugene Latch Key Program, Inc. include the formation of a program liaison committee at each school site as an option available to individual programs. The suggested committee would include the school principal, the community school coordinator, the program director, and board members and administrators of the overall program.

Meetings. The time of year when annual meetings are to be held should be stated specifically in the bylaws—for example, "in the month of March." The procedure for calling additional meetings of the members also should be spelled out (how many members must request it, etc.).

Amendment procedures. The bylaws should include a description of the process necessary to amend them. For example, "amendments to these bylaws shall be proposed in writing by any committee member one month in advance of a meeting, and shall be made by a quorum (two-thirds) vote."

8. Hold the initial, "official" meeting. At this meeting the name of the corporation is adopted, the articles of incorporation and the bylaws are approved, there is an election of the initial officers and board of directors (who serve only until the first meeting of the members), and a vote is taken to file the articles of incorporation. You must take formal minutes of the above proceedings. These minutes can be in the form of a one-page list of all the items voted upon with the names of those who voted. Each incorporator dates and signs the minutes.

9. Sign and file the articles of incorporation and other papers, and pay the filing fee. After conducting the initial incorporators' meeting, you may sign and file the articles and other documents required by your state. Some states require only one incorporator's signature; others may require up to three. Most states require that you file the bylaws. Filing is usually, but not always, done at the same office that provided you with the original forms. At some point, you or others who have signed the forms as incorporators may be visited by the police or any other public official charged with establishing your "credibility"—that is, that you do indeed reside at the address you have included on the form, and so on. Some states will not require this check.

10. Once the incorporation process has been completed, you will be notified by mail that your application has been approved. This can take from a quick ten days to a laggardly six months.

■ *Legal Requirements after the Program Is Incorporated.* Assuming that your incorporated organization has been granted approval by the church or school board to open your program, there are legal requirements you must comply with. First, obtain an employer identification number. This is required of every organization that pays regular salaries to employees. You must obtain this number even though you have probably not yet hired any employees, and the program is not yet in operation. The number is required of all nonprofit organizations before they can file for tax exemption. To obtain it, file with your District Internal Revenue Service (IRS Form SS-4). The form is short, and there is no fee.

Register with the state unemployment insurance office. (Different states may call this office by different names.) When you wish to begin hiring employees and operating the program, most states will require you to register with the unemployment insurance office. You will have to fill out a questionnaire. Two methods of paying unemployment insurance are available to you. For a discussion of each method, see Chapter 9, "Budgeting."

Seeking Tax Exemption

Once you have legally become a not-for-profit corporation, you can file for tax-exempt status with the federal and your state government.

■ *Why Should You Apply for Tax-Exempt Status?* There are many good reasons. Being a tax-exempt organization means that the program:

- Will not have to pay federal or state income taxes,
- Will not pay state sales tax,
- Does not have to pay state unemployment tax (as long as no employee makes a claim),
- Can use space owned by another tax-exempt institution (a church, a school) without imperiling that organization's status,
- Will be eligible for the lowest postage rates,
- Can allow employees to choose not to pay Social Security taxes (FICA),
- Will be able to accept contributions from individuals, foundations, or corporations (these contributions are tax-deductible to the donors).

This last advantage is considerable. It means that your tax-exempt status will encourage contributions from others. You are therefore more likely to be the beneficiary of donations and of grants.

Here are some disadvantages to tax-exempt status:

- There is more time and expense involved in initial (and ongoing) paperwork and recordkeeping. You will have to have an annual audit, and you will be examined by state regulatory agencies.
- The amount of time you can spend in lobbying activities will be limited by law.
- If you go out of business, any assets must be given to another tax-exempt organization.

It's clear that unless these points are more crucial to you than the advantages listed above, exemption is the way to go.

■ *When Should Application Be Made?*   You may begin filing for tax-exempt status as soon as you have received notification that your program has been approved as a nonprofit corporation. You can obtain a booklet on filing from the IRS. It is not necessary to file for tax exemption immediately, but it is probably a good idea to continue the legal process once you have begun—especially if you have the good fortune to have the services of an attorney who can provide the continuity between the tasks of filing for nonprofit incorporation and the tasks involved in applying for tax-exempt status.

■ *How Long Does It Take to Get Approval?*   It takes two to six months between the time the application is filed with the IRS and the time you are notified that the application has been granted or denied. Tax exemption becomes effective on the date the program was incorporated, so you will not be liable for taxes after the date of your incorporation. However, this is true only if the application for tax exemption was filed within fifteen months of the incorporation date. After fifteen months, your tax-exempt status will be effective as of the date of application for tax exemption, and you may be liable for taxes incurred during the interim months.

How Do You File for Tax-Exempt Status?

You file separately for federal and state exemptions. You must file for and be granted federal exemption before you can apply for and be granted state exemption. For federal exemption, request an application and file with the district office of the IRS. There is no fee. For state exemption, file with the appropriate bureau in your state (at its department of corporations or department of taxation, or the office of the secretary of state). There is a small fee or none. In some states you must file two separate applications, one for exclusion from income tax and another for exclusion from state sales tax. When you receive exemption from sales tax, you will be given an "exempt purchaser number" that you will present when you are making purchases for your organization. The seller will not charge sales tax, whether for poster paints or for a bus.

■ *Filing for Federal Exemption.*   The mechanics are simple, but the way you carry them out is complex. First, obtain a form (Form 1023) from the IRS district office and a book of regulations (Technical Information Release—TIR-1417) from your district office, or from the Department of the Treasury, IRS, Washington, D.C. 20224. This booklet explains the different categories of exemption under which you may file. Then consider, and choose carefully, the one category under which you will file your organization. Under 501(c)(3) the choices are "a charitable, educational, literary, religious, or scientific organization." We recommend that, if possible, you file as an educational organization. (The IRS booklet will tell you the exact language to use.) There are two subcategories under "educational"— schools and nonschools. We advise filing your program as a school. You'll have an easier time obtaining exemptions if you file as an educational organization that is a school.

To qualify under 501(c)(3) as a school, you must:

- Maintain a regularly scheduled curriculum,
- Maintain a regularly scheduled faculty of qualified teachers,
- Have a regularly enrolled body of students in attendance at a place where the educational activities are regularly carried on,
- Meet the provisions of the IRS vis-à-vis administrative and procedural processes (including publication of your program's policy of racial nondiscrimination in local newspapers).

Remember that when you submitted your articles of incorporation to become a nonprofit corporation, you made a statement of the organization's purposes. That statement *should be worded so that it will fit, or qualify the program for, the category under which you are now filing for tax exemption:* either educational institution or charitable organization. *The category you choose for tax exemption must be justified by the statement of purpose you made in your articles of incorporation.*

To file successfully under 501(c)(3) as an educational institution, your earlier statements in the articles of incorporation *must* describe your purposes as primarily educational, rather than as primarily providing child care for working families or others.

In general, programs that file as "charitable" have more difficulty in gaining exemption.

Since IRS decisions are not always consistent from one state to another—or even within the same state—check with other organizations, especially other SACC programs which have successfully received tax-exempt status, for tips on the best approach in your area. You will receive a letter notifying you of the IRS's decision.·

Can We Appeal a Negative Decision?

If you are denied tax-exempt status, you may file an appeal with the IRS National Office, Exempt Organizations Branch, Washington, D.C., and have a hearing at which you can present your case. It may be possible to refile an application using a different description of your organization. (If you filed as an educational organization and the IRS denies your application, you may be advised to file as a charitable organization.)

Licensing and Liability

Every program must have liability coverage and other protection in case suit is brought against it. Any partnering agency, but particularly schools, will want to be assured that, in case of lawsuit due to accident or negligence on the part of the SACC program or staff or board, the agency offering space or other in-kind (or purchased item) will not be held responsible or liable for financial obligations.

It is important that you investigate licensing and liability coverage *before* you go for approval because, in most cases, your program will not be approved unless it can demonstrate that (1) liability insurance will be provided for under a specific agreement with another partner institution (the school, the agency), or (2) it will and can obtain its own insurance. However, you cannot obtain insurance until you have demonstrated that you can comply with the licensing codes of the bureaus. And, generally, you cannot be licensed until you have obtained formal approval from the empowering board. This sounds like "Catch 22," but the fact is that the licenses and insurance needed for approval must be obtained as soon as you receive approval from your school or church board, and before the program is in operation.

This is the time to determine whether the program must be licensed; by whom; what the application process is, including timetables; what the regulations and codes are with which you must comply; how the program can qualify for and obtain liability insurance and other coverage; and what kinds and amounts it will carry. There may be specific stipulations you'll have to comply with, and these may affect the design of your program, including its budget and the number of children it can serve. Obtaining licensing and adequate insurance is also important if your group plans to apply for federal or state money or grants. You will have to meet certain regulations in order to be eligible for funding.

If your program does not comply with legal requirements, it may be prevented from opening on schedule, or ever. One program coordinator told us:

> We first had the building inspected by the state licensing people and the state building inspectors—fire, plumbing, etc.—to be sure the building was functional in terms of construction. They found a hole in one of the fire walls in each of the two schools, and to the embarrassment of the schools, they had to then fix them. This slowed us down approximately two months.

Cultivate good relationships with members of licensing and other regulatory bodies.

Licensing

Most states do not allow child-care programs to open unless they are licensed and have adequate insurance coverage. As you plod through the bureaucracy, remember that its many requirements have been created to safeguard children.

■ *What Kinds of Licensing Will We Need?* Investigate:

1. State regulations for licensing of day care centers.
2. Possibly city codes—New York and Denver are two examples of cities that have their own codes.
3. Local codes. These apply to the use of the building. Such local (and/or state) codes may include health and/or sanitation and nutrition; fire; safety; building.
4. Zoning ordinances or codes. These are separate from licensing and other local codes. They probably will not apply to many SACC programs, but check it out.
5. Special codes and policies such as those of your state or local department of education if your program is school-based, or agency guidelines if you're agency-operated.

■ *Must We Be Licensed?* It is sometimes possible to operate without a state license; it will depend on the policies of your individual state. A few states have no licensing regulations for child care programs, but you will probably still have to comply with state and local building, health, and other codes.

There are also certain cases where state "regs" for day care centers will not be imposed—you may not need to be licensed if your program is housed in a church, for example. Some states permit school-based programs to operate without a license, while others have a policy that SACC programs must call themselves "day camps" before they will be permitted to open in schools. In one state, exemption from licensing is granted to child welfare agencies and facilities operated by state, county, or municipal governments.

Some centers choose not to be licensed because they do not wish to comply with regulations they feel are inappropriate to SACC programs. One way they avoid licensing is to call themselves by another name, such as "recreation program," which means they are not subject to the requirements for "day care" programs. But remember that if you don't call your program "day care" and don't get licensed, you may not receive tax-exempt status and may be ineligible for Title XX funds.

Other centers choose to be licensed, even if it is not necessary. One organizer pointed out, "If it's not clear whether you should be licensed, do it anyway and then you'll have no trouble later," and another said, "The schools don't have to have a license. But I want to have a license. It gives us credibility."

■ *How Do We Get Licensed?*   Licensing of SACC programs, as well as the enforcement of regulations and the renewal of licenses, is done by state governments. All state legislatures, and the governing body of the District of Columbia, have their own regulations, and groups that wish to offer child-care services to the public must comply with them in order to obtain a license.

First, call your state house to find out which of its agencies is responsible for licensing. This may be the department of welfare, of public health, or of education. In Massachusetts, for example, it is the state's Office for Children.

Call or make a personal visit to the licensing board—people there have been of great help to groups starting up. They will generally tell you what other codes you must comply with and what other bureaus you should get in touch with. They may also give you explicit tips on how to conform with regulations.

Find out from whom else you must get approval. Generally, states will not grant licenses unless you can show that you can meet local codes. Find out which local bureaus are responsible for licensing the program—health and/or sanitation and nutrition may come under the aegis of the public health or sanitation department.

Ask for copies of all codes and regulations, including any specific guidelines for programs such as the cne you are planning. Study the regulations. Learn them. Make sure you can comply with them. Call the licensing board and ask further questions, if necessary. Discuss with your group any changes that will have to be made in your design.

Apply for licenses. (This is generally done after your program has obtained formal approval.)

In this prelicensing period, your state licensing supervisor will visit the program site, not only to see that health and safety standards are being complied with, but to review your complete program plan. This may include its organization, its physical site, and the program itself. You can expect visits from other officials later—for example, from local health and fire departments. You will have to obtain permits from these officials, but at this early stage you will probably not have surprise visits from them.

Find out if you will need to obtain a provisional license so that the program can open and begin to operate before the regular license can be obtained. Most states will grant a provisional license when the applicant cannot yet meet all the regulations. The license is granted with the understanding that the program will work toward compliance within a specified period of time—generally six months. You will have to present a plan to show how you will solve the problems that have held up your regular license. Most states will renew a provisional license one or more times.

When you are granted your license, a certificate will be issued to you. You may have to pay a fee. The license is generally valid for one or two years. You will have to renew the license before it expires, and usually you'll be given ample notice (and sent a new form) by the bureau(s).

States (and local departments) can revoke either provisional or regular licenses on certain grounds. You have the right to due process, including appeal, and to be granted a reasonable amount of time to correct any problems before steps are taken to revoke the license. If your license is denied or revoked, you must be informed in writing of the reasons, and of how you can appeal the decision. A hearing may take several months. If the denial is for your first regular license, you will not be able to operate unless you have a provisional license that has not been revoked.

The licensing process takes a long time, and whether you will be granted a license by one bureau hinges on the approval of others. It's a good idea to find out from each group how long it will take from the time you make application until your program is inspected, is granted approval, or you can apply for appeals and be granted provisional licenses. Then, allow for this when you are planning your opening date.

■ *SACC Problems with "the Regs" and Policies.*   These are the most common:

State regulations. The regulations that state licensing bureaus impose generally fall into the following categories: staff:child ratios, group size, physical space, equipment, staff qualifications, and requirement of written records.

The standards different states require vary tremendously, on a scale from the sublime to the ridiculous. In one state, for example, the only requirement to qualify an applicant for a staff position is that he or she have no criminal record. In many states, regulations that were created for preschoolers, or even infants, are used for SACC children. Sometimes they are only slightly modified, or an "addendum" is attached with standards to cover SACC programs. Such standards may require staff:child ratios of 1:25.

Generally, state licensing standards require minimal standards to be met and don't take into account the developmental needs of school-age children. You will probably find these standards inappropriate for your program, and you may wish to approach the licensing bureaus about changing their regulations.

Zoning boards. Zoning permission is not the same as licensing. It is permission to use city or town land, according to that government's rules relating to *land use*. The city's land is divided into districts, and certain categories of buildings or other uses of the land are restricted or permitted in each zone. Examples of categories are "commercial," "community service," or "preferential treatment," which includes religious (church-based) or educational organizations. An example of a restriction is: "No commercial buildings are permitted in Zone A." If you have any questions about whether your center will be permitted in the location you've chosen, call or visit your local zoning board and get the answers now.

Most programs of the type discussed in this book will not have problems in getting approval from a city or town's zoning board. A few programs may run into snags because the zoning board will claim that the zone in which the program wishes to establish itself is off-limits to a day care center, which they may view as a commercial enterprise—whether or not it is a for-profit organization. You must argue that day care is a community need, your program provides a community service, and, as such, should be given the same treatment as schools—that is, be set up throughout a town, wherever needs are located. Therefore, the board should not put you into the "commercial" category, but rather, into "community service." For SACC programs, the "community service" category is preferable to "preferential treatment." If you plan to build a facility, however, you should make sure that the site you have chosen is in a district that is appropriately zoned. Also, you should find out which regulations and conditions will be imposed upon your program.

There are other related issues. Must you provide for off-street parking? If you are to be housed in a church, and are considered as, or are a part of, a religious institution, are there special rules for picking up and delivering children by car?

It will not hurt, if you meet with the local zoning authorities, to bring along one of your supportive political contacts, such as an alderman or town committee person.

If you are not granted a zoning permit as a "day care center," you may still apply for a permit under "non-conforming use" or "special use." Or, you can apply for a variance. All of these routes are time-consuming, and involve petitions and public hearings.

Causes of problems. In many communities SACC is a new concept. Like an adolescent whose growth is unexpected and rapid, "the authorities" aren't sure what the beast's nature is, which regulations or policies to apply to it, or even which local bureau should handle its licensing. Officials not only decide under which category of regulations your program comes, and then issue the appropriate guidelines, but often they interpret how the regulations apply to your program.

It is important that you check state and local statutes to learn whether there are any obstacles to setting up your program in the location you want. And if no one seems to know who should be responsible for licensing your program, persist until you either (1) find out, or (2) are able to establish, for the first time in your community, a policy on who the empowering agency should be.

In one west coast city, when the YMCA wanted to operate its programs in a number of public schools, they found that the state's licensing guidelines were geared toward preschool care: staff:child ratios were inappropriate for school-age children. The director had to negotiate alternative standards with the state—it took three months to obtain a provisional license. In addition, they needed a zoning variance in order to allow a "day care" program into the elementary schools. That meant obtaining a zoning variance for each school. It took three months to obtain them. However, it was possible for the programs to be "grandfathered" in under old zoning codes. The director then began to work with the schools so that variance could be more easily obtained for new school programs, thus avoiding future delays.

Very often, much of the confusion described above is created because in some communities, counties, or states, there are *no* existing policies on SACC programs. This affects particularly those programs that wish to use or rent school space.

There is, sometimes, a silver lining to these clouds of obfuscation. Some groups have seized the lack of clear policies as an opportunity to be creative. They have requested and obtained changes—and sometimes have brought about the formation of policies, where before there were none—to legitimize SACC's existence and its use of public school space. In the Northeast, an office of child care proposed a change in the statutes of education legislation in order to permit the board of education to rule on the use of school space for before- and after-school programs. If you feel that the current regulations in your area are inappropriate for school-age children, see if you can change them. Groups have successfully done this.

Liability

If a group of citizens, parents, or representatives of social service agencies gets together to organize a SACC program, it takes on a set of responsibilities. This means that the group is accountable—legally, as well as morally—to parents whose children will use the services provided, to businesses that may sell goods to the program, and to employees hired by the group or by others designated by the group. It is important that the members of that organizing group, as well as any others who end up being responsible for the program once it is operating, be protected from any personal or institutional liability. And it is important for the program itself.

What can go wrong that might result in personal liability? Unfortunately, almost anything can go wrong. For example, a child might fall from a swing in the playground, break an arm, and require hospitalization. That child's parents might decide that "someone" should pay for those medical costs not covered by the family's insurance. The family is entitled to sue the program—or anyone else they feel might be held responsible.

All programs, regardless of their administrative structure (partnership or nonpartnership) or location, must recognize that suit might be brought against them, and must protect themselves. All programs must have insurance, whether they are new or are added as a service of an already existing agency.

No school board or city or town governing body will grant approval to an applicant program unless the program can demonstrate that it can and will obtain insurance. Often, you must specify in your proposal who will be responsible for which liabilities.

One parent organizer remarked:

> We knew the school board would ask us "What about liability?" so we went to the town counsel for her advice. When we appeared before the board, it was one of the first questions they asked. We could tell them that we were able and prepared to take out insurance, and that reassured them.

The fear of being held liable has been a real obstacle to collaboration—especially by schools—in setting up SACC programs. Potential partners are concerned about financial losses or the threat of public loss of credibility. That's one reason why it is especially important for the agency or group that will be administering the program to look and act accountable, not only by having a good record of responsible actions behind them, but also by obtaining adequate insurance policies. All written agreements between a separate administering agency and a partner should include a clause referred to in legal language as a *save or hold harmless* provision. One lease policy (Montgomery County, Maryland Public Schools) reads this way:

> The lease for each user group shall include appropriate language to save the Board of Education and the school system harmless against any and all claims, demands, suits, or other forms of liability that may arise out of this use of school space.

To insure your program's health, we advise you to take proper precautions: decide—with utmost clarity—*who* will be responsible for *which* coverage in case suit is brought against the program, determine *what kinds* of coverage you will need, and obtain the right kinds and *adequate amounts* of protection. Remember, however, that you cannot actually *obtain* insurance until you have been licensed.

- *Protection from or Limits on Liability.* Who is liable? The program and, sometimes, the people within it can be held liable. If your program is incorporated, the individuals who run it are protected from *personal* liability, and you can adopt an indemnification statement in your bylaws to provide your officers with further protection. However, any corporation members who have been judged to be negligent or fraudulent in their actions are excepted. Board members can be held personally liable for the failure of the corporation to pay withholding taxes or employees' salaries or state unemployment taxes (in some states), and for gross negligence which results in financial loss to the organization.

In addition, a few states have a "charitable immunity doctrine" that applies to incorporated, not-for-profit organizations and that limits the *extent* of liability to the program. Inquire about this at the state bureau where you filed your incorporation papers.

One town counsel has suggested that it might be possible to name the town (or school system, school committee) under the provisions of the insurance policy as an additional insured party. The program would pay for the policy, which would cover any liability incurred during that period of the day when the programs operate. And perhaps the program could exchange this coverage for rent-free space or busing.

■ *Responsibility for Liability.*   Who carries the policy(s)—and, thus, assumes the liability? In the case of a new program that will be administered by an existing agency, the agency can just extend and/or increase its insurance so that it covers the new program. Generally, an umbrella organization carries the policy(s). Schools may carry fire and theft insurance and extend this "umbrella" coverage to all programs held on its sites. In one southern state, every child in the extended-day programs held in schools must purchase school insurance. If you choose to do this, you must make sure that the children's regular school insurance will cover them on a day when school isn't in session, but the program is; for example, on a snow day.

Often, you will have to check the regulations of the organization that sponsors you. If you don't abide by their rules, they may not extend their insurance coverage to your program.

> Each program is pretty individual. But we all have to be in line with school board policies and the policy regarding field trips, health, and safety. We can't do things that are contrary to their policies and stay within the liability insurance that we have. (*Director in Midwest*)

The answer to who is liable is not so simple when a brand new entity—especially a partnership—is created. Since SACC, and especially SACC partnerships, are new concepts in many communities, there is no precedent or protocol for handling the liability issue.

Let's take the situation where a school-based program is run by an outside group. The school has insurance for its students who attend during regular hours. But because the school isn't running the program, it may not accept responsibility or liability for children who use school property before and after regular school hours, and who are supervised by nonschool personnel. Nor will it be perceived as liable by potential litigators. In one western city where the YMCA is in partnership with the community schools department, and programs are based in schools, the director of the program was named liable— and sued for $75,000—when a child who was standing on top of a shed during program hours fell off and was injured.

In this case, which was eventually settled out of court, there was a division of legal responsibility. Schools are liable if the buildings are not safe; the Y, however, has responsibility for accidents that are the result of failure on the part of the program's staff. In this case, no school department or community ed staff person had a job description that included responsibility for child care.

■ *What Kinds of Liability Can Programs Incur?* For SACC programs, liability can result from acts that are legally wrong according to civil law. (These are different from results of criminal acts, which we need not discuss.) The most important such act, from a program's point of view, is negligence. Another might be "breach of contract," which results in financial loss to the contractee.

■ *Which Individuals Are Legally Responsible for Negligent Acts?* Even though your program is incorporated, individuals can be held responsible in some cases. Whether an individual or the program is liable depends on the contractual aspects of the employer-employee relationship. You should consider these contractual relationships when you are deciding what kinds and amounts of insurance to purchase, and when you are thinking about staffing your program. Program employers are *not* liable if they hire an independent contractor, he or she installs a fixture improperly, and it falls on a child. The program *is* liable if a regularly-employed staff person installs the fixture. You may want to think about how you can transfer liability—for example, by contracting for some services rather than having the program's own staff perform them. You might rent a bus (after determining exactly what the owner's liability includes), rent space, or hire someone to come in to cook meals.

■ *What Kinds of Insurance Should We Consider and in What Amounts?*

Liability. This will protect you from the results of negligence. Programs should purchase a general liability policy that provides a high amount of coverage. It does not cost much more to buy $100,000 to $300,000 worth of coverage than it does to buy $5,000 to $10,000 worth.

Automobile. This kind of liability coverage is required by most states. Be sure that your insurance covers transportation, not only for regular operating times, but for such special days as school vacations or early dismissal times. If your program owns vehicles or allows staff members to transport children, purchase high amounts of insurance —if there is an accident, the program is potentially liable. Find out whether your van must get a "school bus" license, and what the insurance requirements are.

Many programs permit employees to transport children in their own cars. Does the program buy *all* the insurance? Does it pay the employee the difference between his or her personal coverage and the higher rate? The best solution is to have the program reimburse the driver for the difference between the cost of the premium that person pays for his/her own coverage and the cost of coverage the program feels is necessary ($50,000 to $100,000 or $100,000 to $300,000).

Fire and theft. This may be in two separate policies. There are two kinds of fire insurance—one covers loss caused by fire or lightning, and the other, "extended coverage options," covers loss from natural phenomena such as smoke, or unnatural acts such as a riot or a helicopter colliding with your building.

If your program is located in a large metropolitan area with a high crime rate, theft insurance may be unobtainable or prohibitively expensive. However, federal crime insurance with low-cost premiums is now available. It is sold by private agents, and they *must* sell it to you if you fulfill the government's guidelines.

Fidelity bonds. These protect the program from the potential financial sins of employees—stealing or embezzlement.

How do you decide what amounts of insurance to buy? SACC programs are usually financially strapped, but adequate insurance protection is vital. If you cannot obtain "umbrella" insurance, or if there are no specifications issued by the licensing bureaus, state laws, or funders, the decision is yours alone. You must weigh the amount of potential risk against the amount of financial loss you may incur. If both are high, obtain high amounts of coverage. If both are low, low coverage is sufficient. But when they are unequal, you must determine: How much insurance can the program afford? If you don't have insurance, and are sued, how much can it afford to pay from its own pocket? And will the premiums cost more than a lawsuit would? Perhaps in this case you can get a policy with a deductible, so that you will pay a smaller amount if you are liable, with the insurance paying the rest.

Generally, the more kinds of insurance policies you buy from one company, the cheaper the entire bill.

Developing Agreements

Now that you are a legal entity, you are able to enter into legal agreements, such as contracts and leases. It is time to firm up and clarify any promises and agreements your group negotiated for tangible goods and services. Get them in writing! Written agreements do not insure rose gardens, but in the beginning stages of program operation they can prevent some thorny problems and strained relations. Spell out exactly what you are asking for and what you expect to receive.

All collaborations require some formal structuring. One of the ways to strengthen good relationships with a partner agency is to formalize the agreement; not so the relationship is cast in stone, but so that *everyone is clear about where the lines of responsibility fall.* As one SACC organizer told us:

> When we first started getting into the school system, it was a learning process for the school and for us. We didn't have a lot of things in writing; there were a lot of unclear relationships and questions, such as: What's the janitor's responsibility? What is ours?

First, it is necessary to have written documentation of your agreement with the policy- or decision-making body which has given you approval to use school space. That permission should be put into writing, as should the school committee or board minutes of the meeting when approval was granted. Personnel who will be "living with" each other on-site on a daily basis will want to consider some written agreements or contracts that spell out the details of their relationship (program director and agency director or principal). Each of these types of agreements does essentially the same thing—it shows the program and its partner specific limitations and boundaries—and opportunities—of the partnership. Such agreements professionalize a process which, for many groups up to this point, has been an informal and somewhat arbitrary one. Many groups have depended on the goodwill of a partner agency and on "gentlemen's agreements," as well as on political allies to turn to in a pinch.

Written agreements provide an opportunity to anticipate problems that may come up in the course of time; spell out the specific details of the sharing of resources and responsibilities; and provide a reference when, at a later time, the rationale for a particular decision is questioned.

Records and minutes of meetings should be kept for later reference: since your program may experience several transitions in its lifetime—either in space use, location, staffing, or administrative structure—a written record, coupled with updated agreements and contracts, will keep you on solid ground.

Agreements Between the Program and Its On-Site Partners

Just as the formal agreement between a governing board and a partner program must anticipate as much as possible problems or changes that may arise, so too should the people who are directly working together on a day-to-day basis formalize their roles and responsibilities by means of written agreements. A common technique is a *contract* between the two people who will be most responsible for the day-to-day operation. This is usually the on-site program director and the person in charge of the partner institution—the principal, the minister, the community school director, or the recreation leader—in whose space a partner program may operate. While many people in collaborative situations have developed good, informal communication, it is nevertheless important to put it all in writing. A contract can include specific names of individuals involved on-site; the areas and functions for which each may be responsible; some explicit rules about cleanup or use of a special area, or use of particular specialized equipment. The on-site contract also may function as a way to clarify the relationships between and among others involved. While a school board agreement with the YMCA may say that the program and the school shall "have a close working relationship" as one of the items in their agreement, it is left to the people involved to figure out how to do that. On-site contracts will help that process which, as we have mentioned, results from hard work and open communication all around.

Agreements with Policy-Making or Governing Body

Several kinds of agreements can exist between a program and its sponsor or partner. *Letters* can be exchanged, spelling out the details of the partnership; *memos, agreements, permits,* and *contracts* can be signed by the governing bodies of the partner agencies; and *leases* can be drawn up, stipulating all the minute details of the terms of the agreement. At the minimum, all written agreements should contain the following information:

The purpose of the program. Descriptive statements about the program: the age group served, hours of operation, and a statement of the goals and philosophy.

Specific resources to be used. The name(s) of the school or church or other facility to be used; specific reference to other space to be used (common areas, specialized areas, playground, etc.); any other resources to be shared as might require written permission.

Management and administration. Each partner's area of responsibility, such as legal issues: Is licensing required? If so, the agreement should so state; liability and the need for appropriate liability insurance should be spelled out; any other insurance the program is required to have should be specified; if insurance will be shared or provided by partner agency, this should be stated. The *save or hold harmless* provision discussed previously should be included.

■ *Agreements Should Anticipate Problems.* Try to anticipate problems or changes in your written agreements. Here are some examples of the kinds of issues covered by some partners in their documents. Note how specific the points are:

In a letter of agreement between a church board and its partner program:

> You will be issued two sets of keys. Children are to enter by the Merrit Avenue door and go directly to their rooms; children will not be permitted in other areas of the building. The gymnasium may be used by scheduling it through the church office and paying the regular hourly fee.

And in a school board memo:

> The cafeteria can be made available five afternoons a week as the basic homeroom for the program. To clear this room will require the relocation of Girl Scout activities to another area of the school.

Future changes are anticipated and planned for; one lease includes the following:

> It is understood that if a food facility is available at the designated school, then a separate agreement shall be made between the parties as to costs and services.

In one community, the school board developed a contract for use by the YMCA which can be used, on a school-by-school basis, each time the Y expands into a new site. The contract leaves blank spaces to be filled in to designate which school spaces and equipment the program is allowed to use.

■ *What Type of Agreement Is Best? Leases or Contracts? Permits or Letters and Memoranda?* In general, the more specific you can be, the better. *Permits* issued by school systems are often very general, with rules that apply to a wide range of groups seeking permission to use school facilities. Permits usually follow a standard form (name of group, cost of overtime, custodial, number of people to use facility) but aren't designed to reflect the complexities of a partner relationship. While some programs may prefer the latitude this type of agreement seems to provide, it is probably best to develop a more comprehensive agreement; the issues will come up eventually and you had best be prepared beforehand.

Many programs use standard *leases* as agreements if they are renting or are given free space. Leases can serve as the major written agreement between partners, but there are some things to be careful about if you use a standard lease format for your agreement. Month-to-month leases probably should be avoided, since they do not provide the kind of security that most SACC programs need. Make sure, if you are the landlord, that you do not wield too much power in the lease—which you might be tempted to use *instead of* negotiation if problems between partners come up. If you are the tenant, make sure you do not give away too much power—giving a school administrator or principal the authority to suspend your use of the playground, kitchen, or other shared facilities may seem like a gesture of good will at the time, but you may regret it. Leases should mention summer or vacation use of space. One program's lease read "September 1– September 1"; but a lawyer, who reviewed the lease before it was signed (a good idea), noted that nothing in the document mentioned continuing the program during the summer months. If the program was not planning to use the space, were they still expected to pay for the monthly rental during the summer?

Whether you use agreements, contracts, leases, or memoranda, the contents are a statement of each partner's responsibilities. Agreements should be specific about the day-to-day operation and administration of the program. A suggested *contract* between a Madison, Wisconsin school and the Madison After School Day Care Association, for example, set up some clear boundaries for a program operating in shared space:

The After School Day Care Program will have access to the all-purpose room ½ hour before the program starts for set-ups and preparation and ½ hour after the program ends for cleanup and planning.

The contract mentions school personnel and their responsibilities with the program:

The school secretary will receive mail for the After School Day Care Program, accept calls, take messages and transmit the above to the lead teacher . . . . The custodian will confer at least once weekly with the After School Day Care Staff regarding the functioning of the program and the needs of each.

Contracts and agreements should include, where possible, a mention of the specific holidays the custodians in a school building will have so that the program can plan in advance to close on those days or to take an extended day trip.

In our discussion of liability, we stated that breach of contract is one ground for suit to be brought against the program (as well as cause for a program to bring suit). It is unlikely that either of these actions will happen, but as you are now a legal organization entering into agreements, there are some points you should keep in mind.

- An agreement does not have to be in the form of a contract or lease for it to be regarded as legal. An exchange of letters, or a purchase order, is a binding legal document.
- You don't have to exchange money in order for a legal act to take place—the promise of a service in exchange for another service can be a contract. In other words, if you offer a parent free tuition for her child in exchange for her providing hot lunches for a group of children, you have made a contract.
- An agreement need not be in writing to be legal. Oral contracts, including those made by phone, are legal. Of course, it is more difficult to charge breach of contract—and to prove it in court—if the agreement was made orally. This is why, for everyone's protection, we urge that you get it in writing.

Don't, however, take a casual attitude to breaking informal contracts—programs *have* been pulled through the courts by people who have claimed that their informal contracts were not honored. Although in most cases their suits were unsuccessful (because evidence was lacking or unclear), the time, energy, and emotional drain involved are very costly. Most important, such breaches may bring about ill will in the community and harm your reputation.

No matter how much care is given to verbal or written communications, the key to success will be your willingness to work at relationships with those people and bureaus whose help you seek. Sometimes, however, good contracts make good neighbors. Caveat contractee!

Part Four

HOW TO MANAGE
THE PROGRAM

INTRODUCTION

You've been approved by the "Big Board" and your group has already tackled several important managerial functions, such as incorporating as a nonprofit organization and investigating licensing requirements. What comes next is the nuts and bolts of managing the program. In the following chapters we will examine the work to be done and the solutions different programs have found. We begin with one of your most important tasks—establishing policies and procedures—and we explain why these small gears are so important to help your program run smoothly.

Effective program management, however, encompasses more than actual tasks such as setting up procedures or preparing a budget. Chapter 7, "Administration," discusses the need to establish a structure within which the program can operate. We examine different kinds of administrative frameworks, and how to choose and set up the one that will best accomplish the work of your program. Next we chart your specific managerial tasks and look at the crucial human factor—the groups and individuals who generally handle different facets of management.

Chapter 8, "Personnel," delineates the tasks program staff will need to accomplish. It presents guidelines for hiring staff who will best serve the program, and then suggests ways to decide upon and implement staff policies that will best serve your staff.

In Chapters 9, 10, and 11, we tackle the Waterloo of many programs—finances—and show you how to emerge victorious: how to budget effectively, develop resources, and how best to accomplish financial managing and planning so that your program can survive and grow.

Once you have established your program's structure, chosen the people who will make it work, and determined how the money will come in and go out, you are two steps away from announcing to the community that you are "open for business." Chapter 12 examines the uses of publicity to bring children into the program, and the enrollment process that should be in place before they actually enter. Also, before the first child arrives, you will need to establish many specific policies and procedures, and this is the subject of Chapter 13.

If you are planning to open your program in September, provide enough time so that you can set up the logistics and actually do the work in a consistent, thoughtful way—not with a "crisis mentality."

It is, indeed, a great deal of work. All of your tasks will be lightened if you keep in mind that their accomplishment will provide a program that, by taking care of itself, really does take care of its children.

Chapter 6

GUIDELINES FOR SETTING POLICIES

> policy: *a general but definite course of action decided upon and adopted for the sake of expediency, facility, etc.:* what you will do.
>
> procedure: *a particular mode of action to be followed:* how you will do it.
>
> *A set of guidelines that articulates the formal decision-making procedures may appear needlessly bureaucratic, but in the long run it is vital. Nothing dooms a center to confusion and tension so much as vague generalities about who does what and how it should be done.*[1]

Every program needs to have clearly established policies, as well as the procedures that will be used to carry them out. It is particularly important for new groups to think about and set the program's policies in advance. These are the nitty-gritty, day-by-day courses of action upon which the wheels of the program run. You must now make formal, specific decisions about how it will operate, setting up guidelines and rules so it will run as smoothly as possible.

For example, you can't begin enrolling children until you've established a policy about whom the program will accept. In addition, you can't admit or enroll anyone without setting up the process for doing so: Who will do it, and will you hold personal interviews? Will you accept applications by mail? What information will you require, what will the forms look like, and how will they be kept on file?

If your program already exists, but is operating in confusion

---

[1] Barbara Schram, "Parents and Staff: Sharing Program Decisions About Their Children," in *School-Age Child Care: Programs and Issues,* eds. Andrea Genser and Clifford Baden (Urbana, Ill.: ERIC/EECE, 1980), p. 32.

with many mini-crises that demand constant decision making, review your standing policies and rules, using the guidelines and tips in this section. Some changes or additions may simplify the program's operation.

It is so important to establish clear, formal policies and procedures. Doing so:

- Helps prevent disputes, conflicts, and crises from developing. If conflicts do occur, formally established policies create basic guidelines that can help settle these problems.
- Facilitates future decision making because basic guidelines are in place.
- Helps ensure consistency in the operation of the program.
- Ensures fair and equitable treatment and guarantees that the program is not run in an arbitrary manner. This means that you must stick to your policy for *everyone,* or be prepared to open a Pandora's box.
- Protects the program, parents, staff, and children from abuse. One of the most prevalent forms of abuse is the late pick-up: it's 6:10, and some parents have not yet come to get their children. This is an abuse of the staff, who are not being paid for the extra time and who have their own commitments to meet, and of the children. A firmly held policy on when children are to be picked up, backed up by a reasonable fine, may help prevent such an abuse. The East Hartford Branch YMCA Latch Key Program, East Hartford, Connecticut, has the following rules:

PICK-UP FOR AFTER SCHOOL LATCH KEY

1. All children must be picked up no later than 5:45 P.M. Any child who has not been picked up by 5:50, will be automatically charged $1 per family for every 15 minutes of lateness.
2. If, for any reason, a parent is not able to pick up his child by 5:45 P.M., the parent should call the "neighbor designated for emergency pick-up."
3. If a child is not picked up by 6:00 P.M., the site coordinator will call the "neighbor designated for emergency pick-up" on the registration form.
4. Children will only be released to those persons listed on the registration form as authorized persons to pick up. Any other person coming to pick up should have a note signed by the parent.

- Protects the integrity of your program from pressure by larger groups. When small groups have created and adopted their

own policies, this action may protect them from pressure by larger institutions (who may be providing financial or other important assistance) to adopt more standardized policies that may be antithetical to the basic philosophy of their program.
- Provides a basis for the formation, communication, and discussion of values when parents and the center have different points of view.

How to Set Policies and Procedures

Sometimes it's obvious that certain subjects require policies. Often it's not—until you come up against a problem that makes it clear that some specific rules must be set. Some of the most usual areas are:

- Admitting and enrolling children
- Setting the days and hours of operation
- Transportation
- Health and safety
- Food
- Discipline
- Parent involvement and children's behavior

Policies and procedures relating to staff and finances are discussed in Chapter 8, "Personnel," and Chapter 9, "Budgeting." Chapters 12 and 13 discuss those that relate to the day-to-day operation of the program. Program personnel have told us that these were areas in which they had had trouble. However, few policies can be considered without taking financial and staff policies into account.

When people consistently come up with the same problem or complaint, it is time to make a policy. For example, in one program in the Southeast, children kept coming to school in "flip-flops"—thonged rubber sandals. This flimsy footwear kept breaking, so—since it is very difficult to run in them—the children took to running barefoot, sometimes injuring their feet. The director decided to institute a policy that children had to wear footgear that enclosed their feet. She explained the reasons for this policy to the parents—that it protected their children and enabled them to take part in all activities—and they complied. Parents don't get upset when the reason for a policy is communicated to them, and when the reason is a good one.

Every program's policies and procedures will vary because they should reflect:

- The particular values, philosophy, and goals of each group, especially those groups in which parents take part in running the program.
- The nature of the community the program serves, including its cultural and economic background and the realities of the lives of everyone involved.
- The sources of licensing and funding and their "regs."
- The policies of your cosponsor—for example, the church, school board, or agency.
- The availability of people to implement the policies.
- What other services are available, and their nature.
- The "reasonableness" or "acceptability" of the policies to the program's constituency, that is, will the policies "go"?
- Other local conditions, such as geography, climate, weather, etc.
- Specific aspects of the program, such as finances, type of space used, whether transportation is provided.

As you can see from the above list, most programs "inherit" some rules from external sources. For example, licensing bureaus, federal or state agencies who fund the program, or the school, church, or agency that provides space or other resources may impose certain policies and regulations. Remember that when licensing requirements impose standards—such as limits on the number of children in a certain-sized space, or the staff:child ratio that must be maintained —these are usually minimum standards. Use them as a guide, but don't hesitate to upgrade them by superimposing your own, more stringent standards, and formally codifying your own standards in your policies.

■ *Policies and Procedures Should Reflect the Realities of People's Lives and the Nature of the Community the Program Serves.* The Adventure Club in Robbinsdale, Minnesota, established this policy on medication, but provided, with precise and stringent rules, for the reality that sometimes it is necessary to make exceptions.

Use of Medication: A. We prefer not to give *any* medications to children.
B. Under very limited circumstances, we may administer only personal prescriptions filled by a pharmacist on a label bearing the physician's and child's names and directions for administration. The parent (only) must give this to the teacher *and* fill out a form.
C. Do not send *any* medication with your child.

In a crowded metropolitan area, an inner-city program that is barely meeting the need and demand for SACC will not set the same stringent admission criteria as a program in a community where there are other services and programs for school-age children.

In one community with school-based SACC programs, each school prepared a civil defense plan designed to shelter students in the safest areas in the school building in the event of severe weather.

Policies and procedures are a telling public relations statement about what kind of program you run. Haphazard or inconsistent methods of handling early dismissals—for example, allowing any child to leave when he or she feels like it, without bringing a note to inform the teacher, conveys the message that the program's attitude toward its children and their parents is at best haphazard, and at worst highly irresponsible. Clearly spelled out and strictly enforced procedures—"Children who wish to leave before the program's regular closing must have a consent note that specifies who will pick them up"—convey the message that the program cares about the children's welfare and the parent's peace of mind, and that it is a well-run, safe place for children.

Special Tips for Setting Policies and Procedures

■ *Set the Rules Up as Early as Possible.*   It is easier to set up a good policy at the beginning than to change or revoke a bad one later. One parent group in the process of setting up its program felt that:

> An important concern was the fact that precedents would be set in the first year. In other words, policies and attitudes set within the first year would be difficult to change and therefore should be well thought out in advance. So a "keep it simple" approach was maintained; one in which an emphasis was placed on observing children's interests, listening, and not "biting off more than one could chew."[2]

Another fine example of forethought is this policy on early school dismissal or emergency closings:

> If school is closed because of severe weather or utility emergency, WCCO radio will carry the announcement by 6:00 A.M. There will be no Adventure Club program if school is closed for an emergency.

---

[2] Cynthia E. Wilson, "The Director's Perspective," in *School-Age Child Care: Programs and Issues,* p. 66.

■ *Keep the Policies Very Broad and Simple.*   At first, you will not know what rules will be needed. You should set up broad policies to provide freedom within limits so that you won't have to change your policies every time a valid exception or a new circumstance arises. This gives the administrator the freedom to make internal adjustments according to the realities of that particular program.

■ *Procedures Should Be Uniform and Created Only to Solve Problems or Avoid Situations That Could Be Complicated or Troublesome.*   They should not be obvious: no one needs a detailed procedure for serving snacks, but everyone does need a clear, step-by-step procedure for emergency evacuation of a building.

Policies cover general mechanics: procedures deal with fine-tuning. Procedures—the way you do things—will affect the day-to-day operation of the program in a more obvious way than policies. They are more detailed than policies, but they should still be simple to follow. If a procedure is too difficult or time-consuming, people will circumvent or ignore it. A staff member who must fill out a form in triplicate each time she uses the program's duplicating machine will either disregard the form or stop sending out printed notices.

■ *Policies and Procedures Should Have a Life of Their Own, Not Be Arbitrarily Decided by Individual Discretion.*   The following is an example of a "policy that is not a policy." It says that the program is available to anyone, but actually leaves it up to the director to accept or reject a child:

> The After School Program is available to any family in need of such service without regard to race, color, sex, religion, or national origin. We, however, must reserve the right to accept or reject applicants based on our ability to provide adequate services. Interested parents should meet with the director to discuss the child's needs prior to submitting a registration form. Within these limits the program is available on a first-come, first-serve basis.

■ *The Reasons for Policies and Procedures Should Be Valid and Justified.*   This may seem obvious—certainly no one wants to spend time creating an unnecessary policy. But remember that some of your policies and other rules will be questioned by community members, parents, staff, and/or children. You should be very clear in your own mind as to why they are important, so that you can explain their rationale. A parent may question the justice of charging a full-time fee for a child who attends only part time. If the program management firmly believes that this is the only way it can afford the quality and number of staff it desires—with minimal use of part-

timers—then it will be prepared to defend itself against charges of
setting unfair fees by pointing out that this policy enables it to set fair
employment wages, ensuring a high-quality staff. The director might
suggest that if the parent can come up with a better way, the board
would be delighted to hear and consider it, with a view toward
changing the policy.

■ *Once Created and Adopted, Policies and Procedures Should
Be Firmly and Consistently Adhered to.*   If they are not, confusion,
conflict, and charges of unfairness will ensue. Seventeen directors of
day care programs in Georgia were interviewed by the Child Care
Support Center, which is devoted to improving management skills
and offering support. The report they published pertained to admitting and enrolling children, but the advice given by these directors
who are "on-the-line-of-fire" can be applied to all policies and procedures.

> Experience teaches directors to be clear, firm, consistent, and willing to
> make few exceptions in rules.[3]
>
> Throughout these conversations, one point emerged quite clearly: al-
> though most directors try to be compassionate with parents, and all ac-
> cept the need to make some exceptions to the rules, veteran directors are
> always able to describe *firmly* established, carefully constructed enroll-
> ment procedures with very few problems. On the other hand, the less
> experienced directors who often seem committed to more relaxed ap-
> proaches and who have unclear and often inconsistent procedures, are
> more apt to complain of frequent policy abuses. Obviously, clearly de-
> veloped enrollment procedures are desirable.[4]

■ *If Exceptions Are Made, the Reasons Must Be Sound and
Defendable.*   Of course, there are always exceptions made since
SACC programs want to serve parents and children as well as possible, and crises do occur. It is often left to the director's discretion
and good judgment to waive "the regs" in an unusual situation. In
deciding whether to "disregard the rules, just this once," he or she will
have to weigh the benefits to the individual child and family against
the dangers to the program, its children and families, and bear the
responsibility for the results of the decision.

For example, suppose a program has set policy that enrollment

---

[3] Save the Children, Child Care Support Center, *Recruiting and Enrolling Children* (Atlanta: Save the Children, 1981), p. 17.
[4] *Ibid.,* p. i of Introduction.

will be limited to children 6 to 9 years old. A staff person asks the director to allow her 5¾-year-old daughter to attend, and the director consents. How will she later justifiably defend the exclusion of three other 5¾-year-old children when, two weeks later, their parents demand that they also be admitted? Will she say that this was just a "special case"? She may get away with it, but then another situation comes up. What does she do when the mother of 7-year-old Jimmy, who is already enrolled in the program, must be hospitalized for immediate surgery and the family requests that Jimmy's 5-year-old brother be permitted to attend the program while his mother is in the hospital?

These are difficult decisions, but they are the kinds of pragmatic ones directors deal with on the spot more often than they would like, at the same time that they are making the other decisions that keep the program running every day.

■ *There Should Be a Mechanism for Changing Policies and Procedures, and the Flexibility to Permit and Accept Change.* No one, especially new boards and staff of programs that have not yet begun to operate, knows answers to what the "correct" rules will be. Although some rules may be clear at the start, the need for others will only be learned through trial, use, and some error and conflict as the program rolls—and, more often, bumps—through its first year. And it is only in the first year, or even later, that it will become evident which rules are needed to help the program run evenly and fairly.

Policy makers and procedure setters must be flexible and open-minded. Programs grow and change through time, as will the needs and values of the people who use and work in it. Although we have stressed standing firm, we do not suggest rigidity. Rather than stonily adhering to regs that have become outmoded or have proven to be ill-considered, programs must be willing to accept and consider reasonable changes, while holding fast to those they still consider valid. The following excerpts from a parent newsletter written by the Eugene (Oregon) Latch Key Program administrator illustrate how difficult it is to stand firm, while remaining open and flexible and genuinely welcoming input from parents:

> Christmas care was used by only half of the parents who made reservations. We arranged for staffing for all of the children. The board will consider a policy of charging for space reserved for *Spring vacation.*

> Policies regarding programs, enrollment and charges are made by the parent board of directors. Let us know if you have concerns you would like to see addressed.

Who Sets the Policies and Procedures?

Generally, boards set the policies, sometimes with the advice and consent of the director; procedures are more often established by the director and other staff. But there are no set rules, and it may sometimes be left to the director and staff to set the policies. (See Chapter 7, "Administration.")

Parents who use the program should have input into policy and procedures by being members of the board or by open communication with the board, director, and staff, who should be flexible and receptive to suggestions. Children, too, can help set rules. In a Massachusetts suburb, a committee, together with members of a student union, opened a summer youth center for adolescents. The students came up with the rules and regulations. Younger children are also able to suggest new ways of solving problems to make the program machinery run more smoothly.

Both new programs and established ones that are experiencing much conflict or confusion have benefited from studying, borrowing, and adapting other successful programs' policies and procedures.

If there are many programs at different centers, all under the auspices of one central organization and/or board, it is usually preferable to allow each program to make its own specific policies after inheriting or adopting the "Big Board's" or agency's major policies and regs.

Once You've Set Them, How Do You Institute
the Policies and Procedures?

Policy decisions should be formally voted upon and adopted by the board, director, staff, or a combination of all of them. Make it clear whose rules they are: for example, that the limits on enrollment are set by a private, parent-run group, and not by the school that is hosting the program.

Setting the rules is only a first step. In order to be followed, policies and procedures must be disseminated to those whose cooperation is needed: the community, board, director and staff, parents and children. Sometimes, as in the case of parents whose children are new to the program, this means periodic communication. In addition to written instructions, programs must recognize the need for continuous verbal communication with parents so that mutual expectations are discussed and clarified before conflicts arise.

Communication is a director's strongest weapon against problems. When procedures and policies are recorded explicitly in writing, confusion is minimized, expectations crystallized, and responsibilities harder to ignore.[5]

Here are some of the methods programs have used to make sure their policies and procedures really worked.

- *A loose-leaf binder containing all policies (and updated with changes) is given to each board member.* This binder might also contain all other "policy" information about the program, such as its bylaws, philosophy, and goals. A copy of the information is kept in the director's office.
- *A handbook of the policies and procedures is given to every staff member.*
- *A handbook—or printed or mimeographed information sheets—is distributed to parents.* Here major policies as well as the procedures pertinent to parent-program responsibilities and expectations are clearly stated. This booklet or document is an abbreviated policy statement. Some programs print their pertinent "regs" on one double-sided sheet of paper. This is distributed with the application form. Sometimes it is understood that if the parent enrolls the child, he or she implicitly accepts the policies and procedures. Other programs require that before a child is admitted to the program, the parent sign a statement that he or she has read the regs and agrees to abide by them. This agreement is made binding in the form of a signed, written contract between the program and the parent. Often the program director will discuss policies with the parent at registration time.

Everyone—parents, children, staff—have rights and expectations of each other that are mutually agreed upon. These are often set down in writing. Sometimes they are listed as part of a parent booklet, such as "Rights and Responsibilities of Program and Parents" (see Bibliography), but often they are built into the policies and procedures. For example, a parent has the right (and expects) to be informed of all field trips or other excursions made outside of the program's main site. It is the parents' responsibility to sign a statement giving their permission for the child to go on these trips. Usually this is done upon the child's admission, and is kept on file by the program.

---

[5]*Ibid.,* p. 17.

Having one blanket permission form saves time, energy, and paper-work.

Although pertinent information can be printed on a sheet or two, many programs prepare and distribute parent handbooks. Some programs delay this project until they have the time, money, and—more importantly—a chance to test the validity and comprehensiveness of their policies when the program is actually running. Remember, too, that some of your policies and procedures will be amended, certainly every few years, and this means that the handbook must be constantly updated.

Most handbooks we have seen are simple—mimeographed or photocopied—and inexpensive. Your handbook should be simply and clearly written. In designing and writing it, keep in mind who your readers are, and use that as a guide in deciding how best to communicate with your audience. You might want to use as a model the contents page of the *Parents' Manual* which was developed by parents in Minnesota, making your own changes. (See Appendix.) In addition to specific policies and procedures, many programs also include, usually in the opening pages, the history of the program, the program's philosophy and goals, sources of funding, and a list of the people who are responsible for running the program and for establishing its policies.

Chapter 7

ADMINISTRATION

Running a school-age child care program is just like running any business: you must have an organizational framework that allows you to deliver services, and you must deliver these services in a way that is clearly structured, accountable, and dependable. Any group or agency can run a good program if the planners and administrators develop a program based on an awareness of the needs of children and their families, and maintain a well-organized approach to program management practices.

Who Will Run the Program?

The program may be run by any one of the following groups:

- A community agency
- An independent corporation formed by community groups and parents
- A group of parents
- A preschool day care center
- A government agency
- The schools (as the sole administering group; community schools; as collaborators or partners with other groups)

Remember that no one model is the one best solution. As we indicated in Chapter 1, "Profiles of Different Programs," each community has special resources and problems which will suggest a particular approach, or a combination of approaches, to administrative arrangements. Refer to these profiles to see how the program works under different administrative auspices. As you read about the alternative models in the following pages, consider which conditions sound most like those that exist in your own community, and which option will work best for you.

A Community Agency Runs the Program

Community centers and such organizations as the Y or girls' clubs are often organized into separate branches or district facilities. Each of these may have its own board and a branch manager or director. The agency's main office may handle program and budget planning, and may perform some centralized administrative tasks. A branch director or agency manager may have a good deal to say about the placement of a SACC program at a local branch. Therefore, if the central administrative staff of the parent agency wants to run or sponsor a SACC program at a local branch, there is likely to be an administrative "layer" already in existence that manages the affairs. In such a situation, the SACC program may require only an on-site director in charge of the day-to-day program management, while the central office takes care of other tasks. The director or manager of that branch must be included in the planning and decision making. There may not always be the same enthusiasm at the local level as at the central—and vice versa.

   ■ *What Are the Advantages?*   Programs run by the Y, a neighborhood settlement house, a social service agency, or by girls' or boys' clubs have some particular strengths as administering groups of SACC:

- There already exists an administrative structure which may be able to accommodate a new program component.
- The agency is already incorporated, tax exempt, and insured.
- The organization's good reputation in the community will help to interest parents and others in the SACC program.
- The agency may be already receiving financial support from community, state, or federal sources (United Way, Title XX, United States Department of Agriculture, etc.).
- Specialized staff may be already available (bookkeeper, accountant, social worker, cook, recreation or arts specialists, bus drivers, etc.).

- The agency has a good track record with other institutions and is perceived as a good "risk" in any partnership SACC program.
- Resources already available would be open for use by the children in the SACC program: transportation, swimming pools, gymnasium equipment.

■ *What Are the Disadvantages?*   People designated to perform administrative tasks for the "new" program must have the knowledge, time, and willingness to perform them. If they do not, the program may end up as an afterthought, with the larger agency's services taking priority. If it *is* the case that you do not have sufficient administrative staff to handle the work, consider hiring a person to have sole responsibility for the SACC program.

There may also be some problems when an agency expands its services but isn't quite sure how much commitment to make to a new program. It is hard to "make money" providing school-age child care. Agencies which do not know this in advance tend to withdraw their support when it becomes clear that the program isn't going to add funds, but will, in fact, require some—especially at the beginning, or if licensing criteria must be met.

But the program doesn't have to lose money! Community agencies with a philosophy of "service to all, regardless of ability to pay" sometimes get into trouble because they don't run a SACC program like a good business. If parents perceive that an organization, because it is large and has a traditionally flexible policy about fees, will absorb late payment of fees—or even nonpayment—then the capacity of that organization to deliver a quality program and sustain itself will be reduced. For example, one YMCA was forced to close some of its programs when they showed a deficit. But, in the words of the program director, "We simply didn't pursue people who didn't pay."

It may be difficult to "shift gears." School-age child care is different from recreation programs, and some agencies have a problem identifying the differences. They assign staff who are terrific on the playing field, but may not be aware of the six-year-old's need to sit on a staff person's lap and have a long heart-to-heart talk after school.

It may be harder for parents to be involved. If the SACC program is not an integral part of the large organization's mandate, its boards sometimes do not adequately represent the interests of parents whose children are in the agency's SACC program. This lack of representation may be a real problem for parents.

TIPS

- Designate someone in the agency to administer the program; be aware of staff's, children's, and parents' needs; and be accountable for efficient management of the day-to-day operation.
- Institute enrollment and financial policies that clearly state your expectations of parents and what your program will or won't do—for example, state a late-payment policy, scholarship plan, etc.
- Take time to plan and design the new program and learn how it will differ from your agency's on-going activities in other areas.
- Find in the community—or develop—training programs for new staff. Or retrain existing staff to be reassigned to the program. Don't assume that a staff member well qualified in his or her field can automatically shift to the child care role.
- Establish (and support) a parent group at each program site. If there are programs in several locations, parent groups can select a representative(s) who can serve on your board; or, a separate parent advisory committee can be established, advising the agency board on SACC program policy.

An Independent Organization Formed by Community Groups and Parents Runs the Program

Community organizations (voluntary, membership organizations such as the League of Women Voters or the PTO) are often involved in the early stages of organizing a SACC program. These groups occasionally choose to administer the program—frequently under the leadership of members who are also parents that need the SACC service. In general, a community group will form a nonprofit organization and will seek to incorporate and to obtain tax-exempt status, like other agencies or service organizations that deliver social services. The administrative structure usually includes a board of directors with formal authority for making policies and for hiring and designating staff to administer those policies and manage the daily operation. This board may consist of the original organizers, or a new one may be formed just to administer the SACC program.

Community groups should be aware that a lot of cramming will be necessary to get an instant education on program administration, "officialese," and curriculum planning. But there are some pluses for groups that choose to set up an independent program. As one program coordinator in the South told us, "Doing it on your own takes more work, but it is a better use of the money than if you are part of a bureaucracy. There's less red tape, more control."

Often community groups will turn over the administration of the program, once off the ground, to another group. Parents and community group members may jointly form a board of directors, for example, or an agency may take over. In one community the original planning group sought administrative support from their county office for children. Forming an umbrella administering body may be one solution in the event that several programs are involved. Parents and others started programs in Madison, Wisconsin, and later formed the Madison After School Day Care Association, which runs the programs.

Parents Run the Program

This model of administration is one typically used when a group of parents whose children are in the same school form a planning group and elect to run the program themselves. While in many ways it is a creative solution and can make for high quality programs for children and definite skill building for parents, it also has its liabilities.

■ *What Are the Advantages?* Here are some of the pluses in parent-administered programs as stated by parents themselves:

- There is a feeling of being a group, of having a collective purpose, of making progress on meeting personal and collective needs.
- Parents are responsible for decisions that affect their own children and other parents and their children; policy is made by those it affects.
- Parents' perspective and values can be reflected in the program policies and design.
- Decision making is democratic and representative.
- Parents have significant "clout" in the community.

■ *What Are the Disadvantages?* Parents are busy with work and family responsibilities; the board asks time and energy. Regarding parent-run programs, several SACC organizers reported that:

- It is hard to keep on going and rejuvenating a volunteer group that has serious responsibilities for kids and for being a coherent business.

- It is a minor part of most parents' lives, so it's hard to get a commitment.
- Parents as administrators must know about licensing, incorporation, tax exemption, and management (organizational and financial), and have to deal with institutional structures.
- Parents have to look at it as a business.

Two organizers recall the problems in managing their programs:

> No one anticipated the amount of administrative work that went into coordinating five or six programs scattered throughout the city, such as: delivering snacks, picking up snacks, dealing with the personalities of many different teachers and principals, coordinating a staff of teachers throughout a large area.
>
> If you look back at some of the forms that we first used, you'll find that they were totally inadequate. If you look at our bookkeeping system, you'd laugh compared to what we have now. It was a sheet of paper with a list of children and with a sliding fee scale, and no way to check to see how many days they were there. The same thing happened with staff salaries. We just didn't think it through. We just sort of went in, and as problems came up, we tried to solve them.

TIPS

- Set realistic expectations and goals. Agree among yourselves about length of meetings and the tasks to be undertaken by board and by staff. In meetings (and there will be many), use parliamentary procedure and create an atmosphere of respect for divergent views.
- Match up tasks with parents' skills. No one will be more likely to "drop out" than a person who is given a task that is too difficult or unfamiliar, and is not given training.
- Multiply and distribute the responsibility. This will help to prevent parent "burn-out." For example, financial tasks can be shared. One parent might send out bills, receive payment, and record receipts—and then pass that information on to another parent, who has the job of retrieving past-due bills.
- Help each other out. Develop a back-up system of parents who have been informed about specific duties and are ready to lend a hand to a parent who may need help at a critical moment.
- Make sure everyone—parents and staff—is clear about roles and responsibilities. *Use written documents* for education—a parent board handbook, a set of policy statements, guidelines for making decisions, etc. Allow parents who are not on the board

to participate in decisions that affect them. Include names and phone numbers of board members—and convenient times to call them—in literature distributed to new families. Make sure your literature spells out who actually runs the program. Some parents may think the program is run by the schools or the church because that's where it's located.

- Develop procedures for transitions. Decide when to have elections (fall and spring allow for easier transition of new board members). When a position becomes available on the board, all parents should be notified. *Train the new board and committee members*. Outgoing members should pass on all written records and share information that may be useful, no matter how trivial or obvious it seems.

- Politicize the board. If it's a parent-run organization, parents must go down and work with the school board candidates, attend fundraisers, and do all those basic grassroots political things.

- Develop the program as an organization that can function on its own. Even though the program does depend on individuals for their time, energy, and commitment, no one person is "indispensable." Create roles and tasks which can be held by any parents who are given thorough training and correct information. The jobs should remain constant—the parents can be interchangeable. "Keep yelling and screaming. " Go as far as you reasonably can to get work done. Too much is at stake to let one person's paralysis stop the action.

A Day Care Center Runs the Program

Preschool day care centers may choose to expand their services to include "graduates" of the preschool who have entered elementary schools in the community. You may have sufficient space to run the SACC component in the same location, or you may have to find another location more suited to the needs of older children.

■ *What Are the Advantages?*   It offers continuity for children, many of whom may have attended the same program since they were infants. It provides an "extended family" of other children and adults who have known and grown up with each other over a period of years. It also means that parents with more than one child can have all their child care needs met in the same location by the same agency.

It offers continuity and variety for staff who want to stay with the center but who can move on to the new program either because of interest in school-age child care or to provide continuity of care for the children. The SACC staff can supplement their hours with part-time work at the center.[1] It also offers flexibility: no matter what school a child attends, he or she can still go to the center for child care.

The school-age component may receive the benefit of center administrative support, fund raising, budget management, transportation.

A day care center may have more stability and longevity in a community than newly formed parent or community groups which band together to start a program for a particular group of children in a particular neighborhood. The center, to stay financially viable and credible, must respond to the changing needs of parents and children.

■ *What Are the Disadvantages?* Transportation may be a problem. Unless the center is located close by neighborhood schools, children will have to be picked up from school (or delivered in the morning). This will be costly and complicated if many schools are involved, and children may have to travel long distances.

Older children may resent being "back" with preschoolers at the day care center, perceived as a "baby place" by some children trying out their new independence as older kids.

The day care center program may not be flexible in designing a curriculum or in finding suitable space which reflects the difference between preschool and school-age child care. While there are some common elements between the two, there are significant differences in environmental design, in program materials, in staffing—and even in the way equipment and materials are stored and available to older children.

There may be problems getting on a solid administrative ground if the center director has too many programs to run; the SACC program may get short shrift.

Financial management can be complicated. Usually each center component (infant, preschool, school-age) has a budget which reflects costs associated directly with that component, and program planners try to make each component largely self-supporting. A SACC program may be seen as a way to shore up the finances of the parent center. But it should not be designed to do this, since the SACC program will sacrifice its quality, and will not be available to low-income

---

[1]Roger Neugebauer, "School Age Day Care: Designing an Effective Structure," *Child Care Information Exchange*, No. 13 (April 1980).

families, who cannot afford a high tuition that subsidizes the parent center.

Access to public school space may be denied. Schools may see the day care center as too entrepreneurial, preferring their "own" parent groups to use space or school resources. Unless the schools have something to gain (income from rents and other fees charged), schools may not select a day care center as a tenant group if faced with a choice between it and another group perceived as part of the school "family."

TIPS

- Make sure that the program is planned to reflect the differences between younger and older children. Hire staff with skills and experience in working with older children. You might want to start with a younger population of school-agers (kindergarten through second grade).
- Design a space that is special for the school-age children—with no constraints on them, such as having to keep super quiet because younger children are sleeping or having to be extra careful, when they come bounding in after school with pent-up energy, of projects that have been started in the morning by preschoolers.
- Be careful to avoid staff burn-out. Don't ask staff to work additional hours (even though it means more pay). When the older school-agers arrive at the day care center, they should be greeted by people who aren't worn out from a morning of running after two-year-olds.
- Make some board positions available to parents with children in the school-age program. This will help to ensure that the school-age children will have advocates when administrative or policy decisions are considered, and that parents' needs are heard.
- Try to assign a head teacher for the school-age program who can spend some nonteaching time handling daily administrative tasks and who can be available for parents and staff.

A Government Agency Runs the Program

City, county, and state agencies can be involved in SACC administration in several ways. Some government agencies administer programs directly, while others can be involved as initiators of programs, providing technical assistance and funding. In Fairfax County, Virginia, the County Office for Children administers SACC programs in collaboration with the county public schools. Policy is made by three groups: the Fairfax County School Board, the County Board of Supervisors, and the Child Care Advisory Council to the County Board of Supervisors. Until recently, the Baltimore, Maryland, Department of Social Services ran its own school-age programs, funded by federal and state social services money.

The initiator approach was taken by the state of Connecticut: there, the state Office of Child Day Care administered funds set aside by the state legislature for innovative program grants to community-based day care programs operated by groups and agencies in the community. The role of the state agency, the Office of Child Day Care, was to help programs with start-up, provide some financial support, and assist in developing policies for operation and parent payment.

▪ *What Are the Advantages?*   The government agency is seen as "official," and therefore other government agencies and bureaus view the program as legitimate. This official status may increase the opportunity to share resources, and may help the program move quickly through red tape. In most areas of the country, government agencies do not license each other.

Centralized services (computer, billing and accounting, other administrative supports) and specialized personnel (social workers, information and referral staff, etc.) are generally available.

County- or city-run programs are usually financially sound and do not always have to make the rounds for money that many community-based groups must. Staff salaries are in line with other county or city salaries, and fringe benefits are usually available for permanent employees.

Staff may be hired to perform supervisory tasks with program directors and other staff, and may be available to add the extra something many staff need to make their programs better. For example, regional supervisors in Fairfax County programs are available to program staff for training, resource sharing, and networking along with their official jobs (hiring, supervision, monitoring, etc.).

▪ *What Are the Disadvantages?*   Programs may be seen by parents as institutional, not "homey." Programs run by government agencies tend to be just as vulnerable as other organizations when social services budgets are cut. Government agencies *are* bureaucracies; there may be many forms and several different layers and levels of decision making. Children's eligibility for the SACC program may be restricted if government funds are the sole source of funding for the program.

Parents may not be involved as much as they are in other types of structures. Typically, program administrators in *all* types of program models seek to involve parents, but it may be harder when the city or county runs a program. Parents sometimes feel uneasy with "officials" and may worry about their continuing eligibility for the program. This may conspire to inhibit parents from feeling free to complain or criticize.

Schools as Sole Administering Agency

Throughout this manual we have discussed the reasons schools and school districts decide to administer their own programs, including problems in the school community, such as vandalism, racial imbalance, and declining enrollments. Some have perceived that children's needs cannot be compartmentalized.

> You cannot just be interested in the cognitive development of the child. There are some affective needs that have to be served. And if they aren't served properly, there's going to be some spillover in the instructional program. (*Principal of a school-run SACC program*)

Some school personnel feel they have a "vested interest" in helping families with child care needs. Others see a "natural community of interest" between schools and day care, with SACC as a logical extension of the school program.

When schools do decide to get into the day care business, there are some administrative responsibilities that will result for the school system. These may include making policy decisions and becoming involved in day-to-day management. Unlike the relationship between school boards and programs administered by an outside group, the school board is likely to be more involved in policy level decisions affecting budget, salaries, hours and days of operation, placement of sites, and expansion or reduction of sites. School-run programs may be receiving in-kind resources and some budgeted funds, in addition to other outside-school revenues supporting the program. Along with use of school funds may come a higher degree of school board involvement. One school board member told us, "If I'm administering the dollars, I want to administer the program."

Similarly, the school system superintendent will generally have a greater role in making policy as well as administrative-level decisions.

■ *Day-to-Day Administration: The Principal's Role Is Expanded.* When schools choose to administer their own programs, the principal will be the program's chief administrator. Usually, the program will also have a coordinator responsible for administrative tasks and day-to-day operation. One principal estimates that she spends 20 to 25 percent of her time involved with the after-school program. She handles budget and personnel, and is generally the point of information for inquiries, complaints, and problem solving. The program coordinator can assist the principal by screening job applicants, managing registration and enrollment procedures, and helping with staff supervision and program planning. Principals of schools that run their own programs generally make final hiring decisions.

■ *The Parents' Role.* Typically parents in school-run programs do not take an active role in administration, but they may serve on advisory boards. In individual schools, some parents may be asked to advise the principal or the coordinator. PTO's may also have a seat reserved for a parent who represents the extended day program, or a parent representative may serve on a school-wide advisory committee.

■ *Staffing.* School personnel who decide to run their own programs must decide who will staff them. Most school systems do not hire regular school staff to work in the day care programs; salary and benefit levels of regular school personnel often make it too expensive. One school administrator told us, "Schools can price themselves out of the market." Another concern is the hiring of regular school personnel for the day care program. Elementary school teachers may not have had the kind of experience that is required to work with children in informal settings. Also, while it may be tempting to offer an afternoon job to a kindergarten teacher, it may not be fair to children in the SACC program—or to the kindergarten teacher, who has already put in hours of planning and classroom time with the kindergarten class.

Some school-run programs do, however, offer jobs to regular school staff. In one school, a physical education teacher, an art specialist, and a guidance counselor work with the day care program. This approach works well since none of these people has five-day, full-time classroom responsibilities. Part-time school personnel (aides, for example) are hired by some schools to work in the SACC program. This enables part-time people to have full-time employment, and may also permit flexible schedules for some who do not work every day in the program.

There are both pluses and minuses to the dual role of teacher in the regular school program and staff person in the SACC program: "You really get to know the children and parents very well. But, it's a long day. It takes more than money for you to want to do it."

■ *Salary and Benefit Issues.* School-run programs must grapple with the questions of equitable salary levels for personnel. If child-care staff are hired who are not regular school personnel but do have either certification or experience, or both, a reasonable salary should be offered which is in line with established scales. The California Children's Centers, for example, are part of the education system, and salary scales for staff, though not identical to teachers', do reflect the awareness of the school system that their work is important and deserves recognition. There is a tricky balance to be maintained, since school finances may not be able to stretch to include the day care staff at the same level as regular staff. If parents are paying for the program, the fees should not be so high that they cannot afford to enroll their children. Chapter 8, "Personnel," discusses other staffing problems.

■ *What Are the Advantages?* They provide continuity for the community. An associate superintendent of schools in the South asks:

> What happens to the next generation? That's one reason the location of choice was the public schools. You have the dangers of public school rigidity and shortsightedness, but you have the advantage of continuity. The school role may increase significantly when the original citizens— who started the program—leave because you'll lose a sense of history.

They provide continuity of care for children and parents. Children and parents benefit from the consistency of school-run programs; parents don't have to make different arrangements for their children each year, and children benefit from the stability of their care. Staff may stay with the program longer; also, regular school staff and program staff have the opportunity to communicate regularly about the children, increasing the likelihood of meeting their needs.

The program offers learning opportunities to older children. Older junior high school and senior high school students may elect to work with the children in the program as part of their academic plan or in work-study after-school jobs. A California program which has satellite family day care homes that serve school-age children has sometimes asked older children to work with younger ones, reading with them and tutoring them in the family day care homes.

A range of school resources is available. Administrative legal and financial services will be available to the SACC program when it is a

part of the regular school program. Tying in with the school's purchasing program, the school food program, and staff training resources are additional benefits.

The program may help to attract families to the school. At a time
when school enrollments are decreasing in some areas of the country
(due partly to low birth rates and higher enrollment in private
schools), the SACC program may attract families to the schools.

■ *What Are the Disadvantages?*   In the early stages of some
programs there can be initial resentment from some principals and
teachers who say, "I'm just here to run an academic program and I
don't need this bother." Even when schools run their own program, it
may be resented by school staff. Different teachers will have different
attitudes toward the program. According to one principal in charge of
an extended day program, some are "resentful of the intrusion of the
program because day care program children have special needs. It is
essentially a territorial issue."

Tight school budgeting might mean that school-funded or
school-supported programs would be cut back or that parents might
have more costs passed along to them—rent or utilities charges, for
example. Even when the program is largely self-supporting, there will
be costs to the schools. One school board member says:

> If schools are going to be responsible, the budget has to reflect the addi-
> tional costs. For example, the use of the school's secretary's time. It is not
> just what the direct costs are . . . there are indirect costs in our schools—
> phones, secretaries, etc.

There may be a problem of definition. Ambiguity about how the
program "fits" with school system categories may create difficult salary and benefit issues. Part-time work in a program may not be considered as professional experience, so it may not count toward salary
or job upgrading. This may mean high staff turnover, and a loss of
continuity for the children and the program.

Schools are bureaucratic, and it may be hard to get things done
without going through a few miles of red tape. One program director
spoke of the double set of guidelines—one for the schools, another
for the programs, and "rules on top of rules." Not to mention paperwork, which goes along with large systems of any type.

Parents may not have input into the program. Parents' work
schedules may not mesh with school schedules, and usually parents
need vacation and school holiday care. If school policy does not allow
for child care to be provided at those times, parents are inconve-

nienced and children may have no other options. Schools may feel unwilling to go the "whole way," as one person told us:

> There is constant pressure from parents to have the schools take care of kids when school is not in session. That provision has been resisted and it's good public policy to do that because we then don't become competitive with private day care operators. We are an extension of the school program. This is a continuing source of friction; it surfaces whenever we have snow days, teacher in-service days, or parent-teacher conferences.

School-run programs run the risk of being too much like school. It's important for schools to *be* schools, providing academic programs and instruction for children. But if the day care program is too much like the regular school day, with too much tutoring and remedial work, children will not be happy—and may resist coming.

TIPS

Many of the tips and advice that apply to school-based partnership programs also apply to school-run programs. However, these are some ideas for school-run programs that school personnel have shared:

- Stress the pilot approach. One staffer pointed out, "If we had said it was going to be in every school in the community, it probably would have met with opposition."
- Choose the schools carefully. Identify one, two, or three principals who are sympathetic and supportive. Maybe you need to find a principal who has had personal experience with the need for SACC in order to start an extended day program.
- Orient your staff. "Let your staff know the good things and the difficult things about extended day, and build a feeling of appropriate anticipation for the program." (*Principal*)
- Preplanning is important. "There has to be a lot of preplanning in terms of movement of students, scheduling of bodies in and out of rooms, and planning of activities, so that when children arrive—even if you've never seen them before—you know where to direct them, the easiest way to orient them, and the most efficient way of getting the program started." (*Principal*)
- Involve parents and others in the community in organizing the program and serving as a policy advisory group. This will help to provide a broad base of continuity and concern in the community, not just a base of those parents whose children are currently in the program and will eventually grow out of it.

- Make the program part of the school family; don't have two separate programs. Try to avoid "typecasting" and stereotyping of children as "day care kids."
- Keep the program out of the school system instructional budget. Large school budgets are going to be increasingly unpopular with taxpayers, and, ultimately, with school boards. A program tied in with the school budget could be cut if the school board were to eliminate nonacademic programs not directly related to the primary mission of the school system. Arrange for programs to be included under community activities budgets or similar nonacademic services. Make sure that equal, or at least substantial, funds come from outside the schools so the program won't die if school funds are cut. As one school superintendent said: "If you just use school funds, you're going to have a fatal flaw."
- Tutoring and remedial work should be optional. Provide the option for parents, children, and classroom teachers to request tutoring and help with homework, but don't force it on children. There are some real advantages to families if parents don't feel pressured to help children with homework after the parents return home from work, but children also need some free time to play after school without feeling pressured about academics.
- Program staff should be child-care-oriented. Hire staff who have a clear idea of the differences between school and child care, between formal and informal learning environments!

Community Schools Run the Program

Many states, cities and towns support the philosophy that schools are a valuable community resource that ought to be available to all members of the community, adults as well as children. Legislation exists on the national level (Community Schools and Comprehensive Community Education Act of 1978), and some states also have legislation promoting the community education concept.

Almost any tax-supported school can be designated a community school, but the community has to decide that it wants to support the concept. In some cases, municipal government is the prime sponsor for community education; in others, it is school systems, or collaborations between the school systems and other groups. By making maximum use of public school facilities, the idea of "making the best use of tax dollars" is supported.

If you are planning to set up a community-school-run program, actively seek citizen participation—both to find out what needs exist, and to involve citizens in decision making through their participation in community school councils and planning groups. Also try to cooperate with other agencies and groups in the community. Work closely with agencies to provide needed services and avoid duplicating existing services.

Community schools that are tied in administratively with a sponsoring school system may receive some financial and in-kind support from the schools: use of space; bookkeeping, accounting, and billing functions; sometimes personnel salaries and benefits; sometimes special staff, materials, even transportation. In many ways, community school programs are in the same boat as many SACC programs; both must become as self-supporting as possible. When community education (CE) programs provide school-age child care programs, it is either as the administering agency or as a partner with a community group. When programs are run by community schools, financial support is usually derived from parent fees or from contracts and grants with social service agencies. When community schools act as partners, they can provide space, some portion of administrative time, technical assistance, and some sharing of school resources.

■ *Setting Policy.* In keeping with the traditional community education philosophy of involving the community in policy and decision making, in which a community education advisory group advises the school board and the administration, many SACC programs set up community councils. Elected or appointed citizens help to set policy on issues affecting a particular school. School-age child care programs are often considered by CE to be simply another service offered to the community, and as such there may be no separate SACC policy group. This depends on the genesis of the program, however. The Adventure Club of Robbinsdale, Minnesota, was started as a partnership between parents, the community schools, and the city's recreation department. Since then, parents have played a vital part in setting policy and in administering the program.

■ *Administration.* When only one or two community schools are involved in running or hosting programs, the community school coordinators may serve as the overall program coordinators and work closely with the program's on-site director. When many schools are involved, it may be possible to have a system-wide coordinator of the programs. If financial resources are adequate (when the schools are the chief administering agency), each school may have an on-site program coordinator.

This is the case in Robbinsdale, where the community education program administers its own latchkey programs. The overall coordinator is responsible for supervision of each of the programs, each with its own director. The Eugene (Oregon) Latch Key, Inc. programs are an example of another approach: the *partnership* with community schools. There, the Latch Key director is in charge of administration of their eight programs located in the schools. The community school coordinator at each site works closely with the director and considers the Latch Key Program as one of the several activities offered by the school to the community, even though CE doesn't run it. Typically, the CE administrator of SACC programs in community schools is an employee of the CE department, paid from that budget and not from SACC income.

■ *What Are the Advantages?*   Whether run by the community schools or by partnerships, SACC programs that are located in community schools have some distinct advantages. Many of the "pluses" we mentioned relative to school-based programs apply to community schools as well. In addition, SACC programs benefit from the relationship between CE and the school system. As one community school director comments, "When you're part of the system, it's always easier to get things done."

As an official part of the school system, CE programs may have easier access to school facilities and resources, and can absorb all or some of the cost of building use.

In Portland, Oregon, the school board's policy for joint use of facilities allows community school–affiliated programs to pay no rent for use of school space; unaffiliated programs *do* have to pay rent. A Portland school administrator says: "It's cleaner in terms of relationships and communication to have SACC under the community school umbrella." Because the nature of community education is somewhat less traditional than regular school administration, it is usually more flexible.

No formal school board approval may be required! A SACC program placed in a community school (or run by CE) is a natural extension of the CE program, and therefore may not always require board approval.

Running or sponsoring a program may be a natural extension of other CE activities for school-age children. Precedents may exist in many communities for partnerships with outside groups to use community school facilities. It may be natural for school boards or others charged with making decisions about SACC to place a program under the CE umbrella, since that body has had experience with outside groups and is a logical sponsor.

Parents may be able to play a more active role; there is increased community involvement. This is especially true of CE programs which use the community council approach to decision making.

Schools see CE programs as a service to the community that has a public relations "payback," since citizens are more likely to lobby to maintain services that directly affect them.

Community school activities are available to children in the program. Children can take advantage of community education activities offered at the school (piano lessons, sports, etc.) while they're in day care and have a "home base" from which to operate.

SACC programs benefit when community schools are partially supported by other funds. All school systems in the state of Florida, for example, receive a state allocation for designated community schools. Further, many Florida community schools receive support from local municipalities and, in some cases, matching federal funds for specified programs (Title XX).

■ *What Are the Disadvantages?*   When community education is in financial trouble, then SACC may be in trouble, and when school budgets fund a large portion of the CE program, there may be a danger of losing funds at budget-cutting time. If various types of in-kind support (rent, electricity, janitors) are assigned actual dollar amounts by the school system and CE involvement is readily seen as a financial liability to the school board, the SACC program may be in trouble. Budget cuts may severely affect the administrative capacity of community schools to run such complex programs as formal SACC. Even partnership programs that pay their own way may feel the pressure.

CE staff may not be familiar with child care issues. CE staff are not necessarily child care experts; this could present a significant difficulty in partnership programs, where the SACC program may exist on the periphery of the CE staff's priorities, outside of their major goals.

The CE staff's lack of clarity about the SACC program, as different in nature and distinct in organization from other CE activities, may be an obstacle.

TIPS

- Community school programs (both school-run and partnerships) should be self-supporting so that budget cuts will not severely curtail operations. Even if school funds are cut from the community education program, the school system may still be willing to provide space, utilities, and other in-kind resources to the SACC program at no or low cost.

- Community schools add another administrative layer to the relationships between the program, the school, and the school system. It is important to have all administrative personnel in touch with each other, and to spell out each person's area of responsibility. The community education director, the community school coordinator, the school principal, the program director—all must work collaboratively, as a team, to be what one community school person has called "operationally committed, not just officially committed" to the programs.

- When community schools assign their own staff to work in SACC programs, training should be part of the process. Not all community school staffers are wise to the needs of day care. Similarly, when community schools hire outside staff to work in the program, attention should be paid to finding qualified and experienced child care workers.

- Community schools partnership programs, in which the schools work with an outside group that runs the program, should try to remain autonomous units, keeping their own distinctive goals, purposes, and operating procedures.

A Partnership Runs the Program

Partnerships, or collaborations, can be initiated by parent groups, community agencies, and by the schools themselves. Such collaborations generally consist of the schools' contribution of space and other resources to a program which is administered by another group or organization. All collaborations must deal with four major issues:

1. School policy on the use of space by outside groups,
2. Financial arrangements for use of space and other resources,
3. Accountability (who is responsible for the program and for any liability in case of injury to child or staff),
4. The impact of the program on the day-to-day operation of the school.

Programs must have enough freedom to develop and offer children opportunities for independence. If a partner institution imposes too many rules which impinge on that kind of freedom, the situation may be untenable. In general, however, most groups can make the tradeoffs necessary to achieve the program's goals and to respect those of the partner.

▪ *Financial Arrangements for Use of School Resources.*   The most desirable arrangement from the program's point of view is for schools not to charge for space or other resources. Schools don't always charge the program when school boards view SACC as having a nonmonetary value to the school system, and when the system can accommodate a program without charging it. School/program collaborations can involve the program in paying for use of space, utilities, and extra custodial time. It is important for school officials to determine the ability of a program to pay rent and still be able to provide a high quality program for children. The idea is to achieve a balance —the schools and the program should feel that their arrangement is equitable and that each "partner" gets something from the partnership.

Many groups can provide care only if there is no overhead expense. This is particularly true for programs seeking to care for children from low-income families or families unable to pay the full cost of care. One staffer asked:

> What will we do if the schools start to charge rent? Everything we can so that we will still have the relationship with the public schools that we have now. We help them and they help us in terms of racial balance and integration. There is the possibility that our Board might offer some contributions towards expenses. We couldn't pay any fee; but we would try to negotiate. We would make an effort, a contribution.

"How much will it cost us?" is the first question school officials ask when a group seeks to run a SACC program in the schools. The answer depends on a number of variables. Is the school building open for other activities until 5:00 or 6:00 P.M.? Do custodial agreements stipulate that a school custodian stay on duty until 6:00 P.M. or later? If so, is this time considered a regular part of the custodian's responsibilities, or are there overtime charges? Will the building be heated and lighted after regular school hours? If school buildings are usually closed at the end of the school day, keeping them open, heated, and maintained will incur additional costs, which must be paid by someone.

Leasing space is a new idea for some school systems. Some school systems do not have a consistent formula for assigning charges. In one school system, the principal of each school which houses a SACC program run by an outside agency establishes a rate for the program in that school; in another community, the SACC programs are charged rent, but none of the other groups using school space have to pay. The school board finally decided to adopt the policy that any program charging fees was capable of paying rent. (See Chapter 10 for formulas to determine charges.)

■ *Accountability.* When school principals are asked what makes a partnership work, most speak of the need for a strong on-site director and an accountable agency partner. Since principals' concerns about having a SACC program often center around the same issues expressed by classroom teachers ("kids will be out of control," there will be a "loose situation" in the buildings, etc.), having strong administrative and program direction will help to allay those fears.

Principals and superintendents also expect the agency or group running the program to assume total responsibility for legal and liability issues. (See Chapter 5.) As one superintendent explained, "We expect the agency to have itself well protected, and not to put us at any risk. We don't want to assume any additional liability because of the program."

Programs administered by groups such as Y's or other organizations which already provide a number of services to the community may be perceived by school administrators as a good risk. Directors of such agencies may be trusted by school administrators.

When there are partnership programs, the general image of the program's administration must be sound. If a school administrator is involved, he or she is vulnerable to criticism; no principal wants to add criticism of a program he or she is not actually running to an already overburdened job. These days, principals are more like managers of complex organizations than ever before; to take on administrative responsibility for running another program is seen by many as too burdensome a task, and probably an unnecessary one, if the agency with whom the school forms a partnership is accountable and responsible for the operation.

■ *The Impact of the Program on the School.* Even when programs encounter smooth sailing in working out administrative responsibilities, the actual experience of being partners is often difficult. Objections from people who were "there first" will undoubtedly surface, and these objections must be heard, understood, and responded to in a respectful way. Program directors and staff may find the arrangement creates a number of problems.

Sharing space is difficult for everyone. Ownership feelings and "this is my turf" attitudes exist in all of us, so it is not surprising that classroom teachers may resist or strongly oppose sharing any space with a program. From the program's point of view, sharing classroom space is not desirable and is to be avoided, but even sharing common areas in the school may present problems. Programs tend to be blamed for anything "off," so that staff have to be superconscious about how the children leave a particular area to avoid being criticized. Some staff say that much of their job is "custodial— cleaning the cafeteria, cleaning the bathrooms; being concerned." Here is one example of why shared space is such a problem:

> The program comes in at 2:35 after the teacher is through, and the next day there are seven pencils out of place and they didn't put two chairs up and the teacher's down screaming at the principal, "They're ruining my classroom." Or, let's be realistic: Sometimes bulletin boards are knocked down, somebody wrote on a desk and somebody took something from somebody's desk. These are the things that go on, no matter how closely supervised kids are.

■ *Who Is Crucial to a Successful Partnership?*   In Chapter 4, we discussed the need to gain the support of key school personnel.

> You must have a superintendent who is willing to share the blame with the principal, knowing that it is not going to be perfect. You must risk materials in the school being disturbed. You have got to hire someone who is capable of running the program and who is not a bother to the principal.

School-based programs must have the superintendent's support! School superintendents may not object to having a program in a school as long as the principal supports it and thus will leave it in the principal's hands. In areas where school boards are not called upon to approve a program's use of school space, the superintendent may have this authority but may wish to be uninvolved after the initial decision is made. Program designers feel that the superintendent must support having a program. One superintendent put it this way:

> You've got to have somebody at the superintendent level who is behind the program in the first place. In my case I was an advocate for the project. That's pretty important. I would say that a principal could conceivably start a program on his own—but probably not, because he'd have to come to the superintendent and get his support initially, anyway. So it works better if you have a superintendent who believes in it. When a superintendent finds something important to him, then you know it's going to show up in the schools—because he tells his area directors who tell their principals who tell their teachers! So that's their chain of command and it works!

Many principals prefer an outside agency to run the program in their schools, but even when the program is run by someone else, the principal has a significant role. Some principals swear that if there are problems, they're still going to end up in the principal's lap. Principals don't get paid any more for having a program in the school, but they acknowledge that, as one principal put it, "the school will be different if a program is there."

The principal is often the chief negotiator between the program and school personnel. Sometimes principals feel caught in the middle between SACC program staff and their own school personnel when the school is sharing space with a partnership program. One principal told a newly hired SACC program director that he would "never go to bat for her." He felt that his first loyalties had to be to his teachers. But, for the most part, principals' attitudes are supportive and they are quite realistic about the benefits and hassles of sponsoring a SACC program:

> I think if you truly believe in the concept, you give more than you get. There's a certain amount of aggravation that goes with having a program. The principal is going to have some problems from time to time; the secretary's going to have some extra work from time to time; the cook is going to have it a little tougher, and the custodian will too. Everyone gives more than they get.

Classroom teachers may resist accommodating a partner SACC program for a number of reasons. Some teachers may have negative reactions to day care: in one school, a principal referred to his teachers as "somewhat like our school board. They worked to keep the school as pure as possible." Other teachers may want the schools to provide day care: the American Federation of Teachers, a national teachers' union, takes the position that it is the schools, and school teachers, who are the best potential providers of day care.

Teachers have concerns about insufficient "control" of children by program staff. They may see the day care children as "hell-raisers" because the program staff doesn't have the same set of expectations for behavior as the classroom teachers do—or they may not know what to expect. If teachers are not informed about the nature and goals of the SACC program, their attitudes about this issue may continue to inhibit harmony between the two groups. If teachers perceive the program as undermining the rules and practices of the school, then it will be harder to gain their trust:

> We had a situation where some of the workers in the program let the children do so much—gave them so much freedom—that then teachers

reported problems with these children in the classroom. You see, if you can misbehave in school from 4 to 6, then what's the difference between 10 and 12, when you're in class. And, if you're in the halls, and literally swinging from the chandeliers after school, then it tends to carry over because it's the same physical environment.

But classroom teachers will often be valuable resources to the program: they work with the same children, can contribute ideas and suggestions, and are certainly important allies to have.

SACC staff have an ambiguous role. "You're one of us, but you aren't one of us." Others in the school may not be exactly sure what the SACC staff person's role entails. This can lead to some suspicion and distance, especially if program staff are seen in the middle, between parents and school. However, when program staff can act as a liaison with the parents on behalf of the school, the child really benefits:

> When parents are angry at the schools, we can come in and kind of be half-way between the school and the parents. We act as advocates for the school principal and for the parents.

■ *Making Partnerships Work.*   Partnerships take time to be acceptable and workable arrangements for those involved. It may take a year or more to feel comfortable when a program uses space in "your" school or agency. Actual *space* is only one factor. Everyone is in some way involved with the program. School secretaries may find that they have more phone calls to answer if the program is identified with the school (as it invariably is, even when it has its own phone and a separate administration). Custodians will have more work—even if the program does most of its own clean-up, the custodial staff is responsible for the overall state of the facility. Custodians are typically the first to arrive and last to leave, so they will be aware of the program's presence in the building. Classroom teachers' feelings about the program also must be considered and respected; and the principal's relationship to the program and his role as intermediary must be addressed. How do program administrators and their partners handle the process of making the partnership work? It takes *time, compromise,* and *communication*, as one SACC program director advises:

> People can't expect to go into a school and expect everything to be perfect. That is why people get discouraged. It takes time, no matter how good your staff is.

Acknowledge that a program's presence is a significant event; it does have an impact! One program uses a "fact sheet" to let parents know that the program staff really is aware of the impact of their presence. The After School Day Care Association in Madison, Wisconsin, prepared a newsletter called: "Our Doors Are Open: The Impact of an After-School Program on the School Building and Personnel." They addressed the issue head on. However, there are other ways in which programs can show their awareness that the new relationship may be difficult for others, and also begin to develop some specific ways of strengthening the relationship. Sometimes it will be important to compromise: not by modifying your own basic goals for the program, but by respecting existing practices and rules. It is necessary that your rules be consistent with those of your partner. One program administrator gave this example:

> Like playground rules—the school doesn't let the kids throw snowballs during lunchtime and recess and so we don't; if they can't bring skateboards to school, we don't allow them to have skateboards.

Make consistency a goal. Schools tend to have more continuity in school management than other organizations do, and this fact made one principal remark that having consistency in program staffing and administration was an important ingredient in the success of his school's relationship with the program:

> I think that [with a consistent staff] we have time to learn a lot in terms of what works and what doesn't work. We had made our mistakes. The custodians began to work the program into their routine, and weren't as threatened by it. The staff would learn to do certain things and the custodians would do other things. The arrangements with parents picking up their kids—those things worked out more smoothly. The fact was that you didn't bother the school office at certain times, you didn't get in people's hair. People learned how to handle that and built their procedures better.

Have meetings! Everyone involved in your partnership should have at least one meeting at the beginning of the program year. Anyone who will touch base with the program should be invited: custodial staff, secretaries, school personnel who may be sharing space with you (the physical education teacher if you will be using the gym, the homemaking teacher if you will be using the homemaking room, etc.). The agenda of this meeting can be as simple or as complex as you need. It might be important just to make introductions all around, so that the program staff and school staff can identify each other and know whom to talk to when the need comes up. Or you may feel that it would be a good idea to review your written agreement or guidelines, spelling out the space you are using, the common areas, and the line of accountability in your agency.

School faculty meetings are another mechanism by which program staff can establish relationships with classroom teachers and other school staff. (If faculty meetings are held during hours when the program operates, send a staff representative.) Some program staff have had some problems with "acceptance" by classroom teachers; others report no problems. The majority, however, feel that it does take time. If program director and staff are invited to attend occasional staff meetings either as a courtesy or, in many cases, to share information about individual children, then a precedent will be set for future discussions and information sharing. Program directors give this basic but important advice:

> Be available to the personnel; always try to be seen in the best possible way. Walk up and down the school hallway, wave to the teacher. Seek out the principal or the assistant principal several times a week.
>
> Give the guy or the gal in the chair some strokes. You'd be surprised how really little reinforcement principals get for the jobs they do. When they have a program at night for potluck, invite the principal, and make a pretty big deal that he or she is here, and that they're really giving support to the program. You need your warm fuzzies once in a while, and when you get those you feel a little more able to give the time that's necessary to make the program more successful.

Communication is the key to success in a partnership effort. Keeping the principal informed is among the most important tasks of the program staff. In general, it is the principal who makes the decisions about which space will be used, what materials will be available for sharing, and the availability of other school resources for use by the program. As soon as problems surface, the program staff should talk with the principal. The principal can act as the "middleman"; he or she can encourage the school staff to be receptive to the program's presence and even to use it as a resource. Classroom teachers and custodians see the principal as their boss, so it will be especially important to keep communication channels open. Touch base frequently, especially at the beginning when you're working out the give-and-take.

Should the principal be involved in hiring program staff? Regardless of who does the hiring for the SACC program, the principal should be free to offer opinions, either officially or unofficially. While some principals want to have veto power in hiring, most prefer to cooperate with the program administration in making decisions. In the final analysis, a principal must approve the choice of the director, and possibly other program staff, if a program is going to get off to a good start. As one principal put it, "It's not an antagonism contest. We're on the same side."

The custodial staff probably tie in more with the program on a day-to-day basis than the principal does. Many program directors report that it is crucial to get their support. One program director has said, "The custodian has the key to the program; he can lock us in or out of our space!" It is important to remember the impact on the custodial staff in a partnership setting: there will be some more work, even if it just means being aware that there's a group of children in the building after school is over.

Sometimes "flak" comes from system custodial supervisors and not from custodians themselves. Even when the custodial contract with a program stipulates that the custodial staff is to work evening hours for the regular school programs when a new SACC program moves in, there may still be resistance. Keeping communication going will make a difference.

TIPS

Here are some tips shared by staff:

- Let the custodians know what you need in terms of space well enough in advance so that your schedule and their cleaning schedule don't conflict. Let them know in advance, for example, when you will be on trips so that they can plan to do some repair or cleaning job in your absence.
- Daily greetings—basic human relations—are most important.
- Invite school personnel into the program area; invite them to any open house or play your kids put on. In one program, the children helped the custodians decorate their rooms with drawings and pictures, and the program gave a party for some custodians who were leaving the school. Custodial staff may even want to participate in your program, as do the custodians in a community-school-based partnership program in a western city: one custodian helped out with some of the kids after his shift was over—he'd go for a walk with a small group, go to the park, and sometimes buy ice cream cones. This kind of interest in a program accompanied the attitude one man expressed:

  > I like kids, being around them. If a kid leaves a mess, that's normal—if an adult leaves a mess, that's different. There is a little extra work, but that's what the school is here for. If they weren't

here, then we'd have no job. It's just part of the job. The room is different from the regular classroom—we understand that—it's even easier to clean because there aren't any desks and chairs.

- Share your resources. The Hephzibah Children's Association had more foster grandparents assigned to them than they were able to use in their program, and some of the schools the program operated in needed help in their kindergarten classrooms. So Hephzibah offered to share this valuable resource with them. The idea is to get away from "what's mine is mine, and what's yours is yours." For example, equipment which belongs to the program or to the sponsoring agency—such as film projectors or other expensive items—could be made available to the partner agency, even if budgets and administration are separate. One program director says of building the relationship:

  > If it goes bad [the relationship with the partner], it takes a long time to repair it. There are two ways to be: friendly or ignore each other. But think, what's the best for the kids?

- A liaison person may help. Some school systems assign a school administrator to provide liaison with partner programs. It is helpful for both programs and principals to have someone at the system level who can help with problem solving—and, importantly, who knows the history and status of current agreements between the two partners. This position can be filled by someone outside both school system and program; for example, a PTO member can be the liaison person. If your original planning group involved members from advocacy groups and service organizations, you may be able to use one of these resource people as the contact person.

The principal, in the end, is accountable to the school system if there are serious problems with a partner program. A southern principal suggests the following tips for other principals. They are based on the acknowledgment that the principal is, in many ways, the chief executive officer of his or her school, and in some ways has the same role in relation to a partner program in the school:

- Establish your authority and its limitations.
- Establish the authority of the program and its limitations.
- Then stand back and let it function, so the program operators can take action without going to the principal every time.

How the Program Is Administered

In this section we pay closer attention to the structures and roles of administration: the board of directors, the program director, the parents. Depending on the type of organizational model you choose, some structures and positions will differ, one from the other, but the basic tasks of administration will be the same. There must be a structure established under which people are empowered to make policy decisions about the program as well as day-to-day management decisions. A set of procedures must also be created to accomplish the tasks.

Ask these general questions to help accomplish your work:

Are there clear lines of authority and accountability? Does everyone involved know what their tasks are, how to accomplish them, and who to turn to when problems come up? Does administrative capacity match the scope of the program—for example, the number of children, the type of funding, the location?

Do the policies reflect the needs of the children, their parents, and the program staff? In order to make policies that are fair and appropriate, the board of directors, the agency board, or the administrator or principal should seek the advice and counsel of parents and other experts. If advice and counsel is sought, will the policy makers listen to it and take it into account in making decisions?

In partnership programs, how much control will the partner agency or institution have? How free are you to design a program that reflects the goals and philosophy of the organizers and parents? Will the partner agency exert its authority over budget decisions to the detriment of good program planning? Will it require excessive restrictions on the enrollment, use of space, or administrative procedures you design?

Collaborating with Your Partner's Board

Program organizers will often have to be concerned with more than one level of administration. Not only will you manage the program itself, but you will also need to develop good working relationships with official sponsor or partner groups. Administrators of these organizations may have the authority to determine if and how your program will be a part of their larger institution or agency. The policies of such groups will affect your program, regardless of your official relationship: a school principal, for example, may run a SACC program in his own school, but he will still have to seek approval from the school board or the system superintendent to have the program in the first place.

The partner organization's previously established policies and ways of doing things may have to bend and stretch to accommodate the new program.

Working out administrative structures requires careful planning. An administrative structure:

- Is a *framework* for the responsibilities, limitations, and freedom within which the program operates;
- Provides a mechanism for institutionalizing a program's relationship with a sponsor or partner;
- Establishes clear lines of authority and accountability within the program itself.

An administrative structure should include:

- Clear guidelines and agreements between the program and its sponsor or partner *and* among those directly responsible for managing the program on a daily basis;
- Flexibility *and* definition so the program can be responsive to the changing needs of the children, parents, and staff and the realities of the community.

The program is very fragile in the beginning. After a while, if it's done right, it's institutionalized.

■ *The "Big Board."*   Regardless of the internal administrative structure you have set up for your program, most likely you will be connected in one way or another to a sponsor or partner institution. There will be a policy-setting authority to deal with. This may be the school board, the community service agency board of overseers or directors, a municipal board of overseers, or the like. Establishing your relationship with this body will be your first task of administration, and it is important to clarify this relationship at the outset. This "big board," as distinct from the board of directors of the program itself, may have varying levels of involvement with your program, ranging from simply giving approval to taking an active part in determining policy about enrollment, fees, scope of service, and staffing. For the most part, programs which operate separate entities—with their own boards of directors and separate administrative staff— generally have a fair amount of latitude in setting the program's policies, even when a "partner" institution is involved in providing space or other resources. However, both those responsible for sponsoring or collaborating with the program and those whose primary task is running the program will want to create a good climate for the relationship; like any relationship, there must be freedom to move as well as clearly defined boundaries.

Institutional boards will want to know that the administering group is responsible and accountable, and capable of running the program at no liability to the institution. Most boards will take the position that if an "outside" group administers a program within the umbrella of the institution, the program will be associated with that institution in the mind of the public. Therefore, any collaborating group should provide good program management, including financial stability. Boards are in the business of making decisions about the larger institution, so collaborative arrangements should be worked out smoothly to avoid complications for the larger institution and for the program too.

Boards also need to know whether and how the new program will affect existing operations, and will want and need documentation on the program's scope of service, and the availability or lack of other resources for school-age children.

■ *Designing the Relationship.*   A good example of a collaborative structure between the board of a large institution and programs separately administered but located in that institution is reflected in the Brookline (Massachusetts) Public Schools' *Guidelines for the Operation of Extended Day Programs.* (See Appendix.) The School Committee approves each program to operate in a school, after receiving tentative approval for the program from the principal and the director of school plant. After the program has been approved, the program board is responsible for all administrative concerns, such as establishing tuition rates, selecting staff, etc. The school committee guidelines also describe in some detail what each side will do for the other, and create some checks and balances. By and large, the programs are administered autonomously, while still "part" of the school system.

Another example is the agreement between the Fairfax, Virginia County Board of Supervisors, the County Office for Children, and the Fairfax County School Board, which allows programs to be administered in school space:

Management is defined in the agreement:

> The County Board shall be responsible for the operation and management of extended day care centers, including budget, personnel, payroll, logistical functions, audit, program development, and evaluation.

The County Board of Supervisors has responsibility for:

Management; liability insurance; use of school equipment; overtime of custodial services; utilities; bus transportation; maintenance; equipment; regulation; procedures for allocation of space and energy conservation.

The School Board, which provides the public school space for the programs run by the County OFC, provides:

Space; annual review by associate superintendent; procedures to grant requests for space; maintenance and custodial services (no overtime); liaison with County Board; billing of County Board for extraordinary use of utilities; information on children's health to extended day staff, if parent requests. Furnishings and equipment, if available, will be loaned.

All of this detail is necessary. It saves time and effort figuring out which group is responsible for what in a crunch situation; it alleviates stress on personnel who really aren't responsible for certain areas. In the example cited, the concise and comprehensive agreement was particularly necessary because administrative responsibility had shifted from one agency to another. It was important to be specific about which agency was accountable for each facet of program management and operation.

TIPS

- Keep the board informed: communicate information about the program regularly and frequently.
- Be systematic about collecting required data, and about presenting information to the board.
- Maintain a running record of enrollment; show how the program enhances the larger institution's goals. The YMCA in Boulder, Colorado, is required by the school board to do a needs assessment every April, along with an inventory of providers in each targeted school area. This is to allay school board concern about taking business away from existing providers.
- Follow the correct protocol in making changes in the nature of the program. If you do make changes and don't need board approval for them, let the board know so they aren't surprised. Make sure you explain your requests for new or additional resources clearly. One director told us,

  We did a proposal for nutrition funds and school board people made us withdraw it because of a lack of understanding of the proposal and how it fits into the program. Later on when school board members were at a fair and saw the exhibit about nutrition and foods, the very board member who had been the deciding vote to nix the proposal came back all excited about what she saw!

- If you or the program is publicized, let the board know. If you have a chance, make a "plug" for the board's support and enthusiasm.
- Involve the board in the program: contact new board members, explain the program, give them a tour, and show them how things work. Invite a board member to sit on your program board or advisory group.

Even programs run by schools must engage in maintaining good relations with the school board. A principal of one such program says that he must also be a public relations expert in order to keep the board informed and aware of the value of the program. He counsels others to:

> Do a lot of public relations. We have developed a slide-tape show which we show to the school board, at teacher orientations, and at parent orientations. You need to promote not necessarily the extended day program but the school in general. You've got to show what the school is trying to do for children.

The Tasks of Administration

Administrative tasks can be divided into three phases or time periods, with certain activities to continue throughout. *Phase 1, the planning period,* is the period during which you will begin to formalize some of the earlier activities the planning group has begun, as we describe in Parts II and III of this manual. During *phase 2, the start-up period,* the program has not yet opened its doors to serve children, but is preparing to do so. The director and other staff are hired and enrollment begins. During this time you will set up the logistics of operating the program: transportation, design of space, purchase of equipment, etc. In *phase 3, operating the program,* you are now ready to serve the children. Enrollment may continue, if the program is not full. Personnel at the partner location are aware of your presence, and your activities are geared to make the placement of the program in "their" space as pleasant as possible. Last-minute changes notwithstanding (you can't use the space promised—for example, another kindergarten classroom is needed because of a sudden influx of kindergartners), your space has been designed, and you know what equipment, materials, or special areas you will be using. Parents have been informed about fees and other policies and procedures.

Figure 7–1 outlines the tasks of administration that are common to most programs. There will be some exceptions and variations, because of the different types of sponsorship and support for SACC programs. For example, some agencies will not hire new staff, but may assign staff already on board to run the program, giving them the responsibility to hire work-study students or to find volunteers or public employment trainees.

■ *Policy Making.*   Some of the tasks involve making and implementing decisions on program policy, including size, the population served, funding sources available, staffing needs, and official dealings with state and federal agencies. These sets of tasks are different, one from the other, but are entwined: Policy may be made by one group and implemented by another, but there must be a basic thread of agreement, communication, and organization which ties them together.

Decisions on policies will affect the present and future success of the program. This task is usually vested in a policy-making body. Depending on the type of program you have, this decision-making body may be the board of directors, the school or church board, or the agency administrator. Parents can be involved in policy setting in different ways, ranging from running the program entirely (parents serve not only as policy makers, but also as managers or implementers of the policies they make) to serving on an advisory committee which reviews policy made by another body.

■ *The Board of Directors.*   The administrative tasks a board of directors should carry out are to:

- Establish a program philosophy; decide on program policies such as population served, balance of races and sexes, personnel policies; make policy statements.
- Establish the board's scope of authority: the program's bylaws, parent participation requirements; the program's role in relation to other agencies or partner institutions; decisions on size, scope of the program.
- Establish a managerial function. Through the standing or ad hoc committees, the board selects a director, participates in hiring other staff, prepares or approves a budget and manages finances; seeks to raise funds, designs scholarship or other financial assistance mechanisms; complies with local, state, and federal laws, if they apply.

Who serves on the board? In a parent-run program, parents may

THE TASKS OF MANAGEMENT*

Who does these tasks? There are no hard and fast rules. They may be done by the planning group or by parents; by the program director or the agency director, or other appropriate staff; by a partner agency board or administrator—and often by some of these groups and people working together.

Task	Task Involves:	When Done? How Long Does It Take?
Complete formal organization	Completing process of incorporation as nonprofit organization; developing bylaws, electing officers, organizing committees; filing for tax-exempt status; other legal business	Incorporation: 10 days–4 months Tax exemption: 2–6 months
Fulfill legal requirements	Completing licensing procedures, other health and safety requirements (building, zoning, fire)	Varies (you may be able to open with a provisional license)
Clarify agreement with partner agency	Preparing written agreements with partner agency, including requirements for reporting, or other management tasks	Varies; an ongoing process, but major agreements should be completed before start-up
Secure insurance: liability, medical (for staff)	Purchasing liability insurance or reviewing existing policy for possible adjustment; investigating medical insurance plan (group) or plan for alternative medical coverage for staff (full or partial)	During and after incorporation process
Prepare budget (develop fee structure and accounting, fee collection procedures)	Designing structure (sliding scale, flat rate, sibling payment policy, etc.) based on earlier work on budget requirements	Before operating program
Hire director	Writing job description; advertising; complying with affirmative action requirements; interviewing; designing and signing of contract	Job description: 1–2 weeks Advertise: 1 week Interview: 1–2 weeks
Develop policies and procedures; develop enrollment plan	Deciding on number and ages of children; race and sex balance, if desired; special needs children; priorities for admission	Before program opens
Prepare written materials on policy and procedures; develop parent information packet	Clarifying policy and procedures (hours, vacations and holidays, fees, parent participation, etc.)	Before program opens

198

Task	Description	Timing
Recruit and enroll children	Advertising program, if indicated; developing enrollment, medical, and other forms (check on children's existing medical insurance which may have been purchased by parents through school system); forming waitlist, if indicated	1 month
Develop transportation plan	Contacting and contracting bus service; designing other arrangements (taxi, staff to pick up children, etc.)	Before program opens
Hire other staff (plan to hire in proportion to number of children projected for first enrollment; you will be able to hire more staff as needed)	Writing job descriptions; advertising; complying with affirmative action requirements; interviewing; designing and signing contract	Advertise: 1-2 weeks Interview: 1-3 weeks
Investigate volunteer staff or public service or youth employment programs: work/study	Contacting community agencies for elderly, CETA, schools and colleges; writing job descriptions; interviewing	Varies
Conduct training	Planning program content based on earlier discussions; involving staff in planning; developing "group" as unit; clarifying tasks, areas of responsibility	1-2 weeks
Design space	Clarifying, with agency staff and director, exact space and other areas to be used; designing space and storage use; making materials checklist	1-2 weeks
Obtain equipment and supplies	Checking if in-kind contributions are available from partner agency, parents, community, local business, etc; purchasing, if necessary	Before program opens
Continue enrollment of children	Additional recruitment, if necessary (advertise with schools, child care I&R services, social services department, etc.)	Periodic; when necessary
Involve parents	Establishing schedule of parent meetings; learning parents' skills to share with program	Ongoing
Develop and maintain links with schools, classroom teachers	Staff meetings with classroom teachers of children in program	Ongoing
Train staff	Creating opportunities for staff to learn new skills, doing self-evaluation as group; visiting other programs; staff support groups	Ongoing
Continue development of policies and procedures as need arises; carry out day-to-day internal administration	Continue development of policies and procedures as need arises; maintain up-to-date records (attendance, personnel, finances, etc.)	

*Although tasks are in a sequential order here, many of them are interdependent and need to be done simultaneously.

Figure 7-1

make up the largest group on the board, but others in the community may also be considered for board membership, especially those who have been part of the original organizing effort. This group may have valuable skills or entrée to important information and/or people in the community and, as your supporters, will advocate on your behalf. A staff representative from the program may also be considered for board membership. In partnership programs, the principal (or agency director, or minister, etc.) should be invited to serve on the board as an *ex officio* member.

In an agency-run program, board members should be selected whose skills, interests, and awareness of day care issues and children and families meet the goals and needs of the program. This is especially true of boards which have an administrative role, as opposed to an advisory one. The "working board," charged with tasks as well as policy making, will require some "experts" whose areas of skill—such as law, health, child development, finance—can be useful to the program.

■ *Advisory Boards.* Some programs have advisory boards in addition to official boards of directors. Advisory boards can be a group of professionals or "movers" in the community who are knowledgeable about the program and can be asked to help in its development.

Most programs, unless they are actually run by a parent board, ask parents to be involved in administration. For some, this means "at a distance"—their main responsibility is to approve, or *not* approve, policies and procedures established by program managers.

Many groups have parent advisory boards, committees, or councils. In multisite programs, each site may have a parent board that elects a representative to a central parent advisory council or board of directors for the entire program. The more parents feel like "owners" of a program, the more they want to continue to be involved, even when their energies are not needed for daily administration. Also, some programs simply want more from the parent advisory group—and set out to get it. Much of this impetus will depend on the auspices and history of the organization running the program. Community schools, for example, have a tradition of involving the community in making decisions, so it is possible for parents to be more closely related to the program. Other agencies may not have a tradition of meaningful parent involvement. And, if the administrative structure is highly decentralized, program management may fall into the hands of the program director and on-site supervisor, while policy is made "higher up." Parents may not fit into that hierarchy very well, unless conscious efforts are made to bring them closer to the seat of power. A director of a program run by a large board of professionals with one parent representative, and by a parent advisory board as another separate body, feels that parents do decide on "real issues—things that they can make decisions about. The parent group can ask the board to change policy, and often the board does so."

The following excerpt from the Madison, Wisconsin, *After School Day Care Association's Handbook* is an example of very clear statements by the program to the parents about their administrative rights and responsibilities:

> The structure within the association shall be a representative democracy, with parents at each center electing representatives to the governing board. It is the right of every element of the association (staff, parents, children) to expect support from every other element, to appeal decisions involving them directly, to sit on the board as a representative or concerned party, to carry through in the objectives of the association for creative, enthusiastic daily care, to express opinions for that potential.

The Board of Parent Representatives: Responsibilities/Duties

Policy	Determination of all policies re: the administration and program goals
	Has the responsibility to request information to determine those policies
	Sets all policies for future of organization as well as present operations
Hiring	Responsible for all hiring/firing of staff (usually in consultation with curriculum coordinator & director)
	Responsible for all hiring/firing of administration staff
	Responsible for committee personnel (volunteers)
Appeals	Hears appeals regarding all decisions, policies, differences with other elements within association
	Hears grievances of all decisions, including its own
Finances	Responsibility to work with director on budgets, fee setting, fundraising, proposals (including appearances before potential donors if necessary), and ascertaining cash flow appropriateness on a monthly basis
Publicity	Aid Central Staff
Committees	Functions of the board are handled by various committees of the board: Standards & Guidelines (Policies), Personnel (Hiring), Financial (Finances), Publicity (Publicity)

| Authority | The Board shall have the ultimate authority and re-sponsibility for all actions of the ASDCA and all decisions of the board are final |
| Officers | Shall be elected according to the bylaws and each officer shall chair one committee |

While programs' formal structures provide guidance for decisions on policies and procedures, much of the day-to-day management will be handled by the director or other staff. SACC programs depend heavily on staff, who generally receive low pay and who do not have the most comfortable working conditions. It is their enthusiasm which often makes the difference between a good program and a poor one. Programs need to officially recognize the contribution staff members make. Especially in shoe-string operations, where people must take on more responsibilities for program administration than is really ideal, staff should be able to voice opinions and share in making decisions about policies and program issues. This does not necessarily mean that all programs should have staff as voting board members—but if you want to contemplate such a process, here are some tips on how to do it:

- One or two board positions can be held for staff (or more, depending on the size of the program).
- Staff as a group can elect or appoint members to represent them.
- Staff positions can be rotated every few months.
- Staff can be nominated along with others for election to the board.
- Staff can be voting or nonvoting members. If nonvoting, then staff serve in an advisory capacity.[2]

Most funding sources, both public and private, do not object to staff as board members; however, some, such as the United Way, do object. Make sure you check with funding sources on their position regarding this issue if you think there may be objections.

If you are concerned with staff representation producing a conflict of interest, board policies can be developed to define the limits of staff participation in discussion or action taken on individual staff, such as personnel action.

When the board makes decisions about salary issues, the staff rep-

---

[2] Roger Neugebauer, "Staff Members on the Board of Directors: Centers' Experiences," *Child Care Information Exchange*, No. 9 (September 1979), pp. 15–16.

resentatives on the board can serve as advisors, presenting their requests but not participating in the ultimate vote.

A small working board (eight to thirteen members) is a good idea; all parents in the program might be members of the corporation and have voting power. An executive committee would be responsible for designing and recommending policy.

The board may first be composed of the original program organizers, whose names are listed on official documents as the program incorporators. When you hold your first annual meeting, election of board members according to your bylaw procedures will formalize the board; and in a new program which begins to attract parents, new people can be elected to board positions. You will also need to elect officers at the annual meeting—president or chairperson(s), vice president(s), treasurer and secretary (clerk).

■ *Committees—The Way the Board Functions.*   Boards of directors, regardless of size, use a system of standing and ad hoc committees to do business. The executive committee is composed of those most closely associated with and responsible for the program. It usually is made up of the officers of the organization, and may include also the chairpersons of other committees. Also, standing committees can be organized for finance, fundraising, personnel, program/ curriculum, nominating, building committees, etc. Ad hoc committees are set up to handle business which comes up infrequently. Chairpersons of various committees may be on the executive committee, as well as someone acting as liaison with the agency or school being shared by the program.

Committees work best when the chairperson clarifies the committee's tasks and goals with other members. Tasks should be clearly outlined; a schedule/timetable will help committee members to feel that the tasks, even if ongoing (such as finance), are manageable. Committee members should each have one or two tasks suited to that individual's time, resources, and skills.

The following description of the work of committees is from the Eakin Care Program in Nashville, Tennessee:

Budget and Finance—General Duties: Plan yearly budget based on projected income and expenses. Would be helpful to have persons with general bookkeeping knowledge and skills and persons with an understanding of taxes. Current project is to close out books for the year and to file financial statement to IRS for Not-for-Profit and tax-exempt status.

Personnel—General Duties: To review applicants for positions available in teaching staff; aid in yearly evaluation of staff members and evaluate performance and skills of staff with the director; make recommendations for raises to Governing Board. Current project is to fill vacancy for lead teacher position and to develop an evaluation form for staff members.

Program Development and Evaluation—General Duties: Evaluation of program in relation to satisfying the needs of parents and children; review relationship of program with Eakin School faculty and staff; work with Director in planning yearly program to meet those needs identified. Current project is to develop an evaluation report to present to Dr. Brooks referring to status of program and progress made since March 1977.

Constitution and Bylaws—Design Constitution and Bylaws for this organization. This committee is meeting during the summer to complete this project.

Secretarial and Telephone—General Duties: Help with copying materials and typing when necessary. Telephone committee is activated when information must be given out on short notice. (In the past, only in emergency situations.)

Volunteers and Refreshments—General Duties: Prepare refreshments for parent meetings and Governing Board meetings; share interests or skills in the Center with the children; provide transportation for field trips.

Nominations—General Duties: Communicate with parents to discover persons willing to serve in an elected capacity on the Governing Board. Current project: nominate persons for Governing Board positions becoming vacant in September (three positions).

■ *An "Association" of Programs.*   In Madison, Wisconsin, two parent-run programs grew quickly from one to nine programs. The After School Day Care Association was formed as an umbrella administrative structure for all programs. Each member program elects a parent representative to sit on the association board to appeal decisions involving them directly: "to carry through on the objectives of the Association for creative and enthusiastic daily care, to express opinions for that potential." The Madison Association Board determines policy, participates in hiring, hears appeals, works with the director on budgets, fee setting, fundraising, proposals, etc., and aids the central staff on other tasks (public relations, for example).

Every board, no matter how it is structured, must have an investment in the program and should keep in touch with the needs of parents and children. Regardless of how well meaning, or how initially involved board members may have been in getting a program started, unless parents' needs and wishes can be reflected in the decision making, programs risk having inefficient and unrepresentative policy—or even decisions about their continuation—made by their board. A YMCA board, for example, approved the start of several programs in a large eastern city which had virtually no organized school-age child care. Two years later, declining enrollment and no evidence that the program would become financially solvent indicated to the board that the Y shouldn't be in the SACC business. Therefore, the board made the decision to disband the programs—but it made no effort to find out how parents felt about the program, or to reassess the program director's overburdened work schedule. In fact, the need and demand for SACC was growing in the community, and the program might have been redesigned to meet the need.

■ *The President or Chairperson.* This role is a pivotal one; the president will coordinate the board's basic responsibilities, including policy making, fiscal planning, hiring and firing of staff, etc. (In some situations, the board will also handle enrollment, billing and collecting of fees, bookkeeping, and other day-to-day functions.) This role might be shared by two people as co-chairpersons.

■ *Managing the Program.* The overall tasks of managing the program may be in the hands of a program director, the head of the agency sponsoring the program, a "district supervisor," or the community school coordinator—again, it depends on the program's location and administrative auspices. Daily administrative tasks must be managed by an on-site program director (or head teacher or recreation leader) who may also have responsibility for working with children, depending on the size and financial resources of the program. Multisite programs usually have an administrator and some additional staff to handle bookkeeping and other administrative work for all the programs, but these programs, too, should have an on-site director or head teacher at each location, in charge of day-to-day program operation.

In multisite programs, on-site directors need a link with each other and support from "above." A special role—"managing director," a board of directors' liaison person, a parent representative—could be created so that there is an advocate/ombudsman for the on-site staff.

The board delegates; the staff implements. Boards delegate a good deal of the daily routine of running the program—and the daily decision making—to the program director. Staff members implement policy made by the board, which is the legally authorized and accountable policy maker. The director is the program's manager, who makes sure that the program runs safely and smoothly. Program directors should be included in policy making; their expertise and insight into families and children are vital in setting policies consistent with the program's goals and philosophy.

The director is indispensable to a good program. Since board members move in and out of administrative roles, often it is the director—the one constant figure—who trains new board members. The director will make recommendations to the board on hiring new staff, on salary and personnel issues, on admission and enrollment questions, on a myriad of other issues. In addition, the director will field negative feedback about the program and will represent the program with school or agency personnel. In short, the director is intimately involved with every aspect of administration, as one program director emphasizes:

> The Latchkey site coordinator really does the administration and paper-work and not the parents. At first the parents wanted the programs so badly that they were willing to do anything. Now there is a sort of complacency. Less attendance at parent meetings, no parent replacement on the board. They assumed that everything was going perfectly. When I came in as after-school coordinator, I said, 'I need you and there is lots to do.' I reaffirmed that it is not my program, but their program.

One disadvantage of board-run programs is an increased burden on the director to involve board members in the program and its operation. Once a program is clearly "in good health," in the capable hands of the paid director, some board members tend to "fade away." One director offers these tips on keeping board members' attention:

- Keep the board informed; give them all the information you have. If there's an article in the paper, they should get a copy. Encourage them to visit the sites, talk with them about what's going on.
- Give the board a cause to believe in. They must believe in what this is all about.
- Give them specific tasks with a deadline.

Prepare a clearly defined job description for the director or administrator:

- Define the policy goals and administrative goals of the board and spell out, as specifically as possible, the policy and administrative tasks which the program director or administrator is hired to perform, and which tasks the board will manage.
- Don't abandon the director as soon as he or she is hired! Keep in mind that the staff person you hire must *feel* supported as well as *be* supported by the board.

- **Getting Community Support.**   Form or join a SACC support group in your area. Independent groups may start programs in several sites in a city or town. This often happens after one hardy group paves the way for the later efforts of others. One way for new managers to learn about the sometimes unfamiliar tasks of administration is by communicating with others who are more experienced. This means making contact with administrators of programs that have been operating for a while. This contact can provide:

- Sharing of information and technical assistance.
- Sharing of resources and personnel (for example, all the programs in town could contribute toward the salary of a trainer or administrative-level staff member, such as a bookkeeper or accountant). Food, equipment and supplies, and transportation might be purchased in bulk. You might save considerable money and time if all the programs would alternate picking up and delivering items.
- Political and moral support. A united group of program representatives makes a compelling showing when it counts. The pooled energies and resources of this group can get parents out to attend public meetings or to attract media attention.

Such an association or group for SACC staff may make a substantial difference in the way your programs work for children. Staff members can share program and activity ideas and plan joint events (intramural sports, shared use of a music or dance consultant, etc.). An association with others doing the same kind of work and sharing problems provides a necessary support system—especially in the relatively low-paying field of child care.

Chapter 8

PERSONNEL

WANTED:

Staff person for after-school child care program. Hours: 3:00 to 6:00 P.M. daily; full-time during summers and school vacations. Qualifications: college degree in education, early childhood, recreation or related field; two years experience working with children in group settings. Must be energetic, hard working, well-organized, mature, responsible, committed to child care; willing to make at least a one-year commitment. Responsibilities include: planning and implementing a full-year after-school program for forty children, ages five to thirteen with co-worker; building links with local community agencies; communicating with public school personnel; conferencing and meeting with parents; supervising student interns, volunteers, teen-agers, and others. Salary: $4.00 per hour. Benefits: one week paid vacation; no health insurance available.

People who might respond to the ad above will note carefully that the candidate is asked to have extensive qualifications—but will be paid at one of the lowest rates for any job in the United States. It is not uncommon in SACC for salaries to be very low and job responsibilities very high! The person who decides to work in a school-age child care program must be aware that there is a "special context" in which SACC programs operate: the unique hours of care, and the low salary.

The working hours in SACC programs most frequently are 7:00–9:00 A.M. and 2:30–6:00 P.M. In addition, most programs have periods—days, weeks, and months—when care needs to be provided for longer hours (early release days, school vacation weeks, summers). These hours of care mean not only that programs have to hire people to work part time during odd hours, but also that staff members often are expected to work longer hours when the program offers full-time care.

In most cases, low wages for SACC staff is the rule rather than the exception. They are caused by the part-time nature of the work and the hourly rate of pay most staff members receive. It is not uncommon for workers to receive $3.50 to $5.00 per hour and to work 15–20 hours per week. Even those staff working full time are generally paid much lower salaries than public school teachers'—and with few benefits.

Teacher . . . counselor . . . activity director . . . recreation leader . . . caregiver . . . child care worker . . . group leader. These are some of the job titles used by staff working with children in group programs; often the different titles reflect the job titles in the agency that runs the program. Sometimes it's not clear, when you are called a "teacher" in a SACC program, just what you are expected to do. Or, if you're a "recreation leader," are you simply expected to lead group games and sports?

In this chapter, we introduce you to the different tasks that program staff will perform and help you to think about what personnel you will need to accomplish them. We also emphasize the "special context" as an important factor when you make decisions about staffing. The last part of this chapter takes you through the process of developing a plan for salary and benefit decisions, personnel policies, and staff training and supervision.

Administrative Tasks

The complexity of tasks and the decision about who will carry out those tasks will depend on the program's size (number of children, staff, locations); the program's structure (affiliation with a sponsor group, its existence as an independent organization); and funds available for administrative personnel with no child care duties.

For example, small single-site programs which are organized and administered in part by a parent group are usually structured so that parents are responsible for some administrative tasks, such as bookkeeping, staff hiring, purchasing of snacks. The program's director or head teacher may have responsibility for such other administrative tasks as advertising for staff, new enrollment efforts, coordination of clean-up crews, etc. Larger one-site programs tend to have a full-time director; or, they may distribute the tasks among different people—

perhaps hiring a part-time bookkeeper, secretary, or educational coordinator. In public-school-run programs, many administrative tasks are handled directly by school department offices or personnel.

All programs will need to have staff who work directly with the children and who plan and carry out the program every day, and one person (a director or coordinator) at the site who is in charge of all program personnel and who either performs or delegates administrative tasks. In one-site programs this person is usually in charge of many of the administrative details, from fee collection and financial reporting to hiring and training the staff. If the program is small (under twenty children), the director or coordinator is often both a teacher and administrator, with the job title of head teacher, teacher/director, site coordinator, or lead teacher. Some multisite programs have well-staffed central offices where the bulk of the administrative work takes place—payroll, hiring, and training are largely done by central office staff. In others, the different sites are highly decentralized—each operating more or less as an independent entity, with minimal staffing and involvement from the central office. However, each has at least one person with responsibility for the administration of that site.

Most SACC programs start small and grow according to the need and the demand. Often, a program that began in one location may grow until it has from ten to twenty sites. If you can foresee growth of this nature, or if you are in the midst of such a spurt, you should plan for increasing numbers of central office staff who can work closely with clusters of programs or who can work with larger numbers of programs in specific areas (for example, nutrition, training).

Regardless of the size or structure of your program, there are certain tasks that must be accomplished—some daily, others periodically, and a few only once or twice a year. Some major nonteaching tasks include supervising and directing program personnel; overseeing program activities; conducting and scheduling regular staff meetings; developing and implementing a process for on-going staff development, training, and evaluation; and publicity.

Administrative tasks will include orientation of new families; establishing and carrying out the enrollment process; maintaining adequate staffing, including participation in the hiring and orientation process for all center (program) staff; maintaining records (for example, attendance, fiscal, individual child); setting up and/or overseeing systems for collection of parent fees and other income and for paying staff and expenses; assisting in development and administering of budget; writing proposals for funding/services; and developing and maintaining public relations with community agencies, site personnel (for example, public school or YMCA staff), and parents.

The director will also be responsible for planning and implementing the daily program for the children in care. This includes:

Planning
- Selecting and gathering materials and supplies as needed (purchasing, collecting, scrounging, etc.)
- Exploring and contacting community resources (Y's, library, skating rink, art center) to determine how/when/if program can plan with them to use their services
- Assessing the needs, interests, and abilities of children in care
- Seeking parent input and knowledge about regular school program
- Scheduling activities and events based upon all information collected about children, available resources, parent preferences, public school curriculum, etc.

Implementing
- Adapting activities/curriculum to the needs/levels of each child
- Creating a safe, predictable, and stimulating environment
- Preparing and serving food/snacks to children
- Establishing and maintaining regular contacts with parents
- Utilizing any/all outside resources as appropriate and possible
- Carrying out a daily program for children consistent with program goals and philosophy
- Maintaining written records and reports as needed on individual children and other areas of program
- Attending staff meetings, conferences, workshops
- Overseeing work of all students, interns, volunteers
- Seeking feedback on the program from all involved—staff, parents, children, board; and making changes as indicated

Working with Children

What should people who work in school-age child care programs be called? Some feel that using the title "teacher" may imply "school," or a formal learning setting. Others may feel that "child care worker" has certain negative connotations. Whatever the title, child care workers are *the* critical factor that distinguishes a mediocre program from one of high quality, and those who staff good programs *are* teachers. When we use the term "teacher," we are thinking of the many opportunities that SACC programs can and do provide for informal learning to take place.

It will help everyone connected with the program if you decide in advance what title your staff will have, be it "staff member," "child care teacher," or other designation.

Who performs the teaching tasks in most SACC programs? It depends upon the program's size and affiliation, if any. A twenty-child program may have one key staff person who does the administration and teaching and is called a teacher/director, or head teacher, and is assisted by another paid person. High school and college students, community volunteers, senior citizens, and participants in work experience programs work with the children from time to time or on a regular basis. Some programs prefer a "team" approach, where all child care staff share the same title (teacher, child care worker, counselor) and divide the tasks equally according to individual strengths or some other criterion. In other cases, programs operate hierarchically, with such positions as head teacher, teacher, assistant teacher, aide, counselor I, counselor II, program assistant, etc.

No matter what titles are given and how the work is divided up, one person or a team of people must ultimately be responsible for planning, carrying out, and evaluating the program daily. This means: thinking about the program with others; gathering/creating the materials and resources to work with; interacting daily with children and their parents; and obtaining feedback in order to make necessary changes in the program. Just what qualifications should you be considering for inclusion in your job descriptions? And what personal qualities are you looking for in the people who will fill these jobs?

■ *What Makes a Good Staff Person?*   Answering this question involves asking yet more questions. What kinds of adults do you want children to become? What qualities do you value? What are the needs of school-age children? Briefly, some of their needs are for security and trust, freedom with clear limits, a flexible structure, respect for individual differences, caring and affection, challenges that can be met, and skills that can be mastered. What type of person can best meet these needs? Two experts give their opinions:

> Young children need optimum association with adults and older children who exemplify the personal qualities we want them to acquire . . . . Children need relationships or experiences with adults who are willing to take

a stand on what is worth doing, worth having, worth knowing, and worth caring about.[1]

A second myth is that almost anyone, if friendly, warm, and breathing can develop and carry out a good program that meets the unique, complex, individual, and group day care needs of school-age children. Of course, school-age children in family day care, group or center care need friendly, caring people supervising them, but they also need to be with adults who have knowledge and understanding of how children grow and develop—adults who can facilitate children's activities, encourage individuality, and stimulate ideas. Children need people who are interested in, feel responsible for, seeing that their day-to-day experiences take place in an environment which promotes growth and learning.[2]

Whether you are hiring the bookkeeper, the director, the bus driver, or the cook, there are certain general qualities that will apply to everyone. It is telling that most job descriptions and other written materials from SACC programs neglect to list or to mention the qualities that they are seeking in their staff—that is, beyond the years of schooling required and the minimum age. However, as we have talked to those involved and observed top-notch people in action, we have developed a profile of our own. The following voices of parents, caregivers, children, and others highlight the qualities essential for everyone who works in SACC programs—in any and all capacities:

> I think there's definitely a personality type that really should work with school-age kids. *These people have no problem sorting out issues of authority, and they really are good at fostering skills.* They kind of assume that the world and all of its objects and arrangements is a really fascinating place, and how could anybody possibly resist getting involved with it . . . . They may have dropped out of school in the 6th grade or they may have a Ph.D., *but they have a certain orientation to kids. (Teacher)*

> Adults are needed who *respect and listen to the children,* who know *what activities are appropriate,* who *challenge their curiosity,* who are *flexible and inspire confidence,* who *do not talk down to them,* and who are *available.*[3]

> I look for people with *a sense of humor* right at the top of the list. School-age kids communicate a lot with their humor. *(Head Teacher)*

> A good school-age staff person helps you, cares about you, helps you when you get hurt, is *fair* . . . sometimes. (9½ year-old child in SACC program)

> You have to have *common sense.* Having your master's degree doesn't mean that you are going to be able to take a group of eighteen kids and

---

[1] Lillian Katz, *Talks with Teachers:* Reflections on Early Childhood Education (Washington, D.C.: NAEYC, 1977), p. 95.
[2] Docia Zavitkovsky, "Children First: A Look at the Needs of School-Age Children," *School-Age Child Care, Programs and Issues* (Urbana, Ill.: ERIC/EECE, 1980), p. 6.
[3] *Ibid.,* p. 10.

one adult to the swimming pool and make it. It doesn't matter how many
books you have read. (*Teacher*)

Parents want people *who are going to stay in the job* and they don't mind
paying for it. (*Parent*)

Along with being able to work with children, you have *to be able to work as a
member of a team and be able to get along with others.* (*Teacher*)

You want people who are willing *to do more than is expected,* who know that
there are going to be times when a parent may be late and we need to stay
a few minutes. . . . One who sees beyond what the job description says.
(*Teacher*)

■ *What Makes a Good SACC Administrator?*   In the words of
one parent board member, "The director is the key position in starting a program. Parents can do the groundwork, but you have to have
a director to make it all happen. The director has to be able to build a
program." We would agree with the parents from this program who
emphasize the critical role played by the director in building a SACC
program. What kind of person can "make it all happen"? A
manager—someone who will run the program on a day-to-day basis,
making decisions and solving problems as they arise. You should also
look for a multifaceted individual, because the director will be called
upon to function in a wide range of roles with a host of different types
of people. The job is demanding, yet challenging; exhausting, yet
exhilarating—all at the same time.

In addition to the general qualities, we would include the following qualifications for a program or site director:

- Prior experience, training, and proven expertise in child care
  or human services, program planning and management (for
  example, staff supervision and development, money management, hiring/firing of staff).
- Ability to work effectively with adults.
- Skills in building relationships with public school personnel,
  federal, state, and local officials, community agencies, funding
  sources, parents, teachers, and other community members.
- Ability to organize tasks, establish systems, and delegate work
  and responsibilities to others.
- Ability to solve problems and take action as needed.
- Ability to function in a variety of roles.
- Ability to engender trust and respect from all—parents, out-
  side agencies, staff, and children.

Because of the administrator's role in designing and implementing training and staff development, as well as her or his role as a

"master teacher," we stress the importance of experience in teaching young children. When directors have taught, they understand, in a very real way, day-to-day life with children in a SACC program. Directors are not out-of-touch administrators. Their planning and management functions are intrinsically tied to the day-to-day needs of parents and children in the program setting.

There are some directors who stand apart. They take the time to value and to appreciate the children, parents, and staff, as well as being linked to every possible community network. They are looked up to as leaders and are approachable and accessible to all. As one staff member said in describing the director: "She can be at the State House testifying one day and here washing the dishes the next." Some other opinions are:

> The director has a big impact on the program. He or she can really help teachers using the teamwork approach. (*Head Teacher*)
>
> If people are glad to come to work, then they feel good about themselves, and then about the job. This comes from the director. (*Teacher*)
>
> An administrator needs to be a caring person to the staff members— value them, respect them, build on their strengths. (*Head Teacher*)
>
> The director needs to be available. When someone says, "Do you have a moment?", find one. (*Site Director*)
>
> I have to trust in her ability, decision making, etc. She is here every day with the comings and goings of the program. She is so involved with community groups, we have to back her up . . . . (*Board president, SACC Program*)
>
> To have a successful agency, the director has to take time with parents, staff, board members, etc. (*Parent*)

■ *What Makes a Good SACC Teacher?*   Many different kinds of people can be successful caregivers. They must know children, however, must be able to plan and carry out a program for them, and should be able to relate well with adults. The following quotes— in answer to our question—represent the combined wisdom of well over 200 years of experience in SACC:

> Quality is linked with who the teachers are—love and caring isn't enough. You have to *understand how children* grow and develop and the meaning of behavior.
>
> Children are really affected by staff changing every six months. You need to have teachers who stay.
>
> Someone who can give kids *freedom to learn,* who can *let kids be in on decisions,* who can *let go of control* and who *knows kids are really going to be able to handle it.* Someone who isn't authoritarian.
>
> A basic *honesty*—you can't lie to the kids. You want them to trust you when they're feeling good, frightened, hurt, etc.

Teachers should be in good health—no back problems, for example. This is important for the curriculum—to be able to get around with the kids.

I look for people who work well on our staff; we need to click; it's a team.

I look for someone who sees the importance of working with parents.

We want people with a professional commitment to day care.

The sort of thing I would look for is a person who can be warm and authoritative. And can be simply matter of fact about kids getting out of bounds, and that it's OK to set limits, and that you don't have to get grim about it . . . . The other thing that I really feel is important as kids get older is adults who have some skills . . . . It's very hard to teach a person how to knit unless you know how to knit.

Someone who's willing to learn something from children. Someone who's recreation-oriented, who has *skills in dealing with large groups of kids.*

A person who likes to use the center as a home base. Likes to go places with kids, who can ask him or herself, "What would kids be doing if they were at home?"

After you've given all the reasons, you have to be willing to say, "You can't jump off the roof of the shed, and that's it."

As a parent, I want someone to talk with. People who *care* for my children . . . not just teachers.

I would say our most successful workers have been happy with themselves, haven't had a lot of problems, and can relax.

■ *The Special Case of the Teacher-Director.*   SACC programs often hire someone who divides his or her time between teaching and administration. No matter what this person's title is, he or she has a difficult job to do. The teacher-director must work with the children alongside the other teaching staff, and must be responsible for all of the tasks of administering the program mentioned previously. This double job is more demanding than either of its parts, and requires the characteristics and strengths needed for each component, plus the added maturity, energy, and perspective to balance the two. The skills needed for teaching are different from those needed for adminis-ration—and vice versa. The fact that someone is an excellent teacher doesn't mean that he or she will be an able director as well. Pay close attention to the skills needed for *both* positions, the tasks to be performed, and whether you think the applicant can handle the combined roles.

■ *Adding Administrative Staff.*   As programs expand in en-rollment and number of sites, you will need to carefully consider adding different types of staff. This may mean hiring an "executive" or all-program director in addition to individual program directors. It may mean hiring regional directors to work as staff developers with numbers of programs: providing staff training, classroom materials, and on-site supervision. Or it may mean hiring a bookkeeper, secretary, administrative assistant, engineer/custodian, cook, or social worker.

We mention these positions because you should consider your staffing needs now and try to project what your future needs will be. We are also suggesting that there is a wide range of ways to organize your program staff, although there is no one "ideal" set-up.

Sample job descriptions for many of the positions we have mentioned appear in the Appendix to guide you.

The Hiring Process

Your hiring process, and all of the details that it encompasses, is more than merely a mechanism for bringing new staff members into the program. In many ways it is a reflection of your priorities, your values, and your philosophy, and so it makes a strong, clear statement about the program to others. How people are treated (form letters vs. phone calls), who is involved (parents, teachers), where and how you advertise, and how the prospective employee is made to feel will communicate subtle and not-so-subtle messages.

Hiring is also a two-way process. Not only are you gathering the information about the potential applicant that will allow you to make a final decision, but he or she is doing the same about your organization. This is an important issue for SACC programs, since the salary, benefits, and working conditions may be less than ideal. You may well have to do a "selling job" to the candidate of your choice.

We cannot stress enough the importance of developing *and* following a step-by-step process of advertising positions, recruiting and screening candidates, hiring them, and orienting them to the organization. A procedure that is uniform and clear will be fair to the applicants, and will guard you against making hasty judgments based on limited or subjective information. Ultimately, your hiring process should be set down in writing, formalized and standardized as a part of your entire personnel policy. Doing so will ensure that all employees are informed and that the process is demystified.

As you begin to think about hiring staff, consider the following questions:

- *Who should be involved?* Will parents, staff, board members, public school personnel take part in the hiring process? Are there others who should have a role? If so, who, and in what ways—reading applications? interviewing? Many programs find it has been helpful to involve different people, who provide a variety of perspectives. Input from staff who may later work alongside the candidate is critical and has future payoffs. In school-based programs, some degree of involvement from the principal tends to build alliances and confidence in the program. The opinion of parent-users is essential, since they know very well what they want for their children.

- *Will different hiring procedures be followed for different positions?* Some programs develop an all-inclusive, lengthy process for hiring the director, and then abbreviate it somewhat for other positions. Others allow the director to make final decisions regarding all hiring, and still others use one procedure for all positions to be filled.

- *How can you be certain that legitimate and legal hiring processes are followed?* Many programs find that they have inadvertently or unknowingly discriminated against an applicant. Find out what you are required to do so that your hiring practices are legal and nondiscriminatory. Funding sources or administrative policy may determine certain hiring practices for you to follow. Being clear about Affirmative Action/Equal Employment Opportunity (EEO) guidelines and consulting an attorney will prevent this from happening.

- *How can the staff be balanced in a way that is best for everyone?* What attempts will be made to reach out to and hire men and women from diverse cultural and ethnic backgrounds in addition to those representing a wide range of ages, social classes, backgrounds, and other conditions? Many programs have emphasized the importance of balancing the staff—hiring young and old, hiring men and women, hiring individuals from different racial and ethnic groups, hiring handicapped individuals, etc. This diversity adds richness to the program and allows for the different relationships that parents and children will build with staff.

■ *How to Design and Implement Your Own Hiring Process.*

When I'm hiring people, I ask them why they want to do it, which age child they feel most comfortable with, what hours they like to work, how they feel about extras—coming for meetings and conferences—and the length of the day. I ask them what things they don't like to do, and we talk about salary. Then I tell them about the program and send them to the centers to see them, to see the head teachers and the program. The key thing is we urge them to come in as substitute staffers. We see if we like each other. (*Director*)

Step 1: Decide who will be involved and how decisions will be made. From the start, everyone needs to be clear about *how* candidates will be hired; whose input will be sought, and how; and what the process will be for the final decision making. Everyone needs to know if there will be a consensus or if one individual will make the ultimate decision. Once clear, these process details should not be changed midstream.

Step 2: Draw up a job description. Develop a clear, concise document that outlines the tasks and the responsibilities. Also include in the description the job title and the qualifications needed for the position in terms of required education, skills, and specific experience. (See Appendix for samples.) Furnish enough detail so that the prospective applicant will know the terms of employment—starting date, hours, salary, benefits—and what type of time commitment (three months, one year) is necessary. A final application date and specifics about how to apply is essential.

Step 3: Recruit applicants. The more careful and selective you can be in your advertising and outreach, the better your chances are of coming up with a pool of viable candidates—individuals who will present you with the opportunity for a real choice. In this case, *quality* triumphs over *quantity.*

We recommend employing a variety of methods, depending somewhat on the position to be filled. The following methods are effective:

- Posting job descriptions at college/university placement offices (especially those with programs in early childhood education, recreation, etc.)
- Using word-of-mouth—spreading the word through parents and others
- Advertising in newspapers—those that are read by the community you are trying to reach
- Listing the position in child care newsletters, with child care organizations, and with child care support agencies (for example, information and referral services, mental health centers, etc.)
- Posting attractive and eye-catching notices on bulletin boards in locations where candidates might see them

Be sure to specify the method of application—"send your application to the director"—and the final date on which applications will be accepted. This will save you from a barrage of phone calls and visits.

If you are trying to attract people with unusual skills, strengths, or backgrounds, a rather aggressive outreach effort is essential. If you are looking for a Spanish-speaking candidate, for example, a bilingual job description and discussions with community members who might know of qualified persons will help. Following EEO guidelines and/or Affirmative Action guidelines will also dictate how you handle this portion of the process. Other agencies, institutions, or funding sources may also have rules or stipulations that will affect your procedures. For example, in Minneapolis, Minnesota, all Latchkey staff must be civil service employees; in the California Children's Centers, specific certifications are needed by some personnel. Many centers follow an ongoing practice of recruiting individuals to be substitutes, and those that excel then become prospects for full-time employment.

Step 4: Screen candidates. (The detailed process following applies to hiring a director or a head teacher, but may also be adapted to hiring other staff.) First, sort the resumes you have received and draw up an interview list.

If you have done well in your recruiting efforts, you will receive stacks of letters and resumes. Since it is often difficult to determine from a resume or a letter if a candidate meets your requirements, we suggest that you set up criteria with priorities to be used by those who sort the resumes. For example, will experience carry more weight than formal training? How essential is a college degree if the applicant has had a myriad of life experiences? Are strengths, interests, or skills in one area more appealing than in another? Are some experiences "better" or more valid than others? Will the candidate who knows someone in your organization receive preferential treatment? Will men, racial and ethnic minorities, or handicapped people be sought out? Take the time necessary for a full discussion of these issues before you begin to sort.

The next steps are to plan the interview—both process and content—and set up interviews with selected applicants. The interview will tell you some very important things about the candidate. In essence, you are going to try to get behind all of the "right answers" and correct phrases to find out what the applicant really thinks, values, and knows, how he or she behaves, etc. This is easier said than done.

Step 5: Hold interviews. You should strive to standardize the interview so that you will have an unvarying basis for comparison among the candidates. As much as humanly possible, the "hiring committee" should remain the same throughout, and a list of essential questions (see box) should be used.

When different people—parents, public school personnel, teachers—participate in the interview, it may be easier to get a true picture of the candidates' attitudes and the actual. ways he or she would interact with these different "constituents." Open-ended questions and those about real situations allow a glimpse at the individual's thought processes and his or her approach to problem solving.

The process of the interview—how the individual interacts with and treats people, as well as his or her style (for example, does he or she come prepared with questions?)—is as important as what the person says.

Immediately after the interview, record your impressions of the candidate. Develop a standard form to use with all your interviews so you can later compare candidates' strengths and weaknesses.

Sample Interview Questions
- Tell us your views on how a school-age day care program is different from school.
- How would you work with children in a group setting when ages range from five to twelve?
- When children fight, do you get involved? How?
- What do you think about day care and its effect on children?
- How do you feel when children call each other names? Call you names? What would you do?
- Describe your past experience in working with others as a team.

Step 6: Select finalists and conduct second interview. Once you have interviewed the candidates, compile a list of finalists. This should probably consist of from three to five names. At this point, you should write to the applicants who have been eliminated and tell them why—for example, they did not have enough experience. Then, two or three personal references per candidate should be checked, and the places of employment and educational experiences listed on the resume should be verified. Staff members (or school or agency staff) should write their observations of the candidate's visit to the program and/or work with children. This should be added to the applicant's file.

This group of finalists should be interviewed a second time. These will be more in-depth sessions, since now the applicants have far more information about the program, the community, and the position being offered. And now you have information about the candidates from a variety of sources. At this point many programs present the finalists to the entire board or to a larger, more inclusive group.

Your questions in this final interview should be directed at filling in the gaps—potential problems, weaknesses, or concerns you may have uncovered; answering the candidate's questions; and taking a second look at each other.

Step 7: Make the final decision. You have collected information, checked references, verified work experience, and observed the candidate in action. He or she has talked to other people in your organization and, possibly, has seen the program in action. All of this contributes to your making the final decision and offering the position to someone.

The applicant you have selected should be offered the job with a specific time frame for a reply and clarification of all of the conditions he or she is accepting if "yes" is the answer. Once the applicant's "yes" is firm, all of the other finalists should be told of your decision. If your first choice refuses the job, you may have a second choice within the group of finalists . . . and so on down the line until you have a positive response. If you or your group is not comfortable offering the job to any of the other finalists, you may either have to make some changes to accommodate the candidate of your choice or begin the entire process again. Keep in mind, however, that settling for someone about whom you have doubts is a mistake you will regret.

Many programs hire staff for a probationary period, which gives them a chance to see how the person works out and to provide close supervision. In other cases, when programs have reservations about a candidate, they overcome these by making specific recommendations. This may mean, for example, hiring a person with the stipulation that he or she enroll in a training program or take a particular course.

Shortly after the candidate accepts the position, you should:

- Send a formal hiring letter or contract to the new employee, spelling out the terms of employment.
- Set up a file for the person—including copies of personnel policies, program policies, benefits, and other helpful documents.
- Make an "official" announcement of the new employee. Depending upon the situation, this may be a notice on a bulletin

board, a memo to school officials, a written and/or verbal announcement of the new appointment, or some combination of these.

- Complete the paperwork that accompanies the hiring—tax forms, emergency information, health insurance, etc.

Step 8: Begin the orientation process. Orienting a new employee takes time. In a new program, you and your staff may be orienting each other, learning together. In an established SACC program, there are people to meet, files to read, and a site (or sites) to get to know. If possible, most ongoing programs try to build in overlap time so that the previous employee can orient the new one. How much time will depend upon the specific situation—for example, the complexity of the position, or whether money is available to pay salaries of both people for a given time.

No matter what the situation, it is important to remember that any new employee will need time; an opportunity to ask questions; a chance to read files and other written information; formal and informal discussions with parents, children, board members, staff, school personnel; and a conscious effort on the part of others to help make the transition a smooth one.

You and your staff will find it helpful to prepare an orientation handbook. Much important information on daily procedures can be put in a staff handbook. While it doesn't have to be fancy, a handbook can help to standardize the orientation process. For example, you could include:

- Fire procedures
- Emergency procedures (including the location of the first-aid kit, the name of the program's physician, the procedure used to notify parents)
- Procedures on release of a child to adults other than a parent
- Day-to-day situations (what do you do if a child wants to bring a friend to the program for a day?)

Staffing the Program

How do we know how many staff members to hire?

If we are providing SACC from 8:00 A.M. until 5:30 P.M., how do we arrange the staff so that any one person doesn't work *too* long a day?

Should the director fill in as a substitute for sick and vacationing teachers?

Why does our staff turn over each year?

How can we effectively use high school and college students as staff members?

The number of staff and their work schedules will reflect the total numbers of children in the program, the size of groups, your staff:child ratio, the ages of children, hours of operation, administrative structure, philosophy, and funds available. When you design a staffing plan, you will probably be forced to balance and weigh a variety of factors such as these. In the best of all possible worlds (where SACC programs are fully funded), you would staff your program with as many full-time, well-qualified caregivers as your ideal staff:child ratio and group size suggests. You would pay staff at a high rate, offer generous benefits, allow for ample *paid* meeting, planning, and training time, and not overload staff by burdening them with too many responsibilities. In reality, most SACC programs have limited funding and must make tradeoffs. We suggest that programs weigh their priorities, goals, and values against the financial realities they face. You may be unable to include everything in your staffing plan, so allow your priorities to dictate, and be certain to consider the long-term effects of your actions.

There should be enough staff to carry out the program, giving children individual time, with consistency and predictability. You will want to be sure that paid staff time is allotted for planning, meeting, and supervising; and that the plan encourages people to make an energy and time commitment to the program. In the long run, a plan that meets these staff needs will ultimately be best for the children. Many parents, however, have only limited income to pay for child care. A plan that pays staff well—including payment for certain nonteaching time, training, staff development, and benefits—is costly. When parents are unable to subsidize care, staff members often are forced to, by being paid low salaries or bearing the brunt of other cost-cutting measures. To avoid this situation, some compromise should be reached.

Programs that are most successful in attracting top-notch staff, *and* in retaining them, hire them as full-time personnel. This may seem difficult, if not impossible, to do in many SACC programs because of the limited number of hours of operation (for example, 3:00 to 5:30 P.M.). However, some of these programs have been able to make "full-time" jobs by combining roles. A teacher may work in the before-school program and double as bus driver or cook; the secretary/bookkeeper doubles as a classroom aide, etc. Creating full-time positions for staff will mean hiring people who see the job as their major time commitment—not, as is often the case, people who are taking a part-time job until a better, full-time offer comes along, or people who accept the part-time position in order to devote the bulk of their time to something else. The more that SACC programs can offer full-time status to their staff members, the more they are making a commitment to the employee and encouraging him or her to take the job seriously. This tends to result in a more stable, long-term, and dedicated core of employees.

Whatever staffing pattern you develop, it is essential that *paid* time be built in for staff meetings, planning with coworkers, parent conferences, staff supervision, and other staff development and training activities. In this case, it is often difficult to balance dollars and "necessity." Although it may be difficult to see the immediate results, money spent this way has a tremendous long-term effect upon staff quality, longevity, program stability, and attitude, and it helps prevent "burn-out"—a disease that is endemic to day care.

Your program's philosophy will have a direct, crucial impact upon the way you staff the program. Will all staff work in teams? Will they be given the same title, earn the same hourly wage, and divide the responsibilities equally? Or will staff be given different titles, different salaries, and varying responsibilities (head teacher, teacher, assistant teacher)? Will all staff work full time? part time? or will there be a mixture of both? If you use student interns or paid, part-time student help, what level of responsibility will they have?

Once you have made decisions about your group size, staff:child ratios, hours of operation, the philosophical issues mentioned above, and you know how much money you have for staff salaries, you are ready to set up a staffing plan.

Three Approaches to Staffing

You must decide now what hours you want the staff to work and how you will set up the schedules. Programs that try to employ as many full-time personnel as possible use three major approaches to staffing: *split-shift systems; staggered, overlapping shifts;* and *job combining.*

Some programs find it financially impossible to hire more than one—if any—full-time staff. If you think that may be your situation, we urge you to read this section carefully, with an eye to thinking creatively about staffing. Although for the purposes of explanation we have created seemingly discrete systems for staffing, think of the process more like a selection from a buffet table than a predetermined dinner. Consider all of the possibilities, combine them as it suits you, and design your own plan.

■ *Full-Time Approaches.*   In a *split-shift system,* the work day is divided. Typically, a person might work from 7:30 to 9:30 A.M., and then return to work from 3:00 to 5:30 P.M.—or, perhaps, other hours are assigned. This system is most often used in programs that have before- and after-school programs, but do not operate for a full day.

Some people find a split work day to their liking—especially parents of school-age children (whose children might attend the program), college and graduate students, and those people who hold two jobs or who want time for other pursuits. Many who find it difficult to split the day by working for two different employers do appreciate that by working different "shifts" for the same program, they now have a full-time job with all of the benefits—vacation, insurance, sick time—that such a position affords. For others, a split shift does not work, and as a result some programs have had more success hiring one staff for the morning and another for the afternoon. If this is done, we strongly advise that *at least* one person work full time, to provide a sense of continuity for the children and to promote information-sharing between the morning and the afternoon staffs. The separate-staff approach does tend to compartmentalize the child's day and means that the child must adjust to three separate environments daily (morning program, school, and afternoon program).

The concept of a *staggered shift plan* is that as many staff as possible work full time in overlapping shifts. This provides coverage that reflects the realities of enrolled children's different schedules, and that accounts for periods during the day—especially transitions—where more staff are needed. In most staggered shift systems, there are a few part-time employees. This type of system is used most effectively in programs that provide care for a full day or close to it—in such cases, no *one* individual could possibly work the entire care day. A staggered-shift staffing pattern for a center that operates from 7:00 A.M. to 5:30 P.M. might look something like the schedule illustrated in Figure 8–1.

Note that in Figure 8–1 all full-time staff work seven-hour shifts. Staff member A is considered the "A.M. kindergarten" person, since he or she is present for the entire morning kindergarten care period; in the same way, staff member C is considered the "P.M. kindergarten" person. Before 3:00 P.M., when only twelve to fifteen children are in attendance, there are generally two staff members present. At transition times—9:00 A.M., 12 noon, and 3:00 P.M.—three staff are always

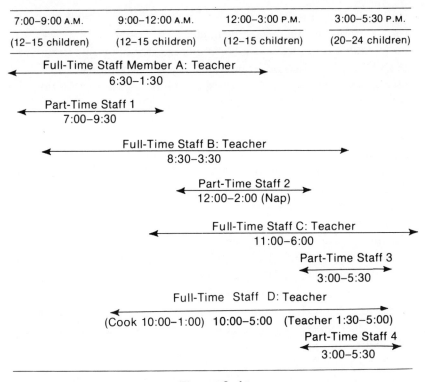

Figure 8–1

present. And in the heavy after-school hours—3:00 P.M. to 5:30 P.M.—a combination of full-time and part-time staff provide the most economical solution. Part-time staff member 2 has been hired specifically to cover the post-lunch, nap time for the children (who will have just come from public school kindergarten and will probably rest for an hour or so). This also allows time for meetings, planning, etc. when all full-time staff are in attendance. This is a critical, although oft-forgotten, component of a staffing plan.

A *job-combining system* is one in which a number of tasks are performed by one person in order to have as many full-time employees as possible. The jobs to be combined will depend a great deal upon the needs of the individual program and the positions that are available. In general, this tends to be arranged on an informal basis and is used effectively by both small and large programs. Often, programs run by, or housed in, schools are able to offer additional hours to people who are already receiving salary and benefits from the schools. In one school-run program, the school guidance counselor also doubles as the SACC program coordinator; in another, a permanent "sub," who is on call daily for the entire school, runs the after-school program. Clearly, there are financial advantages to the program; however, the individual and his or her qualifications are critical to the efficiency of this plan. In multisite programs, jobs in several locations may be combined into one staff person's responsibilities, thus maximizing the full-time opportunities for their employees. For example, a teacher at one site may also serve as the all-program "curriculum coordinator"; the "food and nutrition coordinator" might teach in one program; and the morning kindergarten teacher at one location might be an afternoon teacher in another. The most common use of this practice of combining jobs is found in the majority of smaller, one-site programs, in the person of a *teacher-director*. In fact, most small programs find that the two roles must be combined in order for the program to function cost-effectively (see Figure 8–2).

Note that only the teacher-director works a seven-hour, full-time day; the other two staff work a thirty-hour week, which includes a daily half-hour when all three staff members are present for planning or meeting. In such a system, we'd suggest that staff time be added for the two teachers so that at least once a week they can meet more extensively.

■ *Part-Time Approaches.* Many programs, especially those operating in the after-school hours, choose to hire only part-time staff. If the program is only open for two to three hours daily, sufficient income may not be generated to warrant hiring any full-time staff. Also, the people running the program may think that by

10:30 A.M.	12 Noon–2:30 P.M.	2:30–5:30 P.M.
No children in attendance	After A.M. Kindergarten 12 children	After School 20 children

Teacher/Director

◄——— ADMINISTRATIVE TIME ———►	◄ TEACHING TIME ►
10:30–2:30	2:30–5:30

◄——— Teacher #1 (6 hours daily) ———►
11:30–5:30

◄——— Teacher #2 (6 hours daily) ———►
11:30–5:30

Figure 8–2

employing only part-time people and not offering vacation, sick days, and health insurance, they are doubling their savings. Money saved "off the backs of staff" will most likely result in high turnover, low commitment, and low morale. These are factors that will have a long-term negative impact upon the stability—and hence the quality—of the program.

In some communities, the available labor pool may make it more viable to hire a largely part-time staff. For example, a great number of graduate students are employed in the Madison, Wisconsin, ASDCA. They appear to have found the "perfect complement" to their graduate studies, and make fairly long-term commitments to the agency.

■ *Special Considerations: Nonpermanent and/or Nonpaid Staff.* Given the limited resources available to most SACC programs, often someone gets the idea to supplement permanent, paid staff with no-cost or low-cost labor. The sources most commonly considered are:

Students
- High school students enrolled in child development courses who need an "internship"
- High school students enrolled in youth employment programs (youth enrollment program pays salary and places student in nonprofit organization)
- High school students who volunteer, or those who are in a work-study program
- College students majoring in elementary or early childhood (or in a related field) who need to do a term of internship or student teaching
- College students who are eligible for federal work-study funds (the SACC program only contributes about 20 percent of their salaries)
- Students who are hired at a salary paid in full by the program

Volunteers
- Retired people (often called Foster Grandparents, etc.) who will donate a limited amount of their time to the program
- Parents of children in the program
- Other people (including students) in search of experience with children

Most programs "employ" some volunteers, work-study students, or other low-cost personnel.

It is important to consider the differences between employees who work *daily* and those who work less frequently. Also, there is a great deal of difference between staff who work with the program for a short-term, limited time period (for example, six weeks, one term) and those who are involved over a multiple-year period (a one-day-a-week volunteer who comes for two years).

Some programs are more effective in using volunteers, low-cost, and/or temporary labor than others. Why? Because they use some —or all—of the following approaches and techniques:

Consider short-term or volunteer workers as a supplement to your permanent staff. Individuals who make only a limited commitment to the program should be given limited responsibility. Although many program operators are tempted to have short-term employees fill key roles, they find that turnover and transition undermine the stability of the program. Volunteers and nonpermanent staff may ultimately— through training, experience, and longevity—become vital staff members, but initially they should be considered as supplementary personnel (in terms of staff: child ratio and your program planning). With time, this is likely to change.

Develop written job descriptions that clearly spell out expectations. Be certain that each person knows what is expected of him or her in terms of hours or days at the program, tasks to be done, job responsibilities, and who is his or her supervisor.

Build in a high degree of structure at first. Generally it is best to work with students and volunteers in a structured way, having them start by working with children on a one-to-one basis and performing somewhat prescribed tasks. This way they won't be overwhelmed *and* you can assess their performance—their skills and their strengths—as you slowly help them to take on more responsibility and perform more independently. Some volunteers never get to that stage; others do within a week's time.

Orient everyone to the program. Develop a process whereby new people are given a general overview, made aware of the program philosophy, shown how children are to be dealt with (especially discipline), and given a general sense of the rules. One program director says that this is most successful if she "doesn't assume anything." With students this can mean talking about things like smoking, not teasing children, or the importance of arriving on time.

Ask for a specific time commitment at the beginning. Many program staff find that unless the person is willing to be involved for at least two to four months, it is not beneficial to them to have the person there at all—even if he or she comes at no cost. This is especially true with inexperienced people and when programs have a great number of staff and volunteers.

Provide ongoing supervision and training. In general, the more supervision and training are offered to students and volunteers, the more skilled they will become. Also, time spent will have the effect of enhancing their feelings of self-worth and of importance to the program. That is, the more seriously they are taken, the more they take the job seriously.

Develop a way to evaluate performance and provide feedback. An ongoing evaluation process, closely linked to your initial expectations and the supervisory process, provides workers with both positive and critical feedback which they can use to improve their performance. If someone isn't working out, this allows you to identify the problems, try to solve them, and—if all else—to ask the person to leave. In fact, most programs have the most difficulty, understandably, in "firing" a volunteer.

Have realistic expectations. Many SACC programs have found that students, volunteers, and other part-time people have grown to become invaluable assets to the program. However, you should be realistic about your expectation of part-time staff who have other demands on their time.

■ *Special Considerations: Plan Effectively for Staff Illness, Vacation Time, and Other Causes of Absence.* These can cause problems. For example:

> It is 6:30 A.M. and the director has just been awakened by a phone call from the head teacher who opens the before-school program at 7:30 A.M. Her daughter's ill and she's unable to come to work . . .
>
> Of the three staff members who work in the after-school program, one is on vacation, and a second has just called in to say that he has to go to the dentist. It's noon and the children will be arriving at 2:30 P.M. . . .
>
> A German measles epidemic has been sweeping your SACC program. Not only are half of the twenty-four children in the program out sick, but two of the three staff are home in bed and the director has just been called by the school to come pick up her own child.

A prearranged plan for dealing with staff illness, vacations, or other causes of absence is invaluable. These are the days when makeshift, informal arrangements won't do. If, as is true for many programs, the director is the "ace in the hole," the "substitute for all seasons," what happens if he or she is unavailable, ill, or involved in proposal writing or some other pressing center business? Does the program limp along with fewer staff, possibly engendering the hostility of those staff forced to work doubly hard to cover for those who are absent? Are staff made to feel that they are not allowed to be sick, or even that they should come to work (and infect everyone else)? That certainly generates ill will—especially if one considers the other working conditions staff must endure. Is the director feeling both hostile and frustrated when staff call in sick, instead of providing the empathetic and understanding ear that the sick staff person needs?

Planning for the days when staff are ill, on vacation, or unable to come to work may seem like a minor concern when you consider the actual number of working days in the program. However, a predetermined policy can make the difference between crisis management and smooth operation. Consider the following:

- Can you make funds available for substitutes? If so, has money been budgeted to pay substitutes for those times when staff will not be at the program? If so, what will be the hourly rate of pay for the substitute? If not, is this due to tight money, under-budgeting, or is it an institutional or program constraint?
- What is the size and the scope of your program? Do you have multiple sites? Are you in operation for a full day, part day, or just after school?
- What is the nature of the employee's absence? How much advance notice did you get? And—most importantly—what level of control and flexibility does the program have? Is it a vacation, for which the staff member has given you two months' notice? Is it an unexpected illness or death in the family? Or is it a routine, but necessary, appointment that the employee may be able to schedule in accordance with the program's needs?
- How is your program staffed? Are you staffed to cover just for the numbers of children in care or do you have some leeway—an extra staff member and/or a very low staff:child ratio?
- Who is responsible for staffing? How much time does that person (or persons) have to devote to solving staffing problems?
- Are resource people and other staff available to fill in as needed? Are there people who may be expected to spend time "subbing" as part of their jobs?
- What are some workable staffing plans? There is no one answer that will work for every SACC program.

As these questions indicate, a variety of different factors will influence the range of solutions possible. Before examining specific solutions, we would suggest that all programs make certain that:

- Clear, written policies are developed that spell out the exact process to be followed concerning staff absence from work—who to contact when, and other employee-employer responsibilities. These procedures should be known by all and followed in a consistent manner.
- Concern for staff morale and for treating employees fairly is a guiding principle. Dollars saved in the short run may have long-term negative effects.
- Staff are involved in thinking about and in formulating solutions to this problem.
- Thought is given to what effects the plan or plans will have on children in care and upon the program itself.

We recommend developing a system that can withstand the usual occurrences in day care—epidemics of strep throat, staff illness with short notice—and that takes into account the vacation time allotted to each staff member. How can this be done?

Many programs try to develop a "pool" of available substitutes. One program, for example, advertises in the newspaper for substitutes and then has respondents visit the program and fill out the necessary tax forms. Then, when they have a small group, the director conducts an orientation session (slide show of program, question and answer, written information). If the substitute is still interested at this point, he or she is placed on a "substitute list," to be called when needed. The program's educational coordinator is responsible for calling substitutes. Since her time is flexible and she has no assigned teaching time, she also serves as a backup. Feedback is sought from classroom staff after the substitute has worked for a reasonable period of time.

Another program, one that operates before and after school with two separate staffs, gives the staff the first "dibs" on substituting—at their regular rate of pay—for short-term absences. Staff seem to want to supplement their income, and it is the least disruptive solution, since the children already know the staff.

In another program, where no provision is allowed in the budget for substitutes, staff vacations are limited to the ten months when the program runs part-day. During this time, money is budgeted for extra staff (especially for college students who have been with the program for some time). In addition, this SACC program has three or four resource people without caregiving responsibilities who regularly serve as substitutes. (This function is written into their job descriptions.)

Many small programs plan the job of the cook or the secretary/bookkeeper in such a way that the individual functions as a "permanent substitute" who knows the staff, children, parents, and the routine—and who is available on short notice.

■ *Additional Questions Will Always Come Up.*   Some of them are:

Is it acceptable for the director to act as a substitute? Many SACC programs—especially small, one-site centers—feel that they have no money for substitutes and that the best solution is to have the director "sub." Clearly, there are benefits to occasional substituting by the director, because it adds to the director's knowledge of the children and heightened empathy for the staff. However, consider the *actual costs,* financial and otherwise, of such a plan. Even though it might mean that you don't have to spend additional money, it may mean that other, necessary work isn't getting done. Weigh the costs and benefits—does it make sense to be paying the director's salary for substitute work?

Who should be responsible for finding a substitute or planning the staffing for the day? The director? The head teacher? The person who is to be absent? We feel that asking a sick teacher to worry about finding his or her replacement is somewhat like imposing a punishment for not being available. If you have been sick all night, or have been caring for a sick child, the last thing you feel like doing is making phone calls to find a substitute. We suggest a system whereby one person who is easily reachable acts as the planner and the caller. In most programs this will be the program director, site director, head teacher, or educational coordinator.

How can you keep good substitutes once you find them? Many multisite SACC programs are successful in keeping good substitutes because, among their several centers, they can offer an almost full-time job to a substitute. Many programs, in fact, do just that—hire a permanent, full-time substitute. Other SACC programs band together and work out a cooperative arrangement among centers. Essentially, the key to success seems to be to concentrate on giving a few people a lot of work, rather than spreading it around. Some programs avoid those people who are using substitute work as an entrée to a full-time or permanent position in favor of people who may have limited availability and are choosing to work only sporadically.

■ *Conclusion.*   As a result of their survey on staff working conditions in day care, the Child Care Staff Education Project makes the following suggestions:[4]

Set a decent salary for substitutes.

Let parents know about the center's substitute procedure. They will appreciate your care and attention to staff illness. Take time to orient the substitute. Subs need to know that their time, energy, and talents will make a difference to the program.

Create a substitute handout for each classroom. Include daily schedule, basic goals of the program, where to find first aid equipment, emergency forms and curriculum materials, information concerning children in the class who have special needs.

Let the substitute know clearly that there is someone to ask for help. This "liaison person" can be a coteacher or the center director.

Suggest activities which are "sure successes" but take relatively little preparation time, supervision and clean-up. For example, play dough versus finger painting. If possible have the sub visit the center before the first time she or he is called to work. Pay for the visit at the regular hourly rate.

Introduce the substitute to staff and children. Responses from children will vary. Some may readily attach themselves to the new adult, others are more upset by the presence of a stranger. Meeting the sub through someone they already know may allow them to deal with some of their feelings.

Remember to evaluate your substitute procedure as center needs change. Keep your sub list active; call subs once a month to make sure they are still available.

Make a follow-up phone call to the substitute. Get feedback on how to improve the experience for all concerned.

Quality of Work Life

> I have a strong hunch that we cannot have optimum environments for children unless the working conditions for their caretakers are also optimum. (Lillian Katz, *Talks With Teachers*, p. 30)

A program that has fair, comprehensive personnel policies, salaries as high as possible, and benefits that meet the diverse needs of

---

[4] Childcare Staff Education Project, "Improving Substitute Policies and Procedures," *Child Care Information Exchange,* No. 20 (July/August 1981), p. 25.

employees is communicating a powerful message to its staff. When working conditions are at their best, staff feel respected, valued, cared about, important, and encouraged to remain with the program. When they are not, staff feel demoralized, exploited, and undervalued. This results in high staff turnover, "burn-out," and low morale.

Hiring excellent people is only the first step in building a quality SACC program. The human needs of SACC staff must be given consideration: optimum work environments must be created with attention paid to salary, benefits, and personnel policies, as well as opportunities for training, ample supervision, and meeting time.

In the following sections we will examine salary and benefit issues, training, supervision and development, and the importance of clear, well-developed personnel policies. The quality of work life for staff in SACC programs rests heavily on how these issues are handled.

Salary and Benefits

> It comes down to money—that's the bottom line. If you want people to stay, you have to pay them a living wage. People can't stay in an occupation if they can't live. (*Head Teacher*)

> The low pay is also related to high wastage or staff turnover which, in turn, may undermine the stability of child-adult relationships as well as nullify in-service training efforts.[5]

There is a whole range of other considerations besides the actual salary and benefits received by employees. Some are policies or procedures that take time to set up and implement, but don't actually cost money. Others are a way of thinking about and involving staff in issues and decisions that concern them. Still others are benefits that will ultimately appear on the program's budget as money to be spent. Whatever your policies on salaries and benefits are, they should be in writing so that anyone—existing staff, new employees, parents, and board members—can read and understand them.

Equity and fairness should prevail. This means that a system should be agreed upon that has a clear rationale for assigning salaries that staff feel are equitable and consistent, and that take into account recognition for longevity, provisions for cost of living and merit raises, overtime pay or provisions for compensatory time, prior experience training, and job responsibilities.

Involve staff in all aspects of the process, including decision making. This may mean that there should be staff representatives on the policy-

---
[5] Lillian Katz, *Talks With Teachers* (Washington, D.C.: NAEYC, 1977), p. 29.

making committee, and that they should be responsible for sharing information with all employees and then presenting the employees' views to the committee. If, as in many programs, you decide that the director is to be ultimately responsible for such decisions, we would strongly suggest that open procedures be instituted that include employee input at every step of the process.

Consider and balance the priorities of staff, parents, and the program during the decision-making process. Because there are often concerns that may appear to be at cross-purposes (raises for staff may mean increasing parent fees or eliminating an existing job; adding a paid benefit for staff may mean decreasing field trips, etc.), it is essential that priorities be clarified. Difficult decisions will have to be made and a "bottom line," representing the acceptable minimum, will have to be drawn.

Many programs that are set up within already existing agencies may find that they have to adhere to already-established policies and salary schedules. This may mean that a SACC program has to use predetermined job categories, titles, and pay scales along with the partner agency's benefit package. Or it may mean that you are permitted to employ only part-time staff, and that all employees are to be paid hourly. The range of possibilities is tremendous; consequently, this is an area to research thoroughly when you make decisions about administrative auspices.

■ *Determining Staff Salaries.*   Most board members, parents, and program managers articulate the importance of paying staff well, and yet very few SACC programs, when asked, feel that they have fully accomplished this goal.

Although there may be specific reasons why your program is unable to pay staff as much as you would like, this situation is probably caused by some combination of *limited income* (if you charge too much, you won't have enough children in the program) and *high costs* that you are unable to control in other areas (rent, utilities, etc.). Determining your staff salaries means balancing your other expenses plus your salaries with your income. If you compromise too much in any *one* area, you will tip the scales—and the program, the staff, the parents, or some combination of all three will suffer. *There is no one viable salary system that works for all SACC programs.* Essentially, you want to design your salaries so that you can attract and keep quality staff who feel good about their wage; parents can afford the program; and you have sufficient funds for program supplies, equipment, field trips, etc. In addition to achieving this balance, consider establishing a salary scale that permits yearly raises for employees, that accounts for different experience and training, and that distinguishes in some way among staff that have different responsibilities.

Paying staff by the hour. This policy allows for equity between part- and full-time employees, since the standard for determining the salary is the same. Still, there can be incredible variation within systems that are based upon dollar-per-hour figures. For example, many programs base full-time salaries on a thirty-five hour work week. In one program, staff may be scheduled to work directly with children for thirty hours per week and to use the remaining five hours somewhat flexibly for planning and meeting time. Staff are always paid for thirty-five hours per week (barring overtime or unpaid leave) and it is expected that *they* will monitor their nonteaching time. This is much like a salary system.

Another SACC program pays staff for a thirty-five hour work week that is all direct teaching hours. The ways in which planning and meeting times are handled may vary: there may be an expected unpaid "few hours" per week; staff may keep track and claim overtime at their regular rate; or staff may receive compensatory time off when arranged with the director.

Of course, the way that a payment system is set up is directly linked to the program's staffing pattern. Many programs operate with most employees working on a part-time, hourly basis. However, there can be great variety in the way this is worked out.

Paying staff by the week, month, or year (salary). Many programs pay their employees a set amount per year, month, or week. In this system a program hires someone for an established salary that is based upon a yearly figure and the assumption that a general number of hours per week will be worked. *Regardless of a change in hours, the salary remains constant.* Most teachers in public and private schools are paid in this way.

Most programs combine some aspects of both the "hourly" and "salary" approaches in figuring out a system for paying staff. For example, one such program pays new, first-year, full-time teachers $5.50 per hour for a thirty-seven and one-half hour week (thirty teaching, seven and one-half planning and meetings) for fifty-two weeks per year. This totals $10,725 per year. This amount is then divided in twenty-four equal installments that are paid twice monthly to staff.

When thinking about salaries, many new programs focus on the first year of operation and neglect to project beyond it. If possible, design a system that can be put into effect and built upon year after year. The system itself, along with the policies governing its use, should become a part of your personnel policy. A "great" system that is only intelligible to one person or that has no universal logic behind it is not a great system!

■ *Setting Up Paid Benefits for Staff.*   This discussion of benefits refers to those voluntary benefits provided by SACC programs, not mandatory ones such as Social Security and Workmen's Compensation. Before considering benefits generally, we'd recommend that you find a way to grant some benefits or a percentage of benefits to part-time personnel, especially those people who work in a permanent, part-time capacity.

We know that most programs would like to offer staff a wonderful array of benefits—perhaps as a way of compensating them for the low salary and/or less-than-perfect sites. Very quickly, the people responsible for putting together staff benefits find out that they can be very costly. However, we feel that offering a good benefit package to staff is essential and will help you to *attract* and *retain* quality staff. Here are some of the items we would include in our list of minimum benefits.

Sick, personal, and professional days. No matter how they are labeled, all staff members need paid days for sickness (or family illness) and personal business and for their professional growth in the job. In most programs, most full-time staff seem to receive from eight to twelve sick days per full-time year, one to four personal days, and one to three professional days.

Vacation. Vacation policy ranges from no paid vacation for staff to six paid weeks per year that can be accrued by long-term staff. However, most programs tend to give paid vacations of about two to four weeks. Some differentiate between administrative and nonadministrative staff, with the director given four weeks and other staff two or three weeks. We'd advise two weeks as the minimum to be considered, and would urge you to build in more time for long-time employees, as an incentive for staff to stay with the program.

Health insurance. Although many programs do not offer health insurance because they are too small to constitute a group or because all present employees have insurance elsewhere, we encourage programs to form groups for this purpose. Group plans may be available through the Small Business Administration or local chapters of the National Association for the Education of Young Children (NAEYC).

Many programs pay up to 50 percent of one or more types of

health insurance (Blue Cross/Blue Shield, local HMO, etc.) for single coverage, with the employee paying the remainder. Those needing a family plan should have the option of having one, although the SACC program may not be able to pay a greater amount. In general, the larger the agency or institution, the lower the cost and the more options available to the employee. For example, many school systems cover the full cost of health insurance.

National holidays. Most SACC programs are closed for a set number of holidays per year. In some cases, staff are paid at their regular rate, and in others staff are not paid for the "day off." This often reflects the way that the employee is paid by the program, with salaried people receiving paid holidays and hourly workers being paid only for time worked. However, when the program is closed and employees are unable to work, we'd suggest that employees receive their regular rate of pay for the day if they were scheduled to work.

What additional benefits should be considered? Depending upon your administrative structure, the size of your program, and your partner agency—if you have one—you may be able to offer other benefits to your staff. These might include other insurance (dental, life), pension plans, maternity/paternity leave, discounts on school-age child care for dependents, credit union membership, and tax sheltered annuity.

There is often confusion about the cost of different benefits because people use the terms *fringe, fringe benefits,* or *benefits* to mean different things. What usually shows up on a SACC program's budget next to the line or category item called *fringe* (or *benefits*) generally has to do with payroll, state, or federal taxes and unemployment insurance or Workmen's Compensation. The *voluntary benefits* we refer to are disbursed throughout the budget. For example, the line item for *substitutes* should reflect the hiring of replacements for staff vacations, sick days, etc. Each staff salary should include payment for vacations, holidays, etc. A line item for *health insurance* would indicate the amount the program will pay toward health premiums. As you consider the benefits, try to "cost them out" to see what you are really talking about in terms of dollars spent.

■ *Some Additional Considerations and Some Shoulds and Shouldn'ts.* *What about overtime and compensatory time?* This is a policy issue—and a very important one. Programs that get into trouble in this area are the ones that operate too informally, with no established policy. Many programs find that they cannot afford to pay staff for overtime, so they are very careful to account for all hours in their planning, scheduling, and budgeting. Others simply expect staff to work the extra hours out of the kindness of their hearts. Still others ask staff to keep track of their hours and grant employees compensatory (comp) time off. You should establish clear rules that protect the employee from overwork and arbitrary treatment and that assure fair remuneration.

What about disparities between administrative and other SACC staff? Budget planners, staff, and board members should consider the comparative benefits, salary, and working conditions of all SACC employees. Are there great disparities? Are people treated differently? Use your basic policies of equity, fairness, and staff involvement to help you eliminate unequal treatment. If you have no control over salary or benefits, and find that differences are an issue, we'd suggest being as open as possible and working to resolve them.

Try to make the program a community for staff members. Social events—potluck suppers for staff only, for example—can help staff feel that they are part of a small community that cares about them. Another way of considering staff members' personal needs might be to design a staffing plan that accommodates their family responsibilities. This kind of careful consideration can be an unpaid benefit that helps people feel good about a high-energy, low-paying job!

Personnel Policies

We have already outlined many of the issues and policies that concern SACC staff. Now, we simply recommend that the "rules" governing employees be written down clearly, in one document. Written personnel policies are important because, like all other program policies, they help you to:

- Anticipate problems before they occur,
- Create basic guidelines that are consistently put into action,
- Provide fair and equitable treatment,
- Communicate the value and importance of staff to the program, and
- Protect the rights of staff.

When SACC programs govern themselves informally with no set of written "rules" for personnel, they may find that time is wasted settling disputes or problems, or treatment of employees is arbitrary and unfair; in the long run, this results in a "sloppy" organization.

Overall, well thought-out and clearly written policy and procedure documents help decrease supervisory problems, since they lessen the amount of misunderstanding over job responsibilities or disagreements about the rights and privileges of employment.[6]

■ *Some Things to Pay Attention to.*   The important considerations that govern program policy govern personnel policies as well. The following merit highlighting:

- Staff, parents and board members should work together to develop personnel policies.
- Policies should be written in clear, understandable language.
- Copies of personnel policies should be given to all staff members for current and future reference.
- Policies should deal with and protect all staff. Needs of part-time staff should be taken into account.
- Grievance procedures and methods for changing policy should be included.
- Policies should be reviewed regularly to be certain that they are current.
- ·Policies should be practical and workable—fine words on paper are meaningless unless put into action.
- A program must consider the costs of each policy and be certain that each is affordable.

■ *What Should Be Included in Personnel Policies?*   During the planning stages, brainstorm (with staff, parents, board) and list areas that you think are important to include. Study the personnel policies of other SACC and day care programs. Although there are certainly a great many common areas, different programs will have different needs. Figure 8–3 provides a good guide for policy development. Also see the Hephzibah program's personnel policies in the Appendix.

It may be that your administrative structure comes with an already established set of personnel policies—ones that may or may not be appropriate—and you may have no choice but to comply and "informally modify" the policies.

Personnel policies are difficult to write because they translate into program dollars; because all situations must be considered, from the subtle nuance to the common occurrence; and because individuals with different perspectives are likely to be at loggerheads over certain issues. The final document should represent a compromise, but one that *all* sectors feel is fair, workable, and affordable.

---

[6]Reprinted with permission of Save the Children, Child Care Support Center, *Day Care Personnel Management.* (Atlanta: Save the Children, 1979), p. 13.

**OUTLINE OF TOPICS TO BE
INCLUDED IN THE PERSONNEL
POLICIES AND PROCEDURES
OF A DAY CARE PROGRAM**

I. Statement of Employer Philosophy Toward Employees
II. Process for Establishment and Amendment of Personnel Policies
    A. Description of how a board of directors or its personnel committee will work with staff in the development of personnel policies.
    B. Statement of how often the policies will be reviewed.
III. Employment and Employee Status
    A. A definition of the types of employee status. Permanent and probationary employees are the most common. It may be desirable to define or discuss temporary employee status (e.g., a substitute teacher) and the terms promotion and transfer.
    B. A statement that the program is an equal opportunity employer.
    C. A description of the process by which a vacancy is filled.
    D. A description of the process for resigning, and the required period of notice.
    E. The policy regarding retirement.
IV. Basic Employment Description and Expectation
This includes the length of the workday and workweek; policy for documenting time; statement about when salaries are paid; recommendations or requirements concerning type of clothes to wear; areas in the building in which smoking is permitted or prohibited; whether staff are expected to eat lunch with the children (required in the day care licensing standards in some states) or are permitted a separate lunch period; if desirable, a statement prohibiting employees from eating or drinking foods which the children do not have (e.g., eating candy or coke in the classroom); a statement of health tests (TB, physical, VD, etc.) which may be required for employment in day care; information about parking, or areas of the building which can be used for breaks or planning work; and policies on use of the telephone for personal calls.
V. Salary Plan and Description of Fringe Benefits
    A. Included in the salary plan should be a statement of the employer's philosophy on salaries, how base salaries are established and are reviewed, and under what conditions salary increases will be made available.
    B. Included in the fringe benefit discussion should be a description of required fringe benefits (usually workman's compensation, unemployment insurance and social security) and a description of optional fringe benefits (e.g., medical insurance, life insurance, retirement plan). Information about the pros and cons of choosing various optional fringe benefits should be available and could be included in the Personnel Policies and Procedures document.

Figure 8–3

VI. Attendance and Leave
   A. Definition of expectations regarding regular attendance, proce-
      dure for notifying if employee will be late, policy when an em-
      ployee is absent without authorization.
   B. Definition of vacation and sick leave—how it is accumulated,
      whether unused leave may be carried over at the end of a year,
      how soon to apply in advance for vacation leave, whether sick
      leave must be documented by a doctor's statement, definition of
      other family members whose illness would justify the use of sick
      leave.
   C. Definition of leave for special purposes, such as jury duty, voting,
      serving as an election officer, and attending a funeral. Some pro-
      grams have a policy to cover when the program is closed due to
      bad weather.
   D. Definition of educational leave where applicable.
   E. Definition of maternity leave.
VII. Disciplinary Actions and Appeal Procedure
   A. This should include a description of the process by which disci-
      pline will be administered. It could include the steps of probation,
      suspension, and dismissal, although often it only includes a dis-
      missal process.
   B. The actions of an employee which could cause a dismissal should
      be stated. Some of the most common reasons are: The employee
      uses physical force in disciplining child, the employee has
      falsified employment information, consistent failure to carry out
      assigned duties, failure to comply with the program's licensure
      regulations and, in some programs, the violation of confidential
      information—such as discussing a child's behavior with someone
      other than staff or a child's parents.
   C. A description of how an individual employee may appeal a disci-
      plinary action or other decision related to employment.
   D. A description of how general grievances of employees can be
      brought to the attention of an upper level of supervision or the
      board.
VIII. Employee Evaluation
   A process of periodic evaluation of employee performance is common
   in most day care programs. Discussion should include purposes of
   the evaluation, its frequency, whether the evaluation will or will not be
   used in making decisions about promotion or salary increases, and
   usually a statement that the employee is required to sign the evaluation.
IX. Miscellaneous Topics
   Other possible subjects that some day care programs have found
   necessary to include are:
   A. Policies related to nepotism—that is, whether relatives of current
      employees or board members can be hired or be the supervisor of
      a relative.

Figure 8–3 (continued)

B. Policies of what kinds of political activities an employee can engage in; this only applies to centers which are subject to certain federal laws (Chapter 15, Title V of the United States Code—formerly known as the Hatch Act—and/or Sections 606 (6) and 213 of the Economic Opportunity Act).

C. Special meetings or workshops which employees are expected to attend.

D. Policies of whether an employee's child can be enrolled in the program or not.

E. Statement related to employees' travel and conditions under which they will be reimbursed for expenses.

SOURCE: From *Day Care Personnel Management*, pp. 59–60. Reprinted with permission of Save the Children, Child Care Support Center.

Staff Development: Training and Supervision

■ *What Is Staff Development and Why Is It So Important?*
"Staff development" is a dynamic process of planned supervisory experiences and training activities, with evaluation included as a key component. Examples of activities that might be a part of staff development include:

- Regularly scheduled staff meetings.
- Special meetings with SACC program staff on particular topics or issues of interest (for example, setting up creative art activities, multicultural programing), with staff or outside consultants serving as resource people.
- Conferences between individual staff members and their supervisor to discuss long- and short-term goals, to evaluate themselves, and to receive feedback on their progress.
- Parents and staff participating together in workshops, meetings, or informal discussions on topics of mutual interest or concern (evening workshops, making games or cardboard carpentry, or a discussion on separation or loss).
- Working cooperatively with other SACC programs to form an association for staff development purposes (holding weekly support group meetings, organizing workshops for SACC staff, or researching and passing along information on training resources).
- Enrolling in a course at a nearby college or adult education program (pottery, observing children's behavior, science activities for children).
- An all-program potluck supper where *all* staff have a chance to meet new personnel, catch up with each other, and share ideas.

How does staff development affect SACC programs? Time and attention paid to staff development activities will directly improve the overall quality of the program. It results in increased competence on the job; ability to accept growing levels of responsibility; deepened commitment to the program; improved understanding of SACC; strengthened working relationships and communication skills; and greater personal growth, self-awareness, and feelings of connectedness to the total program. As one long-time director states: "All of us feel that we are growing. We have grown. And we've contributed to the development of the program in creative ways."

■ *Laying the Groundwork: Parents and Board Members Must Understand Staff Training and Supervision and Actively Support It.* Staff development activities can and do occur whether or not money has been budgeted for them. There are other ways in which board and parent support—or lack thereof—can be critical. Quality staff training takes time, and time that is not constantly interrupted by the daily operation of a SACC program. Hiring a director who understands the role that staff development plays in providing quality child care is the first step. Ensuring that staff have ample paid time for supervision, meetings, and other activities is another requisite. These are priorities and philosophical issues that should be debated during the budgeting process.

Someone must be given overall responsibility. A person who "has the big picture" must be responsible for staff development as a part of his or her job. This person needs to consider training and supervision as interdependent activities and coordinate them as part of an overall plan. For example, as a result of an individual goal-setting/self-evaluation conference between the developer and a teacher, they agree that the teacher needs to be more creative in planning for the ten- to thirteen-year-old children in the program. A few weeks later the director is asked for possible workshop topics for a local day care conference. She suggests that "Planning for Older Children in Day Care" be on the agenda.

This individual should develop low- or no-cost ways of meeting the diverse needs of the program and the people within the program. (See the examples of staff development activities at the beginning of this section.)

Advance planning should be done. Planning and coordination are essential: working hours may need to be juggled so that three staff members have no child care responsibilities at a certain, prearranged meeting time; a substitute may have to be hired so that a teacher is able to attend a conference; alternative child care arrangements may need to be set up so that the SACC program can close for two days of staff meetings before the summer full-day program begins.

Besides simplifying the logistics of training and supervision, doing advance planning and making one person accountable also helps to ensure that activities and experiences *build upon* one another and are not just a series of disconnected arbitrary events. Also, given the constant daily pressures on staff to attend to pressing "survival issues," scheduling in advance is often the only way to ensure that training and supervision activities *will* take place.

Planning also allows you to set specific goals and realize them. For example, if improved communication between staff and parents is an important program goal, activities can be planned that provide opportunities for staff and parents to work together, to share ideas, and to build relationships.

Staff involvement in training and supervision should be explicitly built into job descriptions and personnel policies. This serves two major purposes: to highlight the importance of training and supervision, and to let prospective staff know exactly what they can expect. Some staff may be looking for a program where training and supervision are a priority; others may not want to work in such an environment. Clarity will help you to attract staff who see themselves as learners and who want to and will make a commitment to engage in staff development activities.

Depending upon the size of the program, number of sites, and administrative structure, different individuals will have supervisory responsibilities. It is essential that these supervisors have certain skills:

> Supervision requires imagination and creative leadership for both job productivity and job satisfaction of employees. At the same time it requires realism. Working relationships in day care programs do not always flow smoothly; there are individuals or groups of employees who have grievances; there are employees whose work is unsatisfactory and sometimes employees whose poor performance requires dismissal.[7]

Whether part time, full time, or student, every staff member must have someone who "guides" him or her, someone to meet with on a regular basis to set goals, evaluate performance, and receive feedback. By building a positive supervisory relationship, each staff member has an opportunity to identify areas of strength to build upon and areas of weakness that need improvement.

---

[7] *Ibid.*, p. 39.

Expectations should be clearly delineated. The supervisor must be explicit about what is expected of the staff in terms of such issues as hours of work, meeting times, responsibilities during the workday, etc. If specific goals have been agreed to by the staff member and his or her supervisor regarding improvements or changes in some aspect of job performance, it must be clear how assessments will be made. In addition, a time frame should be set up.

Evaluation should be built into the supervisory process. Evaluation often implies something anxiety-arousing or very formal—or a bit of both. Evaluation is essential to the supervisory process, in that the goals set and the expectations outlined are based upon an original evaluation, or an assessment, of the needs of the staff person, the children, *and* the SACC program. Thereafter, staff should constantly be evaluating their own progress, and *a formal process should be developed by the program so that each staff member can measure his or her self-assessment with that of his or her supervisor.* It is essential that criteria upon which such evaluations are based be known and shared by those involved. It's also important that written records of such evaluations be kept by the employee and the program.

Supervisors should strive to achieve a positive tone. A major goal of supervision is to help individual staff members be the best caregiver, cook, bookkeeper, or whatever he or she can become. With this in mind, supervisory sessions should contain positive and negative feedback, if any, with an emphasis on the individual's strengths and specific ways that areas of weakness can be improved.

Supervision should be done both individually and in groups. Group supervision can allow peers to give feedback to one another and to assess their own strengths and weaknesses with help from their team members and coworkers. Clearly, setting up such a situation requires a supervisor who is skilled in working with groups of adults.

Supervision should be given a high priority by setting aside uninterrupted, paid time for sessions for all staff. Although informal discussions and meetings certainly have value, a supervisory style of "catch as catch can" is not one that results in a high quality SACC program. Here is a checklist of important points:

- All staff should have a clear, written job description with responsibilities outlined.
- Each staff member should have a supervisor.
- Staff members should meet individually with their supervisor to receive feedback, discuss progress, set goals, etc., on a regular basis (at least two meetings per month).

- Written evaluations—including self-assessment and supervisor feedback—should be done at least two or three times yearly.
- Team meetings or all-program staff meetings for the purpose of group supervision, feedback, self-evaluation, etc., should be held regularly (at least one a month).

One head teacher gives the following advice to other supervisors: "Know what is going on in the classroom. If you see that there's a problem, work on it as it comes up. Problem-solve all the time. Emphasis is on *our* problems, not *your* problems."

Much of what we have chosen to call supervision is often considered "in-service training." The term *training* brings to many people's minds formal courses held outside of a SACC program. We think of training as all of the opportunities for staff members to learn new things—from each other and from others outside the program. Consequently, training does not have to be expensive or fancy. In fact, some of the best training going on in SACC programs uses the greatest resource—experienced, knowledgeable staff.

School-age child care is an interdisciplinary field, and, as a result, there is no single course of study or background that is appropriate for all staff. *Child development* and *skill in working with groups* are two of the key building blocks of any training to be designed. In addition, staff training should include a variety of different approaches, content areas, formats, levels of difficulty, etc., to meet the range of needs that is typical within most programs.

Know what resources exist within the community and use them. Most communities have many opportunities for learning—some free, and many at low cost. Staff of the American Red Cross might do a session on first aid, for example; a representative of the public library might talk about choosing books for school-agers; a psychiatrist from the local hospital could discuss strategies for handling difficult behavior in the classroom; and an instructor from a nearby college might work with staff, observing and recording children's behavior.

Knowing what exists in your community is critical, but the essential ingredient is, of course, your relationships with different people, groups, and institutions, so that you can work together. Generally, there is something in it for both parties—the key is to figure out exactly what that something is. For example, the librarian may be very willing to do some sessions for your staff if, as a result, he or she knows that a staff member will accompany your children to the library each week—a staff member who knows the library well enough to really help the children and make the librarian's job easier.

Identify the needs of the staff as a whole, and as individuals, and attempt to meet those needs. As one director said, "If I see a need, I find people to come into the center and talk about it. I provide lots of literature and pass it around to the staff." Often, a specific problem with one child may be easily translated into an all-program training need. In one school-run SACC program, a newly enrolled autistic child made many of the staff feel unsure of themselves. They invited the special education people from the district in to talk with them and to provide guidance. From then on, program staff with specific questions or problems had an expert to call.

Make contacts with other SACC and day care programs in the area and explore possible collaborations. Often, an individual SACC program can't generate the resources, both financial and otherwise, to provide certain opportunities to staff. In some communities where a number of SACC programs exist, associations, support groups, or task forces have been formed. Besides the political clout that a larger, more inclusive group can muster, it may also provide opportunities:

- To "buy" training that is out of reach of the individual program,
- To meet on a regular basis to discuss issues of common concern,
- To provide support to each other and mitigate against feelings of isolation, and
- To share strengths by doing workshops and other sessions cooperatively or for each other.

On-site training, based upon the expressed needs of staff, is an effective way to accomplish a variety of goals at once. Staff should be given opportunities to assess and express their needs. Someone within the program should be responsible for doing this *and* for translating those needs into action. Training held at the SACC program can allow staff to work together and build relationships while sharpening skills and learning new things. Staff members will always be more motivated to participate in training if they have had a hand in its design.

Build upon the strengths of your staff; require experienced staff members to train those with less experience. You should consider your staff the greatest resource you have and provide opportunities for them to run training sessions and to share their expertise with others. All staff should have opportunities to be "teachers" and "learners."

■ *Putting It All Together.* Laying the groundwork that we referred to in the beginning of this discussion is necessary in order to design and carry out a successful staff development program. Also keep in mind that staff development is part instructional, part social, and part inspirational. To weave together all of the threads, we suggest that:

- Small programs set aside some of the director's or head teacher's time for planning, coordinating, and implementing staff development activities. Large and/or multisite programs should hire part-time or full-time people (curriculum coordinators, staff developers, training coordinators, etc.) who are specifically responsible for these functions.
- *Some* funds—even if limited—should be set aside for conference fees, materials, consultant charges, etc.
- Programs should work to build in the supervision and training recommendations we have suggested.
- Weaknesses identified through program evaluation should be addressed through staff development activities.

■ *Firing Staff.* Your evaluation process will help employees to learn where they need to improve and how to make improvements. We'd like to guarantee that, if you follow all the steps outlined in the training, supervision, and evaluation sections, you will achieve a 100 percent success rate—but we can't. There will be times when you will have to ask a staff member to leave the program, for any number of reasons. To provide for this, your personnel policies should include specific expectations of all staff regarding their job responsibilities, performance, and accountability. Personnel policies should include procedures for notifying a staff member of unsatisfactory job performance, of probation, and, finally, of dismissal. The personnel policies should be available to all staff, administrators, and board members.

Personnel files. A file on all employees should be kept up to date by the program director or a member of the board of directors. Or, the head of the sponsor agency could be designated to do this for the program's director. The file should contain all written evaluations, communications between you and the staff member, and references submitted during the interview/hiring process. In the case of repeated lateness, inappropriate behavior, or irresponsibility in performance of duties, a note to the staff member should clearly describe the nature of the complaint, and the steps recommended to improve performance. In the event of repeated infractions of rules, a strong written warning should be given to the employee. A copy of this note should also be kept in the personnel file. This sort of written documentation will be very important later if you must ask the person to terminate employment.

Face-to-face meetings. Try not to wait too long before confronting an employee with your dissatisfaction and complaints. Things may not improve on their own! A meeting with the employee—called by the director or by a personnel committee or a combination of both—may be the first step. If no improvement is made, then a second meeting should be called. If you have decided to ask the person to leave the program, this can be communicated in person at the second meeting.

Written notice of termination. As a followup to the meeting with the staff member, prepare written notification to the person, with copies to appropriate committees or agency staff. You should be prepared to give the staff person at least two weeks' notice, but if the firing reflects serious health or safety concerns, you may not want the person to remain in the program during the time of notice.

Handle with care. The firing process should be handled as carefully as the hiring process. Asking a staff person to leave a program may simply mean that that person is just not suited to work with the children in your program—she or he might be better suited to work with younger children, or perhaps should not work with children at all, but might do better in a totally different work setting. The firing process should be helpful to the employee, if possible, and should provide learning opportunities, even though they are painful.

Chapter 9

BUDGETING

How much money do we need to start a program? Where do we get it? How much should we be paying for staff salaries? What other expenses will we incur? And how in the world do we manage it all and keep our books straight?

However competent and confident in planning programs or working with children, many people cower before such questions. They realize that finances are important—indeed, vital—to the existence of the program, but they've never been able to figure out how it all works. The financial side of things seems complicated, difficult, mysterious—like entering a foreign terrain without any road map or road signs to point the way.

This chapter is designed to demystify the financial operations that are crucial to any successful program. In it, we give you an overview of what budgets are all about and help you figure out the sorts of expenses you will incur.

What Is a Budget?

A budget is a calculated plan of expected income and expenses. It is not a record of what actually happened, but your best estimate of what is likely to happen; as such, it provides a way for performance to be measured against projection.

Above all—and this is the point people often fail to recognize—a budget is a tool for program planning. It is a set of guidelines for financial decision making that parallels—and, indeed, derives from—your guidelines for the program you are operating. Carefully thought-out budgets are plans that programs can adhere to. But since they are plans, they often have to be revised during the course of operation—sometimes slightly, sometimes drastically.

Although there are different types of budgets to be used for different purposes, all budgets have two sides—one for funds coming into the program (income) and one for money going out (expenses).

Which Comes First: The Program Design or the Budget?

In the ideal world, a group would think carefully about the program it wants for children and parents, draw up its budget accordingly, and then begin to operate. Some programs do, in fact, follow this course of events. In most cases, however, the program design and financial planning are considered simultaneously, with both program priorities and fiscal realities guiding the budget making. It is a back-and-forth process, but the emphasis must be on those essentials that the group feels will result in a quality program. Otherwise the process will not produce the desired results: a budget that reflects the program's policy, goals, and priorities.

Here are some essential program planning questions that will dramatically affect your budget:

- Who is the program for and when will it operate? How many children? What ages? Can the program accommodate children with handicaps? What hours will the program be in operation? What days?
- What will the activities be? Are there programs and activities in place that the program will tap into, or must the program provide all of its own? What will they be, and what is needed to carry them out?
- Where will the program be housed? What costs are involved in renting, purchasing, and upkeep of the space? What about custodial fees and utilities?
- What is the need for transportation? How will children get to and from the program? Is other transportation necessary?
- What donated goods and services (or in-kind contributions) does the program have? or expect to obtain?

- What teacher:child ratio and group size has been decided upon?
- Who will work in the program? Will staff training be important and necessary? Will volunteers, student teachers, work-study students be used?

Who Should Prepare the Budget?

Many groups underestimate the link between the budget and the program that they offer to children and families. However, the two are deeply wedded to each other. As stated by Gwen Morgan, nationally renowned day care expert from Wheelock College:

> Budget is policy. All our dreams and aspirations for what we want to accomplish for children, for families, for staff are expressed in the budget in the language of money. Every line item in the budget is a policy decision, which directly determines what the program will be. Whoever makes the budget makes those policy decisions.

Who should prepare the budget? At its best, the budget should encompass the different perspectives of all those involved with the program—parents, teachers, board members, and others.

In general, opening up the process insures that everyone has a chance to provide input and has an investment in the final document. Since the priorities of the program will be translated into dollars, don't expect everyone to agree. Compromises and reality must guide the process. In the end, it is recommended that one person or a small committee, depending upon your program structure and philosophy, be responsible for actually drawing up the final version and presenting it to the appropriate "governing body" for approval. Clarifying in advance who will actually prepare and approve the budget will be helpful to everyone.

Start-Up Budgets

One of the most crucial and common mistakes made by new programs is the failure to distinguish between the regular ongoing costs of program operation and the special expenses associated with starting a new program from scratch. Even before you begin to provide child care, you will incur a variety of one-time-only expenses. You might, for example, have to renovate the space you plan to use, or purchase lasting equipment: tables and chairs, easels, record players, carpet, and playground equipment. To meet local licensing requirements, you might have to build an additional toilet, put "school bus" signs on your vehicles, or install a telephone in the public school classroom you are using. You might have to pay a fee just to have the licensing agency come out and tell you what you need!

During the planning period before you enroll children, you will also have staff salaries and other expenses to pay. You will probably want to employ a director at this time so that he or she could begin to hire staff, meet and plan the program, set up and organize the environment, recruit and enroll children, and establish the procedures and routines that are essential to program operation.

When you finally open your doors, no matter what the demand in your community, it is most unlikely that your program will be fully enrolled. Most programs take about six months to work up to full enrollment. But during those six months, you still have to pay for rent, utilities, and other "fixed" costs. To guide you through this beginning period of program planning and early operation, you will need a separate *start-up budget,* a financial plan that considers all of the one-time-only costs—renovation, staff salaries in advance of opening, advertising—and that accounts for the underenrollment that will probably occur. But you should also have a *projected operating budget,* a plan that lets you estimate what your expenses and income will be for a full year, after your program has achieved some stability. In the pages that follow, we will be careful to distinguish between those expenses you should include in your start-up budget and those that fit in your regular operating budget.

Preparing Your First Budget: Expenses

The expense side of your budget is really no more than a list of all the items you will have to pay for in order to run your program. It divides the functions of your program into convenient categories, and then puts a dollar tag on each of those categories.

The sample budget shown in Figure 9–1 is one handy format for presenting your expenses that allows you easily to distinguish between your start-up costs and your regular operating costs. Please note that the budget format we use is not the only one possible or necessarily the best. Formats vary somewhat from organization to organization. If your program is going to operate as part of an existing agency or school system, the budget you prepare may have to conform to their format. However, translating from our format to any other shouldn't present a problem.

SAMPLE BUDGET: EXPENSES

I. *Personnel*
   A. Salaries and Wages
      1. Administrative
         a. Director
         b. Administrative Assistant or Secretary, Bookkeeper
      2. Teaching
         a. Head Teacher
         b. Teacher
         c. Work-Study Assistant
         d. Substitutes
      3. Social Service
      4. Nurse
      5. Cook
      6. Custodial
      7. Driver
   B. Fringe Benefits
      1. FICA
      2. Unemployment
      3. Other
   C. Consultants
      1. Training
      2. Other
II. *Space and Utilities*
   A. Space
   B. Utilities
      1. Heat
      2. Light
      3. Telephone

III. *Equipment, Furniture, Vehicles*
   A. Educational
   B. Administrative/Office
   C. Food Service
   D. Custodial
IV. *Consumable Supplies*
   A. Educational
   B. Administrative
   C. Food Service
   D. Custodial
V. *Food*
   A. Equipment
   B. Supplies
   C. Food
VI. *Transportation*
   A. Vehicle purchase of rental and gasoline
   B. Field trip—bus fares, fees, etc.
   C. Staff travel
      1. Local
      2. Long distance
VII. *Publicity and Advertising*
VIII. *Other Fees*
   A. Licensing
   B. Insurance
   C. Audit
IX. *Miscellaneous*

Figure 9–1

Personnel

Undoubtedly you will have to budget more for staff than for any other item. Most SACC programs find that personnel costs range from 70 to 85 percent of all expenses. That makes sense, though: personnel is *the* key ingredient to insuring a quality program. While there are ways to keep staff costs down, you won't want to skimp on whom you hire. Moreover, in many states licensing regulations will require you to have a minimum staff:child ratio.

■ *Start-up.* The start-up period for SACC can easily take six months or more, involving varying amounts of people's time. After all, someone has to arrange for incorporation, line up available community resources, obtain licensing, and attend to all the other details. Most often members of community groups take on these responsibilities without charging for their services, or agencies assign staff members to work on program development as part of their regular responsibilities.

However, it is very important to decide at what point a paid director, coordinator, or head teacher and other staff will be employed. In order to ensure a smooth opening, a director should be hired from two to four weeks before a program begins. Full staffing is usually not possible until enrollment is high enough to justify it; however, the hiring of a core staff for at least a week of intensive training and orientation will help all personnel work together as a team.

■ *Hidden Expenses.*   Unless it accounts for "nonteaching" time, your salary budget will be way out of kilter. A program that takes care of children for three hours a day, five days a week, typically requires another fifteen hours a week for such tasks as planning, meeting with parents, purchasing and making materials, arranging for field trips, recruiting and supervising staff, and maintaining liaison with community agencies. And that doesn't include the time that may be required for secretarial work and bookkeeping, purchase and preparation of supplies for meals and snacks, transporting children from school, and cleaning up. The decision about how much nonteaching time each staff member's job requires is an important policy decision for all programs, and should be reflected in the budget. Cutting corners on nonteaching time, or expecting staff to donate it, leads to "burn-out," high turnover rates, and general feelings of worthlessness.

One important hidden expense, sometimes hard to estimate, is the cost of substitutes when your teachers are out sick or attending training workshops. A good rule of thumb is to figure that when staff take vacations, you will usually need to hire someone to work in their places. Most programs assume a set figure—usually at or near minimum wage—that they will pay for this time. The anticipated number of hours (the total vacation and estimated sick time for staff positions that must be covered) should be multiplied by the dollar amount to obtain the budget figure.

Many programs find themselves unable to pay for as much substitute time as they really need. In some programs, parents and other volunteers help out; in others, staff is encouraged to take vacations at times of the year when attendance is down or when staffing is higher due to the temporary employment of college or work-study students. In many programs, the director is the "resident substitute" and works in the classroom when staff are sick or on vacation. Sometimes staff cover for each other by taking longer or different shifts. Often this means the other teachers will work for more hours at their usual rate of pay—but many programs find that, although this practice is more costly, it provides consistency in the program as well as a way for their teachers to earn extra income.

Training is another hidden expense related to personnel. Some programs decide to hire a consultant at a certain rate per week. Often, training may take place primarily at the weekly staff meetings that are held during the work day. Others assume that the bulk of the training will take place either at local colleges or resource centers or at special evening meetings that all staff attend. Whatever the case, many programs feel that including money in this category is a "frill" that they cannot afford. We urge you to develop a plan for staff training and to estimate your costs realistically.

■ *How Much Should You Pay for Staff?*   This is perhaps the most problematic question in program planning and budget preparation, and it's a classic chicken-and-egg situation. You want to pay good salaries in order to recruit and retain the best possible employees; but because SACC is so labor intensive, higher salaries translate directly into higher parent fees—which you also want to keep down.

How much money programs actually pay their staff varies tremendously. We found a number of programs using work-study students exclusively—college students whose hours were compatible with that of an after-school program. In those cases staff received minimum wage, and the cost to the program was considerably less because it shared the expense with the college. Other programs have pay scales that are not within their control. This could include programs mandated to employ civil service staff (as in the case of a community education department), or programs in states (such as California) that require certification and set pay scales for most of their teaching staff. In such large agencies and institutions as YMCA's, YWCA's, and school districts, staff may have to "fit into" already established job titles that are linked to salaries.

When there are no guidelines and you have the opportunity to make the salary decisions on your own, you will have to consider cost of living in your area, other salaries for "comparable" work, and what type of person you would like to hire. If the job is part time you may find that you want to pay more so the individual isn't forced to go out and find another position to make ends meet—or you may be able to create a full-time position.

Although we have found wide variation in staff salaries, hours, benefits, and qualifications, it has generally been true that where staff are well paid and given benefits and other financial incentives, quality staffing is the result. The use of work-study students, interns, senior citizens, and other volunteers can lower your costs, but many programs find that in order to maintain the quality they are striving to achieve, volunteer and low-cost labor is only a complement to highly qualified, well-paid staff.

In general, we would recommend paying your staff *as much as you can afford* and to consider the costs of benefits as essential to starting and maintaining a quality program. It is difficult for us to quote exact salary figures since factors such as geographical location and program size, as well as varying staffing patterns and job descriptions, cause great discrepancies. For example, in one eastern city, a salary survey taken in the spring of 1982 revealed that many teacher-directors were being paid at the rate of $5 to $9 per hour, and teachers were in the $4 to $6 range. In addition, hours of paid work also varied from 20 to 40 per week.

■ *Benefits.*   Certain fringe benefits are required by law, while others are optional.[1] Taken together, they can represent a significant expense item in your budget. Benefits include unemployment insurance, Workmen's Compensation, Social Security (FICA), health insurance, contribution to a retirement fund, and compensation for vacation, sick, and training days.

Programs that operate under the umbrella of an existing agency often adopt the benefit policies of that agency. These usually include health benefits. Freestanding programs can usually arrange for health insurance through Blue Cross/Blue Shield or another private insurer; it is not unusual for the employer and the employee to share this cost equally.

A benefit allowance for sick, vacation, and training days should be reflected in the amount of money you allocate for substitute teachers. It is fairly common practice to allow one sick day and one vacation day for each month of accrued work.

------

[1] See Lawrence Kotin, Robert K. Crabtree, and William F. Aikman, *Legal Handbook for Day Care Centers*, pp. 88–98, for a full discussion of the issues relating to mandatory vs. optional benefits.

Space and Utilities

Space and the costs associated with occupancy are probably the expense items that vary the most from program to program. While many programs housed in public schools operate rent-free, at least one program we encountered in New York City was paying a hefty $1,000 per month in 1980. And many programs that have operated in schools for years without having to pay either rent or utilities are now faced with charges for either or both.

During your start-up period you may encounter several one-time-only costs for renovation of facilities. Your local licensing authority may have particular requirements about exit doors and windows or number and location of bathrooms. Whether or not it is required, you should probably have a telephone installed for the program so that parents can reach you (and vice versa) in case of emergency. And if you are in a suburban area, you may have to put up a sign to restrict parking for the program to a certain area.

Whatever space you find, you will probably want to occupy it for at least two weeks before you start operating, and after any major renovations have been done. This will give you time to set up the environment for children. With this, of course, will come the start-up costs of any rent, utilities, and maintenance.

Estimating your utility costs may be difficult, but it is essential if you are to establish a realistic operating budget. Calling the utility companies and asking for the previous year's figures for your location and the expected rates for the coming year should prove helpful. If the space was used differently, try to keep that in mind.

If you must pay a rental fee, be sure to establish beforehand whether it will change during vacations, summers, snow days, or other full-day sessions. Do the same for custodial fees. In schools where union contracts establish the pay scale and hours, custodians may receive time-and-a-half or better for "after hours work." However, you may be able to arrange for your program area to be cleaned first thing in the morning—within contracted hours—rather than at night.

Equipment, Furniture, Vehicles

Any permanent materials and the costs of their upkeep go into this budget category, which can be further divided into different functional areas of the program: educational (chairs, tables, couches, playground equipment), administrative (typewriter, calculator), food (refrigerator, stove), transportation (car or van), and custodial (vacuum cleaner, brooms). Just how much you have to spend for either start-up or operation will depend greatly on what comes with the space you are using and also on the type of activities you have planned: Must there be a chair for each child? Where will children put their things upon arrival? What kinds of equipment does the program want to own? Is it a good idea to have a couch somewhere in the room?

Kitchen equipment is very expensive. If you are equipping a brand new kitchen, the cost can easily run into thousands of dollars. Purchase of a vehicle or additions made to one is also expensive. Many groups lease a vehicle, thus building the yearly costs into their operating budget. Others find that purchase makes more financial sense in the long run. If so, the down payment and other one-time costs should be included in the start-up budget.

Consumable Supplies

■ *Classroom.*   These are the crayons, paint, paper, games, and sundry other materials that children use while they are in the program. They get used up during the course of the year and have to be replaced. Small programs, especially those with two to three staff, tend to lump all supplies—pepper, pots, and paper, as well as entrance fees for field trips—into one category. However, if supplies for cooking are ultimately used for snacks, it may be clearer to consider them a food expense, and include them in your food category. In general, we recommend keeping discrete categories so that you can really keep track of and accurately estimate where and how you plan to spend your money.

Supplies will be an operating expense after the program is under way, but the initial expense of purchasing all supplies is probably going to be greater than the cost of replenishing them in subsequent years. If supplies are ordered at the point when the center is about to open its doors, you can include the cost of most of them in the operating budget. It is helpful if some supplies can be ordered before the program opens and included as part of the start-up expenses, because you are likely to save money if you buy in bulk, and also because you may be able to secure start-up funds for such supplies on a one-time-only basis.

Estimates of cost in this area can be done in a variety of ways. Many programs do a draft of a weekly activity plan, estimate the expenses that go along with it, and then multiply this by the number of weeks of operation—adding a small amount for special projects, full days of care, or one-time-only expenses. Another method is to figure out expenses on a per-child basis, estimating a weekly amount that you can multiply to arrive at a yearly figure.

Many programs are able to cut their costs in this area by collecting "recycled" items to use for projects, by getting donations from local companies (for example, printers are often delighted to give away paper that may be odd-sized or imperfect in some way), and by being careful and cost-conscious. Also, some school-based programs have access to the school's bulk purchasing and can save dollars by buying goods and supplies through the "school store." In some areas, day care programs have gotten together to purchase collectively and have saved considerable sums of money.

Consumable classroom supplies is one of the few budget items that translates into materials entirely used by and for the children in the program. And yet, many groups underbudget this category because they feel they can always scrounge and make do. When considering your needs in this area remember that this money goes directly into the day-to-day program for children and that your staff will be severely hampered if they don't have adequate supplies to work with. The few dollars you might skimp on or save for these supplies will not be significant in the context of your total budget, so it's best to plan for what you think you'll really need.

■ *Consumable Office Supplies.* Another type of supply that you will use up is office supplies—typewriter ribbons and stationery, paper clips and staples. And don't forget all the other office expenses—like postage and photocopying—that you will incur to keep your program running. How much you will need to budget will depend, of course, on the size and sophistication of your organization. Whatever the size of your program, be guided by the fact that you are running a business. You must have money in order to prepare, keep track of, and duplicate important records: proposals, staff evaluations, board minutes and financial reports, etc. You can estimate your costs on a monthly basis, adding more for months when you will probably have more paperwork—when the schools open in September and when proposals are due during the course of the year, for example.

Food

The food you serve will depend a great deal on your hours of operation. If you are providing only after-school care, then this will probably include the costs of making and serving a snack. This can be as simple as buying juice and crackers weekly and having them on hand for the children to eat. Or your program may include cooking as a regular activity—having different children prepare the day's snack from start to finish, from making the supply list to going to the store to cooking the food.

If your program will be in operation during more than after-school hours, or even all day, your needs will be different. Once you add meals and additional snacks, you must be concerned about: Who will do the purchasing and when? Who will get the food ready and cook it? Who will plan and keep track of the menus (and be certain that they meet federal USDA standards if you receive USDA funds)? All of this takes time, time that must be paid for by the program. Hiring a cook and having him or her take care of all of the food-related matters may make the most sense, but may be out of your financial reach. Many programs divide the work and spread it out among the staff. Sometimes parents are responsible for some aspect of the food program. Food services can be contracted with, or the public schools may sell you their food at a reduced rate.

If you have a kitchen at your disposal, then you need to include the cost of cleaning supplies, kitchen utensils, and other incidentals in your budget. Again, you may find that you plan a more limited program at first and that your food needs will change over time. Or, you may find that it isn't worth the dollars and the trouble and ask that children bring lunches and snacks from home.

If you are providing food of some sort, an amount per child will probably be your best rule of thumb for the food costs. Knowing the numbers of children you will care for and approximating the number that will be in attendance at different times should give you a rough figure for your estimated costs.

The USDA child care feeding program guidelines might be helpful to you as you plan your budget. Or you could prepare sample menus and cost out the ingredients. This may give you a ball park figure you can then multiply by the number of weeks of operation. The hours needed by a cook to plan, shop, prepare, serve, and clean up should be carefully considered. For example, if someone is serving lunch and an afternoon snack, budgeting for an average of three to five hours per day would not be unreasonable. This is where other programs in your area can be particularly helpful. Food coops, commodity and bulk buying can save dollars, but they also take someone's time.

Transportation

Transportation budgets range all over the lot. Some programs provide no transportation and are serving their parents and children well; others have extensive before- and after-school routes that cost thousands of dollars but are essential to their operation.

When budgeting, consider all of your possible transportation needs: transportation to the program (consider all of your hours); transportation back home or to school from the program; transportation of children and staff to and from field trips and community activities; and reimbursements to staff for mileage or transportation costs incurred while purchasing supplies or tending to other program-related matters. As you think about the financial implications of your plans, your feelings about what is good for children should be carefully balanced with your "budgetary sense."

Depending upon your community, there are many different avenues to explore to come up with the most economical and efficient transportation plan. Some taxi companies will contract with you to provide this service; their cost estimates will help you to get a clearer idea of the amount of money that you are talking about. You may be able to hire a person who owns a vehicle and pay him or her directly. You may be able to team up with others and do some transportation sharing—perhaps they will loan you their vehicle for a set period of time. Perhaps the schools will consider transporting the children to your program at the end of the day, instead of to their homes. If you are a large, multiprogram agency, perhaps owning or leasing a vehicle will pay off in the long run. Or, maybe your agency already owns a van or school bus and your new program will be able to use it for certain hours. (See Chapter 3 for other suggestions.)

We have found that transportation is a service easier to add than to take away. Start modestly by meeting your minimum needs, and then expand and adapt after you have some experience in operating the program.

Publicity and Advertising

This is an expense you can't afford to ignore, especially during your start-up period. No matter how great the expressed need in your community, new programs always seem to have longer start-up periods than anticipated; it takes six months to a year to really get things rolling.

While the costs of publicity and advertising may be particularly high during your start-up period, you should also be sure to include them in your regular operating budget. You may have to advertise for staff every year, and newspaper ads are one way of doing so and complying with equal opportunity laws. You may want to publicize special fundraising events. (See Chapter 12 for publicity techniques.)

■ *Licenses.*   To obtain the day care license required in some states you may have to pay a license fee, as well as fees for local building approval, fire inspection, etc. In some cases this will be a one-time-only payment, but in others you will have to pay for renewal annually. Because charges vary greatly, we can't offer a rule of thumb, but we urge you to check with your state licensing agency about the costs you can expect to incur during start-up and during operation.

■ *Other Fees.*   Before you begin operating you will need to purchase your initial insurance coverage. This may be financed through your operating budget, but it must be purchased in advance of operation. Chapter 5 discusses the kinds of insurance most programs will need. You will also want to obtain Workmen's Compensation. Once your needs in this budget category are determined, estimates of insurance expenses can be fairly reliable. Local insurance agents can provide you with estimates and can purchase insurance for you from appropriate carriers. Programs that are part of a larger agency may be covered by that agency's insurance.

■ *Audit.*   A yearly audit of your books may not be required, but it is a good idea to have it done anyway. It will certify the propriety of your financial management to parents and board. Such proof will be required almost automatically by foundations or other grant-making organizations if you apply for funds.

Because certified public accountants are well paid, the annual audit for even a small program can run from $250 up. However, as part of their service to the community, accounting firms may be willing to take you on as a *pro bono* client at no charge or at a greatly reduced fee. The local chapter of the American Accountants Association can help you identify a firm that might help.

Miscellaneous Expenses

No matter which way you organize the expenses, it is a good practice to include a category for emergencies and for the few miscellaneous items you might not have considered. Having some unallocated funds you can use for emergency repairs or unanticipated purchases may not be every bookkeeper's idea of a well-thought-out budget plan, but given the nature of child care it must be considered. The budget item for these contingencies is labeled in a variety of ways including: "miscellaneous," "contingency," or "emergency fund," and the money is to be used to bail the program out of precarious situations that never could have been forecasted by even the most conservative and able fiscal planner.

Preparing Your First Budget: Income

Just as the expense side of your budget is no more than a list of the items for which you will have to pay, the income side is a list of the sources and amounts of funds that will, taken together, allow the program to operate and to meet its expenses. It is really your best guess of what revenues will flow to the program, from parent fees, government agencies, foundations, or other sources.

It's probably obvious that each side of the budget—income and expenses—has an effect on the other: many programs plan their budget by figuring out their income from parent fees and any other funding sources and then allocating their expenses accordingly. Although this may seem to be the only course of events open to a group, we advocate that the expenses of the program you have planned be estimated *first*, income *then* should be considered, and the two balanced until a realistic budget is reached.

The "Sample Budget: Income" (Figure 9–2) is one simple format which allows you to distinguish easily between your start-up income and your regular operating income. In each category, we present

SAMPLE BUDGET: INCOME

Source	Start-up	Operating
Parent Fees		
Registration Fees		
Tuition		
Government Funds		
Title XX		
USDA		
Other		
Fundraising		
Foundation Grants		
Individual Gifts		
Other		

Figure 9–2

guidelines that will help you maintain a realistic perspective as you estimate income. For a variety of reasons, each one of your sources of income may fluctuate over the course of the year. Acknowledging this uncertainty, it's best to be conservative and underestimate your income when preparing your budget.

■ *Tuition/Parent Fees.*   Most programs receive some portion of their income from parent fees. In Chapter 10, we will thoroughly discuss the alternate methods by which fees can be set, such as flat rate, sliding scale, and scholarship subsidy. Now, however, we simply caution you that it is important to be realistic, if conservative, in estimating how much income you will actually collect from parent fees. Many programs base their anticipated income upon full enrollment at all times with all bills paid. In fact, few, if any, programs can boast those statistics.

Simply multiplying the number of children by the rate, by the days of operation in a year will not result in a realistic estimate of income to be earned from parent fees. Instead, it will give you a "maximum potential income"—the most it is possible for you to earn. You must ascertain how much of this amount you can realistically expect to collect, so that you can anticipate the income to include on the budget. Programs that have been in operation can look at previous years' figures and calculate the ratio of "actual income" to "maximum potential income." Expressed as a percentage, this is known as the "utilization rate."

New programs should be conservative and assume that all children will take the vacations allotted, that some children will be sick for periods of time, and that once a child leaves the program, weeks may elapse before his or her space is filled. A figure that is 80 to 90 percent of your maximum income is a good rule of thumb in estimating income from tuition—especially if you have set money aside in your start-up budget for early months when enrollment may be low.

Clear policies and procedures on such issues as whether you will permit part-time users; ample notification by parents of changes in children's scheduled use of the program or long absences; and prompt payment of fees will allow you to project the income to be earned more exactly.

If you find as you sit down to plan your budget that you are unable to project your parent fees accurately because you have not, as yet, determined any of these policies and procedures, then your first task will be to make these decisions before you can estimate tuition income. (See Chapter 12 for guidelines.)

■ *Government Funding.* As much if not more caution should be exercised when you estimate your income from government funders. For a variety of reasons, the income you actually receive from any government sources may be less than you anticipated. In many states, reimbursement is linked to attendance. So even though you must have teachers available at all times, you may not receive the money to pay them unless a specific minimum number of children is always in attendance.

In all too many cases, reimbursements from government sources are paid several months behind schedule. To pay your staff or your bills, you may be forced to take a loan from the local bank. But if you take a loan, you'll have to pay interest on it—interest that the government won't reimburse you for. With today's interest rates, late payments from government agencies may add hundreds of unanticipated dollars to your expenses. Moreover, sudden freezes or cuts in funding from government agencies are always possible. For all of these reasons, many programs are wary of depending too heavily on any one government source.

No rule-of-thumb formula—such as our 80 to 90 percent suggestions regarding parent fees—can be used to estimate government revenue. However, we do have a few guidelines for ensuring that you receive as much of the government money you are eligible for as you possibly can.

First, because government reimbursement is so often linked to attendance, it is important to keep current, up-to-date waiting lists, to actively publicize your program in the community, and to keep a watchful eye on attendance patterns.

Second, because the rules for government funding are so complicated, we suggest that you take the time to understand them fully and consider in advance what factors, if any, will affect the amount you receive. For example, if you expect to use USDA Child Care Food Program funds, knowledge of the approximate income levels of the families to be served, the numbers and types of meals to be provided, and the current reimbursement rates in effect will help you to make an educated guess of your income from this source.

Obtaining as much information as possible about government rules and regulations will help you to predict realistically the money coming into the program from each of these agencies.

■ *Fundraising.* Many child care programs find that once they have calculated all of their expenses and figured out the income they can anticipate from all funding sources, there is a gap. This means that unless additional funds are generated, the program will either have to cut expenses or face presenting a budget that is "out of balance." Fundraising—whether it be on a large or small scale—is usually the method that programs employ at this point.

As Chapter 10 explains in depth, fundraising can take many forms, including requests to foundations and corporations, individual solicitations, and holding local events. In setting up your budget, be very realistic about how much money you can raise and equally clear about *who* is responsible for fundraising. When a board approves a balanced budget that includes $5,000 to be obtained by fundraising, be aware that unless this money is forthcoming the program will be $5,000 short. Therefore, as you work out the budget category of fundraising you must also set up a plan for how that money will be raised, or, at least, clarify who is responsible for seeing that it is raised.

■ *In-Kind Services or Goods.*   Such items which are donated to your program do not generally show up on your operating budget. Many programs do, however, try to "cost out," or assign a dollar amount to, the goods and services they are receiving at no charge. You may do this because you want to figure out *exactly* how much it is costing you to provide child care or because other funding sources want the information, or you may want to demonstrate the value of their services to those who are contributing to your program.

Some programs attach a separate in-kind listing to their operating budget. Others list the donated goods and services on the income side of the budget, but don't add the figures in when they tally the totals. If you choose to include in-kind resources as a component of your budget, it is essential that you balance the income with the appropriate expenses. We feel that a more accurate picture will be presented if in-kind resources are listed separately.

■ *Wrap-up.*   Your first operating budget will probably be revised several times during your start-up period as you make different decisions and then have to weigh their financial implications. However, we recommend that at some point a "final version" be approved to serve as the year's budget. This final budget should be balanced—or at least the expenses should be equal to or less than the anticipated income. It is then the program manager's task to use it as a guide for expenditures and income.

At first, the budgeting process may seem to be a huge undertaking, especially because you have limited information and experience. You will find, and most programs confirm, that each year it gets easier—you will know more about what to expect and what happens in the program will be reflected in its budget. In general, it is crucial that you develop a realistic budget and that you overestimate your expenses and underestimate your income. If you are conservative in any one area—this is the place!

The budget categories and sample formats presented throughout this chapter are meant to guide you. They are not "the" way to present your financial information—there is no set or correct method. As you experiment, you will no doubt come up with a format and a way of displaying your budget that works to your advantage— one that is clear to you and communicates well to others.

It is not enough to draw up a budget and then to step back and let the program "happen." Careful management of the expenses and income from day to day, by whomever has this administrative responsibility, will always be necessary.

Interpreting Your Budget

No matter what size your budget is, how your program is financed, or what administrative umbrella you come under, someone, somewhere, will ask: "How much does it cost?" That someone may be the school board wanting to know what it will cost them to sponsor the program or to collaborate with you; it may be the taxpayers who feel that "their" taxes are, in part, paying for the program; it may be the parents who are paying tuition for child care; or it may be a foundation to whom you are appealing for additional funds. In any case, this is a question you will hear more than once from a variety of sources.

Cost Analysis and Determining Program Costs

Figuring out your program costs can be deceptively simple: simple because you can obtain an average cost per child, regardless of how many hours each child attends, by dividing your total expenses by the total number of children who attend. With just a bit more calculation you can get a more useful and accurate figure—the cost per child-hour. This can be determined by dividing total expenses by the sum of all the hours used by each child in the program.

Both of these figures are useful, but they will not help you to adjust your costs or realistically to compare yours to those of another program. To really compare your program with another you have to translate your costs into percentages. You also have to understand the three types of costs each program has.

Factors Affecting Costs

The three types of costs every program has are fixed, variable, and semivariable. Understanding their differences and their relationship to each other is essential to determine the cost of your program.

Fixed costs are incurred no matter how many children are enrolled. They are the costs of literally "opening your doors"—rent, maintenance and utilities, administrative and office expenses (telephone, postage, audit fees), insurance, and some personnel costs (secretary, bookkeeper, director, social worker, cook). Clearly, the arrangements you have made for space and the accompanying utilities and maintenance will have a dramatic impact upon your fixed costs.

Programs that receive donated or low-cost space find that their fixed costs are considerably lower and that most of their money appears to be spent more directly on the children in care. A word of caution, however: there is generally some cost to programs for donated space, although it may not appear as dollars and cents. In some instances the price may be administrative control by another agency, or the necessity of using nonpermanent, shared space.

Very often programs will not pay rent, but will be charged an indirect cost rate—a percentage of the total budget—by the school system or sponsoring agency. Generally this charge covers all of the services that are being performed, whether they be use of the computerized payroll, access to all administrative personnel, or "free" custodial services. Don't be misled: paying a charge or an indirect rate is a cost, and, for you, a fixed cost that must always be counted in.

Another major factor affecting your fixed costs are the hours, salary, and benefits given to the nonteaching staff. Some programs are "top heavy"—having lots of money going for administrative staff time that may be excessive. Since these costs are difficult to change once you have hired your staff, careful consideration should be given to this in advance. You can always add staff and hours, but it is difficult to cut back once you have committed yourself.

Variable costs are the ones directly tied to the numbers of children in care and to your hours of operation: the costs of food, transportation, field trips, classroom supplies, and other materials. Your variable costs are apt to fluctuate from week to week and from month to month, especially in your early months of operation. Once your enrollment has stabilized, these costs will not vary quite as much. However, if your hours increase—especially for those programs that provide full-day care during school vacations and other nonschool days—these costs will also increase accordingly.

Semivariable costs, those that change somewhat with the numbers of children and hours of care, are mainly the costs of the salaries and fringe benefits of your classroom staff. When thinking about staffing patterns and costs, a variety of factors must be weighed simultaneously: you are asked to consider the staff:child ratio you wish to maintain, the group size you are planning on, and how enrollment will affect this balancing act. If you expect to have a ratio of 1:8 and a group size of sixteen children, you will probably want (or need) to hire two teachers whether you have twelve, fourteen, or sixteen children in care. In other words, the staff costs will be the same even though the numbers of children will vary. However, if you have eighteen children, you will need to hire a third teacher.

This example illustrates why classroom staff costs are considered semivariable rather than variable, and why the number of children —along with the ratios you wish to maintain—is critical in figuring your staff costs. The link between cost and quality will become clear as you staff your program. This is another reason to weigh your alternatives very carefully. You must also consider the personnel policies you choose to adopt. If your enrollment dips, will you lay off a teacher? These are not simple considerations, but they are crucial ones for your program.

Another major factor that could affect your classroom staff costs is whether you plan to use low-cost or free personnel. Use of students from a college work-study program, foster grandparents, student teachers or interns, or volunteers can lower staff costs. Our word of caution, however: consider carefully the impact of this plan upon the quality of your program.

Determining Your Breakeven Point

When you are starting a new program, one of the things you will want to know is the point at which your expenses are equal to the money coming in. According to Roger Neugebauer, editor of *Child Care Information Exchange,* "This 'breakeven point' will tell you how many children you need to enroll and how much you need to charge them in order to pay all of your bills."[2]

Your first step in figuring out your breakeven point is to identify and total your fixed and variable costs. Once you have done that, you will be able to do some figuring that will tell you how much you should

---

[2] Roger Neugebauer, "Money Management Tools—Breakeven Analysis," *Child Care Information Exchange,* No. 7 (April 1979), p. 6.

charge for tuition and the numbers of children you must enroll in order for your program's revenues to equal its costs.

How do you figure out your breakeven point? We have said that a program breaks even at the point where

$$\text{Revenues} = \text{Costs}$$

We know that revenues are directly related to the numbers of children enrolled multiplied by the tuition charged for each child in care. We also know that there are two kinds of costs: fixed costs and variable costs. (Note: semivariable costs should be considered as fixed costs when figuring your breakeven point.) So the formula can be restated as:

Revenues per Child × Breakeven Enrollment
$$= \text{Total Fixed Costs} + \text{Total Variable Costs}$$

To figure out the total variable costs for the entire program, it can be said that:

Total Variable Cost = Average Variable Cost per Child
$$\times \text{Breakeven Enrollment}$$

By substituting in the above equation, we get a new equation that looks like this:

Revenues per Child × Breakeven Enrollment = Fixed Costs
$$+ \text{Average Variable Cost} \times \text{Breakeven Enrollment}$$

Solving for breakeven enrollment in this algebraic equation, we get:

$$\text{Breakeven Enrollment} = \frac{\text{Fixed Costs}}{(\text{Revenues per Child}) - (\text{Average Variable Cost per Child})}$$

Don't let the formula scare you. Just remember that all figures must cover the same time period—a week, a month, or a year.

To clarify, let's take the example of a group starting a SACC program that wants to know how many children it needs to enroll and what tuition to charge in order to break even. They have based their budget on an assumed enrollment of thirty children, a total of $2,400 in fixed costs per month, a per-child tuition of $100 per month and an average variable cost per child of $40 per month. Then:

$$\text{Breakeven Enrollment: } \frac{2{,}400}{100 - 40} = \frac{2{,}400}{60} = 40 \text{ children}$$

Clearly, this program has got to do something or it will be in big financial trouble, since the group is only planning on an enrollment of thirty. There are a few possible alternatives. Let's compare the results of several courses of action:

1. Raise the tuition $20 per month:

$$BE = \frac{2{,}400}{120 - 40} = \frac{2{,}400}{80} = 30 \text{ children}$$

2. Lower the fixed costs to $2,000 monthly:

$$BE = \frac{2{,}000}{100 - 40} = \frac{2{,}000}{60} = 34 \text{ children}$$

3. Lower the variable cost per child by $10 monthly:

$$BE = \frac{2{,}400}{100 - 30} = \frac{2{,}400}{70} = 34 \text{ children}$$

In order for the group to keep its enrollment down to *thirty* children, it would have to raise the tuition $20 or so if it did not want to alter the costs of running the program. Or it could do both—that is, raise the tuition somewhat and lower the costs a small amount. Or, it could leave the tuition at $100 and drop the fixed cost to $1,800—a considerable drop of $600 per month. Another option would be to divide the average variable cost per child in halves.

When it is all on paper the group has many possible courses of action from which to choose. In fact, that is exactly the reason for doing a breakeven analysis—to consider all of the options in the *planning* stage so that the program does break even and doesn't run into financial problems when it's operating. The advantages and disadvantages of different courses of action can be weighed, and the group has the opportunity to examine the potential costs and benefits of each. Of course, this is no guarantee of fiscal tranquility, but it does provide a way for you to make major decisions in advance, as your program takes shape.

Chapter 10

RESOURCE DEVELOPMENT

The design of your program and preparation of your budget are in-extricably linked to two very important questions: where and how do you get the money to operate?

A variety of sources support SACC programs. Perhaps the most common source is fees from parents whose children use the program. Funds available through public or government-sponsored programs can subsidize particular aspects of program operation: fees for low-income parents, the purchase of food for meals and snacks, and the salaries of certain teachers. Space made available by public schools can offset the costs of renting space. Contributions from the private sector—from business and industry, foundations, individuals, and local service clubs—may be targeted for specific program uses or for general operating expenses.

In this chapter we will familiarize you with the major funding sources that may be tapped for SACC; explain how the funds may be obtained for your program; and, based on the experiences of SACC programs, discuss the tradeoffs involved in the use of the different sources.

Decisions about using different funding sources will have an un-mistakable impact on your program. For example, a decision *not* to use any government funding and to rely exclusively on parent fees may result in a fee structure that is quite high and that prevents the enrollment of children from low-income families. Conversely, heavy reliance on government funding may produce a program that serves only children from low-income families. Foundation funds might be targeted only for children from single-parent families, while use of school space might obligate you to serve all children on a first-come, first-served basis, regardless of family income or structure. Before you secure support from any source, you must understand what effects on the program, if any, such support will have.

The huge variation from one community to another makes it impossible to specify one "right" approach to funding. It is certain, however, that the more diversified the funding base for a program, the more likely it is to withstand shifts in community priorities or government policy, or the vagaries of the United States economy. This section shows you how to obtain funding from many different sources, but leaves the final decision about the mix of funding up to you.

Parent Fees

Most SACC programs depend on parent fees for a good portion—if not the majority—of their income. The actual percentage will vary, of course, according to the amount of other financial resources or in-kind contributions available.

There are three major systems that SACC programs can use to establish parent fees: (1) flat-fee structures, in which all parent users pay the same set rate for care; (2) sliding-fee systems, where parents pay on a graduated scale according to their ability; and (3) scholarship programs, which generally offer a tuition break to a selected number of parents, while the rest pay the full fee. Within each of these systems there can be great variation. Often, different methods are combined, or an element of one is incorporated into another. There is no reason to urge groups or programs to set up a "pure" method. In reality, most set up hybrid fee structures.

Figure 10-1 summarizes the advantages and disadvantages of all three systems. The text which follows describes each system in detail and then explains how it can be implemented successfully. After looking at all three systems, we will review some general guidelines and tips for designing the fee structure that is right for you.

Flat-Fee Systems

Flat-fee systems are those in which every parent pays the same fee for the same amount of care. In the spring of 1982, programs providing

Advantages	Disadvantages

Flat-Fee Systems

- Flat-fee systems are the easiest to figure out and to implement.
- Programs maintain close control over the amount of money to be collected—guesswork is at a minimum.
- Everyone is treated the same—all tuition payments are equal. (Unless a sibling discount is given.)

- Parents unable to afford the flat rate are unable to use the program.
- No special consideration is given to single parents, those families with unusual medical expenses, or others in hardship situations.
- Flat-fee systems may discriminate on the basis of income.
- Programs using flat-fee systems tend to be more homogeneous and less economically diverse, since all parent users must be able to afford the same fee.

Sliding-Fee Scales

- Sliding-fee scales allow parents to pay according to their ability.
- Parents with a wide range of incomes are encouraged to use the SACC program, thus resulting in a more diverse population.
- A uniform, fair system of fee reduction is used that is systematized and not based upon favoritism or whimsy.
- Once the original work is done, determining an individual parent's fee is fairly easy.

- Often, more families are eligible for the lowest payment than the program anticipated, and the scale will not generate the income needed.
- You don't really know from year to year or from month to month exactly how much money you will collect from parents.
- Some method of family income verification must be decided upon. Do programs need to require pay stubs, bank books, and legal statements regarding child support? Or is the honor system adequate?
- It is often difficult to decide what is to be counted as income (alimony, child support, child SSI payments, etc.).
- It is difficult to decide how particular financial hardship situations should be dealt with (special medical expenses, exorbitant rent, child with severe special needs).
- Some parents may have negative feelings about a fee scale that treats people differently and allows for a range of tuition payments.

Scholarship Systems

- Scholarship programs can allow some children to attend your SACC program who might be unable to do so otherwise.
- SACC programs can offer scholarships of some sort even if they raise just a small amount of money.
- The availability of scholarships can be important to a family in extreme hardship or crisis.
- A scholarship program may result in a more diverse group of children.

- In most cases, scholarship programs are limited, based upon the amount of money raised.
- Due to financial constraints, only those with extreme need may be able to receive any financial assistance.
- In order to have an ongoing scholarship program, programs must obtain and/or raise funds yearly to be used as tuition subsidy.

Figure 10-1

care during the after-school hours (3:00–6:00 P.M.) were charging fees ranging from $12 to $35 per week. In programs providing both before- and after-school care, parents are paying $25 to $60 per week. Some programs using flat-fee systems discount the cost of a second child attending the program. For example, all parents sending one child might pay $25 for the first child and $20 for the second and subsequent children.

■ *How to Make Flat-Fee Systems Work.*   Flat-fee systems work best when in-kind resources (especially donated or low-cost space, utilities, etc.) or successful fundraising have the effect of reducing everyone's tuition payments. SACC programs that are solely dependent on parents for their funds have two major problems: steep tuition and dependence on only one source of income.

Most SACC programs that use flat fees successfully have a parent population that can pay the price. However, flat fees have been used by some SACC programs that provide care to families with a wide range of income levels. This has worked when the program has reduced their costs due to free space, low cost, or volunteer staff, or because the program was extremely successful in obtaining other financial support (from United Way, USDA, or local community organizations, for example) that allowed a reasonable, affordable tuition to be charged to parents. As you will see later in this chapter, another method of making flat-fee systems work is to balance them with some sort of scholarship program for a predetermined number of families in hardship situations.

Sliding-Fee Scales

Sliding-fee scales are based on the principle that fees for SACC are dependent upon the parents' ability to pay. In a sliding-fee scale, tuition payments increase in a series of graduated steps that are linked to increases in family income. A family with an income of $25,000, for example, would pay more than a family with an income of $15,000, which, in turn, might pay more than a family with an income of $10,000.

Although sliding-fee scales can be developed in many different ways, there are two major schools of thought about their design. In the first approach, upper-income families subsidize the tuition of lower-income families. In the second approach, no group of parents subsidizes any other. Instead, families at the top of the income range pay the actual cost of care while all others get some reduction in fee. In such cases, it is important to note, program revenues will only equal program expenditures if some supplementary funds are secured. It is these supplementary funds which, in effect, subsidize the tuition for those parents who do not pay the full cost of care.

We recommend the second approach. In our experience, parents who are involved in subsidizing others, as well as those who are being subsidized themselves, ultimately became dissatisfied with the system. It is more effective to have parents of all income levels working together to bring in additional revenue for the program they all share.

■ *How to Make Sliding-Fee Systems Work.* The SACC program director who said, "It was guesswork at first, and then you can go on past experience," certainly captured the feelings of many who currently use sliding-fee systems. However, the reality is that designing a workable sliding-fee scale demands that SACC programs take a systematic approach—thinking conservatively and carefully about the actual and the potential parent users.

Collect all financial information you need to determine the range and distribution of parent incomes. Information on family incomes and other important data—number in family, for example—will help you determine ability to pay and will insure that your sliding scale truly benefits those who need it. This information will also allow you to avoid a common pitfall—a sliding-fee system where most parents are at the bottom of the slide and money coming in is insufficient to subsidize them.

Determine the actual cost of care—adjusted for reality. The top fee on the scale will be the adjusted actual per-child cost of providing SACC. This is the first figure you must obtain. Simply divide your total expenses by the number of children enrolled. Next, add 10 to 20 percent to this amount to account for the realities of underutilization, bad debts, underenrollment, etc. Then divide by whatever unit you use—week, month, day, or hour—to arrive at the correct adjusted figure for the top of your scale.

Determine a uniform system for expressing and determining how much parents can afford to pay. This is done differently by different SACC programs, but the principle is basically the same. For the most part, the figure that is used is annual gross family income, often linked in some way with the number of children in the family. One SACC program computes an *adjusted income figure* by subtracting $750 for each child in the family. In another, a family of two earning $9,000 pays at the same rate as a family of three earning $10,000, and of four earning $11,000. Whatever method you decide to use for determining what parents can pay, it is essential that you be consistent.

Method aside, how much can families actually afford for child care? Each community is somewhat different—the top amount paid for SACC at one program may be the middle of another program's scale. However, Gwen Morgan suggests 10 percent of family income as a good rule of thumb for what parents can afford to pay for child care.[1] Roger Neugebauer reports that most programs are within the 9 to 12 percent range.[2] Since these figures are for day care in general, we expect that the percentage of family income to be charged for SACC would be somewhat lower. For after-school care, we noted many programs fixing the fee at 2 to 6 percent of the parents' income.

Decide at what income level parents should pay the full cost of care. You already know that your top fee is essentially your cost of care, adjusted for reality (add 10–20 percent). You might express this monthly, weekly, or even hourly—but the formula stays the same. There are several ways to decide at which income level parents should begin to pay the full cost of care. Some programs decide what percentage of family income should be going for child care and use that to set the top of the scale. For example, if it costs a SACC program $1,200 yearly for each child (after school only), and the program would like parents at the top to pay about 5 percent of their yearly income for child care, then the top of the scale would include those with an annual income of $24,000 and up. Others base the scale on state (or city, county) figures on median income, usually setting the figure at the top of the scale at 105 to 115 percent of the median income. Another pragmatic solution is to look at the range of parent incomes, assume that at least 50 percent of the parents need to pay the full fee in order for the scale to really work, and then select the median income of the parent group as the cut-off point. What annual income amount would allow that to happen?

As you consider your cut-off point, you will probably combine a number of these methods. Clearly, you don't want to charge parents at a rate out of line with their income, nor can you afford a scale where not enough parents pay the true cost of care.

Set the bottom of the scale. How do you decide what amount of income parents must earn to be eligible to pay the lowest fee? In 1980, sliding-fee scales from SACC programs across the country generally set the bottom of their scales in the $5,000–$7,500 family income

---

[1] Gwen Morgan, *Managing the Day Care Dollars* (Boston Office of Continuing Education, 1982), p. 38.
[2] Roger Neugebauer, "Money Management Tools—Sliding Fee Scales," *Child Care Information Exchange*, No. 8 (June 1979), p. 29.

range. Some people use eligibility for Title XX as the cutoff, with the assumption that those below the fee scale can be subsidized by Title XX funds. Others set a fixed percentage, as they did for the top of the scale, and apply it to the bottom. *Essentially, the more parents who are at or near the bottom of the scale, the most conservative you have to be in reducing the bottom fee.*

To avoid having the majority of parents at the bottom of the scale you will have to be conservative about your fee reduction, making informed predictions based upon the financial information you can gather from parents. For example, if you expect more than 75 percent of the parents to be eligible to pay the lowest fee, you may decide to set that bottom fee at a figure that will enable you to generate the income you need. The crucial consideration here is whether this altered fee can still be paid by those parents at the lowest end of the scale. What percentage of their total income are they paying? On the other hand, if you feel that the tuition reduction is not substantial enough, you may work backward and try to figure out what fee would be more in line, and either try to cut your costs or raise additional funds to support the scale at that level.

Decide how to figure out the income increments and the corresponding fee charges. Roger Neugebauer outlines the following four-step method for setting the income and tuition increments:

1. Subtract the bottom income step from the income at which parents will pay the full fee and divide the remainder by *nine*. This resulting amount constitutes the income increment for the scale.
2. Subtract the lowest fee from the full fee and divide the remainder by *ten*. This figure constitutes the fee increment for the scale.
3. Add one income increment to the bottom income and one fee increment to the lowest fee. This pair constitutes the second step of the scale.
4. Add eight more income increments and fee increments in pairs. The eighth income and fee increments make up the last step in the scale. The top of this step should be at the cut-off point.[3]

If you don't use a formula such as this one, the important thing to remember is that you don't want to have huge income jumps or income categories that cover too wide a range.

---

[3] *Ibid.,* pp. 27–33.

Will the scale work? Many programs have told us stories of sliding-fee scales that didn't work and almost cost them the program. Once you have set up your scale, simulate what the results would be. Can you operate in the black? Are parents at the bottom of the scale getting enough of a fee reduction? If not, then the scale is not really fulfilling its goals—allowing and encouraging low-income people to use your SACC program.

Try to set up a scale that is clear and simple to use—not everyone has a Ph.D. in calculus! Any family should be able to pick it up, figure out its fee, *and* see some rationale for how it was set up.

Here are some additional words of advice from SACC program directors:

- Set a limit on how much you can subsidize.
- Be clear about your rationale for a sliding-fee scale, since parents may ask (and complain) about the inequities.
- Consider the federal income tax credit when you are setting up your scale.
- If you have limited income to subsidize your sliding scale, just set up a partial scale for those who need it the most.
- Set up clear, all-inclusive policies that make using the scale simpler and seem less arbitrary.

Scholarship Programs

Another approach to lowering the fees that parents pay for SACC is a scholarship system, in which a number of parents who are unable to afford the full tuition are granted a reduced fee. There are a variety of approaches to this method. Some programs have an open scholarship system. Those in need apply to receive the subsidy—explaining why they feel they qualify. A committee or the director examines the requests and disburses the limited funds based upon need. Other programs provide unadvertised scholarships: tuition breaks are based upon hardship or extreme need and result from a discussion between the parent and the program director. Still other programs give fee reductions only if the parent can perform services for the program (teaching, purchasing, carpentry, custodial), while others grant scholarships with no work requirements.

■ *How to Make Scholarship Systems Work.* If you want to subsidize parent tuition but cannot generate enough funds to support a sliding-fee scale, then a scholarship program is in order. There are three major ways to work out the financial details of a scholarship program. The first is to assume that all nontuition income obtained is to be reserved for scholarships. The second is to allocate only a portion of nontuition income or savings as a "scholarship fund." The third is to charge all nonscholarship parents more than the actual cost of care, so that, in effect, the program is generating its own scholarship monies.

Depending upon how much of the program's income is used for scholarships, the tuition fee for parent users will vary. Again, the question is always the same: how much money must be raised from parent fees, so that when it is added to the other sources of income, the total revenues equal costs?

Designing a Parent Fee System That Is Right for You

To design its fee structure, your group has to consider the needs of your community and the programmatic implications—both advantages and disadvantages—of the three major types of parent fee systems. In addition, whatever system you choose, you will be faced with a set of important tradeoffs.

No matter what system of setting fees you design, you must generate enough income to pay for a SACC program that meets your standards of quality. For example, if everyone feels that a certain number of staff members with specific qualifications are essential to your program, then adequate funds must be provided from the program's total budgets. However, paying for the quality you want may translate into tuition fees that appear to be unreasonably high for your population of parents or for your community. This tension between affordability and quality is a common dilemma for SACC, and has no simple solution. To resolve the dilemma you may have to cut expenses or to generate income other than parent fees.

Our advice is that you pay careful attention to the tuition your potential parent users can afford so that you can determine at what point a tuition would be out of reach. There seems to be a pivotal point for SACC program tuition rates—a dollar amount that will keep parents from enrolling their children or that will force them to withdraw them from the program. Once tuition goes beyond this point—which varies from community to community—parents will often have their school-age children take care of themselves or use makeshift, informal arrangements. Sliding-fee systems can help to achieve a balance between quality and affordability, especially in communities where the rates parents can pay vary widely. However, as we have said, too many parents on the bottom end of your scale can undo your SACC program's delicate financial balance. Another method is to acquire some in-kind resources that will have the effect of reducing your expenses and thus of lowering the tuition for all parents.

■ *Setting Fees for Different Program Components.*   How can you charge for different components of care—before-school, after-school, vacations—and be certain your totals add up? Since use is unpredictable, how do you know what to assume? Should different components pay for others?

There are several ways to think about charging for different care components. No matter what system or combination of fee systems you use, a first step is to list, for the entire year, the care options, days, etc. that you are charging for. You will no doubt have done this when you prepared your budget, since it is necessary when estimating your costs.

One option is to base fees upon the actual percentage of the total costs each component represents. For example, the costs of providing breakfast would be assigned to the morning component, costs of providing snacks would go to the afternoon component. Staff time would be divided accordingly, and so on. Dividing up your budget this way will let you approximate the actual cost of each care component, which can be expressed as a percentage, and allows you to price your care accordingly.

Another method is to figure out a per-hour charge for child care. This also demands that you know exactly how many hours are being used for each type of care.

There are still other methods for pricing care components. Many depend upon the results you want—that is, do you want to encourage parents to combine care options, or do you want to encourage them to use part-time care only? Is your before-school program relatively easy and inexpensive to run? Perhaps you want to charge more for it to keep your after-school charge down somewhat.

Don't be afraid to create your own combination of fee structures. One SACC program, for example, has a sliding-fee scale for its after-school component, but charges all parents the same flat rate for before-school care. Another, with a flat-fee system, charges the same rate for before-school or after-school care, but less than the combined rate for users of both components. Others do exactly the opposite.

No matter how you set tuitions for different components, keep in mind the minimum use at which you will allow a component to continue. If only three children out of twenty-five use your before-school care, will you continue to offer it? Will those three parents pay for the entire component, or will parents using after-school care pay some portion, in order to keep it alive? Many programs move slowly, offering one component first, adding others as they have smoothed out many of their problems and can use experience as a guide. This may well be the approach for your SACC program.

■ *Fee Reductions for Siblings.* Most groups starting SACC programs ask about fee reduction policies for brothers and sisters in care. Should they have them? And if so, how much of a discount should be given? SACC programs that provide reductions hope that a reduction in tuition will enable older children in the family to remain in care along with the younger ones. Some say that the cost of providing care is lowered when more than one child from one family is involved, but the reality is that costs are cut only minimally.

Fee reductions are given in a range of ways. Some programs allow parents to adjust their income based upon the number in the family. Many list a base tuition for one child and then a percentage reduction—anywhere from 25 to 60 percent—for the second. Other programs allow discounts for any number of additional children.

Although there is obviously no set formula for fee reductions, they can only be established with knowledge about who will use your program and some guesswork about how many siblings will be included in your figures. The figures of one large program may give you an idea of how the use tends to break down: 1,216 children, including 888 families with 1 child, 158 with 2 children, and 4 with 3 children. This translates into 1,050 full tuition payments (86 percent) and 166 reduced payments (14 percent).

Some programs make an educated guess about who will use the reduction, and raise everyone's tuition a certain percentage to compensate. Others treat fee reduction for siblings like a scholarship program, and raise funds strictly for this purpose. When programs offer sibling reductions and sliding-fee scales, their combined effect in reducing revenue must be considered carefully: the percentage of the full fee at the bottom of the sliding scale will be altered depending upon the number of sibling discounts expected. Some programs also base their fees on fewer children than they plan to enroll, expecting that the two or three siblings (in a small program) will generate income over and above operating costs.

When you consider whether or not to have a fee reduction policy, you must look at the possible impact of not providing a sibling discount. Will you be underenrolled? Will you lose many of the older children from the program? Only you know the community, its needs, and the possible gains and losses of having a sibling reduction policy. If you feel uncertain and afraid to take the economic chance, our advice is to wait a year and see how your program is used and by whom. This will give you more accurate information regarding the impact of a sibling policy on both your SACC program *and* your parent users.

Summing Up

The following advice from SACC programs nationwide should be considered when setting parent fees:

- Involving parent representatives in the fee setting process enables them to explain to other parents why the fee is set as it is and where the money goes.
- Fee structures should be tailored to the individual program and community. You can't borrow a sliding-fee scale from another city and expect it to work.
- Simulate your fee system and ask yourself—"Can Mrs. Jones, who has three children and is making $10,000, really afford to pay that much?"
- If your resources are limited, don't be afraid to restrict your financial assistance to those with the greatest need.
- Know your competition—consider the other options available to parents and try not to promote choice on the basis of fees charged.
- If your structure has different fees for care, be certain that you understand the rationale so that you can explain it to parents.
- Work cooperatively with other child care programs in your vicinity. Try to consider preschool day care fees when you are setting up your structure. If parents of preschoolers find they must pay the same or more for after-school care than for full-day care, your program (not to mention the parents and children) will probably suffer.
- Set a limit on how much you can subsidize.
- Consider your fees and fee structure according to the income generated *and* the design of your program. Be certain both are congruent with your philosophy.

The Schools

Public schools can offer vital and varied resources to SACC programs, including space, utilities, transportation, insurance (inclusion in the school's liability and other policies), food (snacks and/or meals from public school kitchens), and special resources and services (business manager, psychologist, bilingual specialist, nurse, librarian).

Whether SACC programs pay for these school resources—and how—also varies from community to community. In many instances, the public schools absorb the cost of most, if not all, resources, thereby enabling programs to maintain reasonable fees for parents. Such is the case in Arlington, Virginia, where twenty-four out of twenty-six elementary schools operate SACC programs under the administration of the schools; in Minneapolis, Minnesota, where latchkey programs operate within the Division of Community Education and as part of the public school budget; and in Raleigh, North Carolina, which operates an extended-day magnet school. In other locales, such as a few Massachusetts suburbs, the schools charge only for overtime custodial fees, while a community in Virginia passes on the energy costs for keeping the schools open overtime. In still other situations, such as El Paso, Texas, Madison, Wisconsin, and Portland, Oregon, the schools charge SACC programs a rental fee which is renegotiated each year. In one community, all eight school principals even charge each SACC program a different fee!

Financial Options for School Participation

In Chapter 7 we said that schools sometimes have difficulty in determining how—and what—to charge programs. There are no uniform guidelines for each community to follow, but there are several methods of deciding on fair rates. This section explains the four most common arrangements made between school systems and SACC programs: (1) no charges; (2) fees based on the amount of square footage used; (3) fees based on the number of hours a program spends on the school premises; and (4) a flat rate or fixed amount.

■ *No Charges.* Because SACC programs operate on tight budgets, using any cost savings to reduce parent tuition, raise staff salaries, or otherwise improve the program, many school systems simply waive any charges. This is especially the case when other school or community-sponsored activities which require custodians take place after school, or when custodians would normally be at school cleaning up.

In some instances, it may be difficult to figure out what costs should be assigned to SACC; in others, it is clear that the actual costs represent an insignificant part of the school operating budget, while the benefits to the school system are very significant—in both tangible and intangible ways. In some systems, schools that faced declining enrollment stayed open when they started offering after-school care; in others, SACC has given the schools a positive public image and even brought new residents to town.

■ *Square Foot Charges.*   Fees calculated on the amount of space used are usually designed to reflect the cost of maintaining a typical classroom. For example, in Maryland's Montgomery County, a program which serves a maximum of twenty-six children is mandated by state licensing requirements to have a minimum of 35 square feet of space per child. The school rooms that the program uses may be larger than that 35-square-foot minimum, but the program is charged only for the amount of space it uses—35 square feet per child. So although the program may in fact be held in a 1,000-square-foot room, it is charged at the rate of 800 square feet (or twenty-six children × 35 square feet). In this way, the school system charges are kept within reach of the program's ability to pay; the system derives some revenue to cover the costs of providing and maintaining the space; and as the number of children enrolled increases, the rent is proportionally increased.

Not every part of a space figures into the calculation: bathroom and sink space, for example, are not considered a part of the total usable space for the program. Use of other areas in the school building, such as the gym or music room, is negotiated with the principal and not figured into the square-foot calculation.

Establishing a fee policy based on the amount of space a program occupies must be done with caution. If the financial realities of the program are not considered, space charges may well undermine the financial strength of the program. In one city, separate groups of parents run twelve separate SACC programs in the elementary schools. The smallest serves fifteen children; the largest, sixty. The fifteen-child program is in a low-enrollment school with lots of extra space. If charged a fee based on the square footage used (and without regard to licensing), this smaller program would have to charge parents higher fees than a program with more children which uses the same amount of space. A blanket policy on fees based on space use might jeopardize smaller programs while not particularly hurting larger ones.

■ *Charges by the Hour.* This is essentially the same type of formula used in the square-footage method; it can work well only if costs are determined fairly at the outset so as to reflect a program's financial status. Costs would be prohibitive, for example, for a program operating full-day during summer vacations, school holidays, and days off.

Although we refer to this method as the hourly-charges method, it usually involves a square-footage formula to arrive at an hourly rate. In a Boston suburb, for example, a group of parent-run programs is charged in the following way:

1. Total square footage of 11 schools   1,980,400
   Square footage of all programs   11,200
   Day care % of square footage   .6%
2. Operation and maintenance costs for all schools $5,999,938
   Day care share of costs (.6% of operation and $36,000
   maintenance costs)
3. Total day care hours   17,280
4. Cost per hour ($36,000 divided by 17,280) $2.08

Programs thus are charged around $2 per year for the hours after school, which amounts to approximately $1,600 per year. Imagine the cost to these programs if they were to operate full time during July and August as well as staying open on vacation weeks during the school year!

■ *Flat, or Fixed Rates.* In cases where getting information on costs is difficult or where buildings are used by several groups after school hours, some schools and programs negotiate a flat rate. This may be determined by the "going rate" in the community—the amounts that other groups pay (or donate) as rent to churches or schools. The fee agreed upon initially may be adjusted either up or down as it becomes clear what the program's income will be. This is especially good as an interim plan for programs that are just starting.

What Are the Advantages and Disadvantages of Using the Schools?

For the most part, working with the schools offers SACC programs a variety of advantages unavailable elsewhere. However, collaboration also means tradeoffs. We list the most common advantages and disadvantages here:

- Collaboration with the schools usually results in a reduction in program costs, which can often be passed on to parents as reduced fees.
- Collaboration with the schools opens up a wide range of resources and services. One program in suburban Minneapolis is able to tap into a breakfast program served by school staff; another in California can use the school district's curriculum library of films, books, and other materials; still other programs do bulk purchasing through the schools and use school financial management resources.
- In some SACC programs, collaboration with the schools allows SACC staff to receive salaries and/or benefits on a par with public school teachers.
- For some programs, collaboration has solved cash flow problems. In a county school system in California, for example, when the state is late in reimbursing, the office of county schools is still able to issue checks to the family day care providers who do SACC.
- Collaboration can also mean bureaucracy or, as one school-district employee put it, "rules on top of rules." For SACC programs this can mean an endless procession of approvals—all the way up to the board of education—before budgets are approved and money can be spent.
- Unless they can be negotiated, custodial fees can break the financial back of a SACC program—especially where a custodians' union is involved.
- Rising energy costs can also break SACC programs, especially when they are passed on unexpectedly in midyear. In one SACC program, energy costs have only been contained by keeping the thermostat at 55 degrees and having children wear overcoats.

Guidelines for Collaboration with the Schools

Following is a set of financial guidelines designed to ensure fruitful collaboration between public schools and SACC programs:

- School charges to the program should not pose such a severe financial hardship that the program's original purpose—to provide good quality services to children—is threatened. Charges should be tied directly to day care revenues and to the ability of the program to pay.

- Schools can assign priorities to groups of tenants, each with a different set of costs; school boards may choose to recognize the benefits day care programs offer to the system, and might exempt them from some costs.
- Charges should accurately reflect the program's actual use of the utilities or other services. They should not be inflated in order to provide more revenues for the school system beyond covering that portion of costs directly associated with the program's presence in school buildings.
- School systems should develop a policy about the use of specialized nonclassroom areas such as gym, shop, homemaking, and playgrounds. Schools should consider the use of these areas as crucial to the program's quality, and ought to donate such resources as part of the negotiation.
- School systems should incorporate into written policy statements and guidelines all decisions about rental policy, vacation and holiday use, community use of school facilities, and user fees. Policy should be periodically reviewed with those affected by it—and policy should be flexible enough to respond to changing needs and resources. The essence of partnerships is the notion that each partner gets something from the relationship.
- Programs should provide the schools with an accurate picture of finances and projected enrollment as a good-faith way of working out reasonable payment agreements. Both partners must work at the partnership business.

Government Funds

Funds from federal, state, and local government agencies can enable you to hire and train staff, to offer services to low-income families, and to provide nutritious snacks and meals. Many programs, especially those that serve predominantly low-income groups, simply could not exist without one or more forms of government funding. Without such support, others would have to raise fees or reduce services to the point where the value of their continuing would be questionable.

For all their advantages, funds from government agencies can be extremely difficult to obtain and problematic once you obtain them. As you work your way through the bureaucracy, you will quickly discover that government funds always come with strings attached: restrictions on the income of families you can serve, requirements about your tax status, and lots of paperwork and reporting.

Recent policy changes initiated by the Reagan Administration have made government funding even more problematic. Programs such as public service employment provided by the Comprehensive Employment and Training Act (CETA) and Community Development Block Grants (CDBG), that were important funding sources for SACC programs, have virtually ceased to exist. Title XX of the Social Security Act and the United States Department of Agriculture Child Care Food Program continue, but are administered as state block grants with reduced funding. In addition, funding guidelines have become more restrictive. Under the "New Federalism," responsibility for social programs is gradually shifting to the states, which will, in general, mean that less government funding will be available for SACC programs, with keener competition for funds at the state and local levels.

Because most federal funding programs are in flux as of this writing, we suggest that you check the status of these programs with national organizations and offices such as:

>The United States Department of Agriculture
>Food and Nutrition Service
>Child Care and Summer Programs Divisions
>Washington, D.C. 20250
>(202) 447-8211

>The Children's Defense Fund
>1520 New Hampshire Avenue, N.W.
>Washington, D.C. 20036
>(800) 424-9602

>The Day Care Council of America, Inc.
>1602 17th Street, N.W.
>Washington, D.C. 20009
>(202) 745-0220

Or, consult child care information and referral agencies, state departments of social services, etc.

Other Government Funds

A variety of other as yet unmentioned local, state, and federal funding sources are being used by SACC programs around the country. Some of the money or services from these sources may be available to you. If not, it is our hope that hearing about them may inspire you to find something similar in your community or to think creatively about how available money might be used by your SACC program.

- In Connecticut, thanks to support from the governor's office, the Office of Child Day Care (OCDC) made "innovative program grants" as part of a demonstration program for "children of low-income working parents not eligible for the existing program." Each day care program approved for funding by OCDC received a decreasing percentage of state support over a three year period. The goal of this policy was to encourage programs to be cost-effective in using available public school or other rent-free space, and ultimately to become self-supporting.
- In Wisconsin, the Family After School Program in Milwaukee received a $2,500 flat grant from the state for start-up funds. This grant enabled the program to purchase supplies and equipment for its three proposed sites and to pay for mailing and publicity costs.
- In Virginia, a SACC program receives 30 percent of its funds from the County Board of Supervisors. These monies go to subsidize the program's sliding-fee scale so that care is not prohibitive to the parents who need and use it.
- In the Robbinsdale Area Schools in suburban Minneapolis, Minnesota, the Adventure Club program has received flat grants from small cities whose children attend school in the school district. This money was sought when it became clear that Title XX funds were not going to be made available to the Minneapolis suburbs. As one way of subsidizing the low-income children in this SACC program, Adventure Club looked to the cities and found where the children live. They asked them to "help subsidize a sliding-fee scale based on family income" and also asked that "the city's recreation departments work with the Adventure Club program to provide greater recreational opportunities" for the children in care.
- In one Chicago suburb, community development block grant funds were received by a program through the village funding mechanism.
- In Seattle, the YMCA program, like many throughout the country, is able to cut costs by using eligible college work-study students. The program pays a small percentage of the students' salaries while the federal government and the college pay the rest. Many of the students are able to stay with the program for a number of years while attending school, thus adding consistency to the program and increasing the program's return on

any supervision or training that is done. The major drawback of the work-study program is the college calendar's vacations and breaks, which can present severe staffing problems.

To find out about receiving work-study students, contact the financial aid office of colleges and universities in your vicinity.

There is no one tried and true method for obtaining government funds, but it does seem that programs that "pay attention" to the political process can make it work for them. Constant "positive pressure," good public relations, and lots of information sharing are crucial. Having parents, SACC staff, and board members informed about and involved in the funding process can often make a substantial difference in the outcomes. The effect of letters to politicians and other public officials about the importance of the SACC program, focusing on how certain actions will affect the program and ultimately the children served, should not be underestimated.

Understanding how to build and cement links with other community agencies and institutions may help you in your search for government funds. In fact, one program we visited advised others "to write grants in coordination with other local organizations" as a successful strategy for securing funding. We also know of one SACC program that received a two-year Law Enforcement Act Administration (LEAA) grant because it presented itself as a program that would prevent juvenile delinquency and crime. In seeking funding that may cause you to "package" your program differently, the questions you should ask are: How much do you have to redefine yourself and your goals? How much will your goals for the SACC program mesh with or be shared by the funder? And how much autonomy do you—or will you—have?

Some SACC programs are afraid to become dependent in any way on funding from the government or the schools. They feel that unpredictable losses of funding could spell disaster. For this reason—and because of the Reagan Administration's cuts in social programs—groups, agencies, and institutions running SACC programs are increasingly turning to the private sector.

The Private Sector

The private sector refers to nongovernment-related funding sources such as foundations (national and local), corporations (business and industry), community organizations (Lions, Junior League, Kiwanis, etc.), and individual donors. A detailed tour through the various sub-categories of the private sector would require a book in itself, and several good ones already exist. (See the Bibliography.) Instead, we provide an overview of possible private funding sources, their advantages and disadvantages, and the ways they have been used by SACC programs. We do not go into great depth about how to write a proposal or how to conduct a fundraising campaign. We do, however, outline the crucial steps in any strategy for private sector fundraising and refer you to what we think are the best resources for identifying funders and for writing proposals.

Foundations

There are over 21,000 foundations of several different types in the United States. However, most have one thing in common: they disburse funds to nonprofit groups, agencies, or institutions. The most commonly known foundations are the large, national ones such as the Ford Foundation, Carnegie Corporation, and Robert Wood Johnson Foundation. They restrict their giving to programs or projects that are highly innovative, have national impact, and could serve as models to be replicated elsewhere. Less well-known, but more likely to assist SACC programs, are the community and family foundations, which typically focus their giving on a specific geographic area. These foundations are as interested in meeting local needs as they are in funding innovative models.

Foundations are concerned about making sound investments which contribute to public welfare, culture, or knowledge. By and large, however, they are not willing to provide regular operating support for any program, no matter how good that program is. Foundation funds could make a significant contribution to your yearly budget but it would be unwise to think that any one foundation will underwrite your continuing operation. If you have a new program or component, applying to several foundations may be a good strategy. If you need scholarship money on a regular basis, be prepared to write proposals to different foundations every year.

■ *How to Identify Foundations that Might Fund You.*   Information about foundations is very well organized and accessible, thanks largely to the efforts of the Foundation Center, a professional organization that acts as a clearinghouse in the foundation world. The Foundation Center has a nationwide network of foundation reference collections available for free public use. Four of these—in New York City, Washington, D.C., San Francisco, and Cleveland—are operated by the Foundation Center. Over one hundred others are maintained in cooperating libraries or foundations in all fifty states, Puerto Rico, and the Virgin Islands. (Call 800-424-9836 toll free for an up-to-date referral to the collection nearest you.)

Finding the information you need will not necessarily require a trip to an official Foundation Center reference collection. In fact, the development office or library of many universities, colleges, and large social agencies is likely to have most of the publications you will need to start your search.

Your first step, after identifying an appropriate library, is to develop a broad list of prospects—foundations that have previously funded programs or projects similar in some way to yours. Two publications with subject indexes for grants of $5,000 or more, made by about four hundred foundations, make this task relatively easy. Comsearch Printouts is a computerized listing of grants by topical areas such as day care, youth programs, women's programs, etc. Each topical listing is subdivided by state, so that you can quickly identify foundations in your state which have funded similar programs. *Foundations Grants Index,* from which Comsearch Printouts are derived, is a listing of foundation grants by state, cross-referenced by subject areas. The *Index* appears annually and bimonthly as an insert in *Foundation News,* the major trade magazine for the foundation world. While the Comsearch Printouts are the quickest way to identify relevant foundations, they are not as up-to-date as the bimonthly *Grants Index,* so it is important to use both.

There are several other ways to broaden your list of prospects. First, find out if there is a special directory of foundations for your state, region, community, or subject area. In California, for example, *Funding in the Arts* and *Funding for the Handicapped* can help you identify a select pool of prospects. Second, look in the "Fields of Interest" section of *The Foundation Directory,* which lists 3,000 foundations with assets of over $1 million and/or total annual grant giving of over $100,000. Third, and only as a last resort, you can identify foundations in your state—though not by field or interest—by using Volume 2 of *The Foundation Center National Data Book,* which lists all 21,000 grant-giving foundations.

During the prospecting stage of your search, it is important to think imaginatively about the funding categories into which your program might fit. If, for example, you need funds to remodel your child care facility, don't look just for foundations that fund child care; also look for those that fund "buildings and equipment." None may have funded day care programs before, but that may be because none ever applied, not because the foundation has rules against such grants. If a large part of the population you serve is of minority or low-income status, be sure to look for foundations with particular interest in those populations.

After you have cast your net broadly and identified a full list of prospects, it is time to narrow your list down to those foundations which are serious possibilities. Many of the foundations you identified during your prospecting stage will have geographical restrictions that you don't meet; others will, on further investigation, turn out not to be interested in your type of program. You can obtain much of the information you need for the narrowing down process from *The Foundation Directory*.

To further identify those foundations whose interests most closely match yours, you can use three sources. The Foundation Center's *Source Book Profiles* provides in-depth information on the 1,000 largest foundations, including a selection of recent grants. The annual reports published by about 500 foundations will give you the most recent lists of their grantees and will also explain the foundations' purposes and grant-giving guidelines. For foundations that don't have annual reports, as is the case with many family foundations, you can find the lists of grantees by reviewing tax forms 990 AR and 990 PF, which all private foundations must file with the IRS. Reference collections of the Foundation Center have IRS records for those foundations within their state, and the Foundation Center libraries in New York and Washington have them for all foundations in the United States.

Researching foundations isn't an exact science. Many foundations that look as if they should be interested in your program will decline to review your application, saying that day care is outside their program focus. Others that seem only marginally interested in SACC will turn out to be very receptive to your application. You will develop better judgment and a thick skin after you have been at it for a while, but a sense of humor helps considerably if you are getting into the foundation game.

■ *How to Apply to Foundations.* Once you have narrowed down a likely list of prospects, you are *almost* ready to write a proposal—almost because your chances of having a proposal considered seriously will be greatly increased if you can arrange to meet with a foundation representative before submitting your proposal.

Sometimes meetings can be arranged with a simple phone call, but they are not always so easy to set up. Some foundations simply have a policy of not meeting with applicants. Others may meet with you after receiving a proposal if they want further information. Still others that are receptive to meetings before proposal submission are, like most foundations, beseiged with applicants, so it helps to have somebody who can assist in opening the foundation door to you.

There is no surefire method of making contact with the person who can help arrange a meeting, but several strategies occasionally pay off. First, see if anybody on your board or staff knows somebody on the foundation's staff, which is usually listed in the annual report. If there is no staff, see if somebody knows one of the trustees of the foundation. Second, check the annual report or IRS forms to see what other programs the foundation has supported. If you know the director or a staff person at one of those programs, don't be shy about calling to explain your situation and to ask for help with an introduction. Since foundations rarely provide continuing operating support for programs, your colleague's self-interest may not be in jeopardy by helping you out.

A meeting with foundation staff will let you explore mutual areas of interest. Very often foundation funding guidelines are couched in broad terms. A face-to-face conversation will allow you to learn what's between the lines, and to find out if and how the foundation's program of giving is changing. You may find out, for example, that the foundation is interested in some aspect of your program that you hadn't considered. A meeting will help you tailor your proposal in the most effective manner possible.

If you are able to arrange a meeting, be sure to go in with as clear an idea as possible of what you want to do, why, and how much it will cost, and how you plan to continue supporting it. Also be sure that you can explain *why* your program is in line with the foundation's stated interests. You may not be asked all or even any of these questions, but you should be prepared to answer them.

Whether or not you have a meeting, you will have to submit a proposal. Each foundation may have a different format for the submission of proposals, and it is advisable to stick to that format. One may want a three-page letter stating your needs and how you would use the funds, while another may want a ten-page proposal with a detailed budget and a list of board members. Whatever the variation in format is, essentially most foundations are looking for answers to the same common-sense set of questions. They want to know: what you want to do, why you want to do it (that is, why there is a real need for your service), how you are qualified to do it, how and when you will do it, how much it will cost, how much you want from them, and how you plan to raise other funds during or after the grant period. They want all of this information in a style that is brief, clear, free of jargon, and *personal*. Many people forget that foundation officers are real people; they want to know how the money they grant will make a difference in human lives. Putting all this somewhat differently, a good proposal should be a document that is readable and usable by your board, staff, and by you, because it should present a clear plan of action and results.

There are many books and articles available on proposal writing, some of which are available at the cooperating collections of the Foundation Center. However, the single best publication on proposal writing is *Program Planning and Proposal Writing*. It is available in both a brief and an expanded form from The Grantsmanship Center, 1031 South Grand Avenue, Los Angeles, California 90015 (Telephone: 213-749-4721).

■ *What If You Don't Get Funded?*   If you aren't funded by a particular foundation, use the experience to help you. Send a thank-you letter, and ask if you can talk with their staff about the reasons for the denied request; you may be able to learn from the rejection and ease the way for a future application.

Corporations, Business, and Industry

This category refers to the resources that are available from different segments of the business community, including corporate foundations (the "giving arm" of a corporation that has been set up as a separate foundation), large national corporations, large local corporations or businesses, and small local businesses.

As of this writing, corporations are able to deduct up to 10 percent of their pretax profits from their taxable income if they donate it to nonprofit organizations. However, only about 1 percent of the corporations in the United States donate up to 10 percent. In reality, those that do, tend to do so for other reasons: improving the quality of life in their community; directly benefiting employees and their families; and receiving positive publicity for the company.

It is not possible to paint a clear picture of all of the various resources that the corporate world has and is willing to share with SACC programs. Appealing to the business sector for resources is a fairly new approach, and the corporate community in general is a vast, untapped resource. Nevertheless, a number of day care programs have worked successfully with the business world. Here are some examples:

- Corporate foundations have made grants to individual SACC programs that they have used to purchase equipment, renovate space, or to augment the program's scholarship fund.
- A consortium of businesses has supported a needs assessment on SACC.
- A large midwestern company has acquired property in the country, some miles from its physical plant, and set it up as a summer day camp for the school-age children of its employees.
- As part of their fringe benefit packages, many companies pay a certain percentage of an employee's child care costs, and some corporations have established mechanisms for providing information and referral regarding child care options in their areas. Such benefits have been made more attractive to employees with the new tax law, formally known as the Economic Recovery Tax Act of 1981.
- A large company regularly donates truckloads of renewable scrap materials to a central resource center that is freely used by day care centers in the area.
- A printing company donates boxes full of paper to any day care program that will pick them up.
- A national corporation located in a small town whose inhabitants are largely company employees did a town-wide needs assessment and subsequently started an on-site day care center—heavily subsidized by the company—for the children of employees.
- An accounting office provides a yearly audit and other services to a SACC program at no charge.

It is important to note that businesses, unlike foundations, have more than money to offer SACC programs. They also have goods and services. You may want different things from different segments of the business community, and it is important for you to figure out what you want before you make your approach.

■ *How to Identify Prospects in the Business Community.* Compared to the foundation world, the business world is vast, diffuse, and not as easy to penetrate. Corporate foundations can be identified through several publications available at Foundation Center collections, including *Corporate Foundation Profiles.* However, corporations themselves do not have to reveal the recipients of their contributions. Not all corporate sponors seek the high visibility of the companies that sponsor television programs!

Several easily available sources may, however, lead you to potential contributors from the business world. Your local Chamber of Commerce can help you identify businesses likely to be interested in day care. These are often companies with high concentrations of female employees. The Chamber may also lead you to companies that would be willing to share their scrap materials or services with you. The business section of your local newspaper will keep you apprised of new businesses in the community, which might want the publicity attached to any contribution. And don't forget the annual reports of other social agencies. They may list business contributors who could be contributing to you next year!

■ *How to Apply to Businesses.* As with foundations, your best entrée is through a personal contact: perhaps a parent using your program, a board member, or a friend who works for one of the companies you are planning to approach. A sympathetic, supportive insider can give you a sense of how the company works, who has the decision-making power, and what avenue would yield the most positive results. This person might also help you formulate some specific answers to the important question of *what you can do for the company,* and might help arrange a meeting for or with you.

Businesses may not be used to receiving requests from SACC programs, but at some point they will want your application in writing. A brief (two- to three-page) letter answering the same questions as your foundation proposal should do the trick. If they want more, they will ask for it. Remember to keep it clear, personal, and to the point!

Community Organizations

Most communities have local chapters of national organizations such as the Junior League, Kiwanis Club, Rotary International, League of Women Voters, etc. In addition, there are other existing organizations or institutions (church groups, PTOs, etc.) that are involved in community affairs. Most of these groups have a range of goals and purposes that are determined by the members of the organization, but some type of community service is usually a key component of their work. Some of these groups respond to specific funding requests by outside groups, while others assume some portion of the "problem" and attempt to solve it themselves.

If you are considering asking a group or an organization to sponsor your SACC program, to play a major role in start-up, or to donate a large sum of money, the process will probably differ. In cases where community organizations have been instrumental in starting a SACC program, the impetus has often come from within the group itself. For example, in a Boston suburb, the League of Women Voters was interested in starting a SACC program. The members of the chapter took this on as their group's work, and divided up the tasks that needed to be done. In this situation, the community group itself became the "action" group—doing needs assessments, contacting other agencies and groups, and building a coalition of interested community members. However, parents or other interested individuals or agencies can contact community organizations at different points along the way and enlist their support.

In many cities and towns, a directory of community organizations is published by the Chamber of Commerce, the city itself, or an agency such as the Association of Mental Health. If contacting your local government yields no such central listing, then the telephone directory, local newspapers, public library, and long-time citizens of the community can all help you to fill out your list.

■ *How to Apply.*   Because these groups are rooted in the community, it is important to find out who their members are. Any member should be able to tell you what the group's priorities are, in terms of both how and where it spends any money it might have, and how it handles those priorities. For example, is the group apt to give money for something it believes in and let others do the work? Or is it likely that members will want to become directly involved with the project themselves? Or might the group organization be interested in making an in-kind donation? Learning what interests and priorities an organization has will help you to know if it will be interested in your program or project. Finding out how it responds to things it cares about will give you a sense of what you might expect from the organization or what would be reasonable to ask for.

■ *Individual Donors.*   Wealthy community members or others may be willing to contribute substantial sums of money to your program. Some programs, using the accumulated knowledge of many people, compile lists of such individuals and then send personal letters requesting donations. Others adopt a one-to-one approach, tailoring their appeal to the individual. Often this means providing tours of the program, discussions with the staff, or whatever else is necessary to help the potential donor see the merits of the SACC program. One SACC program even tries to get will bequests by having board members talk to community members about including the SACC program in their wills.

In addition to asking wealthy people for large sums of money, many programs appeal to a larger pool of potential donors for smaller contributions. This is generally done near the end of the year, as individuals are thinking about their taxes. Many organizations feel that this is the best time of year to obtain small, tax-free contributions from individuals. Lots of small contributions do add up. Also, you may be able to institutionalize this process so that it happens yearly and your donors become "sponsors" or "friends" of the program. In addition, perhaps you can think up an inexpensive way to give these people recognition. This may act as the impetus for others who will want to join the group.

Fundraising Events

In reality, many SACC programs depend upon fundraising events, both large and small, for the majority of their nontuition funding. Some groups find that with a good idea and many people willing to do their share, a lot of money can be raised. Others find themselves spending hours and hours of time for a project that nets only a small return. If your program needs a small amount of money (under $500), a couple of small events—such as bake sales or garage sales—might just do the trick. If a substantial sum is needed, then a large-scale event or combinations of events will be called for. Whether the events are large or small, there are some common questions that should be answered to insure success.

■ *When Should Fundraising Events Take Place?* The timing of fundraising events is usually an important factor in their success. Proper timing will probably depend upon the nature of the event itself (for example, a Christmas fair will likely be held in December), the other community events that you are competing with, the availability of volunteers to work on the project, and the SACC program's financial needs. Clearly, if you are planning to raise funds for scholarships, your event should be held well in advance of the period when those funds are to be used. If many of your volunteers take their vacations during the summer, this would probably not be the time to expect planning for a successful event to take place.

■ *Who Should Be Responsible for the Project or Event?* The answer depends largely upon the scope of the project and the accompanying tasks that must be accomplished. No matter what the nature of the project is, there must be one person (or a small committee) who is clearly in charge and is able to coordinate all of the different activities. It is also important that enough responsible volunteers be involved in the project so that a few people aren't overburdened and "burned out" from overparticipation. Involving different individuals in a project that has responsible, clear leadership broadens the base of support for the project, commits more people to its success, and provides more of a "fun" experience for the volunteers. Also, the learning that results from any such endeavor can then be shared by more people.

■ *Who Is the Fundraising Project Aimed at?*   An important step often neglected by novice fundraisers is identifying the audience in advance. For example, if your SACC program is planning to sell Christmas trees, you want to be certain that the adult population in your community knows this, that you are well-located for easy access, and that you are "open for business" during the evening and weekend hours when most people buy their trees. In this case, you must also know all of the details about "the competition." This will allow you to compete fairly and raise the funds you need. A roller-skating day at the local rink would demand advertising in places where potential "customers" would be reached: plenty of signs up at shops that sell or rent skates and at rinks. Also, your group might want to bill it as a family event and approach different community groups who are always looking to join in such activities.

Many fundraising events fail because the "audience" isn't clearly defined and the fundraising effort is misdirected. Others fail because they depend too heavily on the goodwill of the SACC program's friends and relatives. Continually tapping the same group of people for funds will eventually result in little or no success. If you have frequent fundraising projects, it is probably best to reach out to different groups of people, offering something that really benefits them and provides more than the opportunity to give to "charity." For example, one day care program sponsored two evening presentations by well-known plant and gardening experts in the early spring when everyone was thinking about their gardens. Tickets were reasonably priced as a series, and plants and books were on sale in the auditorium lobby. They advertised to the general public within a twenty-mile radius of the town, all of the local garden clubs were called or visited, and signs were placed in nurseries and plant and flower shops in the community. The audience was delighted with the evenings, and the day care program made over $2,000. A huge success.

■ *"How Do You Know If a Fundraising Project Is Worth Do-*
ing?"   Many people ask this question after an event they have spent
months preparing for netted a very small return. Was there some
formula they could have used that would have told them not to take
on the project? Should they have known better?

The best way to calculate whether an event or project is worth
doing is to carefully figure out all of the expenses, maximum income
you will obtain after expenses are paid, and "person time" you think it
will take. Be as realistic as possible—include *all* of the costs you can
think of as well as accurate estimates of needed volunteer time. To see
if a fundraiser is worth doing, Roger Neugebauer, editor of *Child Care
Information Exchange,* suggests dividing the total dollars to be earned
by the person-hours needed. You will then arrive at an estimated
dollar-per-hour figure. He says, "If the result is less than $10 per
hour, the project is probably not worth the effort. From $10 to $25
per hour, it is of marginal value. Above $25 per hour, it is clearly
worthwhile. Really successful fundraisers have been known to yield
$100 per hour."[4] Although this formula is not magic, it may provide
some guidance in determining the merits of a particular project.

In general, most people feel that a "successful" fundraiser is
judged by the amount of money raised. However, for your own reasons, you may want to plan an event that you hope is a fundraiser, but
that has other goals that are of more importance. For example, many
programs sell program T-shirts, bumper stickers, and buttons for
purposes other than making a profit. Therefore, when weighing the
merits of a particular fundraising project, allow your priorities and
goals to guide your decision making.

---

[4] Roger Neugebauer, "Managing Your Money, Avoiding the Pitfalls," *Day Care and Early
Education* (Fall 1979), p. 32.

Chapter 11

FINANCIAL MANAGEMENT

Raising the funds to start your SACC program is essential, but your hard work will soon be worthless unless you pay careful attention to managing the funds properly. From our experience, there are some general operating principles that are common to programs that are well-managed financially, regardless of their administrative structure, size, or philosophy.

- Checks and balances are built in: all money that comes in and goes out is recorded in a number of places, and people check one another.
- Formal systems are developed and used: systems for recording funds received and disbursed are set up and used by all.
- Lines of responsibility are clearly drawn: tasks are broken down so they are manageable and they are assigned to the appropriate individuals within the program.
- Procedures are outlined: everyone knows whom to consult about what—and when to do so.
- Information essential for decision making is available: all of the systems and written forms are designed so that information is easy to find and understandable.
- Emergencies have been "planned for." As much as possible, contingencies have been considered and funds set aside so that financial disaster can be averted.
- Detailed records document all financial activities.

To manage a SACC program's finances, you must know exactly what information you will need—and in what format it will be presented—to fulfill your obligations to funding sources. Besides meeting the needs of your own program—board, parents, staff—you must also determine if there are others, such as a school board or umbrella agency, who will need or want financial information about your program. Knowing the answers to these questions in advance will allow you to design systems that work for you and that meet everyone's needs.

Before we discuss how to set up a financial management system, we must introduce you to the two systems of accounting. "In *cash basis* accounting, transactions are recorded at the point where funds actually come into and flow out of the program. In *accrual basis* accounting, in addition to recording transactions resulting from the receipt and disbursement of cash, you also record the amount you owe others and others owe you."[1] In the discussion that follows we assume that most SACC programs will use cash basis accounting, primarily because it is simple to set up and use *and* because the nature of most SACC programs demands close attention to the *actual* cash transactions. Accountants and books on this subject can be most helpful to groups who are having difficulty deciding between these two systems (see Bibliography).

Recording Expenditures and Income

As you attempt to set up a workable bookkeeping system that allows you to keep track of the funds flowing into and out of your program, a range of questions will come up. In this chapter we raise many of these questions and present answers that combine our experience with the advice of others.

Purchasing

- *Ordering:* Who may order materials and/or services? Who must be consulted? Who must grant approval? How is ordering to be done? in writing? via telephone? What recording system is to be used?
- *Direct Purchase:* What are the rules and procedures for buying items directly from a store or wholesaler? Must prior approval

---

[1] Malvern J. Gross, Jr., and W. Warshauer, Jr., *Financial and Accounting Guide for Non-profit Organizations,* third ed. (New York: John Wiley and Sons, 1979), p. 15.

be given? Under what conditions will individuals be reimbursed? Who may purchase what items? What payment systems are to be used?

In both areas, we recommend that programs spell out clearly *who* is responsible for ordering and purchasing supplies and equipment and *what* the procedure is for doing so. In some programs, for example, the secretary/bookkeeper may order all supplies, with the clear stipulation that he or she may only do so upon consulting with appropriate staff, such as the teachers or cook. In other programs, actual purchasing of food and classroom consumables is done by the teachers, cook, or other staff—with the assumption that they are most aware of their needs and that many of these purchases will be made at the last minute.

We recommend either (1) that one person be in charge of all purchasing (which is based upon the needs of others) or (2) that the people who are responsible for different aspects of the program make purchases for their own areas—based upon a budget. For example, the curriculum coordinator or head teacher might buy all classroom supplies and equipment, the cook might buy all food and food service supplies, and the nurse consultant might purchase all first aid materials. Whatever method you choose, there must be one person who is responsible for coordinating purchasing with the SACC program's budget.

Making Payments

What system is to be used when paying for goods and/or services? Who is responsible for such payments? When should payments be made? What records are to be kept—where and by whom? Will checking accounts and petty cash be used? How will they be set up?

All SACC programs—regardless of size—must purchase and pay for some materials. We recommend that programs have at least one checking account. In fact, one legal requirement of incorporation is that a separate bank account be established. A large agency that has a preschool and an afterschool program would probably set up an account for each component.

One person should be responsible for making all payments. This way, he or she can set up a uniform system for recording transactions, can deal directly with individuals regarding accounts receivable, and can pay bills at the same time each month. Bookkeepers, directors, administrative assistants, and parent treasurers at different SACC programs have stressed the importance of balancing the payments to be made with the program's cash position. Although bills must be paid on time, so must staff—and sometimes a choice has to be made between the two. In a pinch, creditors may be called and will usually extend the due date on a particular bill if you explain the circumstances.

Payments that are made should be recorded in a number of places. The cancelled check and the checkbook itself are not enough. Programs should set up a system in which they record all payments and credits as they are made, and in which they record like transactions together (for example, salaries, supplies). If your program does not have access to a bookkeeper who can set up and maintain records of this sort, see the Bibliography for books that can provide some guidance.

We recommend that checking accounts build in a dual-signature system. This means that all checks should literally pass through the hands of two people—one individual should not merely sign a pad of blank checks. Although many centers find it inconvenient for two people to see and sign each check, this procedure goes a long way toward ensuring good fiscal management.

You should reconcile (balance) the monthly bank statement each month. By doing so, any mistakes you or the bank has made are picked up early. If all financial matters are handled by one person—as is the case in most SACC programs—we suggest that a different person look over the books, checks, etc., every month. Although this practice may seem to imply suspicion or mistrust, it is accepted as a necessary part of sound financial management, and is employed by all well-run businesses.

One of the biggest trouble spots in many SACC programs is the handling of petty cash. A petty cash system is usually set up because small, last-minute items are often needed or because people often make out-of-pocket purchases for which they expect reimbursement. We urge you to set up a petty cash system carefully, and to pay close attention to it. Insist that reimbursement will be given only when receipts for purchases are presented. Many SACC programs keep $20 to $50 in petty cash on hand, which means that the cash box, at any one time, never has more than $20 to $50 of cash and receipts. For example, in a $50 fund, the box might contain $23 in cash and receipts totalling exactly $27. When the cash drops to the $10 mark, the person in charge adds up the receipts and writes and cashes a check for the total amount spent.

If too many large purchases or expenses in one area of your

budget are made with petty cash, they will not show up on your expense record and thus will be underrepresented. For example, if every week the cook buys $20 worth of food out of the general petty cash account, then over the year close to $1,000 will be spent on food that might only show up as a petty cash expense—not specifically as a food expenditure.

The payment systems you set up will have to fit the scale of your organization. If you are a large, twenty-site program with a central office managing the financial record-keeping, bills will probably be forwarded to the office for payment, and separate accounts will be set up by the fiscal manager for the different programs. However, a petty cash fund might exist on each site for the small payments that need to be made on the spot. Smaller programs will probably have all of these activities going on within one office. Even though the scale is different, the same care must be taken to document, to record, and to provide double-checks.

Receiving Payments

How are tuition and other funds that come into the program recorded? Once recorded, what is the procedure? Many SACC programs receive funds regularly, with parents' fees comprising the bulk of the cash inflows. Money coming in, just like money going out, must be recorded in a number of locations. In one SACC program, the administrative assistant receives all payments, dates them, and lists them daily, by check number and name, in a notebook set up for that purpose. She then hands them over to the bookkeeper, who records them in the books and lists each payment separately on a checking account deposit ticket. *All funds received are deposited daily*—a practice we advise others to adopt. Also, cash received is *never* used for purchases—it is always deposited at once.

Like all other procedures, those developed for incoming payments must meet your needs. Many programs set up a book or a file with a page for each family or child. Tuition payments received are recorded and dated, allowing easy access to complete information about any individual family's account. Some programs prefer to develop their own forms for that purpose; others use card systems or journals. Whatever the system, the principle is the same—you must know how much money you received on a given day *and* you must have a running record of the total received from different individuals and funding sources.

Parent Fee Policies

Clear, explicitly communicated policies regarding parent fees are essential to your SACC program's financial health. Carefully worked out sliding-fee scales or scholarship programs will be extraneous if tuition money is not collected as needed. Well-thought-out fee collection policies and procedures are as important to your program's well-being as is the fee system itself. Setting the policies is not enough, however; they must be fairly enforced in order to yield the best results. Here are some suggestions for different areas in which policies should be established. Chapter 12 discusses them further.

■ *Decide Who Should Collect Fees.* Many parent-run programs have parents collect fees; others assign this responsibility to the bookkeeper or director. Still others assign it to a teacher. It is important that parents know exactly whom to pay. Failure to establish a policy in this area may result in lost checks. (Didn't I give the check to you . . .? No, maybe I gave it to . . . .) A trustworthy, mature individual should be given this responsibility—with double-checks built in. Many SACC programs have found that combining the teaching and the bill collecting roles undermines both and often results in a strain upon parent-teacher relations.

In one parent-run program in the East, the parent-treasurer collected fees—everyone else's checks, that is, but he paid no tuition himself! Examples like this suggest the importance of setting up a system with checks and balances built in—perhaps where one person collects and records the payments, and another deposits them in the bank. We recommend that a person who has no teaching responsibilities be responsible for fee collection. If possible, a bookkeeper, administrative assistant, or parent-treasurer should have this job, with a clear recording and depositing system built in.

■ *Decide When Fees Are to Be Paid.* Programs must be decisive as to when payments are due. Although we have found a great deal of variation regarding the times at which fees must be paid, we agree with the advice of a SACC program in California: "Make a policy that tuition is to be paid in advance—this has to be a policy in order to survive." This will help your SACC program to be financially stable—after-the-fact payments will have a negative effect on your cash flow.

It is important to choose a payment system that won't overburden the parents but will allow you to have the cash on hand that you need. In setting your timetable, you should think about *when* you will need large amounts of cash—for staff payroll and rent, for example—and try to collect parent fees in advance of these outlays.

What payment systems are commonly used? We have seen SACC programs that collect fees weekly, biweekly, monthly, and quarterly. We have seen some programs calculate the sum of the entire year's tuition payments and then divide the total into equal installments, and we have seen others figure out the exact number of hours (or days) the program will be used and then estimate the fee to be paid. Some SACC programs collect fees following the week of care provided. Essentially, you must balance what parents can manage with what the program needs *and* with the work involved in fee collection itself. Again, we recommend that fees be paid in advance unless your program is run on a drop-in basis, and the care provided is extremely variable.

It is important that you set actual dates or deadlines for payment of fees. It is also important that you have a clear procedure that can be put into motion when and if fees are not paid on time. This is essential, since late payment and nonpayment of fees are two critical problems experienced by SACC programs nationwide.

■ *How Should User Fees Be Collected?*   One SACC program we know of gives parents a book of vouchers with monthly due dates stamped on each; the parent tears one out of the book each month and sends it to the program with the payment. Many other programs send out bills to parents, asking that they be paid by a certain date. Still others ask parents to pay for care by the first of the month and only bill those who haven't done so by the tenth. Again, the method of collection varies tremendously—often depending upon the size of the program and the administrative and other support services available.

We advise you to set up a system that can be managed by your staff and is clear to parent users. A complicated billing and double-entry accounting system may sound like a great idea, but if staff and/or parent time isn't available to keep it up, then it is virtually useless.

■ *Consider Collecting a Registration Fee.*   Many SACC programs collect a one-time-only registration fee. This can range from $5 to $25 and is generally nonrefundable. Some programs apply the amount to the first tuition payment; others collect it as a flat fee for enrollment costs. Many programs have instituted this fee after having spent hours of time meeting with and doing paperwork for children who, although signed up, never did enroll. This fee may cause parents to consider registration a bit more carefully, and it will allow program directors and teachers to feel compensated for the time they spend with new children during the enrollment process.

■ *Consider Requiring a Deposit of Some Kind.* SACC programs have told us stories of children who have left the program, owing tuition. As a way of avoiding this situation, many programs require that parents pay a deposit (one or two weeks' fee) in advance that can be used as their final tuition payment. Again, the viability of this practice depends a great deal upon the parents. Will it prevent parents from using the program? If so, it may not be a procedure you want to adopt.

■ *Decide in Advance and Communicate in Writing to Parents What the Policies and Procedures Will Be.* Most programs set up a regular schedule of care and charge parents whether the child is there or not. Some programs have a policy that allows children to take a vacation of a limited time at no fee, half-fee, or full fee. If this policy is to be fair to everyone, parents must give the program substantial advance notice. Also, some programs give sick children a fee waiver if the sickness extends past a certain number of days. Your policies in this area must dovetail with the rules imposed by other funding sources.

■ *Storm/Snow Days Policy.* Many programs—due to their public school locations—are forced to close on bad-weather days. In such cases, most programs pay staff and collect fees from parents. Some programs only pay staff for days worked. Some refund the money to parents. Many programs are open for a full day on snow days and only charge parents for the hours that care is used. Setting policy in this area is essential. We know of one program where the parents insisted on receiving a refund—a total of over $200—for care not provided. This cost the program hard feelings and funds it did not have.

■ *Policy on Late Pick-ups.* The late pick-up problem is one we heard about at every location we visited. Knowing this, we urge you to develop a strong policy and a penalty fee regarding this infraction of the rules. Many programs charge parents at a rate equal to the teacher overtime; others levy a penalty that is high enough to discourage a repeat of the offense, while still being affordable. In many cases, the first late pick-up calls for a verbal warning—after that, the fee is charged. Although we are not unsympathetic to the causes of lateness or to the problems that are often out of a parent's control, programs tell us with resounding voices that they have developed these policies only because of the many negative effects late pick-ups have on the program and the staff. They consider their firm stance a protection for their staff.

■ *Late Payment or Nonpayment.*　Late or nonpayment of fees can have drastic effects on a program's ability to meet its expenses. Many programs report that they developed policies in this area as a result of problems. We would advise you to develop a system at the beginning and to use it systematically. Many programs try informal, face-to-face interactions as a first step. One program director advises: "Find out why they are not paying the fee." She feels that the reasons will help you to decide upon a next step. However, the overwhelming advice from SACC program directors is to deal with payment problems at once and not to let parents get behind. We would also advise you to put in writing to parents a clear statement of what is owed, when it was due, and your willingness to discuss the problem with them. If you plan to stop providing care by a certain date if parents have not talked to you, this should also be communicated.

Because they are performing a social service, many SACC programs hesitate to take a strong stand on fee collection and policies. We urge you to remember that if you don't have sufficient funds to pay your staff or your creditors, you will be doing a disservice to others. Obviously, you must strike a balance between being fair, clear, and helpful. We are certain that in the long run you will be glad you have policies in these areas so that you can be firm without being arbitrary, and so that you won't open the checkbook on payday to find that you are unable to pay your staff.

Payroll Procedures

Since personnel costs make up 70 to 85 percent of most SACC programs' budgets, procedures for payroll management are not to be minimized. Payroll is handled in different ways, depending upon the size of the program and on whether schools or other large institutions are involved. In many instances, public and community school-run programs have their payrolls done by the school business office, which uses a computerized system. They will charge your program for a set number of hours a week that the central office works on your payroll. In other large programs, a central office does the payroll without the aid of a computer.

We recommend that one individual be responsible for payroll— whether that is his or her major task or only one of many—and that a dual-signature system be used. In addition to entering the payroll amounts in the ledger, you should keep track of the yearly amounts paid to each employee. This may be done by keeping a file system, payroll sheets especially designed for this purpose, or whatever method you prefer.

It is important to keep a running record of individual staff salaries in addition to your total sum of amounts paid out. At the end of the year, you will have to furnish staff with W-2 tax forms that detail their gross salary and amounts withheld for that year. A separate accounting for each employee will streamline this task. You may also have to think about making cost-saving cuts in program expenditures at some point during the year. If so, glancing at each employee's wages earned will prove helpful.

In addition to recording salaries paid out, SACC programs have to decide when to pay staff and set up a proper accounting system to compute and record amounts to be withheld from checks for taxes, Social Security (FICA), unemployment, and health insurance.

The decision about when to pay staff may be more complicated than you imagine. Payment should be coordinated with money flowing into the program, so that the cash is on hand to pay out. This is especially true for programs that are not part of larger organizations, which have more funds on hand. Also, you must consider the needs of your staff and the bookkeeping time involved. Clearly, a compromise will have to be reached.

Many programs pay staff by the hour, while others pay a set yearly salary. Different systems usually call for different methods of computing payroll. One method used is a strict dollar amount multiplied by the hours worked. Any overtime (which was on a time card, signup sheet, etc.) is also computed and added to the amount. When staff is salaried, one method used is to divide the yearly total into equal segments, so that the employee's pay remains constant. Some of the books listed in the Bibliography will present additional possibilities, with information that will help you to figure out which system is best for you.

Computing and recording all of the amounts to be withheld from employee checks can be time-consuming and a bit complicated until you get the hang of it. Your SACC program is responsible for withholding both federal and state income tax. In addition, you may choose to withhold FICA tax (Federal Insurance Contributions Act—Social Security) as well as state unemployment insurance (depending upon claims, etc.). Also, if you require employees to pay a portion of their own health insurance, you will withhold a certain amount for this purpose. The *Legal Handbook for Day Care Centers* and government publications explain in great detail how their systems work and what SACC programs' responsibilities entail. Failure to pay attention to these deductions and payments will, in the long run, catch up with you. We advise you to learn the rules and follow them to the letter.

Billing

Some SACC programs may never need to bill any agency or individual. However, most programs find that they must bill federal or state agencies for funds, and parents for tuition. If this is the case, we advise you to ask the agency for all of its written material regarding guidelines, as well as all required forms. Also, most government agencies are supposed to provide technical assistance to grantees. Have them show you how they want bills and invoices filled out.

We suggest that when you deal with agencies you get to know individuals personally in order to facilitate the processing of your request. Since your bills will often be for large sums of money, it is critical that you attend to all details connected with their payment. One SACC program director told us that he always hand-delivers his bill to the department of social services. He knows the man who processes it by his first name and often receives a call from him when it is completed. In this case, a little time invested by the director goes a long way.

You should keep carefully documented records of all billing. Copies of letters sent, for instance, should always be available.

Reporting Expenditures and Income

All of the care you have taken to document and record your actual expenses and income will pay off when it comes time to report the facts. Essentially, your records will demonstrate how you are actually taking money in and spending it, in comparison to how you thought or hoped you would. You are examining your current practices against your budget, or plan.

However, it is almost impossible to look over all of the different entries in your checkbook, ledger, or journal and gain any insight into your financial position. For this reason, SACC programs should draw up monthly income and expense statements. These statements, in whatever form they are presented, serve as a summary of the month's financial activities.

In order to prepare an income/expense statement, the first step is to total the monthly income and expenses for each of the line items listed on your budget. On one sheet of paper you should reproduce your budget categories with columns headed: This Month; Year to Date; and Budgeted Year to Date. (See Figure 11–1.) The actual amounts for the current month should be filled in, along with the total amount spent in each category since the beginning of the fiscal year. The final column should have a figure that represents the amount you budgeted for the same year-to-date period. This statement, presented on one sheet, will allow you to scrutinize the funds that flowed into and out of the program during the month. It will present the total picture—a snapshot—of how you are actually doing, compared to your budget for the same time period.

These statements should be drawn up and studied monthly. The information presented will help you to identify categories that are "out of sync" with your budget and to make any necessary changes. Since your statement will reflect the actual transactions, your SACC program may appear to be in serious trouble when, in fact, a government check that is late has thrown your income off for the month. Or, if you have line item expenses that are paid all at once (staff training, food service equipment), a look at the expense/income summary may cause unnecessary alarm.

Besides the recording you do for your own use, it is likely that you will need to communicate much of this information to others. Most funding sources require some type of year-end and/or midyear re-

INCOME AND EXPENSE STATEMENT
February 1982

	2/82	Y.T.D.	Budgeted Y.T.D.
Income			
(List all sources)			
Total			
Expenses			
(List all categories)			
Total			
Net Gain (Loss)			

Figure 11–1

port. If you are a part of a larger organization, you may need to submit summaries of some type to the executive director or to the board. Always find out in advance what is required, to ensure that you have collected the necessary information. Once you have the information, putting together a report is fairly straightforward.

Budget Deviation Analysis

Your monthly income and expense statement may reveal that you have drawn up a budget that is not realistic. This may be due to a host of reasons—and it is important that you acknowledge it early in the fiscal year and do something about it as soon as possible. A process that will prove to be invaluable to you if you find yourself in this situation is a *budget deviation analysis*. This is a complicated name for a common-sense procedure: using your income and expense statement to figure out where you are deviating from your budget and by what percentage, in both positive and negative directions.

First look carefully at the large expense and income categories to see how far off you are in those areas. Don't be fooled by the percentages—a $25 line item that is 75 percent off is not as crucial as a $10,000 one that is 5 percent off. When thinking about how and where to reduce your expenses, consider what each one represents in terms of its impact on your program for children and also in terms of its percentage of the whole. Cutting a line item in half may seem to be a viable solution, but when you consider it carefully you will realize that this expenditure may only represent 5 percent of your budget, and all you would save is $100. This is probably the wrong place to look for cost savings when you consider the minor effect it would have on your program.

Once you have figured out your greatest areas of deviation, your group can then decide what must be done. Your first step should always be to try to be more careful about spending, to be certain enrollment is monitored, and to see if your problems really are in managing the money. However, if the comparison between the actual and the budgeted amounts causes you to conclude that you planned incorrectly, or that sudden unexpected changes in expenses or income are the problem, now is the time to revise the budget.

Use all of the information you have gathered to help you rethink the budget, adding and subtracting where reality has indicated you must. Clearly, you have to make some financial changes or the problem will not make it through the year. Like everything else you do, this will be a balancing act. You will be thinking of your priorities and goals and trying to weigh those against the budget items. You may find that your changes seem minor or that you have taken from some areas so that you could add to others. Perhaps you have found that more income is urgently needed or that your program must cut a staff member.

A good rule of thumb is to look at the largest areas of expense and those that represent the heftiest percentages of total cost, and see what a small cut would do. If you feel unable to cut your expenses, then consider all of the different ways to boost your income.

In any case, revising your budget midyear is serious business if you are working with other agencies. It is important to know the process for changing your budget and what they will require of you. It may be that you only need to submit your new budget to them; on the other hand, you might be required to appear in person and justify the need for the changes.

It is always to your advantage to keep a careful eye on your actual income and expenses and compare them to your budget. Making changes during the operating year is far less serious than finding yourself at midyear unable to pay your staff or creditors.

Cash Flow

One of the greatest concerns for SACC programs is how and when cash flows into and out of the program. Why is this so important? As one fiscal manager so aptly stated, "Accounts receivable don't pay the bills." Because SACC programs are "labor intensive"—most expenditures being for personnel—a shortage of cash can mean a payless payday for staff. If money isn't received as planned, SACC programs will be unable to meet expenses. Also, the fact that most SACC programs have limited cash reserves further intensifies the problem. If you have the income "on paper" but you don't have the money in the bank, you have a cash flow problem. This is a serious situation that most programs want to avoid at all costs.

■ *Some Causes of Cash-Flow Problems.* Cash-flow problems are usually a result of late payments and are linked to the types of income that a program has. When a program has income from federal, state, or local governments, it is very common for the actual money to be paid after the service has been supplied. Therefore, the program has incurred (and paid for!) many of the costs already, and has to wait to receive the actual repayment. Because reimbursement procedures are often complex, the lag between the time the money is paid out by the program and the time the funds are received can cause serious cash flow problems. Similarly, when parents do not pay for child care in advance, and/or when tuition payments are delinquent, SACC programs find that they are short of funds and often cannot meet their expenses.

Programs that spend large sums of money at once instead of in small, monthly amounts also tend to have cash-flow problems. For example, we know of some SACC programs that spend 80 percent of their materials budget in September. However, if the program has just begun, there is probably not enough cash on hand to meet this expense.

■ *How to Avoid Cash-Flow Problems.* Careful planning is the key to overcoming cash-flow problems. We recommend that programs look cautiously and with a realistic eye at the money coming in and the funds to be disbursed. Will these expenses and income mesh? We suggest doing a cash-flow analysis as a way of finding out what your actual cash position looks like.

■ *How Is a Cash-Flow Analysis Done?* Your goal in doing a cash-flow analysis is to plan a schedule so that you can match the timing of your cash inflows with your cash outflows. Essentially, you have to:

- Identify your cash inflows.
- Identify your cash outflows.
- Prepare a chart that summarizes—by month—when cash flows in or out.
- Examine the cumulative effect of your cash flow each month: cash inflows minus cash outflows.
- Consider the consequences of the cash-flow pattern as it appears: if there are problems, consider which inflows or outflows can be changed or rescheduled.
- Establish a plan for a positive cash flow.

As with income/expense summaries and other tools, it is how you use the system that really counts. With cash flow, if you can see that you will have certain problems due to large sums to be paid out, late reimbursements, or expected underenrollment, it is important to figure out just what you can do to remedy the situation.

■ *How to Maintain a Positive Cash Flow.* Timing is the crucial factor when dealing with cash flow. To balance your position so it remains positive, do whatever you can to speed up your cash coming in and to slow down your money going out.

This may mean that you rethink the system you currently use or are about to use for parent fees. Since most SACC programs derive a substantial amount of their income from parents, it is essential to consider the impact of late payment and/or nonpayment of fees. Late payments may be creating a negative cash position that you cannot afford.

Another way to maintain a positive cash flow is to time expenses carefully. Perhaps you know that in a given month you will have more cash on hand—this would be the time to plan certain expenditures. Or, perhaps, given the delicate balance you are always striking, you can only afford to purchase supplies and equipment in small monthly amounts. Your cash flow analysis will help you to figure this out. But don't be fooled. Just because you have money in the checkbook doesn't mean that you can buy whatever you like. Checkbook money management is not the way to plan your expenditures.

Another common way of averting cash-flow problems is to adjust your variable costs. This is generally done in situations where cash flow becomes a problem due to underenrollment—when the program receives less income than expected. If this is the case, you must take care to cut costs immediately.

■ *What If You Still Have Cash-Flow Problems?* Many programs do careful analyses of their money situation and still find that they are unable to solve their problems—a most serious situation. If this is the case with your program, your first step is to pinpoint when you will actually be approaching a negative cash flow. What can you do about it? Basically, you need to find a source of funds to get you over the hump, or you need to postpone some expenses. You may have to apply for a short-term loan or plan a fundraising event. Many SACC programs find it essential to develop a cash reserve account—that is, a savings account to be used only for cash-flow purposes, and to which the funds are returned once the late payments arrive. The important thing, however, is to know where you are headed and to plan for that destination. Constantly running to the board or to the bank at the last minute to ask for money to cover monthly expenses is operating with a "crisis mentality." This will wear everyone out and detract from the program planning. The situation is, in effect, the result of poor planning or unheeded warning signals.

Knowing the signs of trouble in advance will go a long way toward managing a fiscally sound SACC program.

Systematically managing the money is crucial to a SACC program's continuation and ultimate quality. Long hours spent carefully organizing the environment, hiring the staff, and talking to parents will be of no use if the program cannot make it financially. To be quite frank, we know fewer programs that failed because their philosophy was "half-baked" than programs that succumbed because they left important financial management details unattended.

Chapter 12

PUBLICITY AND ENROLLMENT

Now that the building blocks of your program are in place, you're open for business. We are often asked, "When should the program open?" The date will depend upon how quickly you can comply with legal requirements and upon your financial situation. Give yourself time to start the program right. The best time for opening is in the fall, with enrollment taking place during the previous spring or at the beginning of the school year.

Often, in order to get the program off the ground, you will have to put some energy into reaching out to potential users. Otherwise, you may attract few children in your first year, or even none. It's happened!

It's obvious that programs can get into great financial difficulties when they are underenrolled, as this director learned:

> Although our teachers had teaching experience, they had no experience in recruiting kids, which was what we really needed. No one was devoting any time to it. We lost $2,000 our first year.

You will also have to establish firm policies and a systematic way of enrolling children before they come knocking at your doors for admission. This chapter discusses the two-part process of bringing children into the program: publicity and enrollment.

Publicity

The amount of advance publicity you will have to do will depend on the extent of need—on how carefully you have studied the needs assessment and designed your program to fill those needs, upon the amount of interest in your program that exists, and on how much publicity you received before you were granted approval. However, public relations work is not only a necessary part of establishing a SACC program, but of keeping it alive and well. Reaching out to and maintaining contact and good relations with your public is vital to the survival and success of any program. In addition to building general approval and support, it is obvious that you must maintain a healthy enrollment. Although some programs may become fully enrolled as soon as their opening is announced, as one parent reminds us, "Publicity and sending out notices about the program should be ongoing. People forget, new people move in."

It takes a long time before operation at full capacity is possible. This is often because many parents adopt a "wait and see if this will be a good program" attitude. The experience of one program in the Southwest, where a number of parents had indicated need and interest on an assessment survey, is typical:

> When the program opened, many parents didn't bring their kids at first—they didn't trust the new service. Once it was there it began to grow—and we called those who didn't show up after two days.

Another reason for lack of interest may be that parents are not aware that financial assistance is available (if it is). It is important to use every creative way possible to let the community know of the new service and to help build trust in its quality.

Public relations is the art of effective outreach to establish this sense of trust, and that takes a long time to build. Don't be discouraged if your early efforts aren't successful in recruiting children for your program. Many directors have learned that time and persistent effort eventually bring the desired results.

Methods for Reaching Out

There are many ways to attract and inform prospective users; you will probably need to employ several of them simultaneously and/or consecutively. Some may be used later when you need to fill certain slots in the program; for example, to achieve a better balance of sexes or races. Be sure to observe protocol by getting permission from appropriate sources to conduct your publicity, as mentioned in the discussion on conducting a needs assessment (Chapter 2). It is also courteous, as well as good public relations, to send any flier, brochure, or other noteworthy publicity to each person who has helped your efforts to get the program rolling. Also, where appropriate, be sure to indicate the name and phone number of a contact person.

Although we discuss a number of different "advertising" vehicles, remember that your best source of PR will be the word-of-mouth advertising of satisfied users—parents and children.

Every method you employ is a presentation of and statement about the character of your program. Even the way you speak to parents who make telephone inquiries conveys an image to them—hurried and careless or considerate and caring.

TIPS

- Call and/or visit parents who indicated interest on the needs assessment in the starting-up phase or more recently. The program might arrange for an outreach worker—perhaps a parent or someone on loan from a community action program or neighborhood center—to visit parents personally by appointment, by phone, or door-to-door. A friendly, encouraging, outreach person can explain the program and help families in need of after school care to work out ways to use the service. In some cases, a summer outreach worker may be the same person who will teach in the program in the fall.[1]

  The director of one community day care program sent letters announcing the fall programs to all parents who responded positively to the survey. The YMCA's CETA employee telephoned or visited the parents who responded positively to the survey. The project coordinator provided the CETA employee with 9 x 12 black-and-white photographs of children participating in an after-school child care program that had already begun. With these visual aids, the discussions with parents were guided by concrete examples of activities. The CETA employee also met with the principals and counselors of the elementary schools in the target neighborhoods to explain the program and ask for suggestions. Newspaper ads were also used to advertise the new YMCA program.[2]

---

[1] From Kay Hendon et al., *The After-School Day Care Handbook: How to Start an After School Program for School-Age Children* (Madison, Wis.: 4-C in Dane County, 1977), p. 50.
[2] *Ibid.*, p. 132.

- Keep a list of names and numbers of all those who made telephone inquiries and follow them up, if necessary.
- Send fliers home with children, through schools, religious classes. Fliers were sent to parents living in a large housing complex in the neighborhood targeted for a program. They were asked to contact their apartment managers if they were interested in the program. Send fliers to social workers. Leave them at health departments, child service agencies, etc.
- Put posters up in supermarkets and other stores, in shopping malls, churches and synagogues, schools, libraries, laundromats, adult education centers—wherever you know parents in your community are likely to see notices. Make them bright and easy to spot and read.
- Mail or distribute newsletters and bulletins through 4-H Clubs, churches, Y's or other community organizations, or put announcements in the publications put out by those groups.
- Take out newspaper ads, especially in community newspapers. One group bought an ad in a town-wide advertising circular. Consider an ad in the yellow pages of your phone book.
- Write newspaper articles and press releases; invite local newspapers to visit your center's open house or program-in-progress.
- Use radio and TV public service announcements. (They're free.) Additional free coverage by local news stations may be possible—if you can convince the news director that your SACC program is, in fact, news. Arrange to be interviewed. If local religious services include announcements of new community services, get the facts about your program opening to the ministers, priests, and rabbis. Ask them to use it.
- Provide brochures. Programs that can afford to may wish to have brochures made. It's a good idea to have the brochure folded in such a way that the outside back flap is left blank so you can fill it out with a mailing address. You may wish to leave out information that changes from year to year, such as exact school dates or prices, or to leave a space where this information may be written in; you might include it in an insert. You may want to include a preregistration blank in the brochures. Supply the same basic information you would in a press release or articles for publication:
  - *Who* sponsors the program; who is it for (ages, other eligibility requirements)?

WHAT IS EXTENDED DAY?

The Extended Day Program provides a before- and after-school accountability program for elementary school age children of parents employed outside the home.

Activities range from recreation and sports to arts and crafts, games, reading or story-telling, music, films, time to finish school assignments, an occasional field trip, and just "free time" for the children to pursue their favorite interests.

Program Supervisors are in charge of each program. Aides are used in every school. There is a ratio of one adult for every 15 children in grades 1-6 and one adult for every 10 children in Kindergarten.

WHOM DOES IT SERVE?

Children in Extended Day are enrolled in the Arlington Public Schools or in a private school serving one of the Extended Day areas.

Parents must live in Arlington and be employed outside the home. If a parent is incapacitated, the child(ren) may attend Extended Day. If there are two parents, the same conditions apply.

Students in elementary schools without an Extended Day after-kindergarten session may transfer to schools with that session if space is available.

The Program, which began with 66 students in three schools in 1969, served 1,200 students in 21 schools in 1981-82.

ARLINGTON
PUBLIC SCHOOLS

EXTENDED DAY PROGRAM

Founded 1969

Excellence through Diversity

Arlington Education Center
1426 North Quincy Street
Arlington, Virginia 22207
558-2884

WHEN IS EXTENDED DAY HELD?

The Extended Day Program operates on regularly scheduled school days, beginning with the first day of school in September.

Sessions are:

Before-school
  opening at 7:00 a.m.

After-kindergarten
  11:45-3:10 p.m.

After-school
  until 6:00 p.m.

Early release days
  1:00-6:00 p.m.

Children may be enrolled for one or more sessions depending upon the needs of the parent(s). Parents may bring children anytime before school starts and pick them up before 6:00 p.m. The fee paid remains the same.

HOW MUCH DOES IT COST?

Fees are on a sliding scale based on the family's income. There are separate fees for each session—for before-school, after-kindergarten, and after-school.

If more than one child in a family is in Extended Day, there are reduced rates.

Fees on a sliding scale are based on income adjusted for size of family. In 1982-83 the monthly minimum and maximum fees for one child range from $13.00 to $89.25 for the before-school and after-school sessions. For the kindergarten session, fees range from $9.25 to $64.75.

CITIZEN SUPPORT

Since its inauguration in 1969 as a result of the efforts of the Health and Welfare Council and other community organizations, the Extended Day Program has continued to have strong citizen support. An advisory committee works directly with the staff on planning and other activities. A parent organization has become very active and representatives from each school are selected or volunteer on the county-wide Extended Day Parent Committee.

HOW DO I ENROLL MY CHILD?

Call your local school if you wish to enroll your child.

WHERE DO I GET MORE INFORMATION?

Call your local school or the Extended Day Office (558-2884) for more information.

or write:
Extended Day Program
Arlington Public Schools
1426 North Quincy Street
Arlington, Virginia 22207

- *What* is an "extended day program," and what is your program all about? (*Brief* statement on philosophy and goals)
- *How* do you enroll a child or get further information? (Phone number and address if possible, for contact)
- *When* is the program run—hours, day, months, vacations, etc.?
- *Where* is it (or are they) located?

In addition, people will want to know what the costs will be (including whether financial aid is available) and whether transportation is to be provided. Some of this information may be given in a general statement, as in the section "How Much Does it Cost?" from the Arlington Public Schools Extended Day Program brochure shown in Figure 12–1.

Keep the brochure simple and attractive—too many words crammed on a poorly-spaced page will not attract readers. People can always call and obtain additional information. Your aim here is to attract attention, pique interest, and present basic facts. The Arlington brochure is a good example.

- Prepare a slide show. One program that was already operating developed a slide show as part of its presentation.
- Give an open house. This can be held before the program officially opens. Plan the party sensitively, taking into account the values and the needs of the population you wish to serve. You should hold your open house at a time that is most convenient for your prospective users; in some neighborhoods this will mean holding it on a weekday evening; for others a Friday or Saturday night, or perhaps a Sunday afternoon, makes better sense. The director and staff members should be on hand. You might use this as a major goodwill effort: be sure to invite fairy godmothers or fathers—all those who have had a substantial concern with the program: members of school or church boards, donors of resources.

  If your program is school-based, you may wish to invite the superintendent, the principal, custodians, and other school staff. Also invite anyone who has responded to your publicity. You might even consider inviting people who have voiced opposition to your project. You may decide to use this open house mainly for enrollment purposes. In that case, be sure to have enrollment forms ready; if you have brochures, these should be displayed.

If your program is already operating, an open house can provide a valuable opportunity for parents and staff—as well as parents who are prospects—to meet others who have a share in the program.

• Run a demonstration program.

One program achieved firm enrollments in May by running a free two-week demonstration program. This required very early organization, but was an effective way of "selling" the program.[3]

Timing of Publicity

It's often difficult to reach families during the summer. If your program is scheduled to open in the fall, it's a good idea to do your initial publicity in the spring, before school closes. Announce your plans to begin operation in September, and tell how a child can be enrolled. When you make these announcements, one person (or more) must be made responsible for handling inquiries, applications, enrollment, and registration.

Enrollment

Once your publicity begins to work, you will be busy admitting children to the program. There is a discussion in Chapter 3 of the decisions that must be made about whom the program should serve (numbers, ages of children, for example) and of the considerations involved in determining priorities for admission during your pilot year. If you have not done so, you should now firm up and formalize these decisions by adopting them as program policies. Next, you must set up the procedures for carrying them out as efficiently as possible; they should be set up before the first child enrolls. (Refer to Chapter 6 for general guidelines on setting policies and procedures.) A good example of enrollment policies and procedures, clearly formulated and concisely presented, is the statement from the Family After School Program of Milwaukee, Wisconsin, shown in Figure 12–2.

We cannot give you the one "right" decision on how to admit or enroll children, because what is best for a close-knit, suburban, parent-run program for twenty children will be totally wrong for an inner-city program serving seven hundred in many sites. We do, however, provide general information and tips that all programs can

---

[3] *Ibid.*, p. 49.

**FAMILY AFTER SCHOOL PROGRAM
ENROLLMENT POLICIES AND PROCEDURES**

I. Statement of Purpose: To provide a quality activities and child development program for children during the after school hours.

II. Enrollment and Registration Policies

    A. The Family After School Program Inc. does not discriminate in its enrollment policy on the basis of race, color, sex, religion, national origin or physical or mental handicap.

    B. Children must be in grades one through five to be eligible.

    C. Children must be attending the school in which the program is located in order to be eligible for that program. (Plymouth Church program excluded.)

    D. Applications will be accepted on a first-come, first-served basis.

    E. Priority is given to full-time participants (four or five days per week) over part-time participants (three days or less per week) until August 24th.

    F. Registration forms are available from the Family After School Program's main office, 2717 E Hampshire, Milwaukee, Wisconsin 53211, or from a Head Teacher at the program site.

        1. A $7.50 registration fee is required. This fee covers the cost of processing and is non-refundable.

        2. If a child cannot be placed in a program because of full enrollment, he/she will be put on a waiting list if so desired.

    G. The following information must be supplied by the parent(s), legal guardian(s) or custodian(s) of the child and returned with signed registration forms to the Family After School Program office:

        1. Registration Agreement (promise of monthly fee payment, paid in advance)

        2. Attendance and Information forms

    H. A Health Form, completed and signed by the family physician, must be returned to the Family After School Program office by the parent(s), legal guardian(s) or custodian(s) of the child no later than one month after the child enters the program.

    I. Registration forms must be completed for each child in the family applying for the program.

Figure 12–2

use, point out advantages and disadvantages of different methods, and, along with those, the advice of many experienced people.

We know of exceptions to almost all of the rules. For example, although generally it is folly to begin a program until you have a certain number of children enrolled, one director began her program in September as planned, although not one child had signed up. Within a few weeks there were seven children at the center, and the enrollment continued to grow until it had reached its numerical limits.

Policies

What factors should be considered when setting admission policies?

1. Standards mandated by external sources—licensing bureaus, government funders, boards, your agency, etc.—in the form of their guidelines and other "regs."
2. Your own standards, philosophy, and goals. These standards will include the optimal size of your program, group size, staff:child ratios, number of staff, and amount of space you have—all factors that make or break the quality of the program.
3. Cost effectiveness. The amount of income in your budget will determine how many staff members you can hire and how many children you can satisfactorily serve.

■ *Nondiscriminatory Clauses and Affirmative Action.* All programs that incorporate as not-for-profit organizations have to make a statement that their admissions policies are nondiscriminatory. This statement is usually adopted as one of the policies. For example:

> Latchkey makes no discrimination in admissions or determination of enrollment on the basis of race, sex, religion, creed, color, or national origin.

Some programs add other nonobligatory characteristics to this list: "It is our policy to register families with no regard to race, creed, color, physical or mental disability, sex, national origin, or income." This is a way of acknowledging that there may be barriers to admittance other than race or ethnicity, and that the program intends to take affirmative action to ensure that it is open to all children.

We recognize that not all programs have adequate resources—financial, staff, physical facilities—to implement such goals. However, a program can establish the goal as a policy toward which it truly aspires and will work, perhaps by including in its original proposal a plan to provide scholarships in the future.

Programs may also have to adopt the Affirmative Action policies of the schools, agencies, or governments (municipal, county) who are their funders, administrators, or hosts in terms of space. They may also adopt and implement, either formally or informally, a policy which enables them to give special priority to certain ethnic or racial groups. In one eastern city, a principal was particularly concerned that some of the Hispanic and black children who attended his school, and who needed SACC, might be inadvertently excluded from available programs. He took special pains to see that a waiting list of these children was established, so that their parents could be notified when there was an available opening.

Setting Priorities for Admissions

Once you have set maximum and minimum limits on enrollment, you may want to establish a policy on admissions criteria. Priorities may be set along the following categories, or some combination of them: age; grade; neighborhood or school; family's employment or other status, such as level of income; special family circumstances; children with special needs; priorities that are unique to the group setting up the program. You may also wish to decide whether you will permit cross-registration or open enrollment.

The following example of a policy that establishes eligibility requirements—that of the Hephzibah Children's Association— illustrates that generally more than one criterion is used:

> The requirements for admission are:
> - The child must be in kindergarten through fifth grade;
> - The child must be a resident of Oak Park or River Forest, or go to school in Oak Park or River Forest;
> - The parents must be working or students.

■ *Priorities by Age and/or Grade.*   Your best guide in setting age limits is probably your recognition of the ages for which need is greatest. Some states have regulations on staff:child ratios based on age. You should check on whether yours does, and, if so, what they are, because states have individual standards. As of this writing, Minnesota, for example, currently requires a ratio of 1:10 for the five-to-six year olds, and 1:15 for the over-sixes.

Setting limits by age is different from setting them by grade. You may want to choose one method or both, as does a program in the Midwest, one of whose criteria for enrollment is that "children must be 5-10 years old or K-5, whichever fits." This would mean that a five-year-old who has not yet entered kindergarten might not be admitted. But, this method has problems, as the director is first to admit: "The policy and practice is that there are exceptions made, and in the past few years there have been more exceptions than rules. This means problems—for where do you draw the line?"

■ *Kindergarten Children.*   Some programs include kindergarten children; others don't. In deciding whether you will admit them, you need to assess the kindergarten picture in your area, which will include the availability of other services. A YMCA program in the

East decided on a policy of "no kindergarten children" because there was no available space in the school when the regular kindergarten session ended. Also, the Y felt that privately operated day care centers were already serving this age group, offering continuity to children who had attended their preschool. External regulations, as well as your own standards, on staff:child ratios and/or group sizes may mean that you will need a larger staff if you include kindergartners than you would if you admit only older children.

■ *Age Limits for Special-Needs Children.* Some programs that serve children with emotional, intellectual, or physical handicaps set different age limits for them. In Fairfax County, Virginia, a school that teaches only special-needs children, ages five to twenty-one, who are mentally retarded and/or multiple-handicapped also offers a SACC program after the regular school day. Initially, the age limits for children in the SACC program were five to eleven, the same guidelines as those for nonspecial-needs children in other SACC programs. However, the limits have been expanded. The principal of the school believes that SACC programs at "special" schools should be open to children of all ages who attend the school.

A program in the Midwest established the following eligibility criteria for children who are developmentally delayed, and who are mainstreamed, or integrated, into their SACC program: "If they are functioning within our age level—5 to 10—we take them."

■ *Priorities According to Neighborhood or School.* Admissions policies based on location—the school the child attends or his or her home neighborhood—will be determined by the size, number of sites, purpose, sponsorship, and capacities of your program. The range can extend from granting eligibility to any child in the city, and then placing him or her in the appropriate center, to limiting eligibility to the children in one public school's neighborhood. Children who live in that neighborhood but attend private school are also included. If programs are school-based, enrollment may be determined by school attended, or residence, or both.

■ *Cross-Registration and/or Open Enrollment.* Cross-registration means that if there are programs at more than one site (usually this pertains to schools), a child who attends school at one site that has a SACC program may be allowed to attend a program at another site. This may be permitted if enrollment is filled at his or her regular school site, if there is no program at that school, or for other special reasons. Transportation may or may not be a problem, and it should be considered carefully: How will the child cross school neighborhood boundaries? Who will or can be responsible for the child's safety while he or she is "crossing?" The goal of the cross-registration policy is to make as sensible and safe an arrangement for the child as possible. Here is one program's policy: "Students in elementary schools without an extended day program may transfer to schools with a program if space is available." (This policy implies that children who attend schools that already have a program get first priority for admissions.)

In an Oregon city, children who attend the school are given first priority, and then enrollment is open to all others who meet the additional criteria. Enrollment policies are very flexible, and cross-registration is permitted. If children need to attend a SACC program, and there is none available at the school they attend, they are permitted to transfer to another school where there is a program. In this way, the children remain at one site for the entire day. In addition, if a child's babysitter lives outside the areas that have a program, the child can transfer to the school in that district so that pick-up (and/or drop-off) is facilitated.

A consequence of the open enrollment policy is that public schools often get additional staff as the number of children who transfer to these schools in order to take advantage of the SACC program increases. The Oregon director sees this as "very important for the survival of some elementary schools."

One SACC program sets admission priorities in this order:

1. Children of parents working or attending school full time,
2. Children attending the school where the program is held,
3. Children whose enrollment forms were submitted earliest,
4. If openings are still available, after two weeks the directors may enroll children from schools that do not have programs, until the program reaches its enrollment limit of twenty-eight.

■ *Financial Levels.* Programs funded by the government will inherit admissions priorities that are often based on a combination of (1) the family's level of crisis and (2) income levels (or their sources of income).

Title XX day care programs in Georgia have a specific list of priorities for enrolling children. The order is:

1. Referrals from the Department of Family and Children's Services for children who are in danger of neglect or abuse,
2. Employed parents who are receiving Aid to Families with Dependent Children,
3. Income-eligible parents who are employed, but eligible for aid because of level of income,

4. Other "income-eligible" clients,
5. Former clients.

Programs that do not have externally imposed policies and are free to create their own will need to consider the economic circumstances of the community they wish to serve and the financial needs of the program.

■ *Special Family Circumstances.*   Many programs, especially those run by community agencies that are funded by federal, state, or local governments, set up admissions priorities that are based on special family circumstances; for example, the mother's employment outside of the home, or a crisis situation, such as the mother's illness.

Social welfare agencies often have their own kinds and order of priorities. Generally, the number of priorities is directly related to the numbers of programs administered and the source of the administration and/or funding. Implementation of these policies requires many forms to be filled out, so the program's administrative services must be sufficient to handle the job.

In one southern city, the department of social services has set up a very complex order of priorities with fifteen categories of eligibility. The director sees the mission of the agency as "social welfare," and top priority is given to abused and/or neglected children; the next priority is for those children who would have to be placed in an institution if they could not be provided with extended day care.

■ *Children with Special Physical, Emotional, and Intellectual Needs.*   Every child has special needs, but some have physical, emotional, or intellectual disabilities that may require more care in handling than others. If a program's philosophy and goals are to provide for the needs of the community by offering its services to *every* child, then its policy should be to open its enrollment to special needs children.

> Special environments and equipment are nice, but they're rarely necessary . . . the most important ingredient in integrated day care . . . (is) the attitude that special children are first of all children.[4]

Families that have children with special problems have a need for school-age child care that is as great—and often greater—as that of other families, yet they often have more difficulty in finding programs that will serve their children. Day care services for these children are

---

[4] U.S. Department of Health, Education, and Welfare, Office of Child Development, *Day Care: Serving Children with Special Needs* (Washington, D.C.: U.S. Government Printing Office, 1972).

"abysmal," to quote one director, and the more severe the handicap, the harder it is to find services.

According to Martha Ziegler of the Federation of Children with Special Needs in Boston, Massachusetts:

> The length of the school day and a lack of after school activities prohibit many mothers of handicapped children from participation in employment or educational opportunities. Such women, especially low- or moderate-income women ineligible for welfare support, are thus in a double bind. Because their children often require costly special services and equipment, they have a great need to earn income; however, they cannot earn that income unless after-school care is available for their handicapped children.[5]

It is important to let parents and the community know that it is the program's policy to accept, or consider for admission, some or all children with special needs, according to your capabilities. Generally, the procedure is that the program director and the parents meet to determine whether an individual child can profit from the program, and it is up to the program director to decide whether the child can be admitted. In some schools or in large agency-run programs, a social worker or an evaluation team may be asked to help in making the decision. In Fairfax County, the EDC coordinator is involved in the enrollment process *only* for special needs children, to be sure that group day care is best for that child.

■ *Unique Priorities.*   Individual programs may set up policies on admissions priorities that they wish to institute or that are mandated by the groups who are granting approval. In one community where parents wanted to run a town-sponsored SACC program, the town requested that the program be open to all town employees. Many programs will give first priority to siblings of children who attend or have attended, or to "old parents," as the parents of these children are often called.

Establishing Procedures

The enrollment and application process involves acquiring all the information fees, and understanding necessary between parents, children, and program before they can join hands officially. The following questions require careful forethought:

- How will application be made? By mail? In person? Both methods?

---

[5] *Child Care and Equal Opportunity for Women* (Washington, D.C.: United States Commission on Civil Rights, June 1981), p. 25.

- Whom does a prospective parent or agency contact? Name a specific person, usually designated by office, not by name: "Call the Coordinated Child Care Satellite Project at the County Superintendent of Schools' Office." Give a phone number. One project gave the local number and a toll-free 800 number as well, and also had a telephone answering machine. It could also be reached at the center. You may wish to limit the hours for phone inquiries, depending upon your status, who is in charge of the process, and the other work that needs to be done. One established program has included the following in its outreach materials:

  > Preregistration procedures can be confusing. Please call the office at (*phone #*) for answers to your questions. You are more likely to find lines open before 9:00 A.M. and after 3:00 P.M. The office is usually staffed from 7:30 A.M. to 6:00 P.M.

- What is required to make application? What information will be on the printed form parents send in?
- Will an interview and/or visit be required? Some programs require them before a parent makes application; others don't. Preapplication visits in the case of special needs children is indicated. Many programs use a preliminary meeting or conference with the parent as an opportunity to discuss the program's philosophy, policies, and "regs," including expectations of parent involvement.
- How will you make notification of admission?
- Will you have waiting lists?
- Will you have trial or emergency enrollments? Preenrollment conferences? Orientation? Will you terminate enrollment for specific reasons?

Be sure to decide who will do each task, including the typing or mimeographing, keeping lists, being "contact person" for the press, answering telephone inquiries, and interviewing. To avoid duplication of effort and confusion, designate a specific person to carry out each procedure. In some centers, especially those that are agency-run, a social worker may be in charge of the entire process. In many others, it will be the director, or the director and teachers. In designating a person or persons, be aware that:

> . . . the process takes a good deal of a day care administrator's time. Simple enrollments involve at least four hours per child; phone inquiries

often require eight to ten hours a week; and dealing with potential parents can take well over five hours every week. Peak enrollment times often demanded the full-time attention of the director.[6]

Once you have determined your enrollment process, communicate it to your public. State the steps as clearly and simply as possible, as in this example from the Hale Reservation in Westwood, Massachusetts:

TO REGISTER

1. Call (program or school name) for information, registration forms, and an interview.
2. Complete and return application form and sign all authorizations.
3. Complete and return the Emergency Medical Permission slip with the application form.
4. Upon acceptance to the program, send:
    a. First payment
    b. One week deposit
    c. Physical examination and health form

The procedures involved in admitting and enrolling children are:
   Preregistration
   Registration
   Admission
   Waiting lists
   Termination of enrollment

Some programs will not use all of these procedures. Some will structure their enrollment process tightly; others are looser in their protocol. Experience teaches us that "tighter is better"—you can always become more flexible later. Begin by establishing procedures that are as simple as possible. As the program develops, so will your refinements.

■ *Preregistration.*   This term is used to describe the practice of allowing a parent to "hold" or insure a place by sending in a fee, usually $10 to $25. Although some programs will refund the fee if for any reason the child is not enrolled, others keep it as payment for the paperwork and other time involved.

Instituting a policy and procedure for preregistration in the spring or summer will help you to determine how many children you can expect in the fall.

---

[6]Child Care Support Center, Save the Children, *Recruiting and Enrolling Children* (Atlanta: Save the Children, 1981), p. 17.

REGISTER FOR 1980–81

Registration for next fall is filling up rapidly. Register *TODAY* in order to insure a place for your child by sending in your registration form and $10 nonrefundable registration fee ($25 for kindergarten) to . . . .

Programs print preregistration notices in their own newsletters, in those of other organizations, or as inserts in program brochures. If you are going to institute a preregistration process, you must be ready to communicate clearly the procedures, as well as your priorities for eligibility, as illustrated by Figure 12–3, a page from the parent handbook of the Fairfax County School-Age Child Care Program, a Virginia agency that provides an individual program for special-needs children.

The fact that a child has been preregistered may not mean he or she will definitely be accepted. If this is your policy, state it clearly, as well as the fact that the preregistration fee is nonrefundable.

If your policy is to admit on a first-come, first-served basis, you will need to have a place for the date of application on the form, and make sure you date forms as you receive them. It's also a good idea to record any informal inquiries, so you don't lose the names of potential program users.

■ *Registration.*   When a child is formally registered, many programs require a deposit, generally one or two weeks tuition, but sometimes tuition for the entire session. Although nonrefundable deposit requests in the cases below are unusually high, the rationale behind them—to protect the program's sources of income—is sound. The nonrefundable fees a program sets up must be reasonable for the community it serves:

> We require a deposit before your child starts—$50 if your child attends 3 to 4 hours, $100 for attendance of 5–6½ hours, $150 for full-time children. This deposit is not refunded if your child does not enroll in the program for which the deposit has been taken.
>
> Full enrollment is necessary for us to meet the costs we establish in our annual budget meeting. If a child is withdrawn during the year, the deposit money covers some costs while we try to fill the space. Unused deposit money is credited to the families' last tuition.

PROCEDURES FOR PRE-REGISTRATION

May 30-June 7, only families currently in Extended Day Care may pre-register for the 1979-80 school year.

Beginning June 8, pre-registration will be open to all special ed. children. Pre-registration will be handled on an individualized basis and total enrollment will be determined by the specific needs of children pre-registered.

Spaces will be strictly limited, and we recommend early pre-registration. Our receipt of pre-registration forms does not guarantee placement in EDC.

A.   Complete the pre-registration form attached, detach it from this brochure, and bring or mail it with your registration fees to the EDC office, 4100 Chain Bridge Road, 10th Floor, Fairfax, VA 22030. (This is the Massey Building behind the County Court House.)

B.   Make checks or money orders payable to "Fairfax County." Write on the bottom your child(ren)'s name(s) and center.

C.   Allow 3 weeks for notification by mail either that space has been reserved for you or that you have been placed on a waiting list.

D.   Final registration forms and further information will be sent during the summer to pre-registrants.

E.   We strongly recommend that new families call EDC's Special Ed. Program Director (691-2924) for guidance in pre-registering your special ed. child.

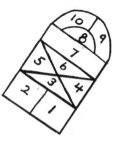

Figure 12-3

REGISTRATION AGREEMENT
Family After School Program, Inc.

1. I understand I am enrolling my child for a total of 36 weeks.
2. I understand that during vacation periods and days school is closed because of bad weather there will be no program.
3. I understand that I am responsible for monthly payment of contracted fees, paid in advance. I will give two weeks notice of withdrawal from the program.
4. I agree to pay_____per month for_____days a week.
5. If my child is having problems adjusting to the program, a conference will be arranged between myself and the staff.
6. In the event of illness, vacation, or other absences such as Scouts, music lessons, and other out-of-school activities, the After School Program staff will be notified and I am responsible for my child and tuition payment. Communication with the After School Program staff can be made through the After School Program's main office (964-5545).
7. The After School Program staff will assume full responsibility for my child from the time he/she arrives at the program until dismissal time. Dismissal time will be 6:00 P.M. or earlier upon my written authorization. The child must sign in upon arrival and sign out or be signed out by an authorized person.
8. I give my permission for my child to participate in hikes and field trips.
9. If a medical emergency arises, the After School staff will first attempt to contact me. If I cannot be reached, the After School staff will contact the child's doctor. If the emergency is such that immediate hospital attention is necessary, the After School staff may take my child to the hospital.

I agree to adhere to the Family After School Program registration policies and give my child permission to participate fully in this program.
Signature _____ Date _____
Send registration packet accompanied by the first month's fee and the $7.50 registration fee to Family After School Program, Inc., 2717 E. Hampshire, Milwaukee, WI 53211.

Figure 12-4

As part of the registration, and before a child is officially enrolled, programs often require that the parent sign a contract or agreement stating that he or she has read the policies and rules and agrees to honor them. The agreement displayed in Figure 12–4 is from the Family After School Program, Inc. in Milwaukee, Wisconsin.

Registration packets. Some programs make a "registration packet," which includes all the forms that must be signed and returned before the child can be officially enrolled. When designing the forms you will need, ask yourself, "What kinds of information about the child and the family will we need?" In addition, state licensing bureaus or other legal bodies require programs to have on hand certain records, such as medical histories and/or examination reports, within a mandatory time; for example, "no later than one month after the child enters the program."

You would be wise to impose your own time limits, such as "two weeks after enrollment," for receiving other forms. Some programs don't consider the registration and enrollment process complete— and will not admit the child—until the necessary information, as well as the deposit, has been provided. You should require that all forms be completed for each child who registers for the program.

Devise a procedure for filing the forms. Your aim is to be able to retrieve exactly the information you need at the moment you need it. Some forms, such as the emergency form or card that gives the name of the child's physician, may not ever be needed, but if an emergency arises, it should be filed in a way that will ensure immediate retrieval. Arrange forms in packets or folders and keep a box near the telephone. Keep everything together and easy to hand out to parents or to send in the mail. Some programs keep all pertinent information about each child in a separate folder; others keep all cards with emergency numbers in one special place and/or put the numbers on specially colored index cards. Whatever procedure you institute, make sure all staff know exactly what it is. Make sure your forms are kept up to date. Periodic reviews may be in order.

Don't inundate yourself with forms. Although there is certain information you must have, often much of it can be contained on one enrollment form, such as the example from the After School Day Care Association of Madison, Wisconsin (Figure 12–5). If you're school-based, you may be able to use the school's forms for some of the information you need.

Following is a list of some forms different programs require. You may not want to use all of them, and will probably think of modifications. It's a good idea, however, to have at least two copies of the forms you do use—one for the program, one for the parent to retain. If there is a central administrative office that serves many sites, it should also have copies of some of these forms.

Enrollment or registration forms. These may be two separate forms, or one and the same. They include names, addresses, and home and work phone numbers of parents as well as the names and numbers of persons to call in an emergency. These forms may also include authorizations (see Figure 12–5). Some programs ask parents to specify "departure procedures" here—how the children are to get home, and who may pick them up.

ENROLLMENT FORM
AFTER SCHOOL DAY CARE ASSOCIATION

OFFICE USE
_____

Today's date_____ First date of attendance _____ Program _____

Child's name	School	Age	Date of birth	Sex	Circle days of attendance	Did child attend ASDCA last year?
_____	_____	___	_____	__	M T W TH F	__Yes __No
_____	_____	___	_____	__	M T W TH F	__Yes __No
_____	_____	___	_____	__	M T W TH F	__Yes __No

Parent(s) or guardian(s) with whom child resides:

Name_____Address _____ZIP _____home phone_____

Name of business _____work address _____work phone _____work hours_____

Name_____Address _____ZIP _____home phone_____
(if different from above)

Name of business _____work address _____work phone _____work hours_____

Person responsible for payment, if different from above:

Name_____Address _____ZIP _____Phone_____

DEPARTURE PROCEDURES: What do you wish the departure procedures to be for your child (Example: Walk home, take a bus alone, wait to be picked up by parent or authorized person, etc.) If you make a change in these procedures later, please inform the staff *in writing* of any new instructions.

PERSONS AUTHORIZED TO CALL FOR YOUR CHILD: Any changes in this list must be received from you in writing.

1. _____Phone_____ 3. _____Phone_____
2. _____Phone_____ 4. _____Phone_____

CHILD/REN'S PHYSICIAN
Name_____Address _____Phone _____

EMERGENCY NUMBERS: Please give the name, address, and phone number of two people that may be notified in case of emergency or illness, when parents or guardian are not available. These people should live in Madison. Please provide a telephone number where these people may be reached *during program hours.*

_____Address _____Phone_____
Name and relationship to child

_____Address _____Phone_____
Name and relationship to child

EMERGENCY MEDICAL RELEASE
If emergency medical care is deemed necessary and I cannot be contacted, I authorize the day care staff to act in my behalf in granting permission for my child to receive emergency treatment.

_____
Signature of parent or guardian

PHOTOGRAPHIC PERMISSION
I DO   I DO NOT   (circle one) give permission to have my child appear in any media coverage approved by the After School Day Care Association. I understand that the lead teacher, in conjunction with the Coordinator, has been given the authority by the ASDCA Board of Directors to determine appropriate requests.

_____
Signature of parent or guardian

Figure 12–5

LATCHKEY INTAKE

Policy Re: Medical Physicals and Immunization Records

We are required by law to maintain current medical records for each child enrolled in the Latchkey program. An immunization record must be on file for each child within two weeks of your child's enrollment in the program.

If your child has had a recent physical, we need a copy of this information, signed by the doctor within two weeks of entry. If your child has not had a physical during the last six months, you must make an appointment with your child's physician at the time of your child's entry into the Latchkey program. The physical must be completed within eight weeks of entry in the program for day care to continue.

I understand the above policy and am aware that if I do not comply, my day care services will be in jeopardy.

Signature: _____

Date: _____

Immunization record will be received by _____
Date of scheduled physical (if necessary) _____
Statement of physical will be received by _____

11/29/79
mkn

Figure 12-6

Health records, including immunization records. These are required by law, and must be updated periodically. Figure 12-6 from the Latchkey Program of Community Day Care, Inc., of Lawrence, Massachusetts is one example.

Dental examination forms may be required by law, if not taken care of by regular school procedures.

Developmental history. Some programs don't take formal histories, but others have very detailed ones, including personal information that the program feels will better help it to serve the child: an inventory of the child's interests, habits, any special home and family situations, etc. In agencies, a social worker or other person—or sometimes a team of professionals—may do this "intake." Programs that are genuinely committed to filling children's needs will want to obtain this information. The example in Figure 12-7 is from the Santa Monica Children's Center in Santa Monica, California.

Authorizations, permissions, and waivers of liability. This form (or forms) delineates *who* is accountable for *what*. It is the authorization for child care and stipulates the hours that the center is responsible

SANTA MONICA CHILD CARE CENTERS
Developmental Information

Date_____

Child's name_____ Birth date _____ Birth place _____
What immediate circumstances make child care services necessary at this time?
_____

Age of child when mother first went to work_____ What have been previous plans for
care of child? _____

PRESENT FAMILY SITUATION
Parents: living together____separated____divorced____parent ill____
deceased____
Age of child at time of above change in family situation_____
If parents are divorced or separated, does child see absent parent?
Never____rarely____periodically (how often?)____regularly (how often?) _____
What helpful information can you offer about how the absence of a parent has been
worked out with the child, and what has been noted about his reaction to these
circumstances? (Use reverse side if more space is needed.)_____
_____

List the names, ages, and any special relationships of other children in the family:
Name _____ age _____   _____
Name _____ age _____   _____
Name _____ age _____   _____
Name _____ age _____   _____

What other persons are living in the household? (Indicate relationship to the child.)
_____

Who cares for the child at home during the mother's absence? _____
In how many different places has child lived?____How long in present home?____
Is present home: apartment_____ house_____ other _____
What play space is available? Indoors_____outdoors_____

Figure 12–7

for the child. The wording on the authorization form used by a Milwaukee, Wisconsin, program is:

> The After School Program staff will assume full responsibility for a child from the time he/she arrives at the program until dismissal time. Dismissal time is 6:00 P.M. or earlier upon parent's written permission. The child must sign in upon arrival and sign out, or be signed out by an authorized person, upon departure.

Emergency medical care. The program should obtain a signed statement from each parent which authorizes it to provide emergency medical treatment, including the administration of anesthesia by a physician. This form usually includes a statement by the program that it will notify the parent before the child is treated, if possible. Some programs ask the parent to indicate his or her preference for physician and hospital, or tell them which hospital they'll take the child to.

This form also includes a statement that the parent is responsible for any expenses incurred, including an ambulance. It makes sense to include a statement of allergies to medications or anesthesia, although this may be on the health form as well. The example in Figure 12–8 is from the Eakin Care Program in Nashville, Tennessee.

Some parents, because of religious or other reasons, refuse to permit the center to provide their child with medical treatment. Some programs require that this refusal be stated in writing. Similarly, if parents refuse to allow their child to be immunized, some states require a signed statement to this effect; in such cases, programs have to follow state licensing regulations. They may also choose to make their own policy about whether to refuse admission to a child who has not been immunized—against polio, for example.

Medication requests. Most programs will administer medication to a child only if they receive a written order from the child's physician and/or written permission of the parent. The medicine must be sent in the original container and have the child's name on it. Some centers insist that the parent hand-deliver the medicine to a staff person.

EAKIN CARE PROGRAM

Authorization for Emergency Medical Care
Date_____
I hereby authorize emergency medical care for my child _____
during attendance at the Eakin Care Program if, in the judgement of the staff, treatment is required for an injury or illness. I hereby also authorize the administering of anesthetics and recourse to other procedures deemed necessary by the attending physician.

I understand that whenever possible, I will be notified prior to medical treatment of my child. I understand that I will be notified at the earliest possible time should prior notice prove impossible.

The physician of my choice is Dr_____;
Office phone_____; Home phone _____.
The hospital emergency room of my choice is _____
My child is allergic to the following medications and anesthetics:

I understand that I am financially responsible for any expenses for medical care or transportation incurred on my child's behalf.

                                                   Parent or Guardian's Signature

A Note on Care During Program Hours:

The staff will administer prescription medicines accompanied by a signed, dated note from a parent or guardian. The staff will not administer aspirin or other non-prescription drugs.

Parents are requested to notify the staff when their child is ill with a communicable disease.

Figure 12–8

Authorized emergency numbers. Parents are requested to supply the name and phone number(s) of a person to call if the parent cannot be reached; for example, if a child becomes ill and should be sent home. This surrogate parent should have a car at his or her disposal. The Parent Handbook of one Wisconsin program specifies:

> For bad weather days, staff and board all have a copy at home of the list of the names and numbers of people, so if the school closes, or if there is no program, or closes early, we can get in touch with people.

Authorized pick-up. Some programs ask that parents designate, in writing, which persons (including and/or in addition to parents) may pick the child up and take him or her from the program's official premises—either routinely or in lieu of regular transportation plans, or in specific instances of early dismissal for music lessons, Scouts, or for other reasons. Often, this "authorized person" must formally sign for the child as in this SACC program:

> Parents or authorized adults pick up their children at the end of the day any time between 5:30 and 6:00 P.M. Parents should sign out their children and check the bulletin board for messages.

Authorization for liability waiver. This is a statement of who will carry insurance for the child—the program, school, other sponsoring agent, or parent. Some programs, or the school districts in which the program is housed, may demand that the parent sign a "liability waiver" against personal or financial claims, covering either their child's participation in the program in general, or on field trips only. However, it is questionable whether courts would uphold the legality of such a statement; in some instances programs could be sued in spite of the waiver. (See "Liability" in Chapter 5.) Here is how one Y handles the waiver:

> The YWCA does *not* provide accident insurance. Please indicate your:
> Type of Insurance _____
> Company _____
> Policy # _____

WAIVER OF CLAIMS

> I hereby for myself and my child waive and release all rights and claims for damages I may have against the YWCA Directors and Staff for any injuries suffered by my child as a participant in the Child Care Program.

Field trips. Permission must be obtained for the program to take the child on trips, use special transportation provided for these occasions, etc. Programs may request a blanket permission form for all

---

FIELD TRIP PERMISSION FORM

Field trips will be planned from time to time as part of the activity of the Adventure Club Program. This will entail walking to nearby parks, wooded areas, stores, etc. Visitations involving bussing will also be planned.

Every possible precaution will be exercised to assure the safety and welfare of your child. However, the school and its authorized agents shall not be responsible, financially or otherwise, should an accident occur.

_____ has permission to participate in the
(child's name)

Adventure Club field trip programs.

_____
(Signature)

Figure 12–9

trips. Some list the places to which children will be taken; for example, "swimming pool at the Y." Blanket permissions save sending out notices each time a trip is planned. The example in Figure 12–9 is from the Adventure Club in Robbinsdale, Minnesota.

Authorization for special purpose: publicity, evaluation. Some programs may be part of a project or course in child development or other study project, or may be visited for publicity purposes. Parents should be apprised of this before they sign their children up, and programs should obtain permission for occasional observation or evaluation on special forms. For example:

> In the event the children in the program are included in any newspaper, radio, or television publicity, I give my permission for my child to be included in the pictures, etc.
>
> *Permission to video-tape, evaluate, etc.*
> I hereby grant permission for my child to be included in evaluation (Developmental, Physical, and Health) and in video-taping and pictures connected with the center program.

Financial information. Parents may need to fill out financial forms to be eligible for partial aid or full scholarships, or to enable the center to take part in a federal program, such as the School Lunch Program. Agencies may require that their own specific forms be completed. In the case of application for federal funds, the forms will be supplied by the appropriate federal agency. If you are creating your own forms, try to obtain information that will help you make your decisions about whether aid is indicated, and, if so, how much (if you are scaling amounts of aid to different needs). A family's income alone may not be a true indicator of need. How many members of the family are there? Does the family have a number of children who need SACC? Does it have other unusually high expenses—medical bills or college tuition for another child or a parent?

Records: access, confidentiality, and release. New laws provide that parents have access to records and that before they are released to anyone else, parental permission must be obtained. The following statements from the Hephzibah Children's Association in Oak Park, Illinois illustrate procedures for dealing with these issues.

> *Records:* Any information contained in your child's record shall be confidential. We will not share information contained in the record with anyone without the written consent of the parent. The parents, however, will have access to all their child's records at any time. Parents have the right to add information, comments, data or relevant materials to the child's record. They also may request that information be deleted or amended. We otherwise comply with all the rules and regulations re- garding student records as established by the state standards for day care centers.

AUTHORIZATION FOR RELEASE OF INFORMATION

> I do hereby authorize Hephzibah Children's Association to exchange in- formation regarding my child/ren with those professional agencies or people concerned with my child's education and health. I fully under- stand that this may entail psychological, social, medical, or educational information.
>
> Signed _____
> Mother's Signature _____
> Father's Signature _____

Notification of admission status. In some programs, registration of the child, accompanied by a deposit, signifies that the child has been admitted. In others, a notification of the child's status is sent. If your program has many sites, you may need to assign each child to a specific one, and notify parents where their children will go.

After enrollment is filled, you will probably wish to place appli- cant names on a waiting list and inform the family of this. The exam- ple in Figure 12–10 is from the After School Day Care Association of Madison, Wisconsin.

Waiting lists. Keep these current and confidential. Go through the waiting list regularly and weed out parents who are no longer in-

AFTER SCHOOL DAY CARE ASSOCIATION, INC.

Dear Parent(s):

We have received your completed enrollment forms, and would like to inform you of the status of your application for your child to attend the After School Day Care program that you requested:

ADMISSION STATUS:

_____Your child/ren has/have been officially enrolled in the _____ program and may attend the program on the date that you requested.

_____The program to which you applied is full, and your child/ren's name(s) has/ have been placed on a waiting list. We will contact you as soon as there is an opening.

_____Full-time enrollments are given priority over part-time enrollments until _____. Since your child/ren is/are scheduled to attend on a part-time basis, we will inform you immediately after _____ whether or not there is space available for your child on the day(s) that you requested.

_____other _____
_____
_____
_____

PROGRAM LOCATION:

_____

We look forward to having your child/ren in the program.

The After School Day Care Association

3200 Monroe St.
Madison, Wi 53711
enc: Registration agreement copy   233-9782
     Enrollment form copy

Figure 12–10

terested, even when there are no vacancies. The procedure you use for compiling your waiting lists will depend on what your policy is: first come, first served; or eligibility priorities.

Centers quite often establish a waiting list on a first-come, first-served basis. For example, there are two ways a director can record the order of parental applications. The most common procedure is to accept applications in order of their appearance. Usually a short form is filled out and more detailed forms are only completed at a point an opening exists. If the waiting list is very long, parents are encouraged to look elsewhere. When vacancies occur, parents are called in order of application.

The second method for handling a waiting list is to screen out parents who are only moderately interested in enrolling their child. This can be done by requiring all paperwork such as medical forms, enrollment forms, etc., to be completed and in the child's folder in order to place a name on the waiting list. When a vacancy comes up, the first family with a complete folder would be considered first. Directors who use this method say that the list is self-limiting and those on the list have shorter waits, since only very interested parents will bother to complete a folder. This method may not work if the wait exceeds six months, since medical information about young children may become obsolete.

Directors (in centers without Title XX funds) usually emphasize that they are extremely strict in following their lists. However, they do have some informal exceptions which are used in an effort to act as a family support or to develop more balanced classrooms.[7]

Because the names and order of priority on waiting lists must occasionally be waived to accommodate emergencies, it is wise to keep these lists confidential. Some programs have discovered that this is difficult, or impossible, to do.

▪ *Emergency Enrollments.*   Sometimes a parent appears at the program door, expecting his or her child to be enrolled. Most directors try to avoid these "emergency enrollments," because they have found that the children often have greater adjustment problems than those who have been better prepared through the regular routes of registration, conferences, and orientation. On the other hand, some situations are emergencies: a parent may be told to report for a job within two days; in cases of child abuse or sudden family illness, social workers may put pressure on a center to accept a child. Every director sometimes bends the rules; in deciding whether to bend them in a specific case, it is best to discuss the problem with the staff, including whether and how they can deal with the unexpected, "extra" child.

▪ *Referrals.*   Because the need is so great, and because centers wish to serve their communities, refusal of admission—either when the program is fully enrolled or when it cannot fill the needs of a specific child—is a difficult act for a director. If it becomes evident at any time in the enrollment process that your program can't serve the needs of a prospective user (the child is too young; the center is inconveniently located, etc.), you may be asked—or feel you have a commitment—to refer the parent to another center. The problems are that there are few referral systems in operation, and you may not have first-hand knowledge of the quality of neighboring centers. Decide now whether you will make referrals; the decision may be to say

<hr>

[7]*Ibid.*, pp. 10–11.

no for the present, or to refer parents to the state or local licensing agency. Some programs do hand parents a prepared list of other community resources, but tell them that they are not necessarily endorsing them. They may tell parents what to look for in order to judge the quality of a program: competent staff, good staff:child ratios, diversity of experiences, etc.

If your program is new, you will find it profitable in the future to become better acquainted with other centers, not only to set up a network for referrals, but to share ideas, information, pleasures and pains.

Special Procedures

Some programs set up special procedures as part of the enrollment process. These may take place before the first day, or may happen on the first day. They may all take place at one time or be staggered. They are set up to ease the child's adjustment to the new experience. The way you conduct these procedures will set the tone of your program for parent and child. Plan carefully. Some special procedures are:

Visits. They enable both child and parent to see programs in operation.

Conferences. Parents of a newly enrolled child must also attend a pre-enrollment conference with the coordinator before the child's first day of attendance. For previously enrolled children, the parent meeting prior to the start of the program is sufficient.

Before-the-first-day or first-day orientation. Set up a consistent plan.

- Introduce the staff, new classmates.
- Have an individual space for the child already set up, with his or her name on it—a locker, cubby, or some section of a storage area.
- Invite the parents to spend some time with the child on the first day, if this is convenient.
- If a new child is entering a program that is already in operation, ask the parent to pick up the child early enough on the first day so that the child is not the last one left.

One program we know of instituted the unusual policy of requiring a two-week trial period before a child was officially enrolled.

■ *Cancellation of Enrollment by the Parent.* The parent should be required to give ample notification (two weeks or longer) to the program and to pay all charges that have accrued. One program stipulates:

> *Withdrawal:* Two weeks written notice is requested for withdrawal for any reason. The original deposit will be applied to the child's last week of attendance. If prior notice is not given, the deposit will be forfeited; this is necessary to protect the program from losses.

■ **Denial of Admission for Financial Reasons.** One director suggests, "Don't accept people who have outstanding bills. Reregister them. They can send the registration card and fee in, but don't take them in the summer program, for example, until they pay their bill from the fall."

■ **Termination of Enrollment.** Although some programs institute policies that enable them to terminate a child's enrollment, none execute it except as a last resort, when all else has failed. Parent conferences are called, and every attempt is made to help solve the problem. Sometimes this may mean changing a policy. With cutbacks in funding for programs, and the strained financial circumstances many families are experiencing, programs may need to review such policies. In the case of financial hardship, the program director who said, "Don't accept people who have outstanding bills," also advised:

> The director should have personal contact. Every two weeks you should get a sheet of unpaid bills, and phone calls should be made by the director. This is the most effective way.
>
> First, look for the reason why parents aren't paying the bill. If we notice the bill is getting high, we write them a letter asking if they want to talk to us about it. Then we hear about all of the family circumstances.
>
> A committee should be established to look at the exceptions. Parents should submit appeals to them.
>
> If you have more than a handful of parents who are asking for fee reduction, your fees are too high.
>
> A child's participation in the program will be terminated if his/her health examination form is not returned to the After School Program office within one month after the child enters the program.
>
> Upon the discretion of the Head Teacher and after reasonable effort on the part of the program staff to integrate a child into the program, a child's participation may be terminated if that child is deemed chronically disruptive to the functioning of the program. The Head Teacher, after consulting the Program Director, will confer with the parent(s) and give notification of termination 5 school days prior to termination.
>
> A child's participation may be terminated if a child is regularly picked up after the 6:00 P.M. closing of the program.

Chapter 13

PROGRAM REGULATION

In this chapter we discuss situations in which programs have experienced operational problems. Establishing policies and procedures will help you prevent many of these problems. You must also institute penalties so that infringement by parents or children is minimized. In addition to informing parents of the rules, send home reminders when they are broken.

Taking a hard line is a means of protecting parents and children, as well as the program's staff and finances. After the rules have been set, stick to them. However, if they prove to be inadequate or unreasonable, you will know it by the number of complaints or requests for change. Then you may need to rethink a certain policy or its procedure.

You will probably need to consider the policies of the institution that is running the program or providing its site, since safety, liability, and legal issues are involved. If you are a school-based program, be sure to consult with the principal—everyone has a different perspective.

The Hours and Days of Operation

There is no greater sea of troubles than the policies and procedures concerning the hours and days of operation. Program managers tell us that their biggest worry is keeping track of children. They always fear that they will "lose" a child. Children may not come on the days they are supposed to be at the program. They may decide to wander off to a friend's, or the parent may neglect to notify the center that the child is ill or is going to the dentist's straight from school. You *must* be accountable: you must set up very strict rules concerning the parents' responsibility to notify the program about absences and changes in the child's schedule and the program's procedures for notifying parents of changes in scheduling or the unexpected absence of the child.

In addition to establishing your schedule, you will also need to set clear policies on fees; for example, will you charge tuition for all or for only some holidays? If you permit children to take tuition-free vacations at a time other than regularly scheduled vacation periods (for which tuition is not charged), and they do not give you enough notice, you may find yourself with too many staff people on hand, and not enough money to pay them. On the other hand, if you decide that tuition must be paid monthly, despite absences for long illnesses or regular school vacation periods, parents may balk. One program encountered resistance from parents who objected to being charged for a day that was cancelled because of snow: "We had to go to work—why should we be charged for a day when the program wasn't in operation?"

What do you feel is fair to the parents, to the children, and to the program—especially to its budget? A program in the Midwest established this policy and included it in the parent agreement:

> In event of illness, vacation, or other absences such as scouts, music lessons, and other out-of-school activities on a regularly scheduled attendance day, the day care staff will be notified and I am responsible for my child and my tuition payment.

Most new programs need to set policies and procedures on the following:

HOURS
- before-school
- after-school
- early dismissals
- part-time

DAYS
- holidays
- summers
- school vacations
- minimum number of days

- drop-in children and guests
- special nonschool days, including emergency weather conditions
- notification of absence

Hours

Programs are very explicit in stating the hours (and days) during which they will provide care. Here is an example from a program in the East:

DAYS OF PROGRAM OPERATION

The Centers will operate within the elementary school facilities, upon approval of that school's principal, beginning the start of the second week of the fall semester and ending the last day of school in May. The Center will operate from 2:30 to 5:30 P.M. on every regular school day. School Holidays and Staff Development days will *not* be center-operating days. The Christmas break and spring break will be the annual vacation time for the Extended Care Center staff; the Staff Development days will be used by Extended Care staff for training.

If you find that a number of enrolled children consistently arrive at 7:30 A.M. when the program officially begins at 8:15, you may want to rethink the hours you've set. If you can provide the staff, and the space is available, think about readjusting the hours to fit families' needs.

The problem of what to do about late pick-ups has been noted earlier. Programs institute financial penalties that are based on what parents can realistically afford—the fees pinch but don't wound. If the practice persists, the child's enrollment may be terminated. One program, obviously much abused, finally instituted the following iron policy:

CLOSING TIME

Centers close at 6:00 P.M. and your fees pay for day care services until that time. Parents whose children remain past 6:00 P.M. must pay an overtime fee, as follows:

1-15 minutes overtime:	$5.00 per child
each additional 1-15 minutes:	$3.00

You will be billed for overtime charges and the fee must be paid before your child(ren) attend the program the next week.

Another program informed parents that the late fee "is given to the teacher who must stay late."

Decide on the hours you will be open when regular school has an early dismissal day. For example:

DAYS AND HOURS OF OPERATION

After School day care programs will run from afternoon school dismissal until 5:30 P.M. Monday through Friday every day that school is in session and will follow the public school calendar. The After School program will begin at dismissal time on regularly scheduled early dismissal days except the last day of school when there will be no After School programs held.

Part-Time Care

Will the hours in which each part-time child attends be consistent? Clearly, variation means that your staff planning and amount of paperwork will be affected. Programs that offer part-time care have found that it is important to have parents work out a schedule ahead of time. One Y had parents send in a schedule each week for the following one. This involves extra recordkeeping.

Be clear on what is meant by "part time." The explanation below is specific:

Rates:

1. A Full Day is 7:30 A.M. to 5:30 P.M.
2. A Half Day Morning is 7:30 A.M. to 12:30 P.M.
3. A Half Day Afternoon is 12:30 P.M. to 5:30P.M.

Days: Holidays, School Vacations, Nonschool Days

Will the program be open whether or not regular school is in session? This decision will depend on whether the facilities you use are available, whether you can make special agreements to keep them open, if you can make alternative arrangements, and on the values and practices of the community you serve. Here are some examples of different policies:

Nonschool Days: SACC is not open on days when school is not open (holidays and vacations). A committee will report on alternative care arrangements. Look for information at the bulletin board or sign-out sheet.

Child care will be available on snow days and on the four nonschool holidays—Rosh Hashanah, Yom Kippur, Martin Luther King, Jr.'s birthday, and Good Friday—when the building is open for use by Extended Day.

On days that teachers work but students do not attend school (i.e., teacher conference days) children may attend the program all day at no additional charge.

Some centers will be open all day during winter and spring breaks from school. All children in the program will be eligible to attend these centers. There will be separate registration and additional fees for these periods.

There are also legal issues to consider. If the building is officially closed to children on certain days because of a teachers' conference or snow, does the program have the legal right to be open? Are the children insured? (If the children are covered by school insurance, is that insurance operative on a day when school isn't in session?) What are your formal contractual arrangements with your partner? Will regular custodial care, snow removal, heat, etc., be provided on these special occasions? Or must you follow the school calendar exactly, including its nonscheduled closings?

Some programs open their doors to the general public during school vacation, when regular enrollment is down: one program advertised openings for vacation week in the local paper.

Programs may set up informal alternate care to cover special days; for example, they make an arrangement with a licensed family day care home, or an agency, that will allow children to attend on special days. A program not ordinarily based at a Y or in partnership with it might negotiate with that agency to provide care for children enrolled in the program. Others might suggest to parents that they contact the Y individually to see whether their children can enter in the agency's activities on a short-term basis. If you can keep your site open, or are temporarily moving to another space, will you have to double up with another program?

There are certain periods when your buildings might be closed for some major renovations or serious house cleaning. Teacher conference days can create another problem. It's a help if the public schools will let the program know, in advance, when these will occur. As a program director in the Midwest said,

> Now the schools are letting the Y know in advance which days would be parent/teacher conference days. The secretaries let the Y know because of individual relationships worked out with the school secretaries.

Summers

Programs that run both school-time and summer programs need to decide whether families are eligible for the school-year program if they don't use the summer one. Parents may fear that their chances for enrolling their child in the regular program will be jeopardized if they don't use the summer one.

Scheduling

Once you have decided on the hours and days of operation, it is important that you present your schedule to parents, help them to work out a schedule for their children, and get them into the habit of communicating it to you. It is equally important to institute procedures by which they can notify you—giving ample notice—of any changes in scheduling, whether it's one day's absence or a long family vacation. Many programs permit great flexibility, allowing children to change their hours from week to week—but they are very strict about parents notifying them of these schedules and any last-minute changes.

> Weekly schedules should be given to the YMCA at time of registration. Any changes in schedules must be called in to the YMCA office prior to the change.

Scheduling for vacation periods creates special difficulties. SACC programs may offer care during Christmas vacation in response to requests, budget for it, and then find that parents either don't use it or that the demand is greater than they can serve.

For these reasons, it is necessary to institute policies and procedures (including the setting of special fees, if there are any) by which parents formally sign up in advance for these sessions, thus giving the program sufficient planning time. This is how the Family After School Program in Milwaukee, Wisconsin does it:

> These are the periods when all-day care is available for After School children:
> 1. Christmas vacation
> 2. February vacation
> 3. April vacation
> 4. Start and end of school year
> 5. School system holidays when the Children's Center is not on holiday; Rosh Hashanah, Martin Luther King Day, etc.
> 6. Public school snow days, if the After School can be opened.
>
> During these periods, we ask parents to sign up according to need for all-day or part-day child care. If a child is half-time and comes all day, there is an extra charge of $7.50 per day. If a child is full-time and comes all day, there is an extra charge of $5.50 per day.
>
> The billing for the extra periods is usually sent out within a month after each extra period. If a parent signs up for time, but doesn't use it, *we still must charge for it*, since we have to hire the number of substitutes ahead, according to the sign-up sheet.
>
> Do watch for the sign-up sheets *before* each vacation period to confirm your child care needs. Last minute requests usually cannot be honored.

A sample sign-up form (from the Eugene Latch Key Program,

CHILD CARE
Spring Vacation

PLEASE RETURN THIS FORM *NO LATER* THAN MARCH 10 *WITH PAY-MENT* IF YOU WANT CHILD CARE DURING VACATION TO:
Eugene Latch Key
P.O. Box 5556
Eugene, OR 97405
345-6358

Remember:

A. Care will be provided at:
    Patterson
    Lincoln
B. Bring a sack lunch on vacation days (no pop or sugar snacks—please).
C. Dress children warmly—the school may be cooler than usual.
D. Bring a swim suit and towel.
E. Vacation hours 7:30 A.M. to 6:00 P.M.
F. Full day rates are $3, $4, $5, $6 extra charge. Payment must be enclosed with reservation.

. . . .

I want child care during Spring Vacation for the following dates:

____ March 17 (Mon)   From ____ AM to ____ PM
____ March 18 (Tues)   From ____ AM to ____ PM
____ March 19 (Weds)   From ____ AM to ____ PM
____ March 20 (Thurs)   From ____ AM to ____ PM
____ March 21 (Fri)   From ____ AM to ____ PM

My site choice is ____ Patterson ____ Lincoln

Figure   13–1

Eugene, Oregon) for a spring vacation session is shown in Figure 13–1.

Special Nonschool Days

Special situations always arise when you cannot or may not be able to provide care. Regular school teacher conference days or release time for your own staff to attend a day-long seminar may or may not mean that you will be open as usual. Some of these times can be foreseen and you can plan for them by establishing policies.

There are also unexpected conditions that may suddenly force sites to close—extremes of weather create such situations. You must decide, very clearly, under what conditions you will stay open, when you will be closed, when you will have early closure, and what procedures you will use to notify parents that these policies are now in effect. In deciding what the correct policy should be, consider what is reasonable for your community. Many areas are faced with "snow days"—school cancellations caused by a sudden blizzard or unexpected icing of streets. Since the safety of the children is the uppermost concern, your policy here will be set with safety as its rationale. In addition, you will need to think about transportation. If you are hiring a bus company, what are its policies on when it will run and when it will not run? If most children will be walking, what are your safety criteria for the streets?

Here are some solutions programs have used:

If the school is closed, so is the program.

Even if school is closed, if the custodians can get in (to clear the walks) the program is open because presumably the streets are passable.

The program will be closed, but it will set up alternative arrangements for those parents who need it: for example, arranging for the use of family day care homes in special instances.

Once you have decided on your policies, plan how you will notify parents of program closings, and put the procedure in writing for them—in a letter, bulletin, or parents' handbook—before you need to use it. Whatever policy you institute, state it simply and very clearly. Try to avoid confusion, unnecessary phone calls, and an overloaded switchboard. Assign the responsibility to announce the closing to a specific person. Some programs tell parents to listen to the no-school announcements on specific radio stations. (You must decide who will call the stations.) Or you can set up a phone chain, the staff can call parents, or the institution you are cooperating with may be delegated to communicate the closing.

Community Day Care, Inc., of Lawrence, Massachusetts informs parents of its policy and procedures in the parent handbook:

The Center is closed due to bad weather on all days when the Lawrence or Methuen school systems cancel classes due to weather. Please listen to your radio (Stations WLLH or WCCM) for No School announcements. If we should close for any emergency reason when the public schools are open, you will be notified early that morning by a staff member.

Notification of Absence

Just as programs are accountable to parents to inform them of schedules and changes, so parents must be held responsible for letting the program know of any alterations in their child's regular attendance, for any reason. Centers must require parents to notify them in the event of any absence. The procedure for notification should be established—either the parent should call in by a certain time to a specific phone number or send a written note.

> I understand that I must call the Program when my child is to be absent (Kindergarten by 9:00 A.M., After Schoolers by 3:00 P.M.—during the summer by 9:00 A.M. for *all* children). I realize that this is for my child/ren's protection and the Program cannot be held responsible for any child who is not at the pick-up point for Kindergarten or not arriving at the day care sites after school.

Responsibility for the child's whereabouts is the major concern, but programs also suffer financially. Centers impose stern penalties for the infringement of these rules, although they are willing to discuss specific problems.

> I understand that if I repeatedly do not call in the event of absence, I may lose day care for my children.
> I understand that if my child(ren) is absent more than five (5) consecutive days (other than for illness) and that if I have not discussed this absence with the program's social worker or director beforehand, I may lose day care.
> All absences or additional days must be cleared through the YMCA office. The YMCA office must be notified by 10:00 A.M. the day of the absence or through the site coordinator the day prior to the change.
> There will be a charge of $1 per family per day if absences are not reported according to the above Schedule Policy #2.
> *Under no circumstances* should absence be reported by phone to the school office. However, a note should be sent to the child's teacher to clarify any unscheduled absence (i.e., a birthday party, etc.).

Generally, programs establish a certain number of paid absence days after which tuition payment may be waived; many programs, however, stipulate that for budget purposes, they cannot waive tuition payments.

> *Illness:* We cannot give credit for absences due to illness. If, however, an illness is serious or protracted, special arrangements can be made.

Signing In

Every program should institute a policy that all children must be checked in and checked out (and thereby accounted for). A specific procedure to enforce the policy should then be set up—either a staff person should take attendance or a parent should actually sign for the child when he or she is picked up and dropped off. Some SACC programs require children to sign themselves in and out, thereby encouraging a sense of responsibility and building in a helpful routine that provides a beginning and ending to the day.

Transportation

Programs need to notify parents exactly when transportation will and will not be available, including special days such as vacations, holidays, or field trips. You must also spell out a code for conditions and conduct in vehicles used by the program, whether driven by a volunteer parent or the employee of a bus company. For example:

> During regular school vacations, transportation is not provided and parents must drop off and pick up their own children.
>
> All children are to attend their regular after-school site and are to be picked up from their usual location. Special notes to parents at the M——— School: Please be aware that there will be no district transportation from your neighborhood on school holidays. If you are unable to bring your children directly to the school in the morning, you may drop them off at the Center by 8:30 A.M. and we will provide transportation to the M——— School.

■ *Field Trips May Require Special Means of Transportation.* Parents should be notified not only of the trip, but of any such special arrangements: "We will be going to the museum by public transportation." If you don't have a blanket form, parents should sign a special permission form which advises them of the arrangements.

■ *Notice by Parents of Changes in Transportation Arrangements.* You should set up a policy whereby, if a child is not going to arrive or leave according to the usual, agreed-upon arrangements, the parent will notify you in proper time and in a proper way. A procedure should be set up so that the parent knows what this "proper way" is, including to *whom* the notice should be made (the bus company, the program director, or whoever takes responsibility for the logistics of transportation) and *what form* the notification should take. One agency's procedure—"If your children have permission to walk home, we request that we have a written note to this effect"—is preferable to a procedure that leaves it up to the child to tell the program staff.

■ *Rules of Operation.* Guidelines that are set up by a public school transportation system or agency—stiff licensing regulations and rules for the condition of its vehicles—help programs ensure safe transportation of children. We worry about those programs that make informal arrangements in which parents and/or staff may use what-ever they can to transport children, without imposing regulations. For everyone's well-being, programs should think ahead about what con-stitutes a safe vehicle and driving situation. Rules should be set up about the condition of the automobiles used, the numbers of children permitted in a car, and where they will sit. The use of seat belts should be mandated. (In some states, the law requires that they be used.) These policies should be strictly enforced. The After School Day Care Association in Madison, Wisconsin, has proposed the following rules:

ASDCA PROPOSED TRANSPORTATION POLICY

1. Number of children per car:
   a. Subcompacts and compacts (Pinto, Vega)
      5 children—1 adult or
      3 children—2 adults
      Subcompact station wagons and intermediates
      6 children—2 adults or
      5 children—1 adult
      Station wagons or vans
      9 children—2 adults
   b. No more than 2 children may be in the front seat of any car.
   c. No children are allowed to ride in the back section of station wag-ons, Pintos, etc., unless there are upright seats in that section.
2. Seat belts must be used if specifically requested by parents.

■ *Rules of Behavior.* Many programs have had to formulate special policies and procedures to deal with misconduct on vehicles. Parents *must* be held accountable for their children's behavior in vehi-cles. Rules of behavior should be drawn up; parents should be notified of these rules and asked to discuss them with their children. Some programs, after notifying a child and his or her parents of mis-conduct, will suspend transportation privileges.

Health and Safety

Every parent wants to be assured that his or her child is in a healthy and safe environment. To provide such an environment for indi-vidual children, programs must set up policies and procedures that will protect the well-being of the group as a whole. These rules cover good health and illness, emergency procedures, and dealing with sus-pected child abuse. As one SACC program clarified:

> Because of the importance of these regulations for both the individual sick child and the children at the Center whom he/she may contact, *they*

must be adhered to strictly. Staff cannot devote the time necessary to comfort and care for a sick child. In addition it is vital to the health of us all that ill children not have the chance to spread an illness.

Health

In addition to requiring proof of immunization, medical and/or dental forms, and special authorizations for dispensing medication, programs have learned that they must set up specific policies on what constitutes illness, and institute procedures to handle different health problems. Decide what conditions will necessitate asking parents (or other authorized persons) to pick up the child and remove him or her from the premises.

> For children who become ill while at the Center, parents will be contacted (see Emergencies) and the child sent home for the following:
> 1. Oral temperature 101 degrees or greater
> 2. Vomiting once
> 3. Liquid stools
> 4. Uncontrollable and persistent cough
> 5. Appearance of acute illness or complaint of severe pain

You should formalize, in writing, the procedures to be used until the child is taken from the program.

> Until the parent arrives, the child will be excluded from activities with other children. The child will rest in the "quiet area" secluded from the main program area, supervised by a staff member.

Also you must determine in advance how the parent or other authorized person will be reached.

> Emergency files will be kept for each child at each site. Parents will be notified by phone from the program staff of any symptoms of impending illness . . . . Parents will be expected to leave work and pick up a child who appears to the coordinator to be too ill to remain in the program unless other arrangements have been made previously between the parent and the coordinator.
>
> The Center expects that if you are called in an emergency, you will come as soon as possible.

Parents have a responsibility to the program to keep children with certain illnesses at home, to notify the program about the absence, and to inform the program of what the problem is. In addition, certain illnesses require special handling. If children have communicable diseases, some programs require that they be informed, so it can be reported to the local board of health when indicated. Programs also stipulate which illnesses will require a doctor's note (stating that the child's disease is no longer contagious) before the child will be allowed back.

Parents may not bring a child to the Center if:

1. The child has a strep throat which has not yet been treated with an antibiotic for 24 hours.
2. The child has any rash of acute onset associated with fever or symptoms of illness.
3. The child had an oral temperature of 100 degrees or greater.
4. Persistent vomiting and/or diarrhea in the 12 hours before the child comes to the Center.
5. The child has impetigo with less than 24 hours of treatment with an antibiotic.

Once the child has been diagnosed with one of the above, we must receive notice from the doctor saying that the child can be allowed back in the Center.

If a child is absent for 5 or more consecutive days, parents of a child who has been ill with a contagious disease, except a common cold, should bring, upon the child's return to the program, a statement from a doctor indicating that the disease is no longer communicable.

When may children who have been ill return to the program, and under what conditions? Guidelines must be set up for communicable diseases:

A child who has had an infectious or communicable disease may return to the Center under the following limitations:
   Chicken Pox: 5 days after the last blister has scabbed.
   Pinworm: Anytime after being on medication for 48 hours.

Parents must understand that they have a responsibility to inform the program of the reason for the child's absence. By the same token, under some conditions the program is responsible for alerting parents about potential "medical emergencies." Here is one program's policy:

MEDICAL EMERGENCIES

Health situations of import for the entire Center will be brought to the attention of the Health and Safety Committee. This committee will have a role in determining Center policy in dealing with the staff and the coordinator of the Center. Parents will be specifically notified by mail of the presence of outbreaks of:

1. Streptococcal pharyngitis
2. Impetigo
3. Measles, mumps, chicken pox, rubella
4. Pinworms
5. Lice

Safety

How should the program handle accidents and emergencies? The first rules to set up when thinking about accidents and emergencies are preventive ones. In addition to using all reasonable measures (including adherence to—or improvement of—licensing standards), programs should print and distribute specific procedures to be used in case of fire or other events that require safe, rapid evacuation of the building. In some cases, programs follow the regulations of the school or agency in whose building they are housed; in others, programs have to devise their own procedures and conduct practice drills. In the example shown in Figure 13–2, the Eugene Latch Key Program in Eugene, Oregon lists exact steps, including *a means for ascertaining that all children are out of the building.*

If your programs will provide swimming, either as a regular activity or a special event, you should think about the swimming rules you will institute: Does the facility housing the pool have its own rules that you can adopt as is, or should you consider the program's additional needs and standards, including special staff:child ratios?

FIRE ESCAPE PROCEDURES

Close windows and classroom door upon leaving room.

Take roll book from file cabinet.

Children Inside
    Line up with staff member and move outside through
       exit doors in playroom.
    Proceed to the ball field adjacent to parking lot.

Children Outside
    Line up with staff member and proceed to the ball
       field adjacent to the parking lot.

Staff member in charge, immediately check roll of students
present.

* Fire extinguisher is located to the left of the playroom
  door exit.

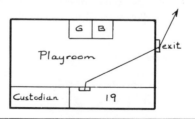

Figure 13–2

■ *When Accidents Happen.*   Every parent and program director knows that even when all reasonable care is taken, emergencies
arise. The program must plan ahead for the measures it will take in
such circumstances, and also distinguish among types of emergencies—a scrape on the knee will not, obviously, be handled in the same
way as a dislocated shoulder. *Parents should be notified* of even minor
injuries, however.

> In case of slight injury, the staff will clean the wound or apply ice or
> bandages, and will fill out an incident report for the parent and our files.

Set up procedures for the staff to deal with the immediate problem. One program keeps a list of instructions, including emergency
numbers to call, and posts it next to the telephone:

EMERGENCIES

RESCUE SQUAD	482-6900
AMBULANCE	482-6211
FIRE	911
SHERIFF	369-2000
POISON CONTROL CENTER	684-8111
FIRST AID	482-3001

In a life-threatening situation: STOP THE BLEEDING
ADMINISTER ARTIFICIAL RESUS-
    CITATION
SEND SOMEONE TO CALL 911
CALL PARENT OR GUARDIAN

In a nonlife-threatening situation: ADMINISTER FIRST AID.

Have the injured child or counselor rest until, in your judgement, he/she
is ready to resume normal camp participation. If a child receives a scrape
during the program, remember to inform the parent/guardian at the end
of the day so that additional attention can be given at home.

Every program should have at least one staff person who has received training in first aid; it is preferable to have all staff trained and
kept up to date on current procedures. Think now about how this
training will be provided, what equipment you should have available,
and where it will be located—and be sure the staff is told the location.
The Children's Center of Brookline and Greater Boston, Massachusetts, states its policy in its parent handbook:

HEALTH AND SAFETY POLICIES

Equipment

The Center has on each floor a single container, kept at a specified location beyond the reach of children, which holds the following items:
    Red Cross First Aid Manual
    Bandaids

Sterile gauze
Adhesive tape
Liquid antiseptic
Scissors
Tweezers
Syrup of ipecac, single dose container
Thermometer

Set up procedures for securing outside medical attention, for getting in touch with parents, and for transportation, as this program did:

EMERGENCY MEDICAL CARE PROCEDURES

In the case of a student injury or medical emergency, the staff member in charge will:

1. Contact parents. Phone numbers are in the student's file in the file cabinet.
2. If unable to reach parent, staff member in charge will contact emergency person listed as emergency contact in student's file.
3. If unable to reach emergency contact, staff member in charge will contact doctor listed on emergency medical care form in student's file.
4. If emergency treatment is needed, staff member will transport student to hospital emergency room listed on student's Emergency Medical Care Form, or will call an ambulance for transportation. Staff member's discretion will be used to determine best possible means of transportation to hospital.

Some programs maintain a separate emergency phone line to facilitate emergency communication. Some will not permit personnel, "under any circumstances," to transport a sick or injured child or staff person. This means the program must call police or an ambulance.

Finally—report and review the incident. In addition to insurance reports and other forms that may have to be filed, many programs have "incident" reports which they turn in to main centers or agencies, and/or use for their own purposes. One of the best forms we've seen not only asks when, where, and to whom the accident happened, but also: "Could this accident have been prevented?" and "What can be done to prevent recurrence of this type of accident?"

Suspected Child Abuse

Many states now have statutes requiring staff who work with children and have "reasonable cause" to suspect a child has been abused to report this to the state bureau responsible for children's welfare. By law, the bureau must then report the case to the police. The director's primary concern and responsibility should be to halt any further abuse. Think now about how such situations should be handled. The centers that have been most successful in dealing with this problem are those that try to work with the families in difficult situations, and/or make every effort to assist them in finding available community resources to help them *before* a crisis situation occurs.

Food

All programs either provide snacks or allow the children to bring something from home for the "snack break." Sometimes the children make snacks at the center. Some programs restrict the kinds of snacks children can bring. One program limited snacks to fruit and nuts and eliminated from its menu foods containing white flour and sugar. The policies you adopt regarding food should reflect parents' wishes and values. The YMCA Child Care Program in Boulder, Colorado decided to use only fresh fruits and vegetables in its menus.

CHILD CARE PROGRAM

The Child Care program will provide a daily snack at approximately 4:30 P.M. The staff will try to avoid processed food items containing sugar and artificial ingredients.

It is suggested that parents refrain from sending their children with sugar foods, soda pop, candy, etc. The erratic energy levels that sugar causes are difficult to monitor in group situations.

If parents have ideas for nutritious snacks, new recipes, and suggestions for places to shop, please contact directors with any information.

Bringing Articles to the Program

Programs have found that they have to set up rules about what children should—and should not—bring to the program. Some children like to bring special books or a soft animal. The problem here is the possible loss of these treasures, as well as possible space limitations. For this reason, some programs request that toys and other personal items be left at home:

Toys, games, records, and books are provided in Latch Key. If these items are brought, the staff will not be responsible for the loss or damage of these belongings.

Other programs are more flexible:

Parents are requested not to send the following items to the center with
their children unless arrangements have been made with the teachers:
toys, live pets, food, and money.

Other rules pertain to clothing. Many programs request that out-
erwear be labeled, including mittens and boots. Some need to specify
that in cold weather, because children play outdoors, they bring warm
jackets, hats, and mittens or gloves. Despite all the labeling, you will
still need to set up a lost-and-found box or other space!

Parent Involvement

All programs must find means of communicating with parents. We
suggested some ways earlier: monthly or biweekly newsletters, announcements in other bulletins, the parent handbook. There are
many ways in which parents can participate in the program; the
problem is not lack of opportunity or interest, but of time. Single parents have the greatest difficulty—although they often find that when
they attend meetings or other activities they receive a good deal of
support in return. (Many program directors we talked with expressed
disappointment that more parents don't become involved, although
they understood the demands on parents' time.)

The policies you establish will be determined by the situations of
the families your program serves and your own needs. Programs that
could not survive without the help of parents may set stiff policies
about their participation. Some programs make one or two conferences a year mandatory, with other more social activities optional.
The Lawrence Extended Day Program in Brookline, Massachusetts,
sets forth suggestions and requirements in its Parent Handbook:

WE NEED YOU

Parent concerns, opinions, and suggestions are encouraged at any time.
Reactions, both positive and negative, help the Program grow. There are
several ways this can be done.

1. Communicating directly with the staff.
2. Calling a Board member.
3. Filling out a Program evaluation form—several times a year a series
   of questions in the form of a written evaluation are sent to all con-
   sumer parents and staff. These forms are returned anonymously to
   the Program Evaluation Committee which tabulates and publishes
   the results and conducts a follow-up meeting with the Program parents and staff.

Each year Program families are invited to participate in special Program events, such as a spaghetti supper, pot luck supper, and an outing at a park.

PARENT PARTICIPATION REQUIREMENTS

1. Responsibilities are divided among various committees to ensure smooth functioning of the Program. It is *mandatory* that at least one member of each family having a child enrolled in the Program actively participate on at least one committee and/or Parent Board. Failure to do so will result in the request that the child be removed from the program.
2. Fund-raising events have been an important source of revenue for the Program. It is *mandatory* that at least one member of each family having a child enrolled work a minimum of 4 hours on a fund-raising event each year.

   By enrolling your child, you automatically become an Advisory Committee member . . . . As a member, you have the privilege and responsibility to make the program fit your needs.

   Remember, we *all* are working parents with limited time! If we are not able to generate strong enough parent participation, fees during the 1979–80 school year will need to be raised.

One SACC program has printed on its registration form:

I will help in the following area(s): (please circle)

fundraising	program evaluation
sliding fee	letter writing
nonschool day care	phone calling
public relations	equipment and supplies
publicity	legislation
typing	

Some of the ways in which parents can become involved in programs are:

- As members of board committees. (See Chapter 7.)
- As resource people, teaching skills and/or for field trips. "We call on all resources—one of our mothers is a police dispatcher and she arranged for us to visit the jail."
- Holding an "international night"—parents prepared a variety of foods from different parts of the world; children made flags, a map of the world; there were songs and dances from different cultures.
- Annual Thanksgiving dinner; a Christmas show; plays and other special events.
- Special family camp weekends.
- Potluck dinners.

- Special discussion groups: for example, nutrition, sex education.
- Home visits as program begins—especially if parents have just arrived in the United States.
- Conferences with parents and children. According to one director, a successful method is to hold a half-hour conference, fifteen minutes of which is with the parent(s) and fifteen minutes with parent and child together. A minimum of one conference is requested with each family, after which either parent or program can request another. "It gives the child a chance to talk about issues at home that have been bothering them or things they don't like about the Center."
- Large programs may appoint a regional supervisor to insure that parent involvement takes place.
- Have an extended day representative in the school PTO advocacy activities—for example, sending out postcards to congresspeople in Washington regarding new or threatened legislation concerning issues relating to day care, lobbying "The Big Board" to keep programs open, etc.

DIRECTORS' TIPS

How do you get parents involved? Look around, make them feel welcome, like a family. I used to feel nervous about calling parents—about the rules, etc. But now I call and it's easier, because I'm more comfortable with them and the guidelines.

Show parents that you care, be friendly, interested, ask questions. But you have to lay it all on the table from the beginning, make the rules clear. You have to know where to draw the line.

Keep the channels of communication open.

You really have to know the children's families. When there is a "concern" about the child, the staff says, "We need some help to work more effectively with the child," rather than "We think something is wrong."

Let parents and children know that we are human and we make mistakes.

The staff really asks questions of parents—"Do you want your kids to go swimming?"—and they really listen to the answers.

Parents feel that if they have a complaint, they can talk to us.

Some programs have found that scheduling meetings late in the afternoon, when work is done, makes it possible for more parents to attend:

We have many meetings for parents. We do it in a series, from 4:30–6:00 every week for four weeks. They come in whenever they can, they don't have to stay the whole time, and the content is from them. It sets up a support system, and the family council facilitates the meetings. This has worked very well.

The PTO was not terribly strong, because people have very little spare time. As a result, PTO meetings are now held at 5:30 in the afternoon. For these special meetings, high school students are used to supervise the children for the extra time while the parents attend the meeting. We limit the meetings to only one hour.

Children's Behavior

Experienced program directors have learned that they must establish, put in writing, and then distribute the program's policies and procedures concerning discipline. In this way they communicate to the parents what the center considers unacceptable behavior and how the child will be disciplined, including the program's policy that physical or other abusive punishment is never used. (Recently, some programs have found it necessary to set rules for smoking, both by children and by staff members.) We have noted that, in severe cases, the child's enrollment may be terminated for several reasons, including continual disruptive behavior at the center or on its vehicles. Dismissal is a last resort. The general rules for policy setting are:

- Define the program's concept of "disciplinary problems."
- Establish procedures for the staff to deal with them.
- If the measures aren't successful, set up a procedure for notifying and meeting with parent(s) to discuss other solutions. Depending on the situation, the child may be asked to attend.
- Establish a policy and procedure for terminating the child's enrollment, when all else fails.

The following is an example of the policy on discipline at the Lawrence School Extended Day Program in Brookline, Massachusetts:

A serious disciplinary problem is defined as one in which a child is hampering the smooth flow of the Program by either requiring constant one-on-one attention; is inflicting physical or emotional harm on other children; is physically abusing staff or is otherwise unable to conform to the rules and guidelines of the Program.

The following policies were developed by the parents who established the Adventure Club program in Robbinsdale, Minnesota and reflect their values; note that involvement of parents is built into the procedure:

Methods of Discipline Used by Staff: Discipline as defined by Webster: "training that develops self-control, character, or orderliness and efficiency."

It is the goal of the Adventure Club program to guide children in becoming happy, responsible, cooperative participants in this program through positive, non-threatening teaching techniques; to increase children's respect for themselves by guiding them to become responsible for their own actions; and to help them grow in their respect for the rights and feelings of other people.

When conflicts over the rights of other people and property develop, it is our goal to work with the individual children, listening to what each has to say and helping to resolve the conflict through effective communication.

If a conflict continues to exist:

1. A child may not be allowed to participate in the particular activity where conflict exists for a period of time.
2. If there is still an unresolved conflict, parents will be asked for ideas on solving the conflict.
3. If problem still exists, parents may be asked to keep the child at home for a few days until the child is ready to cooperate.
4. If conflict still exists, parents will be expected to remove the child from the center. (An alternative to this might be: seeking outside resource such as a family counselor to help all involved to work through conflict.)

   It is our policy never to use methods of resolving conflict by using physical abuse. Similarly, we cannot allow others (including the children) to do so within the center.

During prevacation periods, or at any time when discipline becomes a more general problem, don't hesitate to send a special reminder home to parents.

Part Five

DAY-TO-DAY OPERATION

INTRODUCTION

You are now ready to shape and implement the program as it will operate from day to day. Program building is difficult and challenging. In Part Five, we would like to step back with you to look at the program as a whole, and then look more closely at the crucial ingredients that make a SACC program work. The first step in the building process is *planning*—both the environment and the program for children. Chapter 14 examines the specific needs of children in SACC programs, and discusses ways of designing the environment and planning the activities to meet these needs.

The second step is *implementation* of what you have planned—actually bringing into the program the activities, experiences, and events that will allow you to realize your goals. *Evaluation,* the third step, is an ongoing process that will help you to examine how well your program is working to meet its stated objectives.

Chapter 15 deals with steps two and three. It describes in more detail "the stuff of programs"—types of activities, the use of materials and equipment, and how a program's day is structured. Finally, we suggest methods of evaluating the program.

Before you begin to plan and operate your school-age program, we suggest you take time to follow the advice of Elizabeth Prescott:

> Go back to your childhood—as far back as you can remember—and create an image of a happy memory and of the place where it occurred. Pay attention to the feel of things around you. What was happening to your body? What did you see? What could you touch and feel and taste? . . . The images that you come up with are the starting place for a good model of day care. It's the things that we experience as being good and positive in our childhood that we have the capacity to pass on to the children we care for. You will come up with images that have to do with outdoor places, with cozy places, with smells of good cooking, and with memories of being in physical contact with adults. I hope that your images have reminded you of how powerfully in touch children are with their environments.[1]

Following these suggestions will help to put you in touch with aspects of the program that are difficult for us to describe in words.

---

[1] Elizabeth Prescott, "Dimensions of Day Care Environments," Keynote Address, Day Care Environments Conference, Iowa State University (June 15, 1979).

In many ways, she is talking about the palpable feeling one has upon walking into a top quality SACC program—within a very short time you know it's a good environment for everyone involved, but you may have difficulty in expressing your reasons.

In these chapters we have combined the wisdom of several people who have been working in the school-age child care field for some time, as well as the plans, guides, schedules, lists of activities, program philosophies, and goal statements developed by SACC programs currently in operation.

SACC programs will differ one from another according to the population served, the purposes originally present for the program, the goals parents and staff have for children, and the days and hours of operation. Some programs may reflect parents' and staffs' values that children must be free to travel in the community and attend activities on their own, using the center as a home base. Other programs may be located in a Y or a community center that allows children to use their resources. Still others may take a particular focus (the arts, the environment) and provide activities only within that area. In addition, programs that provide full-day care will have different considerations from those that care for children only two to three hours daily.

Regardless of these variations, SACC programs, if they are truly to meet children's needs, will share some essential ingredients. They will provide ample, interesting, and well-organized ideas, activities, and materials with which children can create "their" program; vast potential for informal learning of new skills and of ways of getting along with children and adults; a way to bring the community into the lives of children (and vice versa) to enrich the overall experience possible for children; and an environment where feelings are understood and valued. Of course, none of these aims could truly be realized without a capable and caring staff.

As we describe the processes of planning and implementing your SACC program, please keep in mind that we are, for the most part, referring to the after-school and before-school hours. Although we attempt to touch upon some of the special issues for all-day programing, we ask that you make every attempt to apply what we say to all of your program hours *and* that you note the special section we've included on full-day programing.

Chapter 14

DESIGNING THE CURRICULUM AND ACTIVITIES

Who Is the School-Age Child?

Why do we need to know about children's developmental needs and stages when we design the content of a school-age child care program?

Children's differences and similarities, along with each child's developmental level and capacity, give us important information when we plan our program's content. The way we design the spaces children will spend time in, the activities they will participate in, the ways that the time they spend in the program is structured and shaped—all of these important program elements must reflect an understanding and appreciation of who children are. Designing a program that will meet their changing needs and be appropriate for their various developmental stages may be a particular challenge, since it will have to be an exciting and special program that can move into a child's "real life" after school without being intrusive. One person who has worked with SACC programs for some time describes it accordingly: "It should be their program, their place, their time. The place should reflect school-age children's needs; it should feel as though it's really theirs."

School-age child care programs provide an environment for children to learn, in an informal setting, about themselves and others. For

Children are different, one from another. Their differences reflect developmental abilities related to age, physical capacity, emotional maturity, and home and culture.

Children are also alike. They share common views of the world, seek to experience pleasurable and challenging moments, feel happy, sad, and bored in a common way—regardless of age, stage, or special physical or emotional circumstances.

there will be "others" who are in some way "different," to whom some children may react with curiosity, with fear, or with hostility.

These informal settings that we plan for, design, and finally live and work in give children and their adult caregivers a chance to see differences and to live with them, to share feelings and ideas. Children who are five and six are observed by children who are nine and ten; the older ones, perhaps remembering their own "childhoods," form protective or nurturing alliances. The younger ones look up to their older friends, emulate them, seek to be with them and to learn. Children with physical or emotional handicaps have the same feelings, needs, wishes, and fantasies as every other child. SACC programs may be an entry point for children into the realities of the outside world, where we must all learn about those differences and live with them.

■ *How Do We Find Out What Children Need?*   First, we consider that children in SACC programs have spent—or will be spending—three to seven hours in school each day. How are SACC programs different from children's daily experiences in regular school?

If you stand at a school building exit at 3:00 P.M., you will most likely see children rushing out, at the first sound of the bell, to begin what many children view as their real life. One school-ager says of school, "It breaks up your whole day."[1] This is a life made up of riding bikes, playing ball, going to other kids' houses, spending pocket money, raking leaves in their own or neighbors' yards, spending hours on the playground, in back yards or sidewalks, choosing sides, gossiping, forming friendships. From a child's point of view, the

---

[1] Gwen Morgan, "Putting it Together: Some Program and Policy Issues in School-Age Day Care," *School-Age Child Care, Programs and Issues* (Urbana, Ill.: ERIC-EECE, 1980), p. 91.

school day often means paying attention, following rules, being in a large group, sitting still and doing your "work." When you ask a child what is his or her favorite time in school, you hear: "recess," "gym," "music," and "lunch."

In many schools, there just isn't time to talk about what children are feeling, to mediate disputes, to engage in the conversation about trivia that makes up the content of most young (and old) minds. SACC provides a unique opportunity within an informal learning environment for children of varying ages to live and learn together. There is no set plan for "covering" specific academic subjects or pressure to do so by a certain time in the year. Instead, it is a chance to enrich what may—or may not—happen in school, and allow children the place and the time to develop relationships, venture out in new areas, or just curl up with a good book or a favorite cuddly bear.

A second way that we find out about needs is to ask others and to make some assumptions. Children have some basic needs and rights. They need and have a right to be safe, healthy, and cared for. We can assume that these "rock bottom" needs are present because we, as adults, hold some shared values about children, and because parents tell us so. Many parents, in answering questionnaires about what is most important to them in child care respond first by talking about safety and security. In addition, children tell us by their behavior that they want to be safe. Many children "hang out" at the playground after school because they are afraid to go home alone. Others in our communities can tell us the same thing: police and firefighters, school personnel, shopkeepers and fast-food restaurant managers—all know that children seek shelter and community with one another.

Children may not be able to express their needs in the same ways that adults can, but they are very able to say what a good program means to them. When children in one program were asked what the program should be like for them they said: "Going to the library, being allowed to bring roller skates, plenty of time to play games, getting help with homework." What they don't like: "When someone invites you home after school and you can't go."

We can find out more about what children are like and what they need to be—happy and always growing—by watching them. We see children teaching each other how to jump rope, play jacks, do the latest disco steps, sing current popular songs, fix each other's hair, throw frisbees, repair bikes, comfort each other, hurl insults, retreat into tears, and bake chocolate chip cookies. We also watch how and at what times they need an adult to console and teach—when there seems to be no way to finish a project or solve a problem without help.

■ *What Are Some of These Needs?*   Since many programs will be used by children who range in age from five to eleven or twelve, the content and style of the program—the way it feels to children of different ages—must speak to these differences in ages. Although the most basic, the need for—and right to—safety, health, and caring is not the only need children have. Docia Zavitkovsky, a pioneer in school-age child care programing, describes some of these different needs:

> Although there is no typical school-age child, there are certain characteristics that seem to stand out for different ages. It is important to know what these differences are if we are to be responsible for planning and implementing programs that meet school-age children's day care needs.
>
> It helps to know, for instance, why five-year-olds in general need more supervision and guidance than ten-year-olds. Five-year-olds stay nearer to home base; they have problems with sharing and losing; they wiggle when sitting and get into all kinds of body positions and screw up their faces when drawing or writing; they are active, busy and vigorous; they know the difference between right and wrong, are easily embarrassed yet can handle most routine situations; they use adult gestures, mannerisms, postures, affectations and intonations; and they act out what they know of the adult world and change roles rapidly to meet the demand.
>
> Ten- and eleven-year-olds, on the other hand, are more sophisticated, but they are also more moody. They tease, test, talk back, are more rebellious, and yet are open to distraction. At one center, the children have a chant: "Don't blame me, don't blame me, I did it 'cause he told me so, so don't blame me." They sing it, dance to it, act it out and laugh when one child admits, "O.K. I did it." They are involved with team sports and competition, with cooking, billiards, puppet shows, records (jazz, rock and roll), joke books, projects, clubs, rituals, riddles and rhymes (like "Inka Bink, a bottle of ink, the cork fell out and wow you stink"). They keep journals, write plays, are interested in making money, and like to move beyond the home base to the community. They want to have the freedom to make choices about what to do and where to go. They are gaining in height and weight. Girls may be menstruating and may be concerned about their looks, especially their skin and hair. Peer relationships are all important. Usually, they are not neat about clothes or rooms.
>
> Planners of day care programs must take these differences between age groups into consideration. I have seen many programs in which children who have been in a center for five or six years are still being fed the same daily schedule that long since has been outgrown—a pabulum, patty-cake program, boring and inviting trouble. However, an activity that is handled well by the staff can be appropriate for children of different ages.[2]

---

[2] Docia Zavitkovsky, "Children First: A Look at the Needs of School-Age Children," *School-Age Child Care, Programs and Issues* (Urbana, Ill.: ERIC/EECE, 1980), p. 8.

As Docia Zavitkovsky says, activities need to be available to meet this range of needs, and should also be interchangeable since eight- and nine-year-olds will want some cuddling time and five's will surely want to climb to the top of the Mount Everest that is your playground's jungle gym.

Basic Program Elements

There are some basic elements—or generalizations, if you will—that you should adapt to fit your program, paying attention to the needs and strengths of your children, the characteristics of your community, the skills of your staff, the days and hours of operation, and the goals you have set.

We have included examples, but you must do the work of generalizing from these specific cases and translating the following broad statements to your own reality.

In planning and implementing a SACC program, programs should:

- *Capitalize on the interests of the children.* Children should have opportunities to take part in activities that capture and extend their interests, as well as experiences that develop new ones. The staff ought to find out what excites individual children—what they want to engage in, learn more about, or explore.

- *Consider the range of experiences an activity can provide.* Many activities can be carried out as a simple "one-shot" experience. However, consider the increased learning that results when an activity is expanded to include the children from start to finish. Cooking is an excellent example. A staff member could select and prepare a recipe, write it up for the children to follow, purchase the ingredients, and take out the necessary supplies and equipment. Then, the children would do the actual cooking. A more exciting and in-depth approach might be: with staff guidance, the *children* decide what *they* want to make; they discuss what *they* think might be the ingredients; they research and bring in recipes; they do the math necessary to convert the recipe so that it produces the amount they need; they purchase the ingredients, organize the cooking, etc.

- *Use the community as much as possible.* This is where your outreach and relationship building efforts pay off. You can take part in already existing events (story hour at the library, skating at the park, intramural sports at the community center, classes at the Nature Center), reorganize regular events so they are specially tailored to your program (Cub Scouts meet at your school, rec department holds some classes at your site, local art center gives SACC program kids a special rate and provides class at a special time to fit your schedule), and/or set up special experiences (trip to a parent's worksite, visit to a nearby bicycle factory, bus trip to a local organic farm).

- *Capitalize on the myriad of opportunities that present themselves for informal, social learning.* Staff in SACC programs can use their informal environment to foster and encourage activities and discussions that deal with feelings, values, and ethical issues. For example, in one SACC program that enrolls physically handicapped children, the disabled child begins to attend the program a week later than the other children. During the first week, before the handicapped child arrives, the other children are encouraged to talk candidly about handicaps—their fears and questions—and they become somewhat sensitized to the feelings of the handicapped child. In this situation the informal learnings are limitless.

- *Build upon the special talents and interests of staff.* Many programs try to hire people with different skills and abilities, in order to provide many options for children. Things that staff know about, care about, and are enthusiastic about will come alive and be exciting to children. (Make sure that activities are appropriate for the children's ages, and that they are consistent with your program's goals and philosophy.) A staff member who is a potter might teach interested children all about different types of clay, how to build and throw pots, about glazes, etc.; a staff member who is an excellent tennis player might have a "tennis clinic" once a week; a staff member who is mechanically inclined might teach some of the older children how to make simple repairs on their bikes.

- *Allow for spontaneity and serendipity.* Although planning is critical to a successful program, it is also important that programs be flexible enough to respond spontaneously to events or special circumstances as they arise. When the first snow falls, children—who have sat watching from their desks in school all day—will want to run and play outside; a fight on the playground may prompt an absorbing and important group discussion; an unhappy child may desperately need the undivided attention of a staff member for a "special afternoon."

- *Agree upon and communicate clear, consistent expectations and limits to children.* Children need to know that there is a flexible yet consistent "set of rules" governing their behavior with each other, with adults, and with materials. When testing limits, children are reassured to find out that staff communicate with each other, and that they cannot go from staff member to staff member until they find one who will "let them get away with it." In such a secure environment, children know and understand the consequences of their actions.
- *Take an integrated, total approach to planning and carrying out the program.* We urge programs to use every opportunity to make connections among things that are happening or are about to happen instead of thinking of all the different activities as independent segments—and thus fragmenting the day. If children are planning to make piñatas to give away at Christmastime, you might put out books on papier mâché, as well as materials for them to practice with. You might find a film that shows how the custom came into being, and the children might spend time planning what they want to fill their piñatas with. Months later, children might be encouraged to write stories or "author" a book entitled, "How to Make a Piñata."
- *Balance the day's activities so that there are structured and unstructured times, teacher-directed and child-initiated experiences, and a range of activity options as well.* Striking this workable balance may appear difficult, but if you consider it while you are doing the planning, it is more likely to happen. As you plan each day, ask yourselves: Are there ample opportunities for children to take initiative and carry out their own ideas? Is the afternoon too heavily teacher-directed? Do the materials available to children allow for unstructured, open-ended use? Do we have the materials and the staff to carry out activities that need some adult supervision and guidance?

Planning Is the First Step

There are three essential elements to consider when planning your program:

- *The environment*—the program's space and the people and materials in that space—should provide freedom to move and quiet, protected areas for children to retreat to.

- *The activities*—the building blocks of the program—should be varied, plentiful, and appropriate for a mixed range of ages. They should be initiated by both staff and children, each taking the responsibility for being well prepared and well organized.
- *Important contacts with the outside world*—the community of which the child is a part—should be developed. Children can be introduced to senior citizens and senior citizens to children; children can partake in community activities; they can learn about unusual (and usual) jobs, and can help to contribute something to their neighborhoods and towns.

All of these are interrelated, and taken together comprise a SACC program's *curriculum*. As defined by one early childhood educator: "Curriculum is what happens in an educational environment."[3]

In some SACC programs this curriculum is often the result of happenstance—the environment, the activities, or the materials are not planned. Or, perhaps, the ways in which all of these interrelated elements interact is not well understood. For example, content-rich programs with the latest recycled materials or shelves chock full of manipulatives, games, and books will not work if staff are not skilled in teaching children how to explore new materials with patience. Rooms that are spacious and free of obstructions will not be much good if children aimlessly wander in search of something to do. By the same token, programs that must make do with shared space in a cafeteria or a corner of a school auditorium can, with creative storage of plentiful supplies, materials, and equipment, create an environment which attracts children and keeps their interest.

Before you construct a plan for your program's curriculum, recall your early discussions about the philosophy of the program. Through planning you translate the philosophy and goals into the actual curriculum. Along with planning, you need an understanding of who your children are—their different ages, stages, cultural heritage; how their parents view your role; the contributions individual staff can make to the program; and the space available to you.

When defining your goals, consider both the goals for the program as a whole and your goals for individual children. The two should be interrelated, each building upon and reinforcing the other. It is not enough just to *set* a goal; everything that happens in the program should work toward realizing that goal. For example, if the pro-

---

[3]Elizabeth Jones, "Introduction: Curriculum Planning in ECE," *Curriculum Is What Happens* (Washington, D.C.: NAEYC, 1970), p. 4.

gram's emphasis is on individuals making choices and taking responsibility for their own learning, then your environment should reflect this. It may be that you set up the room with "learning centers"—special projects and/or interest areas—that children can choose independently. A large felt board that carries a list of all the available choices and has a place for each child to hang his or her name tag may be an organizing tool as well as a way to act upon your goals.

Although the learning center approach may be easier for programs that have exclusive use of their own space, *any* program can plan ways for children to move freely, make their own choices about activities, *and* participate as group members as well.

Most programs set goals for children, but many find it difficult to actually translate them into action. As a part of the planning process, SACC program planners should write down exactly how specific goals and objectives will be implemented. For example:

GOAL—Children will be independent
How evidenced? They will:

- Clean up after work and play.
- Make decisions on their own.
- Take part in activity planning.
- Be a part of group decision making.

How implemented?

- Ample time will always be given for cleanup, so that children rather than adults can take responsibility for this.
- Children will decide on weekly jobs that need to be done and will be responsible for doing their jobs.
- If any child finds that an area isn't cleaned up following an activity, he or she will be encouraged to talk with the children who used the space and request that it be cleaned up—*before* the child approaches a staff member for help.

The Environment

Children need places to play both indoors and out-of-doors, just as they do at home and in their neighborhoods. Both the indoor and the outdoor environment should say, "Come play with me!" It should have spaces within and around it where children can have opportunities for solitude, gentleness, mobility, and challenge. In these spaces the program's activities will happen, but the space itself can provide an activity too—children can participate in planning and designing how the space will be used and make changes in it to reflect changing interests and skills.

The spaces you design, both indoor and outdoor, should mirror the diversity of your children—their ages, their developmental abilities, their different interests, needs, and skills. Some children prefer to spend a lot of time indoors: making things, cooking, talking, and playing quiet games. Others must have more access to physical challenge, to acceptable ways of expressing their energy. All children will at some point want some of each, so your program must make sure that both indoor and outdoor space is available, designed with equal attention and care.

■ *Outdoor Space: What Do You Need?*   When you think about outdoor space, remember that children often seek out their own "turf" where they can, as Elizabeth Prescott writes, "have the opportunity for the legitimate exercise of power, the ability to control territory, and opportunities for risk and daring."[4] If this sounds too much like the *Lord of the Flies,* remember, too, that when you were small, a corner of the yard or playground was an important meeting place— for telling secrets, swapping trading cards, writing your name in sand with a stick.

Outdoor space can be used for special activities. For example, in the Midwest, a portion of a school playground could be flooded to make an ice skating rink in the winter. In temperate climates, outdoor space can be sheltered from the rain and, like the play area in one program in California, be open on three sides, with the roof protecting a ping-pong table and a pool table.

Under ideal circumstances, programs should have outdoor space that is adjacent to their main, indoor area. This allows for a free flow between the two areas and is the easiest for staff to supervise. If adjacent space is not possible, then programs should strive for something that is next door or very close by. The farther away it gets, the more limited will be its use. Outdoor space should be:

- Available to children as an option (one of several) to be chosen when children feel like it
- Safe, but challenging
- Accessible to all children (taking into account age and ability)

---

[4] Elizabeth Prescott, "Dimensions of Day Care Environments," Keynote Address, Day Care Environments Conference (Iowa State University, June 15, 1979).

- Conducive to creative play (a playhouse, hut, etc.)
- Suitable for playing games—softball, jogging, group games, and other sports
- Equipped for climbing, running, jumping, swinging—so it can be used differently by children of different ages and stages of development

■ *Indoor Space: What Do You Need?*   Children need what Elizabeth Prescott calls, "opportunities to be gentle, to play without intrusion." Programs can respond to these needs by creating the feeling of a home base for children—a place that is theirs to relax in and be identified with. Because it is important for children in programs to feel like "regular kids," the home-base space should provide a comfortable, livable place where children can either "fold up" on a couch or can interact with others. Home-base space should offer:

- Safe and plentiful space to move about in (check the licensing requirement in your state, or have a *minimum* of thirty-five square feet of indoor space per child)
- Places for individual and group activities and special projects to be worked on.
- Quiet areas for privacy, reading, and resting.
- Storage for materials, some easily accessible to the children.
- Ready access to the out-of-doors.

This space should feel comfortable to adults and children:

- It should be inviting, warm, and home-like. Fill corners with soft pillows, a rug, an old armchair or couch.
- Children should be able to identify it as their own, by putting their "stamp" on it—their paintings and art creations on the walls, a small pet corner for hamsters, a fish tank or a terrarium, plants, and other living things.
- The space should have some boundaries within it for different kinds of activities and play. Rules about those boundaries should be agreed upon (or initiated) by the children, and clearly communicated and observed (only five children in the block area; no running indoors; the reading corner for quiet work only).
- The area should be used consistently and be easily identifiable by children, parents, and staff from day to day, week to week, and month to month; try to avoid constant moving around from one space to another.

- Feel free to experiment—if something is not working, try a different approach. Keep aware of the changing needs and interests of your children and don't be afraid to make changes.
- Some spaces within the environment should encourage both short-term and long-term projects—places where things can be worked on for one day or over a period of a week or longer.

■ *When You Serve Preschool and School-Age Children.* In programs with both age groups, it is very important that the older children have *separate* space for program activities and for storage of supplies and equipment that is not available to preschoolers. Although this may be difficult if the center has limited facilities, it is essential to school-agers who will balk at what looks like a "baby program" and who need space that is "theirs."

■ *When You Have to Use Shared Space.* A home-base in a cafeteria or corner of an auditorium can be hard to achieve, but not impossible. Large storage closets or mobile storage units that can be rolled away in the evening can hold a multitude of objects which can transform your space quickly. Big pillows, a rug, even plants and other living things (one program's mobile unit houses goldfish in a tank!) can be stored and arranged to create a homey and comfortable feeling. You will make sacrifices, though. Kids' art work may not find a place on the walls; projects may have to be completed in one day, or longer projects may have to be small so that you can store them conveniently. But if it is your intention that your program's space feel good and safe for children, it can happen!

■ *Use Other Areas to Increase Your Space.* When gym, cafeteria, auditorium, or corners of kindergarten rooms are all you have, it is especially important to use other areas in and around your program. Schools may have homemaking rooms, community rooms, special shop or manual arts space, an art room and media center. The recreation center, community center, or Y may have a pool, special gymnastics areas, indoor tracks, and other athletic facilities. The use of these other spaces is important when you have limited home-base space. Children on their way home from school are often free to come and go within their own neighborhoods, and should have the same options available to them in your program.

If no other resources are immediately accessible within the building, you may be able to make arrangements with others to use their facilities on a regular basis:

- *Indoor recreation facilities*—scheduled use of gyms, pools, etc.

- *Library*—weekly visits for story hours, movies, checking out books (small and large groups)
- *Outdoor park facilities*—scheduled use of pools, ice skating, ballfields, etc.

■ **What About Storage Space?**   You should have enough space so that your program equipment and supplies can be stored to maintain them in good working order. Staff should be able to get easily what they need for the day, and children should have access to materials so that their independence is encouraged. Also, both staff and children need places—cubbies, lockers, etc.—to store their personal belongings.

If storage areas don't exist or if what is available is inadequate, consider purchasing inexpensive metal cabinets, or perhaps building something that serves a dual purpose—for example, a room divider/storage cabinet. Many programs that share space find it helpful to have a cabinet on wheels that can be kept in a closet. Others stress the importance of locking up equipment and supplies so that there will be no unbargained-for "sharing."

■ **Consider the Needs of Parents and Staff.**   Wherever possible, make sure there is separate space for the program's director or other administrative staff. This may mean converting to an office a small unused room near the child care area or a large, walk-in storage closet. Or a corner of your program's main home-base space, marked off by a sliding door or screen, could serve as an office. The director should have a desk, cabinets for files and materials, and a place to sit quietly with children, parents, and staff to talk and plan. The director's space should be private, if possible, but close enough to the action so that he or she can keep an ear out and be available when needed.

Program staff also need a place to hang their coats, store their belongings, meet together and with parents, and sit for a moment at break time. Some programs have a staff room that serves as a materials and curricula library, in addition to a meeting place. This is especially important when programs operate all day, during school vacations and holidays.

If you expect parents to pick up their children at the end of the day or drop them off in the morning before school, make sure that there is a space for parents to park cars easily, near your main entrance, if possible. Ideally, there should be a spot for parents to sit, wait for their children to get ready to come home, and talk with other parents and staff.

If your program's space is unavailable to you in the evenings, you will need to plan for a large group meeting area for potluck suppers, staff planning, and training sessions. Such space may be easy to use if you arrange with the host institution in advance. You may be able to arrange a regular schedule for the times you will be using this area throughout the year.

■ *How to Achieve Inviting Indoor Space for Children.* Designing an environment for a school-age child care program is especially challenging because of the diversity—ages, abilities, needs, interests—of the children to be served. In addition, you will be trying to balance how much the actual physical space you have determines the program, versus how much the program determines the space to be chosen. You must *consider the numbers* of children you have planned to serve and whether you need to make modifications based upon the square footage you actually have. You must know *what funds are available* to spend on the space—whether that amount is adequate or whether additional money is necessary. *How much time is needed* to work on the space must be weighed against the time that is available and whether the work will be done by professionals or volunteers.

When adults and children are both involved in making decisions about and in organizing the program's environment, it can become a joint venture that provides an excellent, varied, and unique learning experience, allowing children to feel a sense of ownership and pride in the environment that they have helped to create. This is not to suggest that children should walk into a large, barren room on the first day of a SACC program. Clearly, adults will want to make certain preliminary decisions and will need to ready the environment in some ways before the children arrive. However, children's behavior in a space and their feelings about that environment vary greatly where activity choices are based on *their* expression of what they like to do; they discuss and set the rules; and they help build and paint the furniture. Children of different ages can participate as seems appropriate to their stage of development—with the older children working alongside the younger ones, thus encouraging a "family" group atmosphere.

There is a direct link between how the space is organized and what type of interactions and activities take place. Consider your priorities and the goals you have set for the program as you make decisions about arranging the physical space. For example, if it is important to you that children have a chance to spend quiet time alone (reading, resting, playing), you must be certain that the environment includes some private places where such activity can occur without interruption. If you want children to be as independent as possible, then you must make certain materials (scissors, glue, paper, crayons, etc.) available without the need to involve adults (for example, provide low, open shelves at child's height).

Design the space with the special needs of your children in mind. If there will be children with physical handicaps which make mobility difficult, make sure you have adequate (or extra-wide) pathways for wheelchairs or for children who wear leg braces or other mobility aids.

Assume that there will be times when the outdoor space will be unavailable—the weather is bad, or another group is using it for team sports. The indoor space should accommodate some active play, either a large group activity like dancing and tumbling, or manageable group games ("Take a giant step," "Red light, green light"). If your space simply cannot be adapted for this kind of activity, try to obtain the use of a gym or a nearby recreation center.

Organize the space into distinct activity/special project areas. No matter how large or small the space is, dividing it up into areas for specific types of activity will encourage participation. It will allow children to work productively in small groups without interruptions, and encourage continuity by permitting projects and activities to be worked on over time—for example, special science or woodworking projects. You will be striving to create an environment that is predictable, yet not stagnant. You will want flexibility and change, without the area being in a constant state of flux.

Make the environment beautiful and pleasing to look at and be in. Children and adults should feel comfortable in the SACC environment. This will have implications for the types of furniture in the space, and other materials that will add the "softness" that has been referred to as a critical element in day care environments. As Elizabeth Prescott says: "Pillows, blankets, rugs, bodily contact, laughs, and hugs are important."

Another dimension that is important has to do with organization within the space. Materials should have an order—and an order that makes sense. This will help to teach children how to care for things and will allow them to function more independently in the space. A space that is neat and ordered—blocks stacked with others their size on shelves, rather than dumped in a box—will communicate a message to children about materials, *and* will help children to learn how to take proper care of them.

Define clear boundaries within the space for specific activities. Indoor space should be defined for energy-releasing activities (both noisy and quiet), and you should plan which activities are permitted in what areas. For example, a block area should probably not be right next to the quiet reading area. Some programs that have multiple rooms choose to have "noisy" activities—woodworking, block play, records, cooking—clustered in one room and quieter activities—reading, homework help, crafts projects—in another.

However you organize it, we'd suggest that agreed upon rules be established that govern the numbers of children in particular areas, the behavior allowed (running outdoors or in gym only), and where and how materials may be used.

Display materials so that they are inviting to children. Materials and projects may be displayed so that they entice and encourage children's involvement. For example, many programs set up woodworking areas with hand tools on pegboards, wood and nails in bins, and large woodworking tables for workspace. Others have cooking areas in which cooking utensils and ingredients are arrayed on shelves, with recipes written on large tagboard, easy for the children to read. At times, children are reluctant to try new things unless they are presented in ways that invite curiosity and participation.

As you add different materials or new pieces of equipment, you will find that the total environment may need to be changed. Remember that it takes children a while to become accustomed to the physical space, and to learn the rules. Changes should take place gradually, with time provided to get used to them.

If your program must use shared space which you cannot alter or add to permanently, it is still possible—and necessary—to design that shared space as an inviting environment. When these spaces *are* the SACC environment, they need to be adapted in order to meet the diverse needs of the children in care. Most SACC programs that are unable to change the environment find that locked storage closets, portable room dividers, cabinets on wheels, etc. are essential. One program that operates in a small cafeteria has used ingenuity to provide a rich environment for children: the program has one large metal closet with a lock that contains the supplies and materials needed to transform a small, empty cafeteria into an inviting space. A few rolled carpet remnants and pillows provide softness. Folded blankets can be draped over freestanding tables to allow for private spaces. Children can reach the bottom shelves in the closet to help themselves to the supplies they need; the top shelves are reserved for teachers. A table holds a changing array: fresh flowers, a terrarium, a goldfish bowl, and other things that are aesthetically pleasing for children to look at. On the inside of the door is taped all information that could be needed by a substitute or other staff—emergency phone numbers, the usual daily schedule, etc.

In situations such as this, where space has multiple uses, many programs successfully adapt the environment by including in the daily routine the time needed to set up and "take down" the program—hanging pictures on the walls, putting materials out on the tables, and rolling out room dividers/storage cabinets. When space is shared, it is important that both users agree about how the program can "stake out" its own area, where it will store equipment and supplies, who will clean the space (and when), and in what condition the space is expected to be found by those sharing it.

Designing the Outdoor Space

Outdoor space is essential to your program. Its design should reflect what you already know about children: that they need and like active, physical play; that some children will be more interested in—or more adept at—certain kinds of physical activities than others; that age will determine, to some extent, the kinds of playground activities children will choose; and that all children should have a variety of physical exercise and play available to them.

Planning the use of outdoor space means thinking about both safety and challenge, and about how children of different ages and abilities can use the equipment. For example, climbing structures should allow young children to feel safe and older children to be challenged. An obstacle course might be set up that provides obstacles at varying levels of difficulty.

Your financial and labor resources will also determine how much you can do to your space. You may be able to enlist help from architects or playground designers who are searching for a project for students to work on. Parents and children in the program might work together, both to design and to build the play area. And local businesses, as well as individuals, might donate materials such as huge rubber truck tires, wood, telephone wire spools, and rope.

If you are free to design the outdoor space for your program, there are some things you should consider and do before you build or obtain any equipment. First, visit playgrounds, recreation areas, and other day care programs to see how space is designed and how children use it. Notice which kinds of equipment attract children. It may be that the fancy, expensive pieces aren't really appealing and go unused most of the time, and children cluster around the basketball hoop or a tire tied to a tree branch.

Notice the safety factor: Is the equipment old and in disrepair? Do children play on it anyway? Are the play areas clearly defined and far enough apart to prevent frequent collisions or interferences with activities going on in them? Do younger children get shut out of certain places because the older ones have them staked out? What kind of boundaries between areas are there, and do they work? What's needed to make the boundaries work? Will you have to create lots of rules for playground use in your outdoor space, or can you construct your outdoor environment to minimize excessive rules and regulations?

Look at outdoor space in the same way you look at indoor space. There should be areas for large group games and sports; space for running, perhaps for bike riding and roller skating; areas for climbing structures; and a corner for a playhouse. If you're lucky enough to have a tree, a close-to-the-ground tree house, with ladders for climbing and overhead shelter, will serve as a place where small groups of children can play or that individual children can use for quiet or private time.

Your outdoor equipment should be both single-purpose and multipurpose. Some of the standbys that all children love should be there: jungle gyms, ropes to climb on, swings (either single ones in a corner, or several in a row for socializing), and a sand area that encourages use by the older children as well as the younger ones.

Try to use large equipment that can be rearranged—tires, large planks, wheel sets. As Elizabeth Prescott so wisely put it in a talk at a day care conference, "Anytime you are thinking of sinking anything into concrete, stop and wait and think about it, because once it is embedded in concrete you're going to have to live with it."

Make sure you have enough playground equipment—balls and bats, jump ropes, roller skates (some children may bring their own), etc. Equipment should be in good condition, and there should be enough of it so that sharing doesn't become a problem, with kids having to wait too long in line to use it.

■ *When You Are Sharing a Playground or Outdoor Play Space.* One program staff person advises:

> Have your children feel that they're not different—they can ride bikes on the playground with other kids. The program becomes part of the community, not separate from it.

There may not be an opportunity for you to change the outdoor environment if you are sharing it, so you must use what exists, supplemented by your own movable play equipment. Portable pieces, such as easels or a wading pool, will enhance the activities available, and will help if there's just not enough equipment free to use when you need it.

> One of the things that is really sticky in day care is this question of safety and one of my concerns is that it's very easy to start prohibiting everything. The day you have two children on a swing and one of them falls off and skins his knee, then the next day there's very apt to be a rule. No more two people on a swing. Yet two people on a swing is a neat thing to do and the important thing is that you experiment doing it safely. When you are taking care of other people's children, you have a responsibility that is a little bit different from being mother. This is a sticky wicket that you have to keep re-evaluating because you can't keep limiting children's experience because somebody might have an accident . . . . Climbing trees. Under what circumstance do you let children climb trees? Is it important to let children climb trees?[5]

■ *Make the Space Safe for Children.* Make sure your environment, both indoors and out, is free from hazards. Even when your building meets health and safety regulations, there are bound to be places and conditions which might pose a threat to children's safety: for example, uncovered radiators, slippery stairs, parking areas. Keep your equipment in good working order. If there are sharp edges on climbing structures, rusty edges on small metal cars and trucks or garden tools, fix them or replace them.

Protect your children from adults or other children who are not part of the program or the facility your program uses. Entrances and exits should not be open to all who feel like ambling through. Unfortunately, this is a necessary restriction programs must consider in the best interests of their children.

Make clear rules about how space and equipment is to be used. It is not necessary to ban equipment that might be dangerous (saws, drills, small stoves for wax melting, etc.). It *is* necessary to make rules for their safe use, and to make sure that they are stored in a safe place. While we may not be able to prevent *all* accidents, some are avoidable.

Planning the Activities

> All children will not learn the same thing from the same experience; planning should take this into consideration, particularly for group time.[6]

---

[5] *Ibid.*

[6] Sandra Horowitz, *Curriculum Is What Happens: Planning Is the Key,* ed. by Laura Dittman (Washington, D.C.: NAEYC, 1970), p. 22-23.

Planning ahead means considering both the long and short term. Although you will probably want to keep the program flexible enough so that you can spontaneously respond to an exciting event or circumstance, you will have to do some planning. And planning should be more than a casual—or frantic—answer to the query, "What shall we do this afternoon?"

In *long-term planning* you will think about large chunks of time (months, semesters) and consider what goals you have for that time period. For example, a group that is planning to open a SACC program in September may feel that by Christmas every child should have worked at least twice with each material in the room; should have planned and carried out one in-depth, independent project; and should have gone on at least four field trips. Long-term planning will allow you to schedule special events (trips, play performances by the children, special visitors—a folk dance teacher, a storyteller—to share their skills with the program).

In order to meet long-range goals, the staff will have to integrate them into their short-term planning. This may mean that at weekly planning sessions the staff will always schedule one field trip, carefully keeping track of who went on the last one and what might interest children who are reluctant to sign up. It also may mean that you will plan for clubs or special projects by considering carefully the interests expressed by children, so that no one is left out.

Short-term planning will allow your staff to prepare for activities and projects which may take only a day or a few days to complete, as well as for regular, ongoing activities. For example, if your program participates in intramural sports with other programs, a sports event can be on the schedule several weeks in advance.

As a way of answering the ever-present question "Why plan?", the Madison After School Day Care Association in Madison, Wisconsin includes the following in its curriculum guide:

Children will generally find ways of occupying themselves, even if no plans are made. Why, then, should you bother to plan at all?

1. Planning insures variety for the children. Children will often only choose to do things that are familiar to them. Scheduling new choices opens up possibilities for them.
2. Planning specific activities cuts down on the number of petty conflicts between children. It has long been observed that children can "play" by themselves only so long before things begin to deteriorate. While children need scheduled "free time," they shouldn't have three hours of it.
3. Planning provides a means of assessing the success of the program,

passing useful information on to other staff, and recording for future reference what was done at the center.

4. Planning sets forth specific responsibilities for staff, aides, and volunteers.

5. Planning provides an outline which determines what supplies and materials will be needed on a given day.

6. Planning provides substitutes with information, in the event that a staff member is absent.

7. Planning makes it possible to inform the school administration and staff of upcoming activities. It is important that the After School staff are seen as professionals, and that program plans are available for school staff and administration to see if they so desire.

8. Parents must be informed of program activities, particularly when children will be outside of the school building. Plans should be available at the center for scrutiny by any interested parent. In some cases, it is valuable to post a condensed version of the day's activities so that the children and parents can easily see it.

9. The A.S.D.C.A. Board of Directors and the Administrative staff must be aware of the center's activities. The quality of advance planning is one aspect of staff evaluation.

■ *Your Plan Should Include Some Things That Are Done Every Day, on a Regular Basis.*   Routines are an important part of daily programing. In one program director's words: "Children enjoy a predictable environment if they know when to expect certain regular occurrences, and they will be able to plan many of their independent activities around them."

A staff person from Minnesota describes her SACC program's use of routines:

> Two things about our program never change: We have a circle where we plan for the day, take attendance, do sharing—kids do "show and tell," and we have a survey of what kids are interested in and let them ask questions. The kids have to be quiet and listen to each other, and this happens at first when they come in from school. The other thing is snack—this always comes right after circle time.

■ *The Resources That Are Available to You Should Be Reflected in Your Planning.*   If the swimming pool or gym is only available to you at certain times during the week, then your schedule will allow for those activities. A special consultant—a pottery-maker or a dance teacher—may come to your program weekly or twice a month, so you will also want to plan around those visits. Volunteer staff may only be available twice a week, so in planning you might make maximum use of those extra adults by arranging a field trip or similar activity that requires a greater number of adults as supervisors.

■ *Planning Can Make "Difficult" Times Easier.*   Transition times—the arrival of children in the morning, their departure for school, and their arrival from school in the afternoon—need to be smoothly engineered. Your knowledge of how children will feel at these times will help you to plan for these transitions, as will your knowledge of what staff is on duty and how to use them. Good planning of these difficult times can set the tone for the day.

■ *Incorporate in Your Planning All Information You Can Gather about the Children's School Experience.*   A director in California describes how her program tries to enrich what happens in school:

> If the school class goes to a bank on a field trip, then at the center we try to do things that would extend the experience. It's not an extension of the day, but an enrichment of what they're doing in school. For example, in our dramatic play area, we might help the kids to set up a play bank, with real deposit slips and play money, where the kids could take turns being teller and customer.

When programs plan around school curriculum, staff must have time to talk with regular classroom teachers, and must know in advance that there will be a special unit or part of the curriculum which would lend itself well to the SACC program's curriculum. It is important not to make programs seem like "just more school" to the children, so be careful when you choose this approach that children are really interested in the project or the ideas they have been exposed to in school.

■ *Planning Can Be Based on a Theme.*   Many programs plan their curriculum around certain themes: holidays, events in the community, events planned by the children themselves, or ideas that lend themselves well to involvement by a sizeable group of children. For example, a group of children in one program developed an idea to raise funds for a "Save the Wolf" campaign. They designed T-shirts, made posters, and set up a table at a nearby college campus where they sold the T-shirts and raised enough money to feed and shelter a baby wolf. Such a project springs both from the children and from the philosophy of the program as it is understood, incorporated, and implemented by its staff.

■ *Planning Helps You to Achieve Awareness and Respect for Different Races and Cultures.*   Many program planners and staff want to have a program that is rich in multicultural experiences and awarenesses for children, but somehow it doesn't seem to work out.

To avoid awkwardly "tacking on" discussions about race and ethnicity to another activity, try to weave this goal into your program plan.

It's very important to include the experiences and the perspectives of different cultures in all aspects of the program, not just on holidays or when you host a specific cultural event. This may mean teaching children games that are played by people of different cultural backgrounds, carefully selecting books for your program's library (see resources in Appendix), as well as choosing cautiously the films you show to children. Essentially, you are aiming to present a consistent message to children—that we live in a country where people have different racial and cultural backgrounds and that these differences should be respected.

■ *Planning Helps You to Express Your Program's Values about Male and Female Sex-Role Stereotyping.* If you are particularly concerned that program children see men and women in nontraditional roles, you must consciously plan for your male and female staff members to share the sewing, cooking, building, physical games and sports, storytelling, and woodworking activities. Make sure you do not fall into the trap of assuming that the staff—or the children—will prefer certain activities just because they are male or female. Books and materials used, bulletin board displays—all should be given careful consideration. Children are likely to need lots of encouragement and adult modeling if they are to change their own attitudes. (See resources in Appendix.)

■ *Planning Should Be Flexible.* Don't be afraid to deviate from your plan if it looks as if changes should be made, or to respond to an interesting idea or special resource that comes up at the last minute. As one SACC staff member explains:

> I have a plan. It's not always used. But I need goals and a daily schedule. If no one wants to play soccer and that's what we've planned, that's fine. Then we're flexible to do something else.

Being flexible means that children have the freedom to change the plan if they have a better one, for children are the program's greatest idea makers.

> It is the notion of picking up on where kids are—just being aware of what they are saying, being in tune with them, and being able to change at a moment's notice.

Consider the Different Needs of Children of Different Ages

"Some kids need a pillow, some need a gym." Five-, six-, and seven-year-olds require planning that is different from what you will do for older children. Nine- and ten-year-olds can be quite vocal if they feel that they are attending a "baby" program! However, it is best not to be too rigid in terms of children's ages, for there is a wide range of development, interests, and abilities among children of school age. The staff and the children will be the best judges of what works best. Wonderful things can happen when younger and older children play together—many special opportunities for learning present themselves spontaneously, and many can be orchestrated by skilled staff.

■ *The Younger Child: Five- and Six-Year-Olds.* It is important that younger children have opportunities to learn new things in small groups of three or four, or even one-to-one. The "large group-ness" of public school can be overwhelming for kindergartners and first graders; it therefore is important that the SACC program provide opportunities for individual and small group activity. Most kindergartners need a scheduled rest period. Young children may find all of the activity so exciting that they become overstimulated and overtired if they are not given "time out" from the pace of the day.

Younger children will not have many of the skills and abilities possessed by their older program mates. This means that planned activities must take into account these differences and have varying levels of complexity. When selecting books and purchasing materials, the special needs of the younger child must be considered.

■ *The Middle Years: Seven, Eight, Nine.* The second- and third-graders coming to the program after school are likely to be ready for the playground, *not* for a quiet activity where they must sit for a fairly long period of time. Until the physical needs of the children are met—until they use up some of their energy—a structured activity such as reading may seem like a punishment. Your plan should provide ample opportunities for the seven- to nine-year-old child to make independent choices, work on long-term projects, and define and develop specific interests. Children of this age are particularly interested in learning new skills, doing work that is useful and real, and being with their peers.

In the planning process, this may mean setting up special interest areas that encourage such skill development. Some examples might include woodworking with a "real" carpenter; learning how to take, develop, and print photographs; or performing science experiments.

■ *The Older Child: Ten, Eleven, and Twelve.* Older children's major interest is their peers, and they seek opportunities to work and play cooperatively in same-age groups. Many programs have achieved success by helping children to organize into clubs or special project groups. Others find that thinking of the program as a home base and encouraging the older children to venture out into the community works well. Providing opportunities for children to do *real* work—and perhaps even to earn money—is another successful approach. This could involve having them work as day care helpers with preschoolers, doing odd jobs for community people (raking leaves, cleaning attics, etc.), or organizing a small group "clean-up" project for a nearby recreation area.

Who Should Be Involved in Program Planning?

To be truly curriculum-rich and varied, and to meet the range of needs of the children in care, a program should have input from a variety of sources.

■ *The Staff.* Planning means thinking ahead; it is future-oriented. In order to carefully think ahead, your program director and staff must set aside some time on a regular basis. It is often difficult for school-age child care staff to get to meetings; some may have second jobs and are unable to make an early morning staff meeting; others may have family responsibilities that prevent them from staying late in the evening. Find a time that is mutually agreeable. Possibly you can rotate the time of staff meetings between morning and evening to accommodate everyone's special circumstances. Make it clear to your staff that a part of their job responsibilities—one of the most important parts—is to put in some time thinking about how the program is to work. Program managers can emphasize this by being certain that this time is *paid* time. Without a commitment to the planning process by staff members, your program will suffer. The result will be either chaos—with no one quite knowing what is going to happen next—or the opposite, too much structure and regimentation of children to maintain order. Neither alternative makes for a good program.

All your staff should participate in planning sessions. If the planning role falls entirely to the director without involvement from the other staff, you will not have a program rich in new ideas and activities, and staff will not feel an important part of the program. Participating in planning meetings is a wonderful way for less experienced staff to learn from more experienced people. It is also a way of constantly checking that there is a variety of activities and that there is a consistent approach to difficult situations. In addition, if staff are expected to carry out a plan, their involvement in its design will assure its successful implementation.

■ *The Children.* From the start, all programs should pay attention to children's interests and desires. As one staffer said:

> Unfortunately, our tendency is to say, "I'm having a school-age program, so I'll need balls, headphones, puzzles, etc." instead of listening to the kids and letting them help you figure out what you want for the program.

Instead of telling children what *their* program will be, staff can seek out children's ideas by asking, listening, and watching. Really capable staff members know how to find out from children just what they are interested in, and they know how to support these interests by building a program around them. Involving children in the planning process is vital to shaping a good program, and it encourages children to take initiative, to be responsible, and to respect the needs and values of others. It also transmits an important message to children: what you think is important and will be taken seriously.

■ *The Parents.* Parents should be encouraged to participate in the planning process. They may do this by expressing their desires for their children: "I'd like the children to go to the library weekly," or "I think art materials should be available at all times," or "It's important to me that my son engages in cooking projects." Or, they may show their willingness to actively participate in some way: "I'd like to contribute wool for weaving projects and come in once to show children some different ways to use it," or "I'd like the children to come to my workplace and I'll show them around, introduce them to others, and answer questions."

The key to tapping parents as a resource is to build mechanisms into the program that allow, if not encourage, this exchange of ideas and suggestions. Perhaps you plan to discuss this individually during the enrollment process and during parent/staff conferences; perhaps special planning meetings are held for parents and staff; or perhaps written questionnaires are sent to parents. Whatever the methods used, you must communicate to parents that their opinions and ideas are valued and that you encourage their active participation in the program.

Put Your Plans in Writing

Putting your plans in writing is the bridge between program planning and its implementation. Writing down a daily plan or schedule helps to insure that the process of planning won't be "all talk and no action." SACC programs will want to have several different types of written plans.

All programs should have a daily *schedule* that outlines the different time blocks and that affords a consistent, predictable structure to each program day.

For example, one program may do it this way:

DAILY SCHEDULE

2:30	Free Choice
3:00	Snack
3:30	Group Time/Meeting
4:00-5:00	Activity/Trip Time

The Santa Monica Children's Centers program in Santa Monica, California, operating from 7:00 A.M. to 6:00 P.M., has a broad outline for the entire day, as shown in Figure 14–1.

Programs will also want to have a week-by-week plan, outlining just what activity choices are available each day, what "clubs" or special interest groups meet and when. In addition, programs will want to plan which staff people are responsible for what activities and put that in writing on the schedule (see Figure 14–2).

Keep a long-range calendar that reflects long-term plans and projects, showing when the program meets for full days, and any special events that are anticipated. As discussed, this is especially important for activities that are planned well in advance (yearly talent show, camping trip, etc.) and that need special preparations.

Plans for individual children, as well as their progress and accomplishments, should be carefully recorded. Many staff do this in notebooks, card files, or file folders. Whatever method is chosen, this is an important process, for it will allow staff to have a systematic approach to planning for the individual child.

**EXTENDED DAY CARE FOR CHILDREN
FIVE TO NINE YEARS OF AGE DURING SCHOOL YEAR**

7:00 A.M.	Center opens.
7:00-9:30 A.M.	Arrival of children in accordance with parents' work schedules and the grade school hours.
	Morning program adapted to interests, age levels and hours of attendance in regular school classes.
	Indoor Activities: Construction activities with blocks and accessory materials; music; language and literature with books, stories, discussion, conversation; manipulative materials . . . puzzles, scissors, pegboards, etc.; card games; study area for children who want to finish their homework; records for listening; and cooking experiences.
Noon:	Lunch in the school cafeteria or in the center.
12:45-4:30 P.M.	*Afternoon Program:*
12:45-2:30 P.M.	Kindergarten. Opportunities which help meet physical needs, establish routine habits and positive health attitudes. Rest—washing—snack. Indoor activities.
2 o'clockers:	Grades 1 and 2. Children who return to the Center at 2:00 p.m. Snack. Play inside or outside.
3 o'clockers:	Grades 3 to 5: Children who return to the Center at 3:00 p.m. Snack.
	Indoor Activities: Blocks and accessory materials; puppets; dramatic and housekeeping play; puzzles and card games; music and art materials; reading corner; sewing; craft projects and hobbies; study area; creative dramatics; science and nature.
	Outdoor Activities: Physical activities which involve running, hopping, skipping, jumping, balancing, climbing, such as jump rope, roller skates, kickball, punching bags, circle games, hopscotch, wagons, trikes, cargo net, etc.; team sports and organized games, dramatic play with boxes, ladders, boards, tarps, barrels, blocks and other accessory materials (hats, ticket punches, pulleys, steering wheels, pilot's wheel, etc.); gardening; woodworking; craft projects and hobbies; science and nature projects; sand, mud and water play (weather permitting).
4:30-6:00 P.M.	Inside and outside clean up. Preparation for going home. Individual and small group indoor activities.
6:00 P.M.	Center closes.

Note: Children are released to attend Cub Scouts, Boy Scouts, Girl Scouts, Camp Fire Girls, "Y", Boys' Club, the public library, park activities, to visit friends, etc. Written permission from the parent is required.

Figure 14–1

	Monday	Tuesday	Wednesday	Thursday	Friday
2:30	*CHOICE*: Easels, Blocks, Board Games, WW Table, Outdoors, Art Materials, etc. (Staff A-Floater; Staff B-Outdoors; Staff C-Art Area)				
3:00	*SNACK* Juice & Cookies	Granola & Apple Juice	Bananas & Nuts Apple J.	Apples & Cheese Juice	Cranberry Bread Juice
	(Table 1-Staff A; Table 2-Staff B; Table 3-Staff C)				
3:30	*GROUP TIME*				
4:00–5:00	*ACTIVITY TIME—CHOICES*: • Swim at Y (Staff B,C) • Wood-working (volunteer) • Special Projects (Staff A)	• Floor Hockey (Staff A) • Making Granola (Staff B) • Weaving (volunteer) (Staff C-Float)	• Obstacle Course (Staff A) • Wood-working (volunteer) • Trip to Library (Staff B,C)	• Photo-graphy Club (Staff B) • Cooking Cranberry Bread (Staff C) • Trip to Library (Staff A & volunteer)	• Jogging (Staff B) • Movies (Staff A) • Weaving (volunteer) (Staff C-Float)

Figure 14–2

Chapter 15

MAKING THE CURRICULUM WORK

Activities

If activities are "the building blocks of the program," as Elizabeth Prescott called them in *School's Out,* then SACC staff play multiple roles, functioning as architects, supervisors, and builders. The building blocks they put in place are various: group and individual projects, field trips, clubs, community activities, and interest centers.

Staff must constantly communicate with one another—both formally and informally—to be certain that they agree about what is to happen next and who will be responsible for what. This means discussing changes as they come up; knowing who is responsible for what physical areas of the room and/or what children; enforcing limits; and interacting with children to extend and broaden their learnings. The staff also has an important role in bringing activities, materials, and people to the program, in coordinating community resources so that the greatest number of options are available to children, and in consulting with parents and public school personnel.

■ *Independent Projects.* Many children come to the program full of their own ideas—they want to explore and create on their own. Some may want to continue an activity that they did with the group or that was part of their school day; others may want to work independently, but need adult guidance in selecting a project. What are

> The real challenge to teachers is to develop activities that children will find satisfying over a long period of time rather than momentarily exciting—the kinds of activities that invite genuine and appropriate problem-solving, mastery of the difficult and concentration or absorption, and that even may be a little routine. (Lillian Katz, *Talks With Teachers*)

the range of possibilities for independent projects? Short-term projects may take an hour or an afternoon; long-term projects might last a few days or longer, and may be initiated by staff or by children.

When staff initiates a project, it is often in response to the interests or needs expressed by an individual child. A six-year-old child who has shown an interest in puppets may be helped to build a lap-sized puppet stage to use for small finger-puppets; a child who is fascinated by the stars might work with materials brought in by a staff member to make a star chart that he or she can use for "star gazing"; and the child who is constantly mixing together your cooking supplies might be directed to books on chemistry, with a teacher supervising the actual experiments.

Projects initiated by children are important because children in SACC should feel able to pursue their own interests and to carry out their own ideas, just as if they were at home. In terms of the program, this means that children need time, materials, and adult guidance.

■ *Group Projects.*   Usually group projects spring from the expressed interests of the children, although staff may need to get the projects started and provide ongoing direction. It is important that staff build projects in accordance with program goals, and that projects are chosen or developed that will build upon other activities children are engaged in.

It is the staff's responsibility to see that projects are unified by a common thread. Even such "one-shot" activities as constructing masks for Halloween or building clay pots should be built upon previous experiences and should apply knowledge that children have acquired in other contexts. Many programs find that long-term projects which have a specific goal and involve everyone are perfect for capturing and sustaining the interest of school-age children: for example, a yearly talent show that demands months of preparation, a play that has been written and produced by the children (with some making costumes and scenery), and a Christmas art fair where children's arts and crafts are sold.

■ *Interest Centers.* Many SACC programs divide the environment into "interest centers," organizing the space so that specific materials are to be used in certain physical areas. For example, a science interest area might include an array of shells with magnifying glasses and a list of questions to guide the children's exploration; a block area would most likely be an area away from "traffic" that contains not only blocks but such items as trucks, toy people, and other objects that would enhance children's play; a listening center might contain books, with tapes and records and headphones for individual listening.

An "interest center" means different things to different SACC programs. Some programs think of it as an entire room, with the total space divided into distinct small areas, each containing specific materials for different types of activities. Others consider an interest center to be an area that contains self-directed activities for children. There may be kits that provide all of the materials, including directions, for a science experiment or a specific art project; or perhaps activity cards are placed in a general science area so that the child can select an experiment or activity from a pack of cards.

Whatever your definition, dividing the room into discrete areas and providing children with self-directed activities—both for individual children and for small groups—can offer many rich experiences. For example, you can provide materials that will teach children how to do origami, with four or five sets of directions of varying complexity; or ink and pens for calligraphy, with samples, instructions, and exercises.

■ *Field Trips.* A field trip can range from the simple—walking around the corner to the grocery store—to the complex—a two-night camping trip in the mountains. However, regardless of how easy it is to plan and carry out the trip, you should know why you are taking it and how it fits into the total program. It is important to take care of preliminary business before the event takes place. Talk with the people at the trip location and obtain a briefing about all necessary costs, rules, and particulars. Obtain signed permission slips from parents *and* send reminders to parents regarding the time, date of trip, and supplies (clothes, lunch, etc.) needed by the child. Arrange transportation to and from the site. Go to the site yourself in advance, so that you know exactly what to expect and can anticipate and plan accordingly. (For example, have children bring extra sweaters because it's cold by the water, or snacks because there is no place to purchase anything.)

You should plan with the children so that they can prepare for the trip, whether it be by reading specific materials, deciding what to bring with them, or dressing appropriately. The staff should talk and plan among themselves so that the trip is well organized and, if need be, teachers are assigned certain children and/or responsibilities. You should have sufficient adults (parents and staff) on the trip who know what they are responsible for so that the trip is as enjoyable and uncomplicated as possible. Children should be told what to do if, for some reason, they "lose" the group.

Trips take several forms. There is the local, informal trip that needs very little advance planning and is often carried out with small groups of children—a two-block walk to the library to return books, a trip to a nearby construction site, a purchasing mission at the local hardware store. There are also local trips that do need more specific planning—a visit and tour of the fire station, an afternoon at the roller skating rink, or a trip to an artist's studio. The third type of trip takes a good deal of advance planning and may also require longer or more complicated transportation (trains, cars, rented buses, ferries, etc.). Often, these trips involve months or weeks of planning, preparation, and maybe even fundraising. Examples include overnight camping trips and visits to special sites (Washington, D.C., Plymouth Rock, Disneyland) that may be some distance away.

In your SACC program, children should have opportunities for all these types of trips. When planned well, trips can give children considerable freedom—within established limits—and an opportunity to learn independence by "practicing." Children especially like trips where they can try out new materials, interact with people, and explore new places.

■ *Community Activities.* We recommend that SACC programs truly function as a "home base," reaching out in every way possible to use what already exists elsewhere in the community, rather than duplicating such resources at the program site. What are the possibilities? Some successful collaborative efforts between SACC programs and other agencies or groups are listed:

- A community school agreed to offer a selection of its classes at a school with a SACC program. A SACC program staff member became the additional staff person for the class, and, in exchange, children from the program enrolled in the class at no charge.
- A program received very reduced rates for swimming and classes at the community YWCA because the children were supervised by SACC program staff.

- SACC children attended after-school activities at a local dancing school and at a karate center, combined with attendance at the program.
- Girl and Boy Scout troops met in schools where SACC programs were held so that those children could participate.
- A local nature center worked with SACC programs to develop after-school activities at the center that groups of interested children could participate in at low or no cost.

■ *Clubs.* These groups tend to be organized around a specific interest or topic, for example, photography, weaving, ballet, Chinese cooking, hiking. In addition, clubs are set up to meet over an agreed-upon time period—a month, six weeks, or for a set number of sessions. Regardless of exactly how many meetings will take place, the goals are the same: (1) for children to make a manageable, long-term commitment to a group and to follow through on that commitment; (2) for children to work within a small group that is part of a larger group; and (3) for children to have an opportunity to have an in-depth, long-term experience where new skills are learned.

Many SACC programs have found clubs an excellent vehicle for meeting the special needs of both the younger and the older child. In one program, older children formed a chess club and, with the guidance of a staff member, worked out a fairly detailed set of rules governing club members. When the older children found that the SACC program's noise level was a problem during "club time," they suggested an all-program meeting to discuss and solve the problem. This situation provided the older children with a real way to take initiative, solve problems, and learn about group relations. It also allowed them an opportunity to be in a group with children of the same age, which is especially important to the older child. Of course, this can be tricky, since it could foster a sense of superiority or cliqueishness among the older children that would work against the program's philosophy. This is an example of why staff experienced in "group work" can prove invaluable.

The adult facilitating or leading the club may be a staff person, a parent, a permanent volunteer, or someone brought in just for this special purpose. Most programs combine approaches, and, depending upon the interests of the children and the strengths of the staff, do look outside the program for help. A club can also provide an excellent way to involve community people in the program and to expose children to adults of different ages and diverse backgrounds. Many programs have had excellent results using senior citizens to run clubs; others find that professional artists and crafts people are willing to donate a couple of hours weekly. Certainly, the mix of program staff, parents and outside people can add a whole new dimension to the program.

■ *The Materials.* The variety, quality, and types of materials that you have for children to use determine, to a large extent, what activities are available to kids. We are reluctant to say that every SACC program should contain a specific "set" of materials, because the program goals, the needs of children, and the finances vary considerably from program to program. However, we can recommend that SACC programs always have some of the following materials for children to use without adult assistance.

Materials that are open-ended are excellent as they can be used in a variety of possible ways by the children. These include different types of paper, paints, fabric, scraps, markers, crayons, and clay. Often, these are organized on open shelves or in bins so that children can choose what they would like on their own. Supplies such as scissors, glue, rulers, and pencils should be kept where children can reach them without adult help. Other materials, such as sand, water, and construction equipment (wood, tools) may or may not be available to children without staff help.

Manipulatives, such as Legos, blocks, puzzles, and Cuisenaire rods, often can be used differently by children at varied stages of development.

Books, which should be rotated regularly, should be displayed invitingly at children's eye level. Although some programs choose to purchase a few books of their own, libraries will usually lend the quantities needed.

Materials that encourage dramatic play can be organized in a special play area, and materials such as props and clothes, miniature furniture and people, can be used with blocks and other items to create a store (empty food cartons, tins and jars, cash register, aprons, different types of work clothes).

Games that can be played by individuals and small groups are examples of fairly structured activities that provide opportunities for children to learn to follow rules, take turns, and settle disputes. These include homemade games as well as checkers, chess, Monopoly, Sorry, and similar board games.

Special Program Times

In addition to long- and short-range program planning and activities for children, pay attention to certain times that all programs share: transitions, mealtimes, comings and goings. Consider them when deciding how to organize the day (although the procedures will vary for programs operating at different times of the day, especially full-day programs during no-school days and vacations).

■ *Comings and Goings.*   Depending upon the types of care you offer, your SACC program may have children coming and going throughout the day. It is likely that at major transition times you will either have children coming (or leaving) *en masse,* or that their arrivals and departures will be staggered.

If the arrivals are staggered, you must schedule individual and small group activities first, rather than trying to plan a group time, part of which some children will miss. Programs may begin the day by putting out selected materials for children to use, by designating certain parts of the room as "open areas" for children to select, and by making outdoor space available. Some programs set up a snack table and let children help themselves to snacks as they arrive. Expect lots of informal talking, socializing, hanging up coats, putting away backpacks, and so forth to take place as children make the transition between school and SACC.

Children arriving en masse can be somewhat overwhelming and overstimulating—both to staff and to the children. Those programs most successful in dissipating some of this energy try to offer children a range of options. They can choose noisy or quiet, indoor or outdoor, solitary or small-group activities. Essentially, this allows each child to unwind and relax from the school day, or from the early morning at home, in a way that best suits the child. At a single time, one might see a group of children outdoors, boisterously running and playing; children involved in small-group art and craft activities; and children alone, resting in a soft, quiet corner.

Many programs call everyone together upon arrival for some type of group time—a meeting, the sharing of a snack, or an activity. Because children who have come from school have spent so much time in large groups, think carefully about SACC group time before you schedule it. There are times when everyone *should* come together to discuss issues, plan for events, make choices, and share special experiences. However, it is important that you be certain of your purposes for bringing the entire group together, that the meeting be as short as possible, and that the timing be considered carefully. For example, a group time following school dismissal is often very difficult for children; however, once they have been outdoors running and playing on their own, children will have the attention span for a group meeting that has a clear purpose.

The manner in which children leave the program is determined by where they are going and how they are getting there. In morning kindergarten or prekindergarten programs, children tend to leave in large groups—or even all at once—to walk or be driven to their schools. In after-school programs, where parents are responsible for pick-ups, there is a tendency for children's departures to be spread out over an hour or so.

When you plan, bear these differences in mind. For example, if children are picked up by parents at different times daily, beginning around 4:00 P.M., parents must know about field trips in advance, and often special arrangements and/or plans must be made. When children leave a before-school program in large groups to go to school, time must be allotted for cleanup, for children to collect belongings, and to be certain that they are in the right frame of mind for the school day. This may mean, for example, that a loud ball game in the gym might be followed by a short group story reading before the children walk through the building to their classrooms.

Leaving a SACC program at the end of the day is often difficult for children. In one typical scenario, the parent dashes into the program after a long commute, wanting the child simply to get his coat and leave. In general, this sort of situation needs a bit of staff intervention. The child may need a few minutes to finish something, or at least to do just enough so that the project can be put away. The parent may need a chance to unwind or chat a bit with the teacher.

■ *Transition Between Activities.* Transitions that are disorganized and chaotic will make everyone feel out-of-control; those that are smooth will have a calming effect. When do transitions take place? Every time children move out of an activity or experience they are in transition. In some programs—those that allow children considerable freedom in choosing and moving into activities—there are always some children in transition. In others where the adults have more control over activity changes and the flow of the day, the entire group tends to be in transition at once.

Managing transitions so that they are smooth requires a good deal of planning and communication among staff and between staff and children. Many SACC programs facilitate movement by using mechanisms that encourage children to take the major responsibility for choosing an activity. A chalkboard or a board specially designed for such a purpose is often used, as illustrated in Figure 15–1.

A method such as this allows staff to know *at all times* where each child is—often a difficult task! Another invaluable practice is to remind children what the time is. This may mean telling children ten minutes in advance that in ten minutes it will be time to clean up— and then giving a five-minute warning. This gives children the opportunity to finish, or at least to plan just how much they can do, rather than to end abruptly. Developing a satisfactory system for transitions may take time and trial and error. Don't be afraid to talk this over with children and to try to figure out what works best for everyone in your program.

■ *Meal Times.* Depending upon your hours of operation, you may be serving breakfast, lunch, and dinner, or perhaps a light snack after school. Whatever food is served, you must make provisions for its preparation and consumption. Older children can take an active role in this part of the program by helping with menu planning, shopping, preparation, and set-ups. Many programs give children specific jobs; others expect little involvement. We would suggest that children

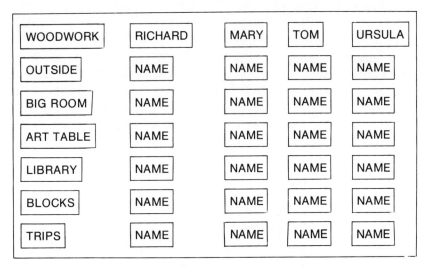

Figure 15–1

be as involved as is possible and appropriate, given the size and complexity of your program.

Meals are served in various ways. In some programs snacks are put out and children help themselves, with little teacher involvement. This may be a way to help children to become more independent, to plan their own time, or perhaps to foster small-group, intimate experiences. In other SACC programs, snack time is perceived as a time for everyone to come together and share in a "family-like" experience. In still other programs no food is provided; children furnish their own snack and meals. Many of these programs make strong recommendations to parents about quantity and quality of food to be brought. In such cases, children have a chance to really experience and practice sharing and cooperation.

Full-Day Programing: Summers, Holidays, and No-School Days

Depending upon your program's schedules of operation, you may be providing full-day care for a substantial portion of the year: not only during the two-month summer break, but during Christmas and February school vacations and spring break. Many SACC programs also provide care on no-school holidays (Veterans Day, Washington's Birthday), on teacher conference days, and on storm days.

Program planning for full days should not be merely an extension of what is planned for after school. Instead, consider the full-day weeks as a time for different types of experiences, because SACC programs are different during summers and vacation weeks. First, staffing changes. Many staff work longer hours, and additional people are added to provide the coverage needed. Often, programs use college (work-study) and high school (youth employment) students as an affordable way to supplement their permanent staff. Because children attend the program for a full day, almost infinite possibilities exist for long-term projects, day-long field trips, and other, more involving, activities. The warmer weather of summer lends an informal atmosphere to the program. SACC programs sometimes refer to their summer sessions as "camp," and plan more outdoor and recreation-oriented activities.

The single full days that are spread out over the course of the school year also require different programing. Since these days are not consecutive, they function as a break in the usual week's routine, with staff working longer hours. These days can be wonderful for special trips, projects or experiences—or they can be very long if not carefully planned in advance.

Your ability to have a satisfying full-day program depends heavily on whether you can leave the center for field trips and outings. Therefore, a cost-effective, practical transportation plan is essential. Some communities have accessible public transportation, or many resources within walking distance—your planning can take this into account. If you must provide transportation, you may be able to cooperate with other community agencies in sharing transportation (for example, jointly renting a van); to pay a reduced rental fee to a local group for the use of their bus; or to make arrangements with a taxi, van, or bus company, as needed.

■ *Summers and Week-Long Vacations.* Many multisite programs bring all of the children to one central location in the summer—a YM or YWCA, recreation center, school—and use that as a home base. Children are assigned to small same-age groups, and partake in scheduled, small- and large-group activities and field trips. Activities may be organized games (softball, volleyball, tag), crafts, (macramé, pottery, needlework), trips to local outdoor recreation areas (parks, lakes, pools, beaches) or other places of interest (bicycle factory, bakery, major-league baseball game).

The Madison After School Day Care Association in Madison, Wisconsin, organizes its summer camp around themes. Each two-week period includes a range of activities revolving around the theme and one major full-day field trip related to it, as can be seen in the schedule shown in Figure 15–2.

A key to successful full-day programing during vacation periods is to have a routine, but one that gives children plenty of choices. More time can be allowed for activities, which may mean that the activities will be more complex. What are the positive qualities about summer programing? Elizabeth Prescott summarizes them in the following excerpt:

> By far, the most frequently mentioned good quality about summer had to do with the difference in its departure from the rigid scheduling of winter. Nearly half of the centers described a summer program which was relaxed, individualized and permitted freedom and a camaraderie between staff and children. The freedom from time constraints seemed to be the major feature which was responsible for this change. One almost needs to see a winter program in action to realize the degree to which time constraints and the schedule of the public school dominate

SESSION I   June 11–20   THE WOODWORKS

Let's look at some of the ways we use wood: architecture, sculpture, woodburning crafts, heat, and more. This will be a good time to construct a wooden driving machine and carve a totem pole. Thursday, June 19 you can get out your woods when we take a trip to a local miniature golf and driving range.

SESSION II   June 23–July 4   TAKING SHAPE

Fitness and nutrition will be the focus of this unit. Biking is great excercise and learning bicycle safety is a must. We will see the Madison Turners give a demonstration, visit Warner Park's Vita Course, learn about good eating patterns, sample varieties of food, and try our hands at making swiss cheese. Tuesday, July 1 we will make an outing to York Farms where we can go horseback riding and explore the farm.

SESSION III   July 7–18   ENVIRONMENT, ENERGY & ECOLOGY

How about taking a little of each and seeing how they blend. We will look at the elements of nature and what it takes to survive, try a few of nature's basic arts such as pottery, weaving and coloring material with dye extracted from plants. Also included will be a visit to the arboretum, experiments with wind energy and solar energy. Steam energy will be the topic Thursday, July 17 when we ride a steam engine and wander through the Mid-Continent Railway Museum.

SESSION IV   July 21–August 1   EARLY IN THE STATE

Wisconsin was not always the way we see it today. We will talk about the who and how of life of various cultures around the state, and look at the area in which they settled. We plan to listen to some tape-recorded histories of early Wisconsin life, listen to folktales, and make up some of our own to pass on. To tie it all together, there will be a trip to Old World Wisconsin on Thursday July 31.

SESSION V   August 4–15   COMMUNICATION & THEATRE

There are so many ways to communicate, and not all are verbal. Body language is fun to observe, sign language is great to learn, and pantomime opens another door of communicating. We will look at movies, radio stations, put together our own theatre presentation, and visit a costume shop as part of our unit. Drawing our summer to a close, the field trip this session will be a picnic at Devil's Lake on Thursday August 14.

Figure 15–2

the program. In the summer, when this rigid time schedule is not operating, everyone seems to switch over to a different system of relating. When the removal of time constraints is also accompanied by a reduction in the number of people using the facility, the resulting change in atmosphere is striking. For example, if a site includes Head Start or Compensatory Education programs, or if the facilities are located on public school grounds, the disappearance of these programs for the summer makes a big difference for the day care program.

Another difference that was described in nearly one-third of the centers was a change in activities, with more trips and special activities such as swimming or picnics in the park. Here again the switchover to new kinds of sensory inputs appears to contribute to feelings of well-being and camaraderie.[1]

■ *No-School and Early Release Days.* Individual full days during the school year give SACC programs opportunities for morning trips, day-long events, or activities that require more time than is usually available. You might consider all-program roller skating parties, field trips to factories (many of which close by 4:00 P.M.), or major cooking or construction projects.

Plan in advance for these long days, because children and staff will have to change their routines. Meals, snacks, and rest time will have to be considered. If the long day is known about in advance, programs can use it in coordination with another project. For example, if the children are planning to have a special evening holiday meal and celebration for their families, you can plan ahead to use a full day for the cooking, purchasing, and other preparations.

Communication

A comment we hear repeatedly from SACC program planners and managers is the importance of effective communication. It is given a high priority by the better programs we observed. Communication—whether in person, via telephone or letter—takes time, planning, and effort.

Programs that are successful in this area build in mechanisms to guarantee that communication will take place: they set up regular all-program or mini-staff meetings; they schedule parent conference periods during the year; they prepare written information about the

---

[1]Elizabeth Prescott and Cynthia Milich, *School's Out! Group Day Care for the School-Age Child* (Pasadena, Calif.: Pacific Oaks, 1974), p. 35.

program to share with school personnel, parents, and other community people; and they see to it that the school principal and program director have regularly scheduled meetings. Staff and parents need to discuss, on a regular basis, issues related to the individual child and his or her progress in the program, including events that affect the child both at home and at the center. SACC staff will want to talk with public school personnel to get a better sense of the school program and, in some cases, to learn more about an individual child.

Real communication is based upon mutual respect and willingness to understand the other person's point of view. Often, personal values and individual backgrounds create a barrier to communication. A staff member and parent may have a conflict over how a particular situation was handled; a public school teacher may be upset because SACC staff will not require children to get help with their homework during program hours. Programs must endeavor to create an environment where everyone is valued—where parents feel that their beliefs about how to raise their children are not being called into question, and where staff are respected for their expertise. Children should know what is expected of them and why, and should have ample opportunity to communicate with adults and with their peers.

Evaluation

Evaluation is the process of measuring how well your program achieves the goals it has set for itself. It is a practical tool and, most importantly, a way to discipline yourselves to take a critical look at your SACC program.

Although we know that many programs and SACC staff are constantly evaluating themselves informally, we propose that, in addition, you set up mechanisms to insure that it is done regularly. Because of all of the daily work that goes into running a program and the details involved in keeping it going, many programs find that they just don't have time for evaluation. Like most things, evaluation could go by the boards if you have not planned for it to happen by carefully building it into your program.

■ *Why Evaluate?*   Evaluating your program in terms of your established goals and objectives will help you to improve the quality of your overall program. You will find out if your program goals are appropriate, if you are adequately meeting the needs of parents and children, and if you have made progress in certain areas.

■ *How Should You Do It?* There is not *a* method of evaluation that we would recommend for all programs. Ideally, SACC programs should develop and use a process that is a regular part of program operation, the results of which are constantly being acted upon to make the program better. Programs should do both *internal evaluation*—the users and those involved in the program (staff, parents, children) do the evaluating—and *external evaluation*—individuals from outside the program come in to do the assessment.

■ *Get Feedback from All Involved in the Program.* In doing internal evaluation, you will have to develop a means for getting feedback about the program from parents, children, and others involved (consultants, social workers, etc.). This is often done through paper-and-pencil questionnaires, program observation, group evaluation meetings, or individual meetings with the director. Some programs choose to have an evaluation committee of the board design and carry out the process; others leave it to the director—being certain also to devise a special process for evaluating him or her. Since the quality of the program rests largely with the staff, an important component of the evaluation process is self-evaluation by each staff member and feedback from others. Some programs find video tape equipment invaluable in helping staff to set goals and to evaluate their progress. Others expect staff to write down their goals, their strengths and weaknesses, and assess their own progress—*and* be evaluated by their supervisor. These kinds of internal evaluation measures should be done regularly. The total program evaluation by parents, staff, and children should be done at least once yearly; evaluation with individual staff members should be done at least three times a year.

■ *External Evaluation Can Help Programs Because It Is Objective.* There is one potential disadvantage to this method: outsiders may not have a sufficient understanding of SACC or they may bring biases of their own. Take care to communicate your program goals to outside evaluators and to choose them wisely.

Inviting outsiders into your program to evaluate it can be very intimidating for those staff who imagine the worst. However, if you are clear about *what* you want in terms of feedback, and set up a plan for getting it, you may find that your program will benefit a great deal from evaluation by outsiders.

No matter what type of evaluation you are involved in, you will probably find that some of your goals are easier to evaluate than others. For example, goals may include encouraging independence in the children, providing an environment that promotes individual choice, and fostering professional growth of staff. It would be difficult to assess whether professional growth is encouraged without talking to staff members and asking them specific questions; however, sitting and observing the program would give evaluators enough information to assess whether children are encouraged toward independence.

The Bibliography includes materials that delve deeper into the subject of evaluation. A look at these resources should provide you and your SACC program with the guidance necessary to design and put into practice a system of evaluation that meets your specific needs.

Chapter 16

CONCLUSION

This Action Manual was written to benefit three important groups: children, parents, and communities. Currently, many of our children have to take more responsibility for their own care than they wish to or should have to. The hours after school and during school vacations and holidays ought to be full of opportunities for children to learn more about their interests, to develop their skills, and to spend time in positive, learning relationships with other children and adults. In this book we offer parents some tested ways of providing alternatives to the long hours of isolation many children endure. We urge parents to work with others—other parents, concerned citizen groups, and professionals—to provide options for their young school-age children.

We intended this book as a tool to help you revitalize the sense of community in your locality. The very act of different groups and individuals coming together, forming coalitions and collaborating to solve a critical problem, is a step in forming a sense of community. A good school-age child care program is also a community for the children who use it, for the staff who work in it, and for all those whose energies directed it into existence.

As this Manual goes to press, many changes are occurring in federal and state funding for children's services, including school-age child care. The redirection of government priorities from social services to other areas is having a drastic effect on low- and moderate-

income families. Many school-age programs which until now have relied on federal funds to serve families may not be able to continue to
do so. The effect of current government policy may be to diminish the
federal funds available for SACC programs. We encourage you to use
the techniques we have described in this book to gain community
support—from business and industry, community groups—and build
strong constituencies for school-age children.

We have described some of these techniques in the Manual, but
new approaches are currently emerging to meet the challenge of caring for young children. Industry support for day care is under way in
a number of cities across the country. Many business leaders are concerned about employees' family responsibilities. (As parents themselves, they may well understand the "three o'clock syndrome," when
workers at all organizational levels rush to the telephones to call children who have just arrived home from school.) In some areas, companies are initiating voucher programs which provide all or a portion
of the day care costs of their employees. Some businesses are looking
at ways they can help community organizations which serve children
by contributing financial support for renovation costs or to support a
sliding-fee scale.

Public school administrators and elected officials are increasingly
interested in accommodating "partnership" programs within school
facilities. The media—both print and television—is a crucial ally in
helping to bring to the public consciousness the "story" of "latchkey"
children. Both school administration and the media are important resources, and we urge you to seek them out as you consider the potential support that is available to you.

If, after reading this Manual, you decide to implement a school-
age child care program, you will have a difficult but do-able task—
that of recognizing the special needs of young school-age children
and turning that recognition into reality. We hope that we have provided some examples of successful organizing strategies so that parents, following these guides, can develop safe and enriching child care
programs—and experience both the elation and satisfaction that
comes with doing so.

We need to let our children know that the adults in their lives are
willing to make the effort on their behalf.

ANNOTATED BIBLIOGRAPHY

Baden, Clifford, and Dana E. Friedman, eds. *New Management Initiatives for Working Parents.* Boston: Office of Continuing Education, Wheelock College, 1981, 201 pages. (Available from Office of Continuing Education, Wheelock College, 200 The Riverway, Boston, MA 02215.) An overview of the most up-to-date information on how employers are responding to the critical needs of working families. Based on presentations from an April 1981 national conference held in Boston. It includes reports on such topics as: on-site child care, family day care systems, child care subsidies, information and referral services, alternative work schedules, etc.

Baratta-Lorton, Mary. *Workjobs: Activity-Centered Learning for Early Childhood Education.* Reading, Mass.: Addison-Wesley Publishing Company, Inc., 1972, 255 pages. This practical volume is chock-full of ideas for developing activities that children can do independently.

Blau, Rosalie, Elizabeth H. Brady, Ida Bucher, Betsy Hiteshew, Ann Zavitkovsky, and Docia Zavitkovsky. *Activities for School-Age Child Care.* Washington, D.C.: National Association for the Education of Young Children (NAEYC), 1977, 85 pages. (Available from NAEYC, 1834 Connecticut Avenue, N.W., Washington, DC 20009.) This is an excellent practical working notebook for those planning daily activities for children attending school-age child care programs. It includes chapters on daily schedules/ activities, routines, cooking, blocks, music and dance, community resources, etc.

Breitbart, Vicki. *The Day Care Book: The Why, What, and How of Community Day Care.* New York: Alfred A. Knopf, 1979, 209 pages. A collection of articles written for a wide audience. Of special note is the section entitled, "How to Start Your Own Child Care Center" which, in addition to highlighting the steps in the process, explores many difficult issues, e.g., politics in the preschool, sex roles, etc.

Children's Defense Fund. *The Child Care Handbook: Needs, Programs, and Possibilities.* Washington, D.C.: Children's Defense Fund, 1982. (Available from Children's Defense Fund, 1520 New Hampshire Avenue, N.W., Washington, DC 20036.) This book documents the range of forces contributing to the need for child care services, presents profiles of a dozen programs and discusses these programs' achievements and practical knowledge acquired. It describes advocates' efforts to expand the quantity, quality, and accessibility of services.

Cohen, Dorothy H. *The Learning Child.* New York: Vintage Books, 1972, 350 pages. This book, written for parents and teachers, provides an in-depth look at the developing school-age child. Although primarily focused on the child within the public school setting, certain of the chapters provide excellent profiles of the child at different ages and stages of development.

COHEN, DOROTHY H., and VIRGINIA STERN. *Observing and Recording the Behavior of Young Children,* 2nd ed. New York: Teachers College Press, 1978. An excellent book that teaches the skills needed to keep anecdotal records on children, helps the reader to understand *what* and *when* to observe, and explains how to interpret the data collected.

Commerce Clearing House, Inc. *Tax Incentives for Employer-Sponsored Day Care Programs.* Chicago: Commerce Clearing House, Inc., 1980, 24 pages. (Available from Commerce Clearing House, Inc., 4025 W. Peterson Avenue, Chicago, IL 60646.) The primary purpose of this book is to help the employer understand the tax consequences involved in the sponsorship and utilization of child care programs. Defined and explained in this detailed guide are tax deductions for business expenses, depreciation and amortization, as well as an examination of the child care tax credit and the taxation of fringe benefits to employees.

Davidson County School Age Day Care Task Force. *Starting School Age Day Care: What Are the Considerations?* Nashville, Tenn.: Davidson County School Age Day Care Task Force, 1978, 20 pages. (Available from the School-Age Child Care Project, Wellesley College Center for Research on Women, Wellesley, MA 02181.) A guide for those interested in starting a school-age program in community settings (church, school, community center). The authors outline important considerations regarding use of space, licensing concerns, staffing, and parent involvement.

Day Care Council of America, Inc. *How to Start a Day Care Center.* Washington, D.C.: Day Care Council of America, Inc., 1981, 32 pages. (Available from The Day Care Council of America, Inc., 1602 17th Street, N.W., Washington, DC 20009.) This publication provides an overview of the steps necessary to start a day care center with an emphasis on the business and management aspects.

DITTMAN, LAURA, ed. *Curriculum Is What Happens: Planning Is the Key.* Washington, D.C.: National Association for the Education of Young Children, 1970. A series of short articles that deal with building curriculum from an experiential base.

FLANAGAN, JOAN. *The Grass Roots Fundraising Book: How to Raise Money in Your Community.* Chicago: The Swallow Press, 1977. (Available from Director of Publication, The Youth Project, 1555 Connecticut Avenue, N.W., Washington, DC 20036.) A practical approach to fundraising at the local level. Since the focus is community based, this book is invaluable to those wishing to start SACC programs and thinking about raising funds to do so.

FLANAGAN, JOAN. *The Successful Volunteer Organization: Getting Started and Getting Results in Nonprofit, Charitable, Grass Roots, and Community Groups.* Chicago: Contemporary Books, Inc., 1981, 363 pages. This is an excellent comprehensive guide to getting nonprofit organizations successfully organized and operating efficiently.

FRIEDMAN, DANA. "On the Fringe of Benefits: Day Care and the Corporation." 1981. (Available from the Center for Public Resources, 680 Fifth Avenue,

New York, NY 10019.) A paper that thoroughly examines the rationale, incentives, and experiences of corporations now participating in child care services for working parents. The author describes the various options a corporation can offer to meet the individual needs of its employees— flexible benefit plans, day care fringe benefits, part-time work, flex time, among others—and analyzes them in terms of their effect on job performance, turnover, absenteeism, and recruitment.

FRIEDMAN, DANA, ed. *Community Solutions for Child Care: Report of a Conference.* Washington, D.C.: U.S. Department of Labor, Office of the Secretary, Women's Bureau, 1979, 104 pages. (Available from U.S. Department of Labor, Office of the Secretary, Women's Bureau, Washington, DC 20210.) This report looks beyond the traditional sources of financial support for child care and focuses on how communities can develop unique solutions to the child care needs of their constituents. Many examples of community solutions are presented along with helpful resources and tools for advocacy.

GENSER, ANDREA, and CLIFFORD BADEN, eds. *School-Age Child Care: Programs and Issues.* Urbana, Ill.: ERIC Clearinghouse on Elementary and Early Childhood Education, College of Education, University of Illinois, 1980. (Available from ERIC/EECE, College of Education, University of Illinois, Urbana, IL 61801.) A collection of papers by veterans and experts, presented at a school-age child care conference at Wheelock College, Boston. Problems in and solutions to establishing and running school-age programs are discussed. The papers provide valuable insights for those starting up and running programs.

GROSS, MALVERN J., JR., and W. WARSHAUER, JR. *Financial and Accounting Guide for Non-Profit Organizations,* 3rd ed. New York: John Wiley and Sons, 1979, 568 pages. (Available from The Ronald Press, Division of John Wiley and Sons, 605 Third Avenue, New York, NY 10158.) An exhaustive text specifically geared for nonprofit organizations; often referred to as the best available guide to accounting practices, budgeting, and other key financial concepts.

HENDON, KAY, JOHN GRACE, DIANE ADAMS, and AURELIA STRUPP. *The After School Day Care Handbook: How to Start an After School Program for School-Age Children.* Madison, Wis.: Community Coordinated Child Care/4-C in Dane County, Inc., 1977. (Available from 4-C, Dane County, 3200 Monroe Street, Madison, WI 53711.) This book is the result of the establishment of five programs. The text focuses on organizing the community for action. The handbook includes sample documents and accounts of the actual start-up process in five communities.

HEYWOOD, ANN M. *The Resource Directory for Funding and Managing Nonprofit Organizations.* New York: Edna McConnell Clark Foundation, June 1982. (Available from Edna McConnell Clark Foundation, 250 Park Avenue, New York, NY 10017.) This excellent directory lists publications and organizations that will help nonprofit organizations raise funds and manage programs.

HIGHBERGER, RUTH, and CAROL SCHRAMM. *Child Development for Day Care Workers.* Boston: Houghton Mifflin Company, 1976, 242 pages. A primer written for those who wish to increase their understanding of child development. Although it focuses on the preschool years, the volume is unique in that it relates child development to the day care environment.

JACKSON, SONIA. *Out of School: How to Set Up After-School and Holiday Care Schemes for Children of Working Parents*. Bristol, England: Bristol Association for Neighborhood Day Care and the United Kingdom Association for the International Year of the Child, 1979. This British handbook aims to help parents of school-age children start programs or find solutions to the child care problem. It includes chapters on staffing, activities, and involving parents.

KATZ, LILLIAN G. *Talks with Teachers: Reflections on Early Childhood Education*. Washington, D.C.: National Association for the Education of Young Children, 1977, 114 pages. A good book for beginning staff members and those supervising them that deals with many of the important issues in staff development.

KOTIN, LAWRENCE, ROBERT K. CRABTREE, and WILLIAM F. AIKMAN. *Legal Handbook for Day Care Centers*. Prepared for Lawrence Johnson and Associates, Inc. pursuant to a contract with the Day Care Division, Administration for Children, Youth, and Families, Office of Human Development Services, U.S. Department of Health and Human Services, 1981. (Available from: Kotin and Crabtree, 6 Faneuil Hall Marketplace, Boston, MA 02109.) This practical handbook covers all of the legal questions that are part of the start-up process and includes tips on smooth (and legal) program operation, particularly incorporation as a nonprofit organization and seeking tax-exempt status.

LEVINE, JAMES A. *Day Care and the Public Schools: Profiles of Five Communities*. Newton, Mass.: Education Development Center, 1978. (Available from Education Development Center, 55 Chapel Street, Newton, MA 02160.) In-depth profiles of five different types of public school involvement with preschool and school-age day care. The book does not evaluate each delivery system, but describes and analyzes the complexities and tradeoffs—the strengths and stresses—within each. The parent-run Brookline, Massachusetts, Extended Day Programs are included as one of the profiles.

MORGAN, GWEN G. *Managing the Day Care Dollars*. Boston: Office of Continuing Education, Wheelock College, 1982, 110 pages. This practical volume provides concrete information on all aspects of day care financial planning and management.

Northeast Child Care Committee of the Greater Minneapolis Day Care Association. "Parents' Rights/Children's Rights." (Available from the Greater Minneapolis Day Care Association, Lehman Center, 1006 West Lake Street, Minneapolis, MN 55408.) This small booklet is an excellent aid in defining program philosophy, setting goals, and establishing policies.

PIEDT, PAMELA L., and M. IRIS. *Multi Cultural Teaching: A Handbook of Activities, Information and Resources*. Boston: Allyn and Bacon, 1979. This book includes sections on self concept, language, and promoting intergroup relations. Included in each chapter are activities and other resources.

PRESCOTT, ELIZABETH, and CYNTHIA MILICH. *School's Out! Group Day Care for the School-Age Child*. Pasadena, Cal.: Pacific Oaks, 1974, 129 pages. (Available from Pacific Oaks Bookstore, 5 Westmoreland, Pacific Oaks College,

Pasadena, CA 91103.) The best book available that describes both the practical and the theoretical issues in SACC. Founded on the developmental needs of school-age children, this volume is especially strong in its discussion of the actual programs for children and quality standards.

PRESCOTT, ELIZABETH, and CYNTHIA MILICH. *School's Out! Family Day Care for the School-Age Child.* Pasadena, Cal.: Pacific Oaks, 1975, 88 pages. The companion piece to *School's Out! Group Day Care for the School-Age Child,* this excellent book focuses on the different roles played by family day care providers and how the system functions for the school-age child.

Save the Children. *Recruiting and Enrolling Children: Tips on Setting Priorities and Saving Time.* Atlanta: Save the Children, 1981. (Available from Save the Children, Child Care Support Center, 1182 West Peachtree Street, N.W., Suite 209, Atlanta, GA 30309.) This booklet includes an outline for a parent policy handbook as well as valuable tips. The Center develops written materials on management and other major issues in day care.

SCIARRA, DOROTHY JUNE, and ANNE G. DORSEY. *Developing and Administering a Child Care Center.* Boston: Houghton Mifflin Company, 1979, 393 pages. A comprehensive text which takes the student in Early Childhood Education through all of the steps essential to starting a child care center. Working papers—or sample documents—are presented throughout.

Southern Regional Education Board. *Day Care Personnel Management.* Atlanta: Southern Regional Education Board, 1979, 82 pages. (Available from The Child Care Support Center, Save the Children, Southern States Office, 1182 West Peachtree Street, N.W., Suite 209, Atlanta, GA 30309.) A complete discussion of personnel issues in the day care setting. Chapters are devoted to personnel laws, written policies, salary planning, employee benefits, etc. Appendices include sample evaluations, job descriptions, and personnel policies.

Texas Department of Human Resources. *The Development of School-Age Day Care.* Austin: Texas Department of Human Resources, 1980, 19 pages. (Available from Extend-A-Care, Inc., 4006 Speedway, Austin, TX 78751.) This action guide is based upon the experience of launching, maintaining, and expanding Extend-A-Care, a private, nonprofit agency serving more than 800 children. A brief profile of the agency is included along with a concise, step-by-step outline for program start-up.

TRAVIS, NANCY E., and JOE PERREAULT. *The Effective Day Care Director: A Discussion of the Role and Its Responsibilities.* Atlanta, Ga.: Save the Children, 1981, 30 pages. Describes ten key management activities of a child care organization, and explains the role of the director in carrying them out. Contains information on the skills and knowledge necessary to be an effective director, and suggests methods of self-improvement.

U.S. Department of Health and Human Services, Office of Human Development Services, Administration for Children, Youth, and Families. *A Parent's Guide to Day Care.* Washington, D.C.: U.S. Government Printing Office, DHHS (OHDS) 80-30254, March 1980, 74 pages. (Available from the Superintendent of Documents, U.S. Government Printing Office, Washington, DC 20402.) The purpose of this resource guide is to help parents select suitable day care arrangements for their children; to enable parents to improve their day care arrangements for their children, and to provide parents with information on what day care should offer their children. This is done in a highly condensed format using a question-and-answer and checklist approach.

U.S. Department of Labor, Office of the Secretary, Women's Bureau. *Employers and Child Care: Establishing Services Through the Workplace.* Washington, D.C.: U.S. Government Printing Office, 1981, 99 pages. (Available from the U.S. Department of Labor, Office of the Secretary, Women's Bureau, Washington, DC 20210.) A practical aid to employers, union leaders, and employee groups who seek information about employer-related child care services. The publication provides guidelines for child care involvement that include needs assessment, cost analysis, and program planning issues. Resource lists for further investigation are also provided.

ZIGLER, EDWARD F., and EDMUND W. GORDON, eds. *Day Care: Scientific and Social Policy Issues.* Boston: Auburn House Publishing Co., 1982. This collection of articles by authors from a variety of disciplines provides a theoretical analysis of day care issues. It combines recent research on the effects of day care with policy analyses on its delivery. The reader will obtain, among other information, a perspective on the history, current needs, and problems of day care in the United States.

BIBLIOGRAPHY

BENDER, JUDITH, BARBARA SCHUYLER-HAAS ELDER, CHARLES H. FLATTER, GAIL A. LINVILLE, MARY E. MATTHEWS, and ROBERT C. SHORT. *The Hours Between: Community Response to School-Age Child Care.* Baltimore, Md.: Maryland Community Coordinated Child Care, 1975, 54 pages.

CARINI, PATRICIA. "Building Curriculum for Young Children from an Experiential Base." *Young Children,* March 1977, pp. 14–18.

COHEN, DONALD J., RONALD K. PARKER, MALCOLM S. HOST, and CATHRINE RICHARDS, eds. *Day Care: Serving School-Age Children.* Washington, D.C.: U.S. Department of Health, Education, and Welfare, vol. 4, DHEW (OHDS) 78-31058, 69 pages. (Available from Superintendent of Documents, U.S. Government Printing Office, Washington, DC 20402.)

Community Schools and Comprehensive Community Education Act. Title VIII of the Education Amendments of 1978. Public Law 95-561.

CRAMER, JAMES P., ELEANOR FELKER, and MARGARET LUCAS. *Latch Key: Developing Child Care Programs Through Community Education,* 1977. (Available from Latch Key, 6425 West 33rd Street, St. Louis Park, MN 55426.)

Department of Human Resources, Metropolitan Dade County, Florida. *An Assessment of Community School and After School Programs.* May 1981.

GARBARINO, JAMES. "Latchkey Children: Getting the Short End of the Stick?" *Vital Issues,* vol. XXX, number 3, November 1980.

HOFFMAN, GERTRUDE. *School-Age Child Care: A Primer for Building Comprehensive Child Care Services.* Washington, D.C.: U.S. Department of Health, Education, and Welfare, DHEW (SRS) 73-23006, 1972, 22 pages. (Available from Superintendent of Documents, U.S. Government Printing Office, Washington, DC 20402.)

JENKINS, PATRICIA. "Guide to Accounting for Nonprofits." Los Angeles, Cal.: The Grantsmanship Center, 1977.

KING, EDITH W. *Teaching Ethnic Awareness: Methods and Materials for the Elementary School.* Santa Monica, Cal.: Goodyear Publishing Co., 1980.

KIRITZ, NORTON J. "Program Planning and Proposal Writing." Los Angeles, Cal.: The Grantsmanship Center. Introductory Version, 8 pages; Expanded Version, 48 pages.

MURRAY, KATHLEEN A. "501(c)(3) Tax-Exempt Status—and How to Get It." San Francisco: Bay Area Child Care Law Project Publications, 9 First Street, Suite 219, San Francisco, CA 94105, 1982.

MURRAY, KATHLEEN A., and CAROL STEVENSON. "Insuring Your Program: Property and Vehicle Insurance." San Francisco: Bay Area Child Care Law

Project Publications, 9 First Street, Suite 219, San Francisco, CA 94105, 1981.

MURRAY, KATHLEEN A., and CAROL STEVENSON. "Insuring Your Program: Liability Insurance." San Francisco: Bay Area Child Care Law Project Publications, 9 First Street, Suite 219, San Francisco, CA 94105, 1981.

NEUGEBAUER, ROGER, ed. "Employer Child Care." *Child Care Information Exchange,* Reprint #9, 16 pages.

NEUGEBAUER, ROGER, ed. "Fundraising." *Child Care Information Exchange,* Reprint #10, 16 pages.

NEUGEBAUER, ROGER, ed. "Money Management I." *Child Care Information Exchange,* Reprint #3, 16 pages.

NEUGEBAUER, ROGER, ed. "Money Management II." *Child Care Information Exchange,* Reprint #13, 16 pages.

NEUGEBAUER, ROGER, ed. "Nonprofit Tax-Exempt Status: Is It Right for You?" *Child Care Information Exchange,* September 1979, #9, pp. 27–31.

NEUGEBAUER, ROGER, ed. "School-Age Day Care." *Child Care Information Exchange,* Reprint #101, 32 pages.

POSILKIN, ROBERT S. "Day-Care Programs Are Optimal Joint Tenants." *Phi Delta Kappan,* December 1980, p. 285.

RUOPP, RICHARD, JEFFREY TRAVERS, FREDERIC GLANTZ, and CRAIG COELEN. *Children at the Center.* Final Report of the National Day Care Study, vol. 1, Cambridge, Mass.: Abt Associates, 1979.

SITOMER, CURTIS J. "Who Cares for the Children?" *Christian Science Monitor,* April 28–May 1, 1981. Reprint June 1981.

SPRUNG, BARBARA. *Non Sexist Education for Young Children: A Practical Guide.* New York: Citation Press, 1975.

STEVENSON, CAROL S. "Insuring Your Program: How to Buy Insurance." *Child Care Information Exchange,* January/February 1982, #23, pp. 7–9.

U.S. Commission on Civil Rights. *Child Care and Equal Opportunity for Women.* Washington, D.C.: U.S. Government Printing Office, June 1981.

U.S. Department of Health, Education, and Welfare, Office of Child Development. *Day Care: Serving Children with Special Needs.* Washington, D.C.: U.S. Government Printing Office, 1972.

RESOURCES

After School Care: A Resource Letter for School-Age Care, Child Development Department, Iowa State University, Ames, IA 50011; (515) 294-1648. (Also see below: *School-Age Notes.*) A newsletter for teachers and directors designed specifically for those in the field working directly with school-age children.

Association for Childhood Education International
3815 Wisconsin Avenue, N.W.
Washington, DC 20016
(202) 363-6963

Bay Area Child Care Law Project, 9 First Street, Suite 803, San Francisco, CA 94105; (415) 495-5498. The project makes available educational materials on legal issues in child care for child care center directors and family day care providers. Topics include liability, insurance, contracts, nonprofit incorporation, tax-exempt status, child abuse, and employer-supported child care.

The Center for Early Adolescence, University of North Carolina at Chapel Hill, Suite 223, Carr Mill Mall, Carrboro, NC 27510; (919) 966-1148. The Center serves as a clearinghouse for information on young adolescents age 10–15 and is dedicated to increasing the effectiveness of agencies and professionals who work with this age group. Resources include a newsletter, publications, consultants, and the development and delivery of workshops.

Child Care Information Exchange, Roger Neugebauer, Editor, C-44, Redmond, WA 98052; (206) 882-1066. This excellent publication is written expressly for day care administrators and staff and takes a practical, "how-to" approach. Past articles cover such topics as sliding fee scales, program evaluation, school-age child care, and employer-supported child care. Reprints are available.

Child Care Staff Education Project, P.O. Box 5603, Berkeley, CA 94705; (415) 653-9889. This project is involved in research and support in the area of working conditions for child care staff. They publish a newsletter, disseminate materials, and are currently writing a handbook for child care workers that has a national focus.

Child Care Support Center, Save the Children, 1182 West Peachtree Street, N.W., Suite 209, Atlanta, GA 30309; (404) 885-1578. The Center conducts regional workshops, offers local training (has a yearly family day care technical assistance conference), and develops written materials on management and other major issues in day care.

435

Child Welfare League of America, Inc.
67 Irving Place
New York, NY 10003
(212) 254-7410

Children's Defense Fund, 1520 New Hampshire Avenue, N.W., Washington, DC 20036; 1-800-424-9602. Distributes pamphlets and publications on child advocacy (e.g., "It's Time to Stand Up for Your Children"; *Where Do You Look? Whom Do You Ask? How Do You Know? Resources for Child Advocates*), publishes a newsletter, maintains an information hotline, and sponsors the national "child watch" project.

Children's Foundation
1420 New York Avenue, N.W., Suite 800
Washington, DC 20005
(202) 347-3300 (food program information)

Council for Exceptional Children
1920 Association Drive
Reston, VA 22090
(703) 620-3660

Council on Interracial Books for Children
1841 Broadway
New York, NY 10023
(212) 757-5339

Day Care Council of America, Inc., 1602 17th Street, N.W., Washington, DC 20009; (202) 745-0220. The only national membership organization for day care. The council provides information on legislation and day care policy issues as well as technical assistance and consultation. Publishes a newsletter and a magazine, and holds a yearly national conference.

ERIC Clearinghouse on Elementary and Early Childhood Education (ERIC/EECE), University of Illinois at Champaign-Urbana, College of Education, University of Illinois, Urbana, IL 61801; (217) 333-1386. A federally funded clearinghouse. Operates an abstracting/indexing service for current literature and publishes a newsletter, occasional papers, and many free resource lists.

The Grantsmanship Center, 1031 South Grand Avenue, Los Angeles, CA 90015; (213) 749-4721. Publishes the *Grantsmanship News,* does training, and makes available a wide range of publications in the area of fundraising, resources, and proposal writing.

National Association for Child Care Management
1800 M Street, N.W.
Washington, DC 20036
(202) 452-8100

National Association for the Education of Young Children (NAEYC), 1834 Connecticut Avenue, N.W., Washington, DC 20009; (202) 232-8777. A large national association with local (AEYC) affiliates. Besides publications by these local groups, NAEYC publishes *Young Children* bimonthly, in addition to books and pamphlets that are of excellent quality. NAEYC holds an annual fall conference.

National Black Child Development Institute
1463 Rhode Island Avenue, N.W.
Washington, DC 20005
(202) 387-1281

The National Commission on Resources for Youth, Inc., 605 Commonwealth Avenue, Boston, MA 02215; (617) 353-3309. The Commission fosters programs that provide opportunities for young people from 10 to 18 to assume responsibility and to make a contribution in their communities. Its resources include a national clearinghouse; films and videotapes; books, guides, and manuals; and a quarterly newsletter.

National Credentialing Program
Child Development Associate Credentialing Commission
1341 G Street, N.W., Suite 802
Washington, DC 20005
(800) 424-4310

National Employer Supported Child Care Project, Child Care Information Service, 363 East Villa Street, Pasadena, CA 91101; (213) 796-4341. Based upon their recent national survey of employer-supported child care, the Project has written a how-to manual (tentative publishing date, December 1982) for employers (including information on needs assessment, cost benefit analysis, existing employer-sponsored programs, etc.) and has up-to-date information on programs across the country.

School-Age Child Care Project, Wellesley College Center for Research on Women, Wellesley, MA 02181; (617) 235-0320, x2546 or x2547. The project provides technical assistance, information, and referral, and distributes a wide range of written materials for those wishing to start school-age child care programs or those in need of assistance with current programs.

School-Age Notes, P.O. Box 120674, Nashville, TN 37212; (615) 292-4957. (Also see above: *After School Care: A Resource Letter for School-Age Care.*) A newsletter for teachers and directors designed specifically for those in the field working directly with school-age children.

APPENDICES

GETTING APPROVAL (Chapter 4)

EDINA PUBLIC SCHOOLS
5555 West 70th Street
Edina, Minnesota 55435   May 20, 1980

TO: Superintendent, School Board, and Community Education Advisory
           Council

FROM: Task Force for Edina School Age Child Care Program:
           Raymond Bechtle, Administrative Liaison
           Ardis Blumenthal
           Pam Keating
           Barbara Nielsen
           Alice Randall
           Gretchen Shanight
           Ardyth Walther

SUBJECT: Recommendation for a School Age Child Care Program for Edina,
           beginning September 2, 1980

CONCEPTS UNDERLYING THE RECOMMENDATION FOR A SCHOOL AGE CHILD CARE PROGRAM FOR EDINA

There is a present and growing need in Edina for before- and after-school child care. At present the needs of many children and their families are not being met adequately. Children with a need for such care are enrolled in private schools which provide such service; some are cared for in the homes of sitters; some are cared for by siblings; and many return to empty homes to care for themselves.

A School Age Child Care Program for children in grades K–6 is proposed for Edina. Such a program would be totally self-supporting by those using its services and would be administered by a parent board. It has been found that the best location for such programs is one central to the community that can be served by existing transportation systems. The best sites are usually schools. Start-up funding is necessary for such programs. The programs then become self-supporting within six months to one year. Such start-up seed money often originates from the city's community resource budget and is reimbursed as soon as possible. Communities surrounding Edina which presently provide such programs include Bloomington, Hopkins, St. Louis Park, Robbinsdale, and Minneapolis. Richfield is developing one.

We believe Edina needs a before- and after-school child care program for children in grades K–6. Such a program would meet the very important needs of our Edina children and provide a source for family support in the community. The program would also benefit Edina in other ways: children who are leaving public schools for private schools which provide such care would remain or return to the Edina schools; younger working families would be attracted to Edina, which would be good for Edina and Edina's schools; the program would provide funds to Edina schools and make use of empty classrooms; and the program would make Edina competitive with surrounding communities as to services provided in this important area of child care and family support.

SURVEY RESULTS AS OF MAY 19, 1980

The purposes of this brief survey are to determine the need for and interest in this day care program and to find out the numbers of people interested in various kinds of service.

Please check the appropriate items:

Results

27	1. I am not interested in this child care program in 1980–81 but would be interested in 1981–82.

127   2. I am interested in this child care program for my child(ren) who will be in grade(s) K = 29, 1st = 26, 2nd = 17, 3rd = 29, 4th = 15, 5th = 7, 6th = 4.

3. I would be interested in service at these times:

68	a. Before school—from 6:45 A.M.
25	{ b. During A.M. kindergarten—9:00 A.M.–12:00 P.M. { c. During P.M. kindergarten—12:00–3:35 P.M.
100	d. After school—3:00–6:00 P.M.
87	e. On school dismissal days—6:45 A.M.–6:00 P.M.
62	f. 5 days per week (exclusive of holidays).
48	g. 1 to 4 days per week (exclusive of holidays).

4. Name your child(ren)'s elementary school(s).

Concord	30	Creek Valley	22
Cornelia	22	Highlands	30
Countryside	23	Our Lady of Grace	7

 125   5. I would like to be on the list for future informational mailings.

  71   6. I would be interested in participating in fund raising _12_ , program
         planning _30_ , serving on the Advisory Board _25_ , serving as a volun-
         teer _4_ .

Number   Your comments (68 responses):

  35   1. Wonderful program, enthusiastic, much needed, etc.

  14   2. A necessity

   3   3. Requests for service in home school—or on East or West Side.

   3   4. Some parents work varying schedules each week and need that flexi-
         bility in scheduling requested hours.

   2   5. There are many young children going home to be alone who need this
         care.

   2   6. Interest in occasional care—not on regular basis.

   5   7. Existence of program would make a difference as to whether children
         attend Edina Public Schools.

   2   8. Opposed.

   1   9. Minimum cost is a factor.

   1 10. Prefer this kind of program to in-home care.

RECOMMENDATIONS FOR A SCHOOL AGE CHILD CARE PROGRAM FOR EDINA

Based on the results of the community survey and on the concepts presented in the accompanying cover information, the Task Force for a School Age Child Care Program recommends the following steps be taken:

1. That a non-profit and self-supporting School Age Child Care Program be established by September 2, 1980.
2. That the School Age Child Care Program be licensed and developed according to the standards of the Minnesota State Department of Welfare.
3. That an Advisory Board for the School Age Child Care Program be established. This Board shall consist of not more than ten people and be composed of parents and community citizens representing such groups as Community Education, Community Resource Pool, PTA Council, League of Women Voters, school principal of site school, district administrative liaison.
4. That start-up funding in the amount of $1,500 to $2,000 be advanced by Community Education, this amount to be reimbursed by the School Age Child Care Program.
5. That the Advisory Board of the School Age Child Care Program be responsible for the hiring of a licensed Program Director.
6. That the Edina School Board authorize the leasing of facilities and contracts for transportation and food services.

LEGAL ISSUES (Chapter 5)

RENTAL AGREEMENT BETWEEN
WINCHESTER CHILD CARE, INCORPORATED
AND WINCHESTER SCHOOL COMMITTEE

1. The area to be rented is on the lower floor of Lincoln School, located at 161 Mystic Valley Parkway, Winchester, MA 01890, and as identified in the attached floor plan. The room marked "x" on the attached floor plan shall be dedicated for use by the after school program. Other areas on the floor plan shall be shared spaces. All shared space shall be left in the condition in which it was found by the director of the after school program.

2. The rental period will commence on January 4, 1982 and will be a tenancy at will. The rental period will end on June 30, 1981. Either party may terminate the rental agreement by giving the other party ninety (90) days' notice in writing of its intent to terminate. The rental agreement shall not go into effect until January 4, 1982.

3. The hours of operation on regularly scheduled school days will be from 2:45 P.M. until 5:50 P.M. On early release-time days the hours of operation will be from 11:45 A.M. to 5:50 P.M., and during vacation periods when the school is not in session the hours of operation will be from 8:30 A.M. to 5:50 P.M., Monday through Friday. During holidays and snow days the after school program will not use school space. During February vacation week and the full days at the end of June following school closing (through June 25), Winchester Child Care, Inc. has the option to relocate the program in order to save costs, with the

Note: This agreement is in the process of revision.

provision that the director of the program shall notify the principal of Lincoln School two (2) weeks in advance. In such cases, the tenant would not be using the school space or school custodial services, and therefore would not be charged for additional custodial services.

4. The rental rate will be as follows:
   A. If the enrollment is under fifteen (15) children on a full-time basis, the rate shall be four hundred fifty dollars ($450) for the term of this rental agreement.
   B. If the enrollment is between fifteen (15) and twenty (20) children on a full-time basis, the rental will be six hundred fifty dollars ($650) for this period of time.
   C. If the enrollment exceeds twenty (20) children on a full-time basis, the School Committee reserves the right to renegotiate the rental.
   D. The rental identified above will include light and heat and routine custodial services performed by custodians during their regularly scheduled hours.

5. The minimal rental for the six-month period shall be a total of four hundred fifty dollars ($450). Rental shall be paid in five (5) installments, beginning on February 1 and ending on June 1, and shall be based on the number of children enrolled full time on the 15th of the month prior to the due date for payment, the first of the month, as stipulated below:
   A. If the enrollment is under eight (8) children, the rental for that period shall be sixty dollars ($60).
   B. If the enrollment is between eight (8) and fourteen (14) children, the rental for that period shall be ninety dollars ($90).
   C. If the enrollment is between fifteen (15) and twenty (20) children, the rental for that period shall be one hundred thirty dollars ($130).
   D. On or before June 15, Winchester Child Care, Inc. will pay the balance of the rental as set by the rental charges identified in Section 4 of the rental agreement.

6. Property insurance for the structure shall be the responsibility of the landlord. Winchester Child Care, Inc., however, will be responsible for obtaining a comprehensive liability insurance policy which provides for a *minimum* coverage of five thousand dollars ($5,000) for property damage (each occurrence) and a quarter of a million dollars ($250,000) for bodily injury (each occurrence). A copy of the insurance policy(ies) shall be furnished to the School Department.

7. The tenant shall be responsible either through payment or replacement for damage to equipment and facilities caused directly by the children or staff of the after school program. The tenant shall not be responsible for normal wear and tear of equipment and facilities. Repair of damage to equipment and facilities caused by circumstances of persons not associated directly with the program shall be the responsibility of the landlord.

8. In the event additional custodial coverage is required, Winchester Child Care, Inc. shall be responsible for payment of the additional time required of the custodian at the rate specified in the Agreement between the Winchester Custodians' Association and the Winchester School Committee.

9. In all cases Winchester Child Care, Inc. must comply with local state and federal regulations.

....
Roger A. Bauman, M.D.
Chairman, Winchester School Committee

....
William C. MacDonald
Superintendent of Schools

....
Jeanne D. Duffy, President

Date: ....   Winchester Child Care, Incorporated

FLOOR PLAN

EUGENE LATCH KEY BYLAWS
(with proposed revisions—3/25/81)

ARTICLE I. NAME

The corporate name of this Agency is Eugene Latch Key whose administrative office is located in the City of Eugene, Lane County, Oregon.

ARTICLE II. PURPOSE

In the exercise of its charter powers, the Agency aims to promote child development in Lane County through:
1. The school year operations of before and/or after-school child caring programs for enrolled Latch Key, elementary-age children.
2. The vacation time (summer, winter, and spring) operation of full day care programs for enrolled elementary-age children.
3. Establishment of board-approved new centers when need is proven and money is available.
4. Assisting other organizations and groups in Lane County to establish similar programs through responding to inquiries, establishing models of high quality, and through technical assistance and information.

ARTICLE III. BOARD OF DIRECTORS

Sec. 1.   The corporate powers of the Agency are vested in the Board of Directors, who shall control all matters of policy and expenditure of funds of the agency.
Sec. 2.   The Board of Directors shall include as a minimum:
a. One parent, elected by the process outlined in Article VI. Sec. 2., of an enrolled child from each school attendance area.
b. One representative from community schools.
c. One representative from Lane County 4-C's.
d. Such other positions as authorized by the directors.
Sec. 3.   Each site shall select, by the elective process outlined in Article VI. Sec. 2., an alternate parent director who shall have voting power on the Board of Directors in the absence of a regular parent representative.
Sec. 4.   A quorum for the transaction of any business shall be four (4) members or their alternates. The act of the majority of the Directors present at a meeting, at which a quorum of Directors is present, shall be the act of the Board of Directors.
Sec. 5.   Parent representatives and alternates shall serve two-year terms, with a maximum of two consecutive terms.

ARTICLE IV. MEETINGS

Sec. 1.   There shall be a minimum of ten (10) Board of Director meetings a year, unless otherwise provided by majority vote.
Sec. 2.   It is the duty of members of the Board of Directors to attend meetings regularly. If a member misses two consecutive meetings without a valid reason, it shall be the responsibility of the Secretary to advise him/her that after the third consecutive absence he/she may be replaced on the Board of Directors.

SOURCE: Eugene Latch Key, Inc., Eugene, Oregon.

Sec. 3.   Members of the Board of Directors shall be notified prior to each board meeting.

ARTICLE V.   DUTIES OF BOARD DIRECTORS AND OFFICERS

Sec. 1.   The duties of the Board Directors are:
  a.   To attend monthly Board of Directors meetings.
  b.   To notify the alternate parent representative of Board decisions.
  c.   To arrange that the alternate parent representative attend board meetings in the event the Board member is unable to attend.
  d.   To represent the interest and concerns of their site's Latch Key clients.
  e.   To serve on Latch Key committees as necessary to further the success of Latch Key.
  f.   To work with the school site director in addressing the concerns and needs of their site.

Sec. 2.   The duties of the alternate parent representative are:
  a.   To attend Board of Directors meetings, as a voting member, when the regular parent representative is unable to participate.
  b.   To inform oneself about Board decisions and other Latch Key concerns.
  c.   To work with the school site director in addressing the concerns and needs of their site.

Sec. 3.   The Directors shall elect annually, in the month of January, from their number a President, a Secretary, and a Treasurer. All officers shall be elected for a term of one year, and no officer shall succeed himself more than once.

Sec. 4.   The President shall preside at all meetings of the Board of Directors and shall represent the Board of Directors for the business and affairs of the corporation.

Sec. 5.   The Secretary shall provide that a record of all meetings is preserved and keep an attendance record. In the absence of the President, the Secretary shall preside and perform his/her duties.

Sec. 6.   The Treasurer shall have the responsibility of keeping the Board informed of the Agency's financial status. The Treasurer shall countersign checks, with the Administrator of the Agency. In the absence of the Treasurer, inability of that officer to serve, or current vacancy of the Treasurer or Administrator, checks may be counter-signed by another officer. Two authorized signatures are required on all checks.

ARTICLE VI.   VACANCIES

Sec. 1.   When a Board member has missed three (3) consecutive meetings and has not arranged for alternate attendance at Board meetings, the Secretary shall notify the Board member, the school site director, and the Board that a vacancy exists in the position. The site alternate shall serve as regular Board member until a permanent selection is made through the following elective process.

Sec. 2.   Upon the vacating of a parent representative or alternate representative position on the Board of Directors, the director of the Latch Key site affected will, within one month:
  1.   Announce the vacancy and solicit nominations to fill the position.
  2.   Publicize the nomination and make arrangements for election of a new parent representative.

3.   Preside over election of the new parent representative.

4.   Notify the Eugene Latch Key Administrator of the decision.

The site director and site parents may participate in the voting. The nominee receiving a majority of the votes shall become the site's representative.

Sec. 3.   In the event of vacancy in an office, a replacement will be elected at the next regular meeting of the Board of Directors.

Sec. 4.   All officer replacements shall serve for the remainder of the term of the officer being replaced.

ARTICLE VII.   COMMITTEES

Sec. 1.   The Board may designate from time to time such standing or ad hoc committees as needed to carry on its business. Chairpersons for Committees and a majority of committee members must be Board members. Other parents or community members may be added. Standing Committees shall include, but not be limited to, Executive, Personnel, and Finance.

Sec. 2.   The responsibility for appointment of Committees lies with the President and is subject to ratification by the Board of Directors. Recommendations for appointment may come from any source.

Sec. 3.   Executive Committee. The Executive Committee shall consist of the elected officers of the Board of Directors and the chairpersons or a committee representative from all standing committees. Executive committee members must be voting members of the Board of Directors. The Executive Committee may act in emergencies between Board meetings on behalf of the Board of Directors. The Executive Committee shall serve also as a Grievance Committee in all program matters and as an appeals board for staff grievances after non-resolution in the Personnel Committee.

Sec. 4.   Personnel Committee. The Personnel Committee shall consist of (at least) two Board members and two staff members and shall meet on a monthly basis.

This committee will recommend policy and procedure regarding salaries, benefits, hours, and working conditions that permit the employment and retention of qualified staff in order to provide quality service.

The committee will also review and when necessary, revise job descriptions and evaluating procedures and keep and monitor personnel policies and procedures so that they are up to date. The Personnel Committee will also act as a grievance committee for staff.

The recommendations of the Personnel Committee shall be presented to the Board of Directors for consideration and adoption.

Sec. 5.   Finance Committee. The Finance Committee shall establish and periodically review all financial accounting procedures and policies and shall take steps, if necessary, to assure that the accounting procedures and policies employed provide an adequate system of checks and controls for the funds of the corporation.

The Committee shall review the budget prepared by the administrator and approve its final form for recommendation to the Board of Directors, review budget adjustments between categories if over 10% of gross amount of administrative budget, review and approve line item adjustments of budget recommended by Administrator.

The Committee shall review and approve any financial transactions of a nonroutine nature.

As feasible, the Committee shall be familiar with disbursements authorized for the corporation's federal and state grant monies.

The Committee shall select an auditor and review the annual audits of the corporation's accounts and transmit a report to the Board of Directors.

The Committee shall review all monthly balance sheets and statements of operation prepared for the corporation's accounts.

The Committee shall keep accurate minutes of its meetings.

The Committee shall review new grant applications and funding requests, consider receipt of new grants and funds as a new budget and make recommendations to the Board of Directors. As feasible, provide leadership in fund raising activities.

ARTICLE VIII. STAFF

Sec. 1. There shall be an administrator and such other members of the staff as the Board of Directors shall deem necessary to carry on the work of the Agency.

Sec. 2. The Administrator shall employ such staff as are required to carry out the purposes and objectives of the Agency in accordance with policies established by the Board of Directors. The Administrator shall keep the Board fully informed on all aspects of the Agency and shall be the medium of communications between all departments of the Agency and between the Agency and the community.

ARTICLE IX. ORGANIZATION

Sec. 1. The work of the Agency shall be organized under the Board of Directors and such committees as may be authorized by the Directors.

Sec. 2. The membership of all committees, excepting the Executive Committee, shall be appointed by the President.

Sec. 3. Liaison Committee. The formation of a program Liaison Committee at each school site shall be an option available to each program. This committee shall consist of the school principal, the school community coordinator (in the community schools), the program director, the Latch Key Board member, and the Latch Key Administrator.

This committee shall serve as a body to consider and resolve program issues. If the program issue requires Board action, this committee may, with a majority vote, request action of the Board. This committee shall serve as the official channel of communication between the program and the Board of Directors.

ARTICLE X. AMENDMENTS

These bylaws may be amended at any regular meeting of the Board of Directors at which a quorum of Directors is present by a two-thirds (⅔) majority vote at such a meeting. Notice of the general character of any proposed amendment must be mailed to the membership at least ten (10) days prior to such meeting.

Signatures of incorporators and Board members:

_____

_____

Appendix 3

GUIDELINES FOR SETTING POLICY (Chapter 6)

TABLE OF CONTENTS OF
A PARENT HANDBOOK

absences
activities
Advisory Committee and
    Advisory Board
after-school activities
breakfast
cost of program
children's rights
children's responsibilities
communication
conferences
discipline
dress
dropping out of program
early dismissal days
emergencies
emergency closings
enrollment
field trips
fees
food and snacks
forms necessary for enrollment
holidays

hours
illness
late fee
licensing
medication
meetings
new student checklist
non-school day care
Parent Assistance Fund
parent participation
parents' rights
parents' responsibilities
personal belongings
programs offered
registration fee
release of children
sliding fee subsidy
snacks
staffing
telephone numbers
transportation
vacations

SOURCE: Contents of "Adventure Club Parents' Manual," for Lincoln, Sunny Hollow, and Neill Adventure Club Programs, Community Education and Services, Independent School District 281, Robbinsdale Area Schools, Minnesota, 1978.

450

WRITTEN GUIDELINES TO FACILITATE
PROGRAM OPERATION

Children's Responsibilities

Children need to be responsible:

1. For learning to take the consequences for their own actions.
2. For respecting the rules that guide them during the school day; for controlling their feelings so that their actions do not harm anyone in the program.
3. For not willfully destructing or harming any equipment or property in the building or anyone else's while they are in the program.
4. For sharing equipment and facilities with all children in the program.
5. For remaining with a staff member at all times and notifying them if they need to go to another area.
6. For signing in when they arrive each day and notifying a staff member when they need to be somewhere else.
7. For coming immediately after school, unless they advise a staff member otherwise.
8. For respecting the rules of the Adventure Club Program.
9. For dressing appropriately for indoor or outdoor play; for having tennis shoes available to wear in the gym.
10. For returning materials and equipment to the place they found them for other children to find before taking out a new activity.
11. For carrying out an activity that they committed themselves to.

Children's Rights

1. Safe and reliable environment.
2. Use all the equipment and space on an equal basis; to find equipment where it is intended and in functioning condition.
3. Have their ideas and feelings respected.
4. Discipline that is fair, equal, and respectful of them.
5. Express their anger, frustration, disappointment, joy, etc. in an appropriate manner.
6. Express their creative ability.
7. Explore and discover.
8. Continue developing their full potential.
9. Have a safe environment free of hazards.
10. Have an environment that offers a variety of choices: physical, quiet, indoor, outdoor, creative, dramatic play, exploring.
11. Have a right to voice their opinion of the rules and the activities.
12. Have staff members that care about them, enjoy being with them, and help them grow.

Reprinted from the "Adventure Club Parents' Manual," Robbinsdale Area Schools, Minnesota.

Parents' Rights

Parents have the right to:

1. Know their children are in a safe environment where they are free to select from a variety of activities.
2. Participate in all levels of decision-making concerning how their children spend the day.
3. Know what types of programs and activities are being planned, and to be offered feedback on the kinds of activities the children enjoy.
4. Share concerns with the staff, Advisory Committee, or board at any time, about anything they do not feel is in the best interest of the children.
5. Know if their child is misbehaving, and to spend time talking with the staff concerning a solution.
6. Know if their child does not report to the program as intended.
7. Know when the children will be going any place other than where the program is usually held.
8. Voice special concerns and considerations not covered in this manual, and to discuss special cases where occasional exceptions may be made from the rules set forth in this manual.

Parents' Responsibilities

Parents have the responsibility to:

1. Let the staff know if their child will not be attending for the day.
2. Observe the rules of the Adventure Club program as set forth in this manual and in any additional policy statements.
3. To share their concerns with staff members and Advisory Council/Board, if the program is not meeting their child's needs.
4. Listen to concerns that staff members have about their child's behavior, and to work through an agreeable solution to any problems that might occur.
5. Know about any change in policy or procedure.
6. Know the discipline procedure of the center as explained in this manual.
7. Replace any equipment that their child is responsible for misusing.
8. Sign out their child at the end of the day; to notify a staff member when taking a child from the center, and to notify a staff member when another authorized person is picking up a child.
9. Inform staff if child has been exposed to a contagious illness.
10. Notify staff of planned vacation and other absences in advance.
11. Notify staff of withdrawal at least one week in advance.
12. Pay fees on time.
13. To keep the child's record up-to-date with changes in phone numbers and addresses.
14. Pick up children on time.

Appendix 4

ADMINISTRATION (Chapter 7)

GUIDELINES FOR THE OPERATION OF EXTENDED DAY
PROGRAMS IN THE ELEMENTARY SCHOOLS
AS PART OF THE PUBLIC SCHOOL PROGRAM
(Revised 3/20/78)

1. Each program shall be approved by the School Committee initially after receiving tentative approval from the Principal and Director of School Plant according to the regulations set forth in the section entitled "Regulations Regarding Use of School Plant by Extended Day Programs."
    a. The Board of Directors of each program shall include as a voting member the Principal of the school in which the program operates.
    b. The Board of Directors of each program shall include, as an ex officio member, a member of the Brookline School Committee to be designated each year by the Chairman of the Brookline School Committee.
    c. Approval renewals shall be granted in accordance with the terms set forth in the School Plant Director's Regulations.
    d. Each year the program shall file with the Office of the Director of School Plant the names, addresses, and telephone numbers of Extended Day personnel *no later than October 1*. After that date, the Director of School Plant shall provide to the Assistant Superintendent of Schools for Curriculum and Instruction a written report indicating the status of records provided by each Extended Day Program.
2. Each program shall be responsible for establishing its own tuition rates and selecting its own staff subject to the following:
    a. A copy of the tuition rates and a yearly financial statement shall be filed with the Secretary to the School Committee each September.

SOURCE: Brookline Public Schools, Brookline, Massachusetts.

      b. All staff shall be interviewed by the Principal of the school in which the program operates and his recommendations made known to the Parent Board prior to hiring.

3. The School Department shall provide through the school budget:
    a. Custodial coverage until 6:00 P.M. daily on all days when school is in session.
    b. Heat, light, and electricity as is required in the areas used by the program.
    c. Regular maintenance of the Extended Day spaces. (See #5.)
    d. One half of the custodial overtime costs (if any) incurred in operating the Extended Day Programs on non-legal holidays when school is not in session as defined in #8.
    e. Custodial coverage until 4:00 P.M. in one school building during school vacations.
    f. Custodial coverage until 11:00 A.M. on Good Friday, when school is not in session because of low attendance.

4. The Extended Day Programs shall be responsible for:
    a. Salary payments to staff.
    b. Equipment of the Extended Day homeroom.
    c. Supplies.
    d. Telephone service and for making certain that the telephone number of the Extended Day Program is widely publicized through fliers home and listing in the regular telephone book along with the School Department numbers.
    e. Any insurance policies as are deemed necessary or are required.
    f. Other miscellaneous costs associated with the operation of the program not specifically covered in #3.

5. Maintenance of spaces assigned to the Extended Day Programs:
    a. If at all possible, space used for regular classrooms during the day should *not* be assigned as basic (homeroom) space for Extended Day Programs. To this end, future building plans shall include specific space designated for Extended Day basic space.
    b. Any request regarding maintenance of these spaces shall be directed to the Principal.
    c. The room(s) used by the Extended Day Programs shall be cleaned, painted, and otherwise serviced by School Department personnel in the same manner and according to the same schedules as are all rooms in the school building at School Department expense.
    d. In order to paint or otherwise make changes in said assigned space(s), the Extended Day Program must obtain written permission from the Director of School Plant after submitting a written statement outlining the proposal. Any work done must meet School Department specifications and shall be paid for by the Extended Day Program.

6. Regulations regarding the use of "other or shared" spaces:
    a. The sharing of such spaces as the gym, library, cafeteria, shop, art, music, and homemaking rooms is encouraged to promote increased enrichment of the program subject to the following regulations intended to assure proper supervision of the children, proper care of such spaces, and a minimum of interference with regularly scheduled classes.

b. The Extended Day Program shall have use of such spaces only with the permission of the Principal, and provided that such use does not, in the opinion of the Principal, interfere with the use of space in the regular school programs.

c. The Extended Day Program director and the classroom teacher shall agree in advance to abide by the following guidelines and with any of the guidelines they deem appropriate.

    i. Students in the Extended Day Program shall be accompanied by a responsible Extended Day staff person while using said areas. It is expected in areas like the shop and gymnasium, where specialized and hazardous equipment exists, that a qualified person approved by the Principal shall be present at all times.

    ii. Shared spaces shall be left by the Extended Day personnel and students in the condition in which they were found.

    iii. Shared specialized spaces shall be vacated by 5:00 P.M. in order to allow the custodian adequate time to perform his regular duties and lock up.

7. Use of School Department equipment:

a. School Department equipment may be used by the Extended Day Program staff only with the permission of the Principal and provided that such use does not conflict with the use of the equipment in the regular school programs.

b. The Extended Day Programs assume responsibility for replacement and repair of School Department equipment damaged or lost while in the custody of Extended Day staff.

8. Operation of the Extended Day Programs during days when school is not in session:

a. The school buildings will be closed on the following holidays: Columbus Day, Veterans' Day, Thanksgiving Day and the Friday following Thanksgiving, Christmas vacation, George Washington's Birthday, and Memorial Day.

b. The school buildings shall be open to the Extended Day Programs on Martin Luther King, Jr.'s birthday, and on Rosh Hashanah, Yom Kippur, and Good Friday, when school is not in session because of low attendance, with one half of the custodial overtime (if any) to be borne by the School Department and one half by the Extended Day Programs. The Director of the Extended Day Program shall notify the Director of School Plant two (2) days in advance of each of the above-mentioned holidays whether or not the program shall operate.

c. During February and April vacations the Extended Day Programs will be assigned to one school building to be designated by the Director of School Plant. One half of the custodial overtime charges will be levied upon and divided equally among the programs.

    i. The Director of School Plant shall notify the Director of each program two (2) weeks in advance of each vacation period as to the school building to be used.

    ii. The Director of each program, in turn, shall notify the Director of School Plant one (1) week in advance whether or not the program intends to operate during the vacation period in question, and, if so, how many children will attend.

d. "No school" (snow) days.

    i. The Directors of the Extended Day Programs will be notified of "no school" (snow) days by the school Principal.

    ii. One school building shall be open on "no school" (snow) days for use by the Extended Day Programs.

    iii. The programs which plan to operate on "no school" (snow) days shall notify the Director of School Plant *no later than October 1st* of each year of said policy. The Director of School Plant shall *by October 15th* notify those programs with such a policy as to the building designated for "no school" (snow) days use.

    iv. In order to insure the safety of the children, parents in such programs shall be required to accompany their children to the designated school and to remain with them until they are safely inside the building and under the supervision of the Extended Day staff.

e. Should more than four extended day programs apply to use the school facilities for vacation and snow days, a second school will be identified for use. The director of adult and community education will be empowered to assign programs to this school if extended day programs report, by January 3, a total of more than 100 students are involved in vacation and snow day activities.

9. Staffing:

a. Each Extended Day Program shall hire its own staff in consultation with the school Principal (see #2). It is expected that sufficient numbers of qualified staff shall be present at all times so as to provide a completely supervised program.

b. Brookline school teachers who participate in an Extended Day Program are expected to meet regular after-school responsibilities and shall make proper arrangements with the Extended Day Programs to do so.

c. In order to accomplish an improved dialogue between Extended Day Program staff and regular school and pupil personnel staff the Principals are encouraged to invite the staff of Extended Day Programs to general staff meetings within the school.

10. Health Regulations:

a. Each Extended Day Program shall comply with the regulations regarding student health records, emergency card file, first-aid training, posted emergency telephone numbers, etc., as set forth by the School Department physician in the document entitled "Health Regulations—After School Extended Day Programs," dated September 30, 1974.

b. Health records and an emergency card for each child in the program shall be available in each program's office *no later than October 15th of each year.* The Director of Child Health shall insure that the school health records are made available to the appropriate Extended Day Care staff for this purpose. The Director of Child Health shall also supply to the Assistant Superintendent of Schools for Curriculum and Instruction a written report indicating the status of records for each Extended Day Program.

11. Insurance:
    a. Parents of children in the Extended Day Programs shall be advised of the availability and coverage of the school insurance policy, and should be strongly encouraged to take out such policy when it is applicable. (Pupils who are enrolled as part of the regular day program are covered also for the afternoon program.) Under the direction of the Principal, the teacher in charge of the program would have the responsibility of soliciting enrollees who are not already covered.
    b. Extended Day Programs staff shall be covered by appropriate liability insurance.
12. Extended Day Program Advisory Committee:
    An Extended Day Program Advisory Committee consisting of a staff member and parent from each program, a school Principal, the Superintendent of Schools (or his designee), a member of the School Committee, and the Child Care Coordinator of the Human Relations Youth Resources Commission (who shall convene the committee) may be set up each year to:
    a. Aid parent groups in schools lacking Extended Day Programs in setting up such programs.
    b. Aid existing groups in sharing resources, ideas, and problems in order to attain and maintain the highest possible standards of Extended Day Programs and to promote the intellectual, social, and physical growth and health of the children enrolled.
    c. Recommend to the School Committee modifications of the regulations set forth herein when deemed appropriate or wise to do so.
    The staff member and parent from each program shall be selected by the program's parent body. The School Committee member shall be designated by the Chairman of the Brookline School Committee.
13. Copies of these Guidelines shall be provided to each existing Extended Day Program and the Child Care Coordinator of the Human Relations Youth Resources Commission.

REGULATIONS REGARDING USE OF SCHOOL PLANT BY EXTENDED DAY PROGRAMS

1. After meeting with the Principal regarding the concept of the program within the school, the parent group shall meet with the Principal and Director of School Plant regarding space for the program.
2. The Director of School Plant will confer with the proper Town Agencies (Building, Fire, etc.) to inspect the locations for compliance with building regulations, building code (Form B-2), and fire regulations of the Public Schools of Brookline.
3. After receiving tentative approval from the Director of School Plant and the Principal, the group shall, through the Principal and via the Office of the Superintendent of Schools, approach the School Committee for approval.

4. After notification of School Committee approval, the group shall request from the Director of School Plant a use-of-buildings application. The group shall file with the Office of the Director of School Plant the names, addresses, and telephone numbers of the officers, program director, and staff and the use-of-buildings application. The above list of telephone numbers shall be kept up to date throughout the year as is necessary.
5. The Director of School Plant, upon receipt of the application and other information under item #4, will file a report with the Secretary to the School Committee, including a description of the physical areas assigned, and return written notice of approval for use of space for the school year to the program director. The Director of School Plant shall arrange for periodic inspection of the spaces by the appropriate Town agencies and, in the case of the Fire Department, for fire drills.
6. Procedures outlined under #4 and #5 shall be repeated annually.
    a. Each program shall report the name(s), address(es), and telephone number(s) of the Extended Day Director and/or Board Chairman to the Director of School Plant at least four (4) weeks prior to the beginning of the program each year.
    b. The Director of School Plant upon receipt of the above information shall forward to either the Extended Day Program Director or Board Chairman a copy of the Guidelines and a use-of-buildings application form. He shall enclose a letter stressing strict adherence to the Guidelines.
    c. The use-of-buildings application form must be completed, filed, and approval received by the Extended Day Program before the program can begin. Approval by the Principal of changes in location of the program must accompany the filed use-of-buildings application form.
    d. In the event that there are changes in the space to be used by the program or changes in the schedule of the program during the year, the program Director must notify the Director of School Plant in writing and approval for the use of space or schedule change must be received from the Director of School Plant *before* the changes may be made.
7. The programs shall adhere to the Public School Calendar regarding vacations, holidays, and cancellations, with the following exceptions, for which one half of the use-of-buildings fees will be assessed:

Two days of low attendance in the early fall and Martin Luther King, Jr.'s birthday	Each school with program shall be open for full day—8:15 A.M. to 6:00 P.M.
February vacation	4 days only, all programs to be consolidated in one school, to be selected by Director of School Plant, to be open for full day—8:15 A.M. to 6:00 P.M.
One day of low attendance in the early spring	Half day for custodial staff, programs shall be open full day—8:15 A.M. to 6:00 P.M.
April vacation	5-day week, all programs to be consolidated in one school, to be selected by Director of School Plant, to be open for full day—8:15 A.M. to 6:00 P.M.

[*Note:* Programs on a daily basis shall have all participants in designated program area by 5:00 P.M. and shall be out of the building not later than 6:00 P.M.]

8. The programs may operate on "no school" (snow) days provided that they notify the Director of School Plant *no later than October 1st* of each school year that that is their intention. On such days the designated building shall be open from 8:15 A.M. to 6:00 P.M.

HEALTH REGULATIONS—AFTER-SCHOOL
EXTENDED DAY PROGRAMS
(September 30, 1974)

1. Child
   a. A copy of the pupil's school health record shall be kept in a locked file in the Extended Day facility. A xeroxed or photographic copy of the record kept on file in the school health office may be made if there is a parental release for this.

      Regulations for continued attendance (required immunizations, health history, record of physical examination by private doctor or school physician) are the same as for public school attendance.
   b. In addition, there shall be an index card for each child, the aggregate to be kept in a box next to the telephone with the required information filled out *in full.* These cards may be obtained from the office of the Director of Child Health Services.
   c. Each parent should sign a waiver enabling the school staff to seek and permit emergency treatment in case a parent, or the parent's designated substitute contact, cannot be located.
   d. If a child needs to take oral medication on a regular basis during the afternoon—on either a long- or short-term basis—the following is required:
      i. A note from the child's physician prescribing the medication, stating the reason for which it is given and including any special directions needed.
      ii. A note from the parent or guardian giving explicit permission to have the teacher (or other personnel) administer the medication.
      iii. If medication is requested to be kept on hand for emergencies only (e.g., for asthma attack), special instructions must be given in letters required under i and ii. In addition, parental conference with the staff should be held.

2. Staff
   a. Health records of staff members.

      A health record of each staff member must be kept in locked file either at the Extended Day facility or in a central file at the Health Department. This includes:
      i. A health history.
      ii. Record of a physical examination.
      iii. Evidence of freedom from communicable tuberculosis.

re: iii.—This may be Mantoux or other appropriate skin test or chest x-ray. Chest x-rays are available free at the Brookline Health Department. Tuberculin tine tests may be arranged through the school nurse at that school.

Evidence of freedom from communicable tuberculosis is to be presented *prior* to starting work and every three years thereafter.

b.   First-aid certification.

At least two staff members will be required to take a basic first-aid course leading to certification. (Courses are available through the Boston Chapter of the American Red Cross.) A yearly updating or refresher course is to be taken by *one* staff member if two are certified.

Whenever the class or part of the class goes on a field trip, a simple first aid kit should be taken along.

3.   General Measures

a.   Emergency numbers (fire, police, poison center) are to be posted near the telephone.

b.   A first-aid kit should be kept in a prominent place on the premises and refurbished as necessary.

c.   Protocols used in public schools for handling major catastrophic emergencies and minor first aid shall be obtained from the office of the Director of Child Health Services and posted or kept in a notebook easily available to regular or substitute staff.

d.   The most recent Red Cross book on first aid and safety should be kept on the premises for reference.

e.   Adequate rest periods and nutritional snacks should be provided according to appropriate guidelines for each age group served.

4.   Available Medical Consultation

The School Nurses and School Physician will be available for (emergency or general) consultation during their respective working hours.

Each school Extended Day Program may also, or alternatively, arrange to use the services of any consultant nurse and/or physician of their choice.

The general school health regulations regarding communicable diseases, impetigo, return to school after strep infections, pediculosis, etc., will, in any case, apply.

School Nurse: On call until 3:45 P.M. daily.

School Physician: On call until 5:00 P.M. daily.

Appendix 5

PERSONNEL (Chapter 8)

LATCH KEY PROGRAM DIRECTOR

  I. Job Description:
    Management of an individual Latch Key Program.
 II. Supervisor:
    Project Administrator
III. Requirements:
    A. Must be twenty-one years of age.
    B. Must have a minimum of two-year associate degree in a related field and a minimum of two years experience in the direct supervision of children, *or* a four-year combination of both.
    C. Must have a minimum of one year experience in adult supervision.
    D. Must have a valid food handlers and T.B. card by employment starting date.
IV. Activities and Duties:
    A. Responsible for the planning and implementation of the daily program.
      1. Responsible for the supervision and teamwork of all program staff.
      2. Arrange weekly team planning sessions.
      3. Responsible for food program.
      4. Post weekly activities and menus.
      5. Insure program meets all licensing and contract requirements.
        a. Insure program meets federal licensing requirements.
        b. Maintain all required USDA information.
        c. Insure positive supervision of all practicum, work study, or volunteer staff.

Source: Eugene Latch Key, Inc., Eugene, Oregon.

B. Coordinate Latch Key program with the school site and insure a positive working relationship.
   1. Follow all designated school requirements regarding school usage.
   2. Maintain positive and effective bi-weekly communications with principal and/or community school coordinator.
   3. Attend school functions as requested and appropriate.
C. Develop interested, informed and supportive parent groups.
   1. Utilize parent letters and parent meetings as needed, with a minimum of bi-monthly formal communications with all parents.
   2. Insure positive parent contact and communication at drop-off and pick-up times.
D. Insure effective communication and cooperation between the program and the Latch Key office and other programs.
   1. Attend and participate in all Latch Key Project meetings.
   2. Assume additional related duties as requested by the Project Administrator.
   3. Timely and neat delivery of all requested program information and forms to the Latch Key office.
      a. Staff time sheets.
      b. Enrollment and drop forms.
      c. USDA materials.
      d. All others.
E. Coordinate Latch Key program with neighborhood groups and programs.
   1. Attend monthly neighborhood Advisory group meetings or Community School Advisory Council meetings.
   2. Stay informed of neighborhood activities and involve Latch Key as appropriate.
   3. Coordinate Latch Key activities with neighborhood programs.

V. Benefits
   A. Paid employee health insurance
   B. Eligible to join SELCO credit union
   C. ½ fee for eligible Latch Key child care
   D. Pro-rata: Vacation days—1 per month
                 Sick days—1 per month
   E. 7 paid holidays
   F. 2 teacher workdays
   G. 2 mental health days

COUNTY OF FAIRFAX OFFICE FOR CHILDREN
EXTENDED DAY CARE

ASSISTANT TEACHER

Starting Pay: $4.96/hr.
Hours: Between 8 and 40 hours per week.
Time: Shift Work—Some mornings and afternoons
    —Some afternoons only—some mornings only
    —Approximately 2 evenings/month
    —Hours approximately the same every day; when hired, you
        will be given a regular schedule
Positions: School Year—most positions are for the school year (the same days
        school is in session).
    Full Year—a few positions are for the full year (including summers and
        holidays).
Starting Date: August 27—orientation week—may be 40 hour week.
Benefits: All Assistant Teachers who work 21+ hours a week are regular part time
    (21–39 hours) or full time (40 hours). These Assistant Teachers are entitled to the
    following benefits:
        — Paid annual leave
        — Paid sick leave
        — Paid County holidays   Based on actual
        — Health insurance   hours worked
        — Life insurance

Probationary Period: One year.

JOB DESCRIPTION

- Assists in planning a daily program of developmental experiences for school age children.
- Provides leadership to children engaged in developmental activities.
- Assists in determining effective use of facilities and equipment.
- Follows procedures to safeguard the health and safety of children in the center.
- Assists in providing nutritious daily snacks.
- Assists in administrative functions of the center.
- Assists in involving families in the center's program.
- Participates in internal staff activities and in special training programs.
- Works under general supervision of head teacher.
- Does related work as required.
- Works extra hours in emergency situations.
- Acts as head teacher when head teacher is not present.

SOURCE: School-Age Child Care Program, Fairfax County Office for Children, Fairfax, Virginia.

SANTA MONICA UNIFIED SCHOOL DISTRICT
Santa Monica Children's Centers

Position: Children's Center Head Teacher

Placement: A teacher with Head Teacher responsibility shall receive a responsibility increment of $1.08 above the appropriate step in Group IV, Children's Center Salary Schedule 73–74.

Supervision:
1. Supervises and directs all center personnel.
2. Cooperates with parents and staff in the development of a quality center program.
3. Supervises the instructional program and encourages staff members to experiment and be creative.
4. Works with parents and staff in the development of assessment and evaluation tools.
5. Conducts staff meetings on a regular basis and other meetings as necessary.
6. Works with the Children's Center Director in the development and implementation of an in-service program for staff and parents.
7. Encourages staff to maintain a personal program of professional growth.
8. Encourages staff to participate in community activities and to enlist the support and cooperation of community leaders.

Administration:
1. Interviews, evaluates, and processes applications of parents for child care services.
2. Orients new families to the center.
3. Assists in the selection of certificated and classified personnel.
4. Orients new and substitute teachers.
5. Collects fees from parents and maintains financial, eligibility, and attendance records in accordance with prescribed procedures (Federal Interagency Agreement, etc.).
6. Maintains records and prepares reports as required.
7. Confers with parents regarding behavior, health, and general development of the child. Follows through as necessary.
8. Enlists the support and cooperation of services in the community, and participates in community affairs.
9. Reports deficiencies in condition of building, grounds, and equipment and promotes safe practices throughout the center.
10. Coordinates articulation between the center and the elementary school or schools involved with the students.
11. Liaison between the home, the school (both center and elementary), and the community.
12. Maintains a personal program of professional development.

Source: The Santa Monica Children's Centers, Santa Monica Unified School District, Santa Monica, California.

HEPHZIBAH CHILDREN'S ASSOCIATION
PERSONNEL POLICIES

I. *General Information*
    A. Statement of Purpose
        1. The purpose of Hephzibah Children's Association as stated in its by-laws is to provide needed care for children without regard to race or creed.
        2. The purpose of the personnel policies is to provide each staff member with clearly defined employment policies as established by the Personnel Committee and approved by the Board of Directors.
            a. Our personnel policies are based on mutual respect and trust among the Board of Directors and our staff. Every position is equally valuable and essential to the well being of our children.
            b. Every staff member will be provided a copy of these policies at the time of employment and whenever policies are revised.
            c. These policies shall be continuously updated to reflect program policy changes.
            d. Any situation not dealt with in this manual will be handled by the Personnel Committee.
    B. Organization Structure
        1. The Board of Directors is composed of elected members from Oak Park and River Forest and is responsible for the operation of the Center. The Board establishes policies and procedures concerning finance, personnel, and general operation of the Center. Members of the Board serve on various committees which are responsible for specific areas of Center operation.
        2. The Executive Director, under the direction of the Board of Directors, is responsible for the performance and conduct of all staff members.
    C. Financial Structure
        1. Community Chest. The Center is funded by the Community Chest of Oak Park and River Forest and complies with the regulations established by the Community Chest Board of Governors.
        2. Other Funding Sources. When additional funding is acquired, changes in financial structure, policies and procedures may be made to comply with recommended regulations.

II. *Employment*
    A. General Procedure
        1. The Center or its designee will recruit, employ, promote, and reward employees on the basis of their capabilities and qualifications for job requirements, without discrimination because of race, color, religion, sex, age, national origin, or disability.
        2. No person shall be considered for employment while he or a member of his immediate family serves on the Board of Directors.

SOURCE: Hephzibah Children's Association, 946 North Boulevard, Oak Park, Illinois.

No person shall hold a job over which a member of his immediate family exercises supervisory authority.

3. Two references are required for each person making application. References will be checked with former employers. Current employers will be contacted only with approval of applicant.
4. For professional positions, school records, college transcripts and/or teaching certificates must be made available.
5. Upon employment, each staff member, at her cost, must have a health examination that meets state requirements.
6. All information becomes property of the Center and will be included in a confidential permanent personnel record maintained by the Director. This record will include but not be limited to:
    a. An application for employment and date of employment.
    b. Letters of reference.
    c. College or high school transcripts, if applicable.
    d. Summary of discussions on job performance.
    e. Formal evaluations.
    f. Personnel action forms (salary range, increments, promotions).

B. Executive Director

The Board of Directors has sole authority over the choice and tenure of the Executive Director. The Board acts upon recommendations of the Executive, Personnel and Finance Committees or delegates to those committees the final authority.

C. Employment of Staff

The Director is responsible for employing professional and supportive staff in accordance with staffing requirements determined by the Personnel Committee.

D. Probation Period

1. The Director and each full-time salaried employee is engaged on a probationary basis for 6 months. Before the end of this period, the Personnel Committee will evaluate the job performance of the Director and, if satisfactory, recommend to the Board that the Director be given permanent status. Upon evaluation and recommendation by the Director, the full-time employee's status becomes permanent.
2. Each part-time hourly employee is hired on a probationary basis for three months. After evaluation and recommendation by the Director, the employee's status becomes permanent.
3. If a part-time employee is offered a full-time position, a new probationary period begins. If any employee changes job classification, a new probationary period begins.
4. If job performance is unsatisfactory, employment may be terminated without benefits.

E. Terminations

1. Resignation. Three months written notice of resignation is required of the Director. Thirty days written notice is required of all other staff members.
2. Dismissal. An employee who willfully violates working rules or for other misconduct is subject to immediate dismissal. A full-time employee who gives unsatisfactory service, who has completed the

probationary period, shall be entitled to two weeks severance pay; a part-time employee, one week severance pay.

   F. Performance Evaluation
1. This is a continuous process. When the Director questions an employee's performance, the matter should be discussed immediately.
2. Permanent employees shall be evaluated once yearly in writing by the immediate supervisor.
3. The employee shall be given opportunity to express his agreement or disagreement with the evaluation, and this shall become a part of the record.
4. Employees shall be evaluated on knowledge of the job, quality of work, interest, dependability, initiative, growth, attendance and punctuality, and cooperation with other staff.

III. *Salary Administration*
   A. Salary Determination

     All salaries will be determined by the Finance and Personnel Committee. They will be commensurate with educational background, experience and job performance, and not be less than the current minimum wage as established by the U.S. Department of Labor.

   B. Salary Adjustments
1. Salary increases are determined by the Personnel and Finance Committees after evaluation of job performance and availability of funds.
2. Adjustments in salaries may be made with acquisition or termination of supplementary funding.

IV. *Employee Benefits*
   A. Eligibility
1. Full-time employees qualify for employee benefits.
2. Part-time employees are eligible for limited benefits as described in the following sections.

   B. Medical
1. Full-time employees are entitled to participate in the Community Chest Blue Cross & Blue Shield Group Plan. Cost of the premium will be divided between the participant and the Center. In case of non-participation, payment in lieu of premiums is not made.
2. Part-time employees who comply with plan requirements may request participation in the Plan at their own expense.

   C. Compensation
1. The Center carries Worker's Compensation for all employees. Any injury, however trivial, occurring to a staff member while performing duty either at the Center or elsewhere, must be reported immediately to the Director.
2. The Center contributes toward unemployment compensation for all employees.

   D. Holidays
1. The following holidays are observed:

Thanksgiving Day	Good Friday	Labor Day
Christmas Day	Memorial Day	
New Year's Day	Independence Day	

2. Each employee receives pay for the above holidays providing the employee worked the regularly scheduled day preceding and following the holiday unless absent from work on those days because of illness. Other religious holidays may be taken as personal business days or without remuneration.

3. If an observed holiday occurs during the vacation period, an additional day of vacation is granted.

E. Vacation
   1. General Provisions
      a. The full amount of vacation allowed each year must be taken within the year.
      b. Subject to Center needs and after six months of continuous employment, vacation time may be taken as accrued at any time during the calendar year.
      c. Upon dismissal, vacation credits are not compensated.
      d. All vacation time is scheduled and approved by the Director.
   2. Director
      a. The Director will be eligible for fifteen days paid vacation after one calendar year of employment.
      b. After two years of employment, five additional days paid vacation will be given.
      c. Director's vacation time must be scheduled with approval of Personnel Committee.
   3. Full-time Employees
      a. Ten working days are given after one calendar year of employment.
      b. After two years of employment, five additional days paid vacation will be given.
      c. Provisions for increase of vacation time may be made for employees having continuous service beyond six years.
   4. Part-time Employees
      Part-time employees are eligible for 5 days paid vacation after one year of continuous employment.

F. Sick Leave
   1. Full-time employees shall be granted ten days sick leave per year for absence from duty due to sickness or injury. Full-time probationary employees will be granted one day sick leave per month worked.
   2. A physician's statement may be requested upon employee's return or during any absence that exceeds three days.
   3. Absences due to illness which exceed accumulated sick leave will be considered leave without pay or may be charged to accrued vacation time.
   4. After one year of full-time employment, unused sick leave may be accumulated on a continuous basis.
   5. Unused sick leave may not be used as additional vacation leave and is not compensable upon termination of employment.

G. Personal Business Leave
   1. Each full-time employee is allowed three personal business days per

year. These days are not cumulative and not compensable upon termination of employment.

2. Requests for personal business leave must be approved by the Director.

3. An employee on probation may request time off without compensation subject to approval by Director.

H. Approved Absences

1. Jury Duty. A full-time employee who must report for jury duty receives the difference between regular salary and the amount received for jury duty.

2. Death in family. Two days leave is allowed a full-time employee for death in the immediate family. An extension of leave may be granted by the Director but this time will be charged to personal business, vacation, or without compensation.

3. Illness in immediate family. A full-time employee may request permission from the Director for absence necessitated by illness in immediate family. Time off may be charged against personal business, sick leave, vacation or without compensation.

4. Staff Development. A full-time employee is permitted time off during normal center hours for educational and development purposes relevant to job responsibilities. All requests for such absences must be submitted to the Director for approval.

5. All time off must be discussed with the Director, or in the Director's case, with the Personnel Committee.

V. *Employee Relations, Procedures and Responsibilities*

A. Grievances

1. In the event an employee has a grievance involving working conditions, this should be discussed with the immediate supervisor who will attempt to resolve the situation.

2. If the grievance remains unresolved, a written statement should be submitted to the Director who will talk with the employee, make every attempt to resolve the situation, and provide a written decision within one week.

3. If upon receipt of the Director's decision, the employee continues to be dissatisfied, or if the employee has been dismissed or suspended and is not satisfied, an appeal may be made in writing to the Personnel Committee of the Board.

4. The Personnel Committee shall afford the employee a hearing within one week of receipt of written grievance.

5. The Personnel Committee shall notify the employee in writing of its decision within one week after the hearing.

B. Working Hours

The Center is open from 7:00 A.M. to 6:00 P.M., Monday through Friday. A work schedule for employees is made by the Director and furnished to the Personnel Committee.

C. Pay Date

Each full-time employee is paid on the basis of an annual salary. Each part-time employee is paid on an hourly basis as agreed upon at time of employment. Payroll checks are issued on the fifteenth and last day of each month.

D. Reporting of Absence

An employee is expected to request approved absences from the Director as soon as possible to facilitate acquiring a substitute. In the case of illness or injury, the employee is to call the center as soon as possible. If another day off is anticipated, the Director is notified as soon as possible.

E. Tardiness

It is the responsibility of each employee to be present at the center at the regularly scheduled time. Persistent, excessive tardiness is a serious neglect of duty and the basis for disciplinary action and/or loss of pay in accordance with lost time. Excessive tardiness is reporting for work after the starting time more than once a month. Five minutes or less is not considered in the employee's punctuality record. If possible, the center is notified whenever an employee anticipates being late.

F. Outside Employment and School Attendance

A full-time employee is discouraged from holding additional jobs or taking two or more courses per semester or quarter. An employee holding a second job or attending school is required to inform the Director. Should job performance be adversely affected by outside employment or school attendance, the employee will be warned and may be dismissed.

G. Retirement

It is mandatory that all employees retire at the end of June the year after they reach their 65th birthday.

H. Student Teachers

Student teachers are assigned by the Director to the full-time teachers. The supervising teacher is responsible for the learning process of the student teacher.

I. Use of Center Equipment or Facilities

Center property is not to be removed from the premises except upon written request to and approval by the Director. Written approval by the Director is necessary for the use of any equipment or the facility outside the school hours.

J. Staff Meetings

A staff member is expected to attend regular meetings, and will be offered opportunities to participate in workshops, in-service training or activities in addition to their scheduled hours.

K. Center Board Meetings

If a staff member would like to attend a Board meeting, a request is made to the Board President.

October 20, 1976

Appendix 6

MISCELLANEOUS MATERIALS

SCHOOL-AGE CHILD CARE PROJECT
TECHNICAL ASSISTANCE AFFILIATES

CALIFORNIA
Tinka Streibert
Santa Monica Children's Centers
Ocean Park Center
2526 Sixth Street
Santa Monica, California 90405
  (213) 396-2367

ILLINOIS
Mary Anne Broeman-Brown
Executive Director
Hephzibah Children's Association
946 North Boulevard
Oak Park, Illinois 60302
  (312) 386-8417

MINNESOTA
Jackie Silver
Child Care Resource
  and Referral, Inc.
1312 NW 7th Street, Suite H
Rochester, Minnesota 55901
  (507) 288-9388

NEW MEXICO
Sheila Bolger, Coordinator
Carino/YWCA School-Age Project
316 4th Street SW
Albuquerque, New Mexico 87102
  (505) 247-8841

NEW YORK
Anita Gitlin Kleiner, Coordinator
The North Area YWCA
2844 Delaware Avenue
Kenmore, New York 14217
  (716) 875-3111

OREGON
Edwina Albright, Administrator
Eugene Latch Key, Inc.
P.O. Box 10625
356 West 8th Street
Eugene, Oregon 97401
  (503) 683-7291

SOURCE: Wellesley College Center for Research on Women, School-Age Child Care Project, Michelle Seligson, Director, January 26, 1982.

TENNESSEE
Richard T. Scofield
School-Age Child Care Technical Assistance Project
School of Education
Tennessee State University—
  Downtown
10th and Charlotte Avenues
Nashville, Tennessee 37203
  (615) 251-1540

VIRGINIA
Roberta Newman, Director
Fairfax County School-Age Child Care
  Program
10396 Democracy Lane
Fairfax, Virginia 22030
  (703) 691-3175

CURRENT STATE DAY CARE CENTER
LICENSING OFFICES

Office of Program Administration
64 North Union Street
Montgomery, Alabama 36130
(205) 832-6150

Department of Health & Social
  Services
Pouch H-05
Juneau, Alaska 99811
(907) 465-3206

Arizona Department of Health
  Services
1740 West Adams
Phoenix, Arizona 85007
(602) 255-1112

Department of Social and Rehabilitative Services
P.O. Box 1487
Little Rock, Arkansas 72203
(501) 371-7512

Department of Social Services
744 P Street, Mail Station 17-17
Sacramento, California 95814
(916) 322-8538

Department of Social Services
1575 Sherman Street, Room 420
Denver, Colorado 80203
(303) 839-3361

State Department of Health
79 Elm Street
Hartford, Connecticut 06115
(203) 566-2535

Department of Health & Social
  Services
P.O. Box 309
Wilmington, Delaware 19899
(302) 421-6786

Licensing & Certification Division
Social Services Branch
1406 L Street, N.W., 2nd floor
Washington, D.C. 20005
(202) 727-0672

Department of Health and Rehabilitation Services
1311 Winewood Boulevard
Tallahassee, Florida 32301
(904) 488-1850

SOURCE: This listing was provided by the Day Care and Child Development Council of America, Inc., Washington, DC 20009.

Department of Human Resources
618 Ponce de Leon Avenue
Atlanta, Georgia 30308
(404) 894-5144

Division of Social Services
P.O. Box 2816
Agana, Guam 96910
(671) 734-9912

Department of Social Services and
  Housing
P.O. Box 339
Honolulu, Hawaii 96809
(808) 548-2302

Department of Health and Welfare
Statehouse
Boise, Idaho 83720
(208) 334-4076

Department of Children and Family
  Services
1 North Old State Capitol Plaza
Springfield, Illinois 62706
(217) 785-2598

State Department of Public Welfare
100 North Senate Avenue, Room 701
Indianapolis, Indiana 46204
(317) 232-4421

Department of Social Services
3619 ½ Douglass Avenue
Des Moines, Iowa 50310
(515) 281-5581

Division of Health & Environment
Building 740, Forbes AFB
Topeka, Kansas 66620
(913) 862-9360

Department of Human Resources
Fourth Floor East
275 East Main Street
Frankfort, Kentucky 40601
(502) 564-2800

Department of Health & Human Resources
P.O. Box 3767
Baton Rouge, Louisiana 70821
(504) 342-6446

Department of Human Services
Augusta, Maine 04333
(207) 289-3455

Department of Health and Mental
  Hygiene
201 West Preston Street
Baltimore, Maryland 21201
(301) 383-4009

Office for Children
120 Boylston Street
Boston, Massachusetts 02116
(617) 727-8956

Michigan Department of Social
  Services
116 West Allegan
P.O. Box 80037
Lansing, Michigan 48926
(517) 373-8300

Department of Public Welfare
Centennial Office Building, 4th Floor
St. Paul, Minnesota 55155
(612) 296-2539

State Board of Health
P.O. Box 1700
Jackson, Mississippi 39205
(601) 982-6505

State Department of Social Services
Broadway State Office Building
303 W. McCarthy Street
Jefferson City, Missouri 65103
(314) 751-2450

Montana Department of Social and
  Rehabilitation Services
P.O. Box 4210
Helena, Montana 59601
(406) 449-3865

Department of Public Welfare
P.O. Box 95026
Lincoln, Nebraska 68509
(402) 471-3121

Division of Youth Services
505 East King Street
Carson City, Nevada 89710
(702) 885-5911

Office of Social Services
Hazen Drive
Concord, New Hampshire 03301
(603) 271-4402

New Jersey Department of Human
  Services
1 South Montgomery Street
Trenton, New Jersey 08623
(609) 292-1879

Health and Environmental Department
440 Chamisa Hill Building
Suite S–3
Santa Fe, New Mexico 87504
(505) 827-3431

New York State Department of Social
  Services
40 North Pearl Street
Albany, New York 12243
(800) 342-3715

Office of Child Day Care Licensing
1919 Ridge Road
Raleigh, North Carolina 27607
(919) 733-4801

Children and Family Services
Russell Building—Box 7
Highway 83 North
Bismarck, North Dakota 58505
(701) 224-3580

Bureau of Licensing and Standards
30 E. Broad Street, 30th Floor
Columbus, Ohio 43215
(614) 466-3822

Department of Public Welfare
P.O. Box 25352
Oklahoma City, Oklahoma 73125
(405) 521-3561

Department of Human Resources
198 Commercial Street, S.E.
Salem, Oregon 97310
(503) 378-3178

Pennsylvania Department of Public
  Welfare
Room 423, Health & Welfare Building
Harrisburg, Pennsylvania 17120
(717) 961-4371

P.O. Box 11398
Fernandez Juncos Station
Santurce, Puerto Rico 00910
(809) 723-2127

Department of Social & Rehabilitative
  Services
610 Mount Pleasant Avenue
Providence, Rhode Island 02908
(401) 277-3446

South Carolina Department of Social
  Services
P.O. Box 1520
Columbia, South Carolina 29202
(803) 758-7620

Department of Social Services
Richard F. Kneip Building
Pierre, South Dakota 57501
(605) 773-3227

Tennessee Department of Human
  Services
111-19 7th Avenue North
Nashville, Tennessee 37203
(615) 741-3284

Texas Department of Human Resources
P.O. Box 2960
Austin, Texas 78769
(512) 441-3355

Division of Family Services
P.O. Box 2500
Salt Lake City, Utah 84110
(801) 533-5031

Department of Social and Rehabilitative Services
81 River Street
Montpelier, Vermont 05602
(802) 241-2158

Department of Social Services
P.O. Box 539
Charlotte Amalie
St. Thomas, Virgin Islands 00801
(809) 774-0930

Department of Welfare
8007 Discovery Drive
Richmond, Virginia 23229
(804) 281-9025

The Department of Social & Health
  Services
State Office Building #2
Mail Stop 440
Olympia, Washington 98504
(106) 753-7160

Department of Welfare
1900 Washington Street, East
Charleston, West Virginia 25305
(304) 348-7980

Division of Community Services
1 West Wilson Street
Madison, Wisconsin 53702
(608) 266-8200

Division of Public Assistance
  & Social Services
Hathway Building
Cheyenne, Wyoming 82002
(307) 777-7561

INDEX